THE
HOUSE
BOOK

INCLUDES MORE THAN 250 INSTANT DECORATING IDEAS,
WITH OVER 2000 PHOTOGRAPHS AND ILLUSTRATIONS

MIKE LAWRENCE
with Stewart and
Sally Walton

southwater

This edition is published by Southwater, an imprint of Anness Publishing Ltd, Hermes House, 88–89 Blackfriars Road, London SE1 8HA; tel. 020 7401 2077; fax 020 7633 9499

www.southwaterbooks.com
www.annesspublishing.com

If you like the images in this book and would like to investigate using them for publishing, promotions or advertising, please visit our website www.practicalpictures.com for more information.

UK agent: The Manning Partnership Ltd; tel. 01225 478444; fax 01225 478440; sales@manning-partnership.co.uk
UK distributor: Grantham Book Services Ltd; tel. 01476 541080; fax 01476 541061; orders@gbs.tbs-ltd.co.uk
North American agent/distributor: National Book Network; tel. 301 459 3366; fax 301 429 5746; www.nbnbooks.com
Australian agent/distributor: Pan Macmillan Australia; tel. 1300 135 113; fax 1300 135 103; customer.service@macmillan.com.au
New Zealand agent/distributor: David Bateman Ltd tel. (09) 415 7664; fax (09) 415 8892

Publisher Joanna Lorenz
Editorial Director Judith Simons
Project Editor Katy Bevan
Photography John Freeman, Graham Rae
Designers Michael Morey, Simon Wilder
Additional Contributions Jan Eaton, Catherine Tully, Judy Smith, Andrea Spencer, Diana Civil

Ethical trading policy
Because of our ongoing ecological investment programme, you, as our customer, can have the pleasure and reassurance of knowing that a tree is being cultivated on your behalf to naturally replace the materials used to make the book you are holding. For further information about this scheme, go to www.annesspublishing.com/trees

Publisher's note
The authors and the publisher have made every effort to ensure that all instructions contained in this book are accurate and safe, and cannot accept liability for any resulting injury, damage or loss to persons or property, however it may arise. If in doubt as to the correct procedure to follow for any home improvements or woodwork task, seek professional advice.

CONTENTS

USE
BOOK

ABOUT THIS BOOK

Home improvement has never been as popular as it is today. For a start, there are more homeowners than ever before, according to the latest statistics, and the majority of them want their homes to look attractive, to feature the latest furnishings and decorations, and to have a sense of style that reflects their personalities.

The media also has home improvement high on the agenda. Terrestrial, satellite and cable TV channels offer an ever-increasing variety of do-it-yourself and home improvement programmes, covering every aspect of the subject from demolition to decoration – and creating a new stable of celebrity designers in the process. The newsagents'

stands are filled with home interest magazines, which give guidance on creating every home style imaginable from period living and country cottage to modern minimalism. Books deal with every practical topic, from do-it-yourself basics to self-building, and also offer style and interior design advice to suit every taste. The degree of choice available is almost overwhelming, and making clear decisions about what to import

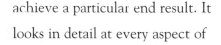

into the home becomes increasingly difficult as a result. Venture
into the home improvement superstores, and there are more
choices to be made. Which type of paint? What colour? How about new
wallpaper, or tiles, or flooring? What kind of bathroom and kitchen equipment should you
choose? And what about light fittings, soft furnishings, or shelves and storage solutions? It
is hard to know where to start… but help is at hand.

This book is designed to simplify the decorating and home improvement
challenge. It takes the reader through a process of analysis,
treating the existing home as a blank canvas and
making it easier to assess precisely what is required to
achieve a particular end result. It
looks in detail at every aspect of ➤

every room in the house, offering advice on choosing and using a varied range of decoration, features, fittings and furnishings to give each room its own sense of style and unity.

The second half of the book presents a range of creative makeover ideas. These are quick and easy projects that can be completed in a weekend, so they are ideal for busy working people, allowing you to achieve lasting results with the minimum of time and effort. This section is divided into six chapters. Windows show you how to transform your home with

modern fixtures and fittings, quick drapes and stylish tie-backs. The chapter on Walls and Floors demonstrates original decorating ideas that will give your home a visual lift, from original wall hangings and fabulous rugs to panelled walls and stencilled flooring designs. Beds and Bedding gives you step-by-step instructions for revamping your bedroom from fabulous cushions and pillows to decorative headboard ideas. Chairs and Tables looks at decorating furniture, Light and Shade gives ideas for updating and making

new lighting arrangements, and Containers has creative storage ideas to keep your home and work station tidy.

The emphasis throughout is on combining style and practicality, so that every job can be approached confidently from planning to execution. With clear instructions and detailed step-by-step photography, everything is eminently achievable.

The information provided aims to help everyone, from the absolute beginner to the more practised homeowner, to achieve sensational results by getting things right from the very start, with no wasted effort or money. It is a source book for every aspect of decorating and styling the home, and it will guide the reader unerringly from concept to completion time after time.

PART ONE

PRACTICAL DECORATING

INTRODUCTION

The interior of a home is like a giant mirror, reflecting the owners' character, taste, aspirations and interests – even their little foibles. The purpose of this book is to help in making decisions that will create a home that reflects the personality of the owners, and one that they are happy to live in.

It starts by explaining how to examine the present state of things, and to work out what should be retained and what would be better changed. This first chapter assesses the benefits of some basic internal alterations, such as reorganizing the use of space or how the furniture is arranged, and goes on to plan new decorating and furnishing schemes in conjunction with another very important but often overlooked factor: lighting. The next stage is to plan in

in detail how to carry out work in a well-organized and strictly methodical way, which is vital to success.

The rest of part one contains chapters that deal with every type of home improvement task, from the use of paint, wall coverings, tiles and floor coverings to features and fittings, soft furnishings and storage, and it closes with a look at the routine maintenance and repair jobs that every householder has to face from time to time. Each chapter gives full information on the tools and materials that will be used, and covers a wide range of techniques and projects. Full-colour step-by-step photographs appear throughout the book, plus explanatory illustrations, useful charts and a wealth of practical advice on creating the ideal interior.

DECORATING
DECISIONS

The hardest part of any do-it-yourself project is deciding precisely what is wanted and planning how to achieve it. The decision may simply involve a choice of colour or pattern, or may be more complex, perhaps involving major changes to the style, layout, features and fittings of a room or rooms.

For example, it may seem likely that better use can be made of the interior space that is available. An easy way of doing this is to rearrange or change some of the furniture, whether it is freestanding or built-in – but a more radical approach may bring even more dramatic gains. Partitioning some rooms, linking others, even changing the use to which individual rooms have previously been put, can revolutionize the way a home works. This approach is particularly relevant as the occupants' needs alter over the years, since a house that worked well with young children will not suit a family with teenagers, and once the children have flown the nest their parents will want to use the house in a different way again.

On a smaller scale, even the way in which individual rooms are decorated and furnished can have a major effect on the way they look and feel. Many people find that achieving the style they want is often a process of evolution rather than revolution; few people can get everything right first time. The secret of success lies in understanding the basic rules of colour scheming and in learning how to make the best use of the wide range of materials and techniques available to the interior designer today.

Lastly, it also means taking a close look at what lighting contributes to the scheme. Few homes make use of the possibilities explored so imaginatively in many public buildings, yet some minor changes to lighting could bring a home alive. Some interior designers even dream of the day when they can create and change interior colour schemes with the flick of a switch. However, until that day the big decorating decisions are still the same as they always were; this chapter should render them somewhat easier to make.

Opposite: The art of successful decoration lies in marrying materials that protect and enhance the various surfaces around the home with a touch of decorative flair and originality that will give every room a style all its own and reflect the owner's personal taste and lifestyle.

MAKING AN ASSESSMENT

The best way to get an objective view of a home's interior condition is to imagine that it is up for sale and to view it in the role of a prospective purchaser. The aim of the exercise is not to give rise to a severe bout of depression, but to make it clear what exists in the home and what could be done to change or improve it.

Start at the front door, and step into the hallway. Is it bright and well lit, or gloomy and unwelcoming? A lighter colour scheme could make a narrow room appear more spacious, and better lighting would make it seem more inviting. Decorating the wall opposite the front door would make a long hall appear shorter, while changing the way the staircase is decorated could make it a less – or more – dominant feature. Is the staircase well lit, for safety's sake as well as for looks? Opening up the space beneath the stairs could get rid of what

Above: Choose an integrated decorating scheme for hallways, stairs and landing areas. Bring down the apparent ceiling height using a dado (chair) rail or decorative border.

Below: The living room has to be light and airy during the day, yet cosy and comfortable in the evening. The fireplace and a central table provide the main focal points here.

is typically an untidy gloryhole (storage room), taking up space without saving any. Lastly, are the wall and floor coverings practical? The hall floor is bound to be well trodden, and needs to be durable and easy to clean as well as looking attractive.

Now move into the main living room. This is always the most difficult room in the house to decorate and furnish successfully because of its dual purpose. It is used both for daily life and to entertain visitors. It must be fresh and lively by day, yet cosy and peaceful in the evening. One of the chief keys to success is flexible lighting that can be altered to suit the room's different uses, but the decorations and furnishings all have their part to play too.

Look at the colour scheme. How well does it blend in with the furnishings, the curtains and drapes, the floor covering? Are there any interesting features such as a fireplace, an alcove, an archway into another room, even an ornate cornice around the ceiling? Some might benefit from being highlighted, other less attractive ones would be better disguised.

Next, examine how the room works. Are traffic routes congested? Are the seating arrangements flexible? Are there surfaces where things can easily be put down? Does any storage or display provision look good and work well? Can everyone who is seated see the television? Does everyone want to? Assessing the room in this way reveals its successes and failures, and shows how to eliminate the latter.

Continue the guided tour with the dining room – or dining area, if it is part of a through room. This is often the least used room in the house, so its design tends to be neglected. Since it is usually used for just one purpose –

eating – it needs to be decorated in a way that avoids visual indigestion. Warm, welcoming colour schemes and flexible lighting work best in this location; strident patterns and harsh colours are to be avoided.

Now turn to the kitchen. Whatever type of room it is, the most important thing is that it should be hygienic, for obvious reasons. Are the various surfaces in the room easy to keep clean, and to redecorate when necessary? Are there dust and grease traps? Is the lighting over the hob (burners) and counter tops adequate? Is the floor covering a practical choice? Since the kitchen is often the hub of family life, it needs to be functional but adaptable, and also pleasant to be in so that the cook does not mind the time spent slaving over a hot stove.

Bathrooms have their own special requirements, mainly revolving around combining comfort with a degree of waterproofing, especially if there are young children in the family. Are the decorations and floor covering suitable? How do they complement the bathroom suite? What about the space available within the room? Could congestion be relieved by moving

things around? – or by moving them out altogether: having a shower instead of a bath could create lots of extra space. Could a second bathroom be created elsewhere in the house? Otherwise, putting washbasins in some of the bedrooms could take the pressure off the family bathroom during the morning rush hour.

Lastly, bedrooms. In most, the bed is the focal point of the room, so the way it is dressed will be the main influence on the room's appearance. The colour scheme also has its part to play in making the room look comfortable and relaxing; remember that the room's occupant will see it from two viewpoints – on entering, and from the bed – so take this into account when assessing it. What about the ceiling? In the one room where people actually spend some time staring at it, does it deserve something a little more adventurous than white paint? Is the floor covering warm to the touch of bare feet? In children's rooms, is it also capable of withstanding the occasional rough and tumble or a disaster with the finger paints? Lastly, is the lighting satisfactory? Most bedrooms need a combination of subdued general

lighting and brighter local task lighting for things such as reading in bed, putting on make-up or tackling school homework. Some changes may make the room work a great deal more satisfactorily.

Once the tour of the house is complete there should be a clear picture of its condition and how well it works; and some ideas as to how it might be improved. Above all, it will have been viewed as a whole, not just as a series of individual rooms. That is the first step towards creating an attractive, stylish and above all practical home.

REORGANIZING SPACE

If a home does not function well, there are three choices. Two of these are thoroughly defeatist and may also be impractical: learn to live with it, or move to a more suitable house. The third is much more positive; alter it so that it gives the extra living space and the additional features needed.

The average home is basically a box, within which internal partitions create individual rooms, doors allow movement and windows let in light and air. Various services are included within the structure – heating, plumbing, wiring and so on. All these features can be altered, within reason, to make them work better.

When planning alterations, there are two considerations which should constantly be borne in mind. Are the changes feasible? And are they legal? It is essential to check with the local planning (zoning) and building control bodies to find out whether the work requires official approval.

Where to improve

Alterations to the use of space in the home are of two kinds. The first is to create new living space. The second is to alter the present layout of the interior and to change or improve the services. Here are some of the possibilities.

In the attic, unused space beneath a pitched roof could well become valuable extra living space. Remember, though, that providing access to the new rooms will mean losing some space on the floor below.

In the existing upstairs rooms, rearranging internal walls could create an extra bedroom or bathroom, while providing plumbing facilities in bedrooms could ease the pressure on the existing bathroom.

Above: Subdividing large rooms can help to create more effective use of space, by redefining traffic zones and providing more wall space for furniture.

Left: Bathing facilities are often over-stretched, especially in family homes. Finding the space for an extra shower cubicle can greatly relieve the traffic jams.

Right: Redesigning the kitchen provides the opportunity to rationalize both storage needs and work patterns. Modern fitted kitchens can cater for every individual requirement.

Downstairs, removing dividing walls to create large through rooms or partitioning large rooms to create two smaller ones, moving doorways to improve traffic flow, or altering the kitchen layout could all be considered. It might even be possible to turn an integral garage into extra living space.

Look at the possibility of changing the use to which individual rooms are

CONVERTING AN ATTIC

A full-scale conversion into one or more habitable rooms – that is, bedrooms and the like rather than just play or hobby space – is one of the biggest and most complex indoor home improvement projects. It involves altering the roof structure to make space for the rooms, strengthening the existing attic floor, providing access from the floor below, installing roof or dormer windows and extending existing services into the new rooms. Professional advice is needed here, and it is advisable to hand over the main structural alterations to a builder or specialist conversion firm. That still leaves plenty of scope for do-it-yourself finishing and fitting of the new rooms.

In many older homes, the space beneath a pitched (sloping) roof can be used to provide valuable extra living space, often with spectacular results.

put, especially if the family is increasing or decreasing in size. Reorganization can bring dramatic improvements to the way the house works.

Creating a through room

Creating a through room means removing an existing dividing wall, and may also require the repositioning of existing doorways and the formation of new windows. If the existing wall is loadbearing, a steel beam will have to be installed to carry the load, and lintels will also be needed over new windows and over new doors in other loadbearing walls. It may be necessary to reroute existing plumbing and electrical services that cross the wall that will be removed. Once the new opening has been formed, there will be extensive replastering to be done, and the floors in the two rooms will have to be linked smoothly. The original colour schemes of the two rooms will also probably be different, which may entail complete redecoration.

Partitioning an existing room

Subdividing an existing room into two smaller ones means building a new wall, possibly adding a door or window to one of the new rooms, and perhaps altering or extending existing plumbing, heating and electrical services to serve the two separate rooms.

The new dividing wall will generally be built as a timber-framed partition wall faced with plasterboard (gypsum board), but a solid blockwork wall could be built on suitable foundations, which may well need to be inserted.

Creating a new door opening

If the new opening is to be made in a loadbearing wall, a lintel must be used to bridge the opening. However, if the wall is a non-loadbearing partition, simple alterations to the wall framing are all that will be needed. The job will also involve some replastering work, making alterations to skirtings (baseboards) and floor surfaces, the fitting of architraves (trims) around the opening, and possibly alterations to existing plumbing, heating and electrical services if pipes or cables cross the area where the door will be installed.

Altering the kitchen layout

The amount of work depends on how extensive the rearrangement will be. At the very least there will be new base and wall units (cabinets) and counter tops, and these will probably involve some work on wall and floor surfaces. If repositioning sinks, cookers (stoves), dishwashers and the like, there will have to be alterations to plumbing and electrical services.

USING COLOUR, PATTERN AND TEXTURE

After redesigning the house layout and reorganizing each room, the next task is to start planning the colour schemes. To do this successfully, it helps to understand the basics of colour theory, and how to use pattern and texture to good effect.

When putting a colour scheme together, a device called the *colour wheel* can be used to help plan the various decorative effects. All colours are made by mixing together varying proportions of the three *primary* colours – red, yellow and blue. Mixing them in pairs creates three new *secondary* colours, with red and yellow making orange, yellow and blue making green, and blue and red making violet. Imagine these six colours making up segments of a circle in the order red, orange, yellow, green, blue and violet. Mix adjacent pairs together again, and you create six *tertiary* colours – red/orange, orange/yellow, yellow/green, green/blue, blue/violet and violet/red. Adding these to the circle gives the basic colour wheel of twelve segments.

There is one more ingredient to add to these colours: colour intensity or tone. By adding different amounts of white or black, you can produce lighter or darker shades of the original colours in almost infinite variety. And you can also, of course, use white, black and varying shades of grey as colours in their own right.

On the wheel, the twelve colours split into two groups. The colours from violet/red round to yellow are known as *advancing* colours because they appear to make wall and ceiling surfaces look nearer to the viewer than they really are. They make a room seem warm and welcoming, but also smaller. The remaining colours are known as *receding* colours because they have the opposite

THE COLOUR WHEEL

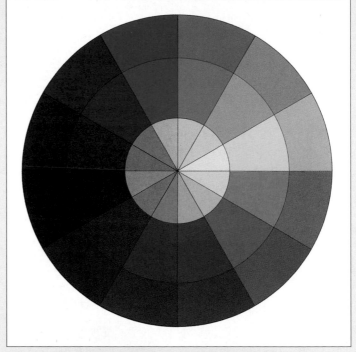

An understanding of colour and colour mixing will be invaluable when choosing a new colour scheme. The colour wheel is divided into 12 segments, and the central ring shows the primary, secondary and tertiary colours described in the text. The outer ring shows darker tones of these colours and the inner one lighter ones.

Left: Blues, greys and plenty of white space create a cool, airy colour scheme that is the perfect complement for wooden fixtures and furnishings in a light shade of pine.

Left: Blues and greens are naturally cool, receding colours, ideal for well-lit south-facing rooms, but can be warmed by splashes of contrast in orange and yellow.

visual effect, making a room look cool, and also larger than in reality. Which group is chosen as the basis for a colour scheme depends on the overall effect that is wanted in that particular room.

The colour wheel also helps to create colour *harmony* or *contrast*. Colours next to or near each other are said to be in colour harmony, giving a restful effect. However, too much colour harmony can become visually rather dull; it needs livening up with some elements of colour contrast, which come from using colours at opposite sides of the wheel. Colours exactly opposite each other, such as red and green, are called *complementary*. The ideal colour scheme is usually considered to be a basically harmonious one, with contrast added by the judicious use of contrasting or complementary colours for some elements of the design. Soft furnishing, such as scatter cushions or blinds and shades, chosen in a fabric to contrast with the overall colour scheme can add just the right amount of contrast to brighten up a room.

Below: Nothing succeeds in creating a feeling of cosiness as well as the red/pink section of the colour wheel. Surface texture plays its part too, as does warm, natural wood fittings.

Above: Neutral tones – beiges, creams and browns – create a colour scheme that is restful on the eye and can be teemed with almost any accessory shades.

USING COLOUR, PATTERN AND TEXTURE *(continued)*

Left: Bold splashes of colour can add interest and definition to a colour scheme that is basically neutral.

Below: Wall coverings with a vertical pattern element can help to make rooms appear taller, but work well only when the walls are perfectly square.

Colour can also play tricks on the eye, which can be used to good effect in colour scheming. For example, painting a high ceiling in a dark colour makes it appear lower. The same effect applies on walls, where using dark colour on opposite walls makes a wide room seem narrower; conversely, using it on the end wall of a long, thin room and lighter colours on the side walls helps to make the room seem wider to the eye.

Using pattern
Pattern on walls, ceilings and floors adds visual interest to a colour scheme, either in harmony with the overall effect or to provide contrast – for example, by having a patterned wall covering on one wall, and the rest painted. Pattern as well as colour can cheat the eye and alter the apparent dimensions of a room. Wall coverings with a distinct horizontal pattern make walls seem wider and ceilings lower; strong vertical designs such as stripes have the opposite effect. The same applies to pattern in floor coverings, which can make a room look wider or narrower depending on which way the pattern element runs.

Pattern size has its own contribution to make. Wall and floor coverings with large pattern motifs make the surface they are on seem to advance and so make the room appear smaller, while tiny motifs have the opposite effect of making the surface appear to recede from the eye. Choosing patterned fabrics for cushions, curtains and drapes or bed linen is an ideal way of enlivening a decor with plain walls and woodwork.

Above: Small, random patterns are a better choice than larger motifs for small rooms, and are ideal for decorating areas where perfect pattern matching can be difficult.

Left: Luxurious fabrics used for curtains, cushions and upholstery are often the ideal medium for adding patterned elements to a decor.

Using texture

Surface texture – in other words, a surface that is not completely smooth – helps to add variety and visual interest to your colour schemes. Wall coverings with a textured or embossed surface generally have a comparatively low relief which helps to soften the decorative effect of the material, while texture paints can be used to create effects that have quite a high relief and consequently look particularly striking when lit from the side. Textured finishes also have another benefit, of helping to disguise slightly irregular wall and ceiling surfaces.

Right: Sometimes richly textured upholstery and floor coverings benefit from the simplest of settings. Here textured walls and painted floorboards in pure white are the perfect backdrop.

LIGHTING BASICS

Below: Where lamps are visible, it is best to use types such as candles and globes that look attractive whether lit or unlit.

Good lighting can play an important role in bringing a home to life, as well as making it easier for the occupants to work and engage in leisure activities. Few homes take advantage of the design possibilities that good lighting can offer, preferring to rely on the traditional central pendant light in each room and the occasional table or standard (standing) lamp.

The following pages show some of the many versatile and attractive lighting effects that can be achieved in different rooms. Before embarking on a radical redesign of a lighting scheme it is important to understand some of the basics of lighting design.

Light is provided by lamps and tubes of various types and wattages. *Wattage* is a measurement of the amount of electricity the lamp consumes. The amount of light each emits is measured in units called *lumens*. Conventional

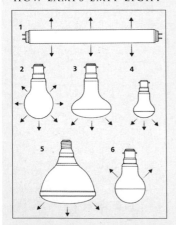

HOW LAMPS EMIT LIGHT

Fluorescent tubes (**1**) and GLS (general lighting service) lamps (**2**) emit light in all directions. Silvered reflectors emit it either forwards (**3, 4, 5**) or backwards (**6**).

tungsten-filament lamps – that is, ordinary lightbulbs – are much less efficient at producing light than are fluorescent tubes. For example, a 40-watt lamp emits about 400 lumens, or 10 lumens per watt of power used, while a 40-watt tube emits almost 2000 lumens, or 50 lumens per watt.

The amount of light that is needed depends on the surface area being lit. As a general guide something in the region of 200 lumens per sq m (20 lumens per sq ft) is needed in work areas such as kitchens, half that figure in other living rooms, bathrooms and in access areas such as halls, landings and stairs, and a quarter of the amount – 50 lumens per sq m (5 lumens per sq ft) in bedrooms.

Above: Individual spotlights on ceiling- or wall-mounted track provide the maximum flexibility when highlighting particular room features.

There are other factors to take into consideration when working out how much light is needed, such as the colour and reflectivity of the surfaces being lit and whether lighting is direct or indirect, but they are somewhat complex for the lay person to work with. As a rough guide for general background lighting, using filament lighting emitting around 10 lumens per watt, aim to provide about 20 watts per sq m (2 watts per sq ft) of floor area. As an example, a living room measuring 6 × 4 m (20 × 13 ft) would need 6 × 4 × 20 = 480 watts of lighting. For fluorescent tubes giving 50 lumens per watt, you need 4 watts per sq m (0.4 watts per sq ft) – that is, just under 100 watts of lighting for the same room. Regard any additional local task lighting in the room, for reading or studying perhaps, as supplementary to this basic figure.

Left: Globe lamps have an opaque spherical envelope that is perfect for use with pendant fittings, and look good whether the light is on or off.

Above: Downlighters (**left**) and PAR reflectors (**right**) can cast a narrow spotlight beam or create a border floodlit effect, according to the type of lamp fitted.

HOW LIGHT FITTINGS EMIT LIGHT

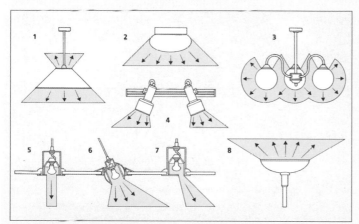

The type of light fitting or lampshade used affects the way light is distributed. Shown here are a pendant lampshade (**1**), a ceiling-mounted diffuser (**2**), wall lights with diffusers (**3**), spotlights on ceiling-mounted track (**4**), a downlighter (**5**), a recessed eyeball (**6**), a wallwasher (**7**) and an uplighter (**8**).

Above: Wall-mounted uplighters are used to wash ceilings with light. When fitted with a crown-silvered lamp, the light source is invisible even with the lamp at eye level.

LIGHTING FOR LIVING AND DINING ROOMS

The key to success with any lighting scheme is to ensure that it meets two criteria: it must give light where it is needed; and the effect it creates should enhance the room's appearance by creating a balanced mixture of light and shadow. The type of light fittings chosen has a major part to play, and so does the positioning of the fittings. The illustration shows how the type and positioning of ceiling lights can create different lighting effects on room walls.

The first basic guideline to observe is to ensure that naked lamps or tubes cannot be seen, by the judicious choice of shades and diffusers. The second is always to provide an acceptable level of background lighting throughout the room, even when additional local lighting is employed, to avoid creating pools of hard, dark shadow. The third is to use lighting to highlight individual features of the room – an attractive alcove, for example, lit by a spotlight, or a run of curtains (drapes) illuminated by perimeter lighting.

In addition, many rooms in the house will probably need local task lighting, for reading, writing, sewing or other work. The kitchen in particular has its own special lighting requirements. Some task lighting requirements can be satisfied by the use of portable plug-in lamps, while others may need more permanent arrangements.

Living rooms are among the most difficult areas to light successfully, because of the many different uses to which the room is put. The aim should be to provide background lighting that can be bright or dim according to the

Above: Globe lamps with 'jewel' finishes sparkle attractively when lit, and look striking when the lamp is off too.

Above: A rise-and-fall fitting provides glare-free light over the dining table, while a freestanding uplighter casts a gentle glow across the ceiling.

Right: Recessed eyeball spotlights allow light to be focussed closely on individual features or objects in a room, and can be adjusted as required.

Above: For lighting with minimal glare, team an opaque central fitting with strip lights behind pelmets (valances) to light up a cornice (crown molding) and the ceiling surface above.

Opposite: Pastel-shaded lamps in opaque lampshades help to create soft background lighting effects that complement the room's colour scheme.

mood of the moment, and then to add separately controllable feature lighting to highlight the room's focal points, and local task lighting where required. The accent is on flexibility. Choosing fittings in keeping with the style of the room will help to ensure that its lighting looks good by day or by night.

Dining rooms have slightly different needs. The main requirement is a table that is well lit without glare, which you can satisfy with a rise-and-fall fitting or carefully targeted downlighters. The background lighting should be subdued, preferably under dimmer control – note that fluorescent lights cannot be easily dimmed. Additional lighting from wall lights or wallwashers can be used to illuminate the serving and carving area, and uplighters for dramatic effect.

WASHING WALLS WITH LIGHT

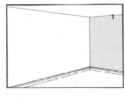
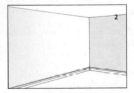

A row of wallwashers of the same wattage create a perfect wash (**1**); decreasing wattages along the row give a graded wash (**2**). A row of downlighters can create a scalloped effect (**3**); a single downlighter casts a parabola (**4**).

LIGHTING FOR KITCHENS AND BATHROOMS

Below: Kitchens are difficult to light because most tasks take place round the perimeter of the room. Lights above counter tops are the perfect solution.

Kitchens pose special lighting problems mainly owing to the wide use of the fitted kitchen. In the old days most food preparation was done on a central table, so a central light was generally adequate. Now almost every task is carried out close to the perimeter of the room, and a central light – still the standard fitting in many homes – is now useless, condemning the cook to working in his or her own shadow.

What a modern kitchen needs is lighting tailored to provide good illumination at each of the main work stations – the cooker (stove), the sink and the food preparation area. There should also be a reasonable level of general background lighting, plus lighting to illuminate the insides of cupboards (closets). These requirements can only be achieved by separate, flexible and independently controllable light sources.

If the cooker has an extractor hood over it, one containing a downlighter will illuminate the hob (burners) satisfactorily. Otherwise the aim should be to provide ceiling-mounted lights positioned so that they shine directly on the hob without casting a shadow. The same is needed over the sink. Ideally each of these lights or sets of lights should have its own switch so that it can be switched on and off as required. For counter tops below wall storage units, lighting is best provided by striplights fixed beneath the wall units and shielded by baffles to prevent glare. Walk-in cupboards and open display units can be lit by recessed downlighters, and base units can be lit by small interior lights with automatic switches worked by opening the doors. If the kitchen is also used for eating, provide a rise-and-fall fitting or recessed downlighters over the kitchen table so

that the rest of the kitchen lighting can be turned off – not least to hide the cooking debris during the meal.

Bathrooms are much less demanding. The basic requirement is for a modest level of background lighting, provided by a close-mounted central light or some recessed fittings. If the washbasin area is used for shaving or applying

make-up, add a wall strip (fluorescent) light over the basin to provide good, glare-free illumination there. Do not install a fluorescent light if it is to be used for applying make-up. Even the best types give a slightly inaccurate rendering of some colours. There may also be a need for a splashproof recessed light fitting in a shower cubicle.

Above: Track lighting is a versatile solution for kitchens and utility rooms, since individual spots can be adjusted to cast light where it is most wanted.

Above: In bathrooms, enclosed fittings are a must for safety reasons. A central fitting with an opaque diffuser will cast a soft overall light.

Left: Recessed downlighters can be used in bathrooms to provide some additional illumination above areas such as vanity units.

LIGHTING IN BEDROOMS

Bedroom lighting requires a combination of restful background lighting and easily controllable local lighting to cover separate activities such as dressing and undressing, applying make-up, reading in bed, or perhaps watching television. Remember that every fitting must look as good from the viewpoint of the bed as from elsewhere in the room.

Background lighting can be provided by wall lights, by table lamps on bedside tables, by recessed downlighters or, very appropriately for bedrooms, with the wall- or ceiling-mounted fittings known as uplighters, which throw light onto the ceiling and completely conceal the lamp when viewed from below. The general light level can be lower than for living rooms, as long as the task lighting does its job. Bright,

glare-free lighting is needed at a dressing table, and good light from above to check clothes. Fluorescent lighting should not be used here, because it falsifies certain colours, so choose ordinary lightbulbs.

Bedside reading lights should be directional so that they illuminate the page adequately but do not disturb a sleeping partner. Lastly, make full use of two-way switching so that lights can be turned on and off without having to get out of bed. Again, choose light fittings to complement the room's decor and colour scheme.

Children's rooms, especially nurseries, have slightly different requirements. Good task lighting is essential for jobs such as changing or dressing a baby, and young children will want a higher overall lighting level

than in an adult's room when playing. They may also need a low-wattage night light for comfort and safety. Finally, older children will want portable task lighting for activities such as hobbies and homework.

The landing and stairwell should not be forgotten. This is one area of the home where good bright lighting is essential; safety is more important than mood here, ensuring that all parts of the staircase are clearly lit without glare. For the best effect, fittings should be positioned so that treads are lit but risers are in shadow. Make sure that any suspended fittings do not impede passage up and down the staircase, and check that recessed fittings are readily accessible – it is irritating to have to get a ladder out to reach a high-level fitting whenever a lamp fails.

Above: Recessed downlighters are the ideal light source for children's rooms, providing good illumination of play and storage areas yet remaining safely out of harm's way.

Left: An opaque shade on a bedside light prevents glare while providing gentle background uplighting and enough downlighting for bedtime reading.

Right: In bedrooms, light fittings need careful selection because they must look as attractive from the bed as from elsewhere in the room. Globe lamps look good and are free from glare.

Below: In nurseries, low-energy fluorescent lamps offer the ideal combination of long life and safety, since the lamp envelope is cool to the touch.

Above: Halls and stairwells need good illumination for safety reasons. Here recessed downlighters illuminate every tread of the staircase and highlight the hall's features too.

Above: A wall-mounted downlighter can also be used to safely light a staircase, casting the risers into shadow and so making the treads more clearly visible.

LIGHTING FOR DISPLAY AND SECURITY

Most of the lighting schemes mentioned so far have concentrated on illuminating individual rooms and providing good task lighting for the various activities carried out in them. However, lighting can also be used as a means of decorating rooms and highlighting their best features.

Spotlights offer great flexibility here. They are available as single, double and triple spot units for wall or ceiling mounting, as individual spotlights designed to fit on lighting track, or as recessed 'eyeball' ceiling fittings. The beam direction can be adjusted to 'wash' walls, curtains (drapes) or ceilings with light, which may be coloured instead of white; or to illuminate an individual area of the room such as a fireplace, an arch, an alcove, a display unit (cabinet) or some other feature.

Small spotlights, especially the recessed eyeball types, can be used to illuminate individual pictures or picture groups on your walls. Alternatively, a traditional picture light – a small strip light in a wall-mounted holder – may be set above or below the picture.

Shelves or closed cabinets displaying china, glass or other *objets d' art* can be lit in several ways. Spotlighting is one, but this can look harsh. What often works better is either backlighting via small tungsten filament strip lights fitted beneath the shelves or, where glass shelves are used, a lamp behind a frosted glass panel at the top or bottom of the unit.

That last area of lighting that is well worth considering is indoor security lighting. It is well known that intruders are deterred by good lighting outside the house; this also applies indoors, for several reasons. The first is that if a would-be intruder sees an indoor light,

he can never be sure whether the house is occupied or not, especially if the curtains are drawn. Even if the owners are out, he will be less keen to break in and risk being seen from outside.

There are several types of programmable controls which can be used to switch both fixed lighting and plug-in lights on, either at preset times or at sunset. Some can then mimic human behaviour by turning lights on and off at random during the night, and will switch off at dawn. Others turn lights on – and can also trigger a burglar alarm – if they detect the body heat of an intruder, much like the sensors used out of doors. All give extra protection, especially if combined with electrically controlled curtain closers.

Above: Coloured lamps can help to accentuate a room's colour scheme, while concealed lighting in display alcoves makes the most of china and other treasures.

Above: Pictures can be brought to life if highlighted by an individual spotlight or a linear picture light.

Opposite: Low-voltage tungsten halogen lighting sheds a crisp white light that is perfect for highlighting a collection of ornamental glass.

Left: Use a combination of small clip-on spotlights and freestanding fittings to cast individual pools of light on decorative objects within an alcove.

PLANNING THE WORK

Once it is clear exactly what work is to be carried out in the home, it is essential to plan the job properly so as to do things in a sensible order. This will not only ensure that the work proceeds smoothly, with the minimum of disruption to family life; it will also help in estimating accurately the quantities of materials needed for each phase of the job, and to check that all the necessary tools and materials are to hand, including hired equipment.

Where to start depends on how extensive the work is. Begin with any major internal alterations such as building partition walls; creating through rooms; relocating rooms; adding or blocking off windows and doorways; removing, blocking or opening up chimney breasts; and lowering ceilings. Then carry out any alterations that are needed to the services – for example electric wiring, plumbing or heating pipework – whether this is to improve them generally or to cope with the alterations. If merely repainting or covering a wall, remove existing furniture, fixtures and fittings in order to strip out any materials that are to be replaced, or to prepare existing surfaces. At this stage, there is an opportunity to tackle any general repairs that may be required to make good the wall, floor, ceiling and woodwork surfaces, before starting work on the new scheme.

Finally, complete the work in each room by replacing the fixtures and fittings, followed by bringing in existing or replacement furniture and adding the soft furnishings.

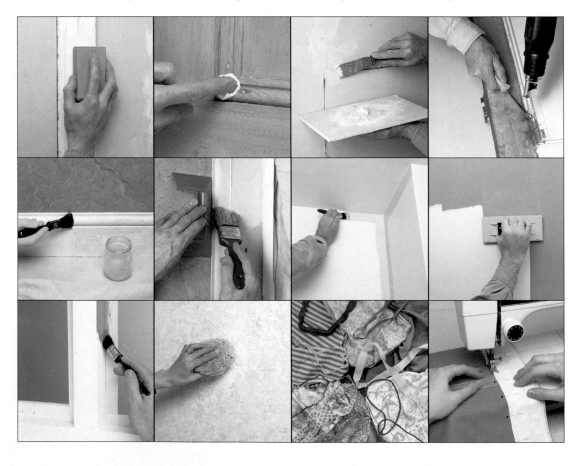

STEP-BY-STEP CHECKLIST

Use this checklist to help in organizing each numbered stage of the work and to draw up a record of the tools, equipment and materials required.

Task	Materials	Tools/equipment
1 Remove furniture from affected room(s)		
2 Remove fixtures and fittings: go to 7 if not carrying out major work		
3 Carry out structural alterations		
4 Relocate room contents		
5 Alter/extend/Improve services		
6 Replace features (doors, mouldings/trims etc.) being altered		
7 Remove old wall and floor covering materials being replaced		
8 Make good any damaged surfaces		
9 Wash or rub down painted wall/ceiling surfaces		
10 Wash or rub down painted woodwork		
11 Clean floors, level surface if uneven		
12 Paint or paper ceilings		
13 Paint or cover walls		
14 Paint woodwork		
15 Fix wall tiles/cladding (panelling)		
16 Add decorative mouldings, borders etc.		
17 Replace fixtures and fittings (light switches shelf brackets, curtain (drapery) track, built-in furniture etc.)		
18 Lay new floor coverings		
19 Reposition furniture		
20 Add soft furnishings (curtains/drapes, blinds/shades, cushions etc.)		

PAINTING

Painting walls, woodwork and other surfaces is, so all the surveys reveal, by far the most popular do-it-yourself job. Modern paints and improvements in the design and manufacture of decorating tools have certainly made the task less arduous than it was in the days of traditional oil-bound paints and distemper, and have also made it easier for the amateur decorator to get professional-looking results.

One major shift in paint technology is the trend away from using solvent-based varnishes and paints for wood, towards water-based products which do not give off harmful vapours as they dry. Water-based finishes are not as durable as solvent-based ones, but are no longer as far behind them in performance terms as they once were, and they have other advantages such as faster drying times, virtually no smell and easier cleaning of brushes, rollers and pads. It is therefore likely that their use in the home will become much more widespread.

No amount of clever technology can eliminate the need for proper preparation of the surfaces to be decorated, even though this part of the job is far less enjoyable and often more time-consuming than the actual painting. In many cases it will involve little other than washing the surface down, but sometimes more thorough preparation will be called for.

This chapter describes the various types of paint, varnish and stain on the market; which to use where; how to prepare surfaces for redecoration; how to apply the new finish – especially to the more awkward surfaces such as windows and panelled doors – and how to create a range of special paint effects that can be a dramatic and inexpensive alternative to wall coverings.

Opposite: Paint offers a huge palette of colours, and complementary and contrasting shades can create the subtlest and most restful of colour schemes. It is the easiest finish to change too when a room needs a new look.

TYPES OF PAINT, VARNISH AND STAIN

Paint works by forming a film on the surface to which it is applied. This film has to do three things: it must hide the surface underneath; it must protect it; and it must stay put. All paint has three main ingredients: pigment, binder and carrier. The *pigment* gives the film its colour and hiding power. The *binder* binds the pigment particles together into a continuous film as the paint dries, and also bonds the film to the surface beneath. In traditional paint this was a natural material such as linseed oil in oil paints, or glue size in distemper; but modern paints use synthetic resins such as alkyd, acrylic, vinyl and polyurethane. The third ingredient, the *carrier*, makes the paint flow smoothly as it is applied, and evaporates as the paint dries.

The ratio of pigment to binder in a paint affects the finish it has when it dries; the higher the pigment content, the duller the finish. By adjusting this ratio, paint manufacturers can produce paints that dry to a flat *matt* finish; to a silky sheen, *eggshell*; or to a high *gloss*. The choice depends on personal preference, tempered by the condition of the surface: high-gloss finishes highlight any imperfections, while matt finishes tend to disguise them.

Paint types

The paint types used in the home have different carriers. Water-based paint has the pigment and binder suspended in water as tiny droplets. It is an emulsion, like milk, and is usually called *emulsion* paint. (In the USA it is

Above: The yellow water-based paint chosen for the walls of this kitchen creates a basically warm colour scheme that is off-set by the gloss paint in cool colours selected for the woodwork. Solvent-based (oil) paint is ideal for surfaces which need washing down regularly.

Left: There is nothing like a hint of strong contrast to bring a neutral colour scheme to life, as the bright red bedposts and picture rail do so dramatically here. Paints specially formulated for steamy locations should be used in en-suite bathrooms.

Right: Blues and greys are cool, fresh colours that particularly suit a well-lit children's room. The brightly painted ladder provides the perfect contrast. Painted surfaces need to be able to withstand some rough treatment in these locations.

Paint systems

A single coat of paint is too thin to form a durable paint film. To provide adequate cover and performance there must be a paint system consisting of several coats. What these are depends on the type of paint used, and on the surface being painted.

The first coat is a *sealer*, which is used where necessary to seal in things such as the natural resin in wood, or to prevent the paint from soaking into a porous surface.

The second is a *primer*, which provides a good key for the paint film to stick to. On metal surfaces, this also stops the metal corroding or oxidizing. A primer can also act as a sealer.

The third is the *undercoat*, which builds up the film to form a flexible,

Above: A palette of yellow shades adds up to an irresistibly welcoming colour scheme for a baby's nursery.

often called *latex* paint.) As the water evaporates the droplets coalesce to form the paint film. Solvent-based *alkyd* paints have pigment and binder dissolved in a petroleum-based solvent, and take longer to dry than water-based paints. (In the USA these are known as *oil* or *oil-base* paints, though the term 'alkyd' is used for some primers of this kind.) These paints give off a characteristic 'painty' smell as they dry, which many people find unpleasant and to which some are actually allergic. Because of growing awareness of the health risks of inhaling some solvents, the use of these paints is declining in popularity and is already legally restricted in some countries.

Paint also contains a range of other additives to improve its performance. The most notable is one that makes the paint *thixotropic* or non-drip, allowing more paint to be loaded onto the brush and a thicker paint film to be applied; one coat is often sufficient.

Left: Paint is not only for walls, ceilings and woodwork; it can also help to enhance the crisp lines of ornamental plasterwork.

TYPES OF PAINT, VARNISH AND STAIN *(continued)*

Below: Plain painted walls can be given a personal touch with hand-painted embellishments. Decorators with unsteady hands can use stencils instead.

Above: Sponging a second colour over a complementary base coat creates a soft broken-colour effect.

Above: Rag-rolling is another broken-colour effect that can look especially attractive when applied in stripes over the base colour.

non-absorbent base of uniform colour close to that of the fourth and final layer, the *top coat*, which gives the actual finish and colour.

On walls, for which water-based paint is generally used, the system consists simply of two or three coats of the same paint unless there is a need for a sealer or primer to cure a fault in the surface such as dustiness, high alkalinity or excessive porosity. The first coat is a *mist* coat of thinned paint. A primer is also used if walls are being painted with solvent-based paints.

On woodwork, the first step is to apply a liquid called *knotting* (shellac) to any knots to prevent resin from bleeding through the paint film. Then comes a wood primer, which may be water-based or solvent-based, followed by an undercoat and then the top coat. To speed up the painting process, paint manufacturers have now perfected combined primer/undercoats, and have also introduced so-called *self-undercoating* gloss paint which just needs a primer.

On metal, a primer is generally needed. A zinc phosphate primer is used for iron or steel, and there are special primers for aluminium. This is then followed by an undercoat and top coat, as for wood. Copper, brass and lead can be painted directly without the need for a primer so long as they are brought to a bright finish first and are thoroughly degreased with white spirit (paint thinner).

Varnishes and wood stains

Varnish is basically paint without the pigment. Most contain polyurethane resins and are solvent-based (like oil paint), although water-based acrylic varnishes are becoming more popular for health and environmental reasons,

CLEANING PAINTING EQUIPMENT

Paint is thinned or diluted if necessary with water or white spirit (paint thinner) according to the paint type. Wash tools and equipment in soapy water if using a water-based paint, and with white spirit or a proprietary brush cleaner for solvent-based (oil) paint. Soak hardened paint in paint remover overnight, then wash out the softened paint with hot soapy water.

Above: Coloured varnishes help to enhance the colour of the wood grain without obliterating it completely, as paint does.

Above: Varnish is a hardwearing alternative to paint on wood with an attractive grain pattern, and the surface shows marks less readily than paint too.

just as solvent-based paints are losing ground to water-based types. Varnishes are available with a satin/silk or a high-gloss finish, either clear or with the addition of small amounts of colour. These coloured varnishes are intended to enhance the appearance of the wood, or to give it some extra colour without obliterating the wood grain, as paint would do.

Varnish is its own primer and undercoat, although it is best to thin the first coat with about 10 per cent white spirit (paint thinner) for solvent-based types, or water for acrylic types, and to apply it with a lint-free cloth rather than a brush so that it can be rubbed well into the wood grain. When this first coat has dried, it is *keyed* or roughened by rubbing very lightly with fine abrasive paper (sandpaper), dusted off, and a second, full-strength coat brushed on. For surfaces likely to get a lot of wear, it is advisable to key the second coat as before and apply an additional coat.

Wood stains, unlike paint and varnish, are designed to soak into the wood. They may subsequently be sealed

with clear varnish to improve the finish and make the surface more durable. They are available in water-based or solvent-based types in a wide range of colours and wood shades; different colours of the same type can be blended to obtain intermediate shades, and the stain can be thinned with water or white spirit as appropriate to give a paler effect.

Stains are often applied with a brush or a paint pad, but it is often quicker and easier to get even coverage by putting them on with a clean lint-free cloth. Quick work is needed to blend wet edges together, and to avoid overlaps which will leave darker patches as the stain dries. A water-based stain will raise fibres on the surface of the wood, which will spoil the evenness of the colour. The solution is to sand the surface perfectly smooth first and then dampen it with a wet cloth. This will raise the surface fibres. When the wood is dry these fibres are sanded off with extra-fine abrasive paper, ready to receive the application of stain.

Above: Varnish can be used to enhance the natural beauty of wood throughout the home, from floors and fire surrounds to storage units and other items of furniture.

PAINTING TOOLS AND EQUIPMENT

Two groups of tools are needed, one for preparing the surface and one for actually putting the paint on. For a masonry wall, the minimum preparation is to wash down any previously painted surface. This calls for a bucket, sponges and cloths, strong household detergent or sugar soap (all-purpose cleaner), and rubber gloves to protect the hands.

If the washed-down surface has a high-gloss finish, or feels rough to the touch, use fine abrasive paper (sandpaper) and a sanding block to smooth it down. Wet-and-dry (silicon carbide) paper, used wet, is best for sanding down existing paintwork; rinse off the resulting fine slurry of paint with water afterwards. Use ordinary abrasive paper for bare wood.

Defects in the surface need filling. Use a traditional cellulose filler (spackle) for small cracks, chips and other surface blemishes, and an expanding filler foam which can be shaped and sanded when hard for larger defects. To apply filler paste use a filling knife (putty knife).

To strip existing paintwork, use either a heat gun – easier to control and much safer to use than a blowtorch – or a chemical paint remover, plus scrapers of various shapes to remove the softened paint. For removing wall coverings in order to apply a painted wall or ceiling finish, a steam wallpaper stripper will be invaluable. The small all-in-one strippers which resemble a large steam iron are the easiest type to use.

Painting tools

The paintbrush is still the favourite tool for applying paint to walls, ceilings, woodwork and metalwork around the house. Most are made with natural bristle, held in a metal ferrule which is attached to a wooden or plastic handle, but there are also brushes with synthetic fibre bristles which are sometimes recommended for applying water-based (latex) paints.

Brushes come in widths from 12 mm ($^1/_2$ in) up to 150 mm (6 in). The smallest sizes are used for fiddly jobs such as painting glazing bars (muntins), while the widest are ideal for flat uninterrupted wall and ceiling surfaces. However, a wide brush can be tiring to use, especially with solvent-based (oil) paints. There are also long-handled

PREPARATION EQUIPMENT

The following tools and equipment are the general items needed to prepare for repainting: steam wallpaper stripper (**1**), liquid paint remover (**2**), paste paint remover (**3**), cellulose filler (spackle) (**4**), expanding filler foam (**5**), rubber gloves (**6**), bucket (**7**), sugar soap (all-purpose cleaner) (**8**), sponge (**9**), cloth (**10**), spray gun (**11**), abrasive paper (sandpaper) (**12**), sanding block (**13**), shavehooks (triangular scrapers) (**14**), scrapers (**15**), heat gun and attachments (a directional nozzle and two integral scrapers) (**16**).

brushes with angled heads for painting behind radiators, and narrow brushes called *cutting-in* (sash) brushes, which have the bristle tips cut off at an angle for painting into internal angles. For the best results, buy good-quality brushes and look after them, rather than buy cheap ones and throw them away after finishing the job.

Paint rollers are used mainly for painting walls and ceilings with water-based paints, although they can be used with solvent-based types too. They consist of a metal roller cage mounted on a handle, plus a hollow sleeve that fits onto the cage and actually applies the paint. Some can be fitted with an extension pole, which is useful if there are high ceilings or stairwells to paint. Most rollers are 180 mm (7 in) wide;

larger sizes are available, but can be harder to 'drive'. There are also slim mini-rollers for painting awkward-to-reach areas such as walls behind radiators. For any type, a roller tray is used to load paint onto the sleeve. Solid water-based paint is sold in its own tray.

The sleeves are waterproof tubes with a layer of foam plastic or cloth stuck to the outside. The second type may be made from natural or synthetic fibre, and have a short, medium or long pile. Choose the pile length to match the surface being painted: short for flat surfaces, medium for those with a slight texture and long for heavily embossed or sculpted surfaces.

Paint pads are squares or rectangles of short-pile cloth stuck to a foam backing

and mounted on a plastic or metal handle. The pad is dipped in a shallow container, or loaded from a special paint container with a roller feed, and then drawn across the surface. Pads come in a range of sizes.

Paint and varnish are also sold in *aerosol* form. This is ideal for small areas or fiddly materials such as wickerwork, but too expensive to use on large areas.

Lastly, do not forget the decorating sundries. A *paint kettle* is needed for decanting the paint and straining out any foreign bodies. Hand-held *paint masks* or *masking tape* are invaluable aids to getting straight edges and keeping paint off adjacent surfaces. Above all, remember to provide *dust sheets* (drop cloths), which perform better than plastic sheets.

PAINTING EQUIPMENT

This selection of equipment includes: brushes in various sizes (**1**), aerosol paint (**2**), long-handled brush for use behind radiators (**3**), hand-held skirting (baseboard) masks (**4**), slimline mini-roller (**5**), roller extension pole (**6**), a full-sized roller with short-pile sleeve and roller tray (**7**), dust sheet (drop cloth) (**8**), white spirit (paint thinner) (**9**), long pile and textured roller sleeves (**10**), paint shield (**11**), masking tape (**12**), paint kettle (**13**), paint pads in various sizes and shapes (**14**), paint-loading containers for paint pads (**15**).

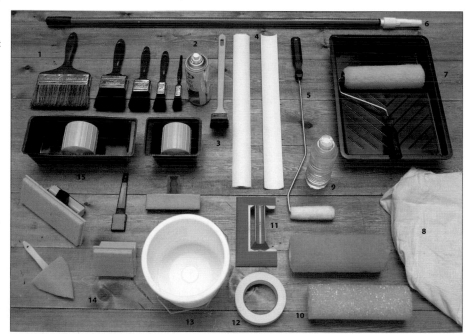

PREPARING SURFACES FOR PAINTING

Modern paints have excellent adhesion and covering power, but to get the best performance from them they must be given a good start by preparing the surface thoroughly.

Wash surfaces, which have previously been painted, using a solution of strong household detergent or sugar soap (all-purpose cleaner). Rinse them very thoroughly with clean water, and allow them to dry completely before starting repainting.

Remove areas of flaking paint with a scraper or filling knife (putty knife), and then either touch in the bare area with more paint or fill it flush with the surrounding paint film by using fine filler (spackle). Sand this smooth when it has hardened.

If the surface shows signs of mildew growth due to persistent condensation, wipe it over with household bleach, or refrigerator cleaner containing a fungicide, to kill off the spores. Wash

down the surface with detergent and rinse thoroughly.

If knots are showing through on painted woodwork, sand the paint film back to bare wood and apply knotting (shellac) to the knot, then prime and undercoat to bring the new paint film level with the surrounding paintwork. Sand between coats. Resinous knots may produce stains which can only be prevented by drying the knot out with a blowtorch.

PREPARING PAINTED WOODWORK

1 Use fine-grade abrasive paper (sandpaper) wrapped around a sanding block to remove 'nibs' from the paint surface and to key the paint film ready for repainting.

2 Wash the surface down with detergent or sugar soap (all-purpose cleaner) to remove dirt, grease, finger marks and the dust from sanding it. Rinse with clean water, ensuring that no detergent residue is left as this will inhibit the new paint film.

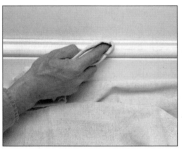

3 Use a proprietary tack rag or a clean cloth moistened with white spirit (paint thinner) to remove dust from recessed mouldings and other awkward corners.

FILLING DEFECTS IN WOOD

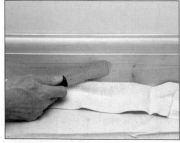

1 Fill splits and dents in wood using filler (spackle) on painted surfaces, and tinted wood stopper (patcher) on new or stripped wood that will be varnished.

2 Use the corner of a filling knife (putty knife), or even a finger, to work the wood filler into recesses and other awkward-to-reach places. Smooth off excess filler before it dries.

3 When the filler or wood stopper has hardened completely, use abrasive paper (sandpaper) wrapped around a sanding block to sand the repair down flush.

FILLING CRACKS IN PLASTER

1 Use the corner of a filling knife (putty knife) to rake out loose material along the line of the crack, and to undercut the edges slightly so that the filler has a better grip.

2 Brush out dust and debris from the crack, using an old paintbrush. Alternatively, use the crevice nozzle attachment of a vacuum cleaner.

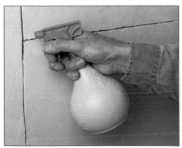

3 Dampen the surrounding plaster with water from a garden spray gun to prevent it from drying out the filler too quickly and causing it to crack.

4 Mix up some filler on a plasterer's hawk (mortarboard) or a board offcut to a firm consistency. Alternatively, use ready-mixed filler or wallboard compound.

5 Use a filling knife to press the filler well into the crack, drawing the blade across it and then along it. Aim to leave the repair slightly proud.

DEALING WITH STAINS

If ceilings have been stained by plumbing leaks, seal the affected area with a proprietary aerosol stain sealer to prevent the stain from showing through the new paint film. Alternatively, paint the affected area with white gloss (oil) paint – it will seal just as well and is usually already on hand. It can be overpainted with water-based (latex) paint.

6 When the filler has hardened, use fine-grade abrasive paper (sandpaper) wrapped around a sanding block to smooth the repair flush with the surrounding wall.

STRIPPING PAINT

Every time a surface is repainted, this adds a little more thickness to the paint layer. It does not matter much on wall or ceiling surfaces, but on woodwork (and, to a lesser extent, on metalwork) this build-up of successive layers of paint can eventually lead to the clogging of detail on mouldings. More importantly, moving parts such as doors and windows start to bind and catch against their frames. If this happens, it is time to strip off the paint back to bare wood and build up a new paint system from scratch.

It may also be necessary to strip an old paint finish if it is in such poor condition – from physical damage, for example – that repainting will no longer cover up the faults adequately.

There are two methods of removing paint from wood and metal surfaces. The first is using *heat*, traditionally from a blowtorch but nowadays more often an electric heat gun. The second is to use a *chemical paint remover*, which contains either dimethylene chloride or caustic soda. Heat works well on wood, but may scorch the surface and can crack the glass in windows; it is less successful on metal because the material conducts heat away as it is applied. Chemicals work well on all surfaces, but need handling with care; always follow the manufacturer's instructions to the letter.

HOMEMADE PASTE REMOVER

Add caustic soda to water until no more will dissolve. Thicken to a paste with oatmeal and use as for proprietary paste remover. Be particularly careful when using this corrosive solution. If it splashes on the skin, rinse at once with plenty of cold water.

USING A HEAT GUN

1 Play the air stream from the heat gun over the surface to soften the paint film. Scrape it off as it bubbles up, and deposit the hot scrapings in an old metal container.

2 Use a shavehook (triangular scraper) instead of a flat scraper to remove the paint from mouldings. Take care not to scorch the wood if it is to be varnished afterwards.

3 Remove any remnants of paint from the wood surface with wire wool soaked in white spirit (paint thinner), working along the direction of the grain.

4 Use a hand vacuum cleaner to remove any remaining loose particles of paint from the crevices in mouldings and from any other inaccessible areas.

5 Sand the surface of the wood lightly to remove any raised fibres or rough patches, then wipe it over with a clean cloth moistened with white spirit.

6 Seal the resin in any exposed knots by brushing on a coat of liquid knotting (shellac). Leave this to dry thoroughly before priming the wood.

7 Apply a coat of either wood primer or a combined primer/undercoat to the stripped wood surface to provide optimum adhesion for the subsequent top coats.

USING LIQUID REMOVER

1 Wear rubber gloves and old clothing. Decant the liquid into a polythene (polyethylene) container or an old can, then brush it onto the surface you want to strip. Leave it until the paint film bubbles up.

2 Use a flat scraper or shavehook (triangular scraper) as appropriate to remove the softened paint. Deposit the scrapings safely in an old container.

3 Neutralize the stripper by washing the surface down with water or white spirit (paint thinner), as recommended by the manufacturer. Leave it to dry.

USING PASTE REMOVER

1 Paste removers are especially good for removing paint from intricate mouldings because they dry very slowly. Apply the paste liberally to the surface.

2 Give the paste plenty of time to work, especially on thick paint layers. Then scrape it off and wash down the surface with plenty of water to neutralize the chemical.

USING A PAINTBRUSH

The paintbrush is the most versatile and therefore the most widely used tool for applying paint. Choose the brush size to match the surface being painted. For example, for painting glazing bars (muntins) on windows or narrow mouldings on a door, use a slim brush – or perhaps a cutting-in (sash) brush if painting up to an adjacent unpainted surface such as glass where a neat edge to the paint film is needed. For expansive, flat areas select a larger brush for quick coverage. Remember that the largest wall brushes can be tiring to use, especially with solvent-based (oil) paints.

Get rid of any loose bristles in a new brush by flicking it vigorously across the palm of the hand before using it for the first time. Wash previously used brushes that have been stored unwrapped to remove any dust or other debris from the bristles, and leave them to dry out again before using them to apply a solvent-based paint.

Always check that the metal ferrule is securely attached to the brush handle, and hammer in any projecting nails or staples. Check too that the ferrule is free from rust which could discolour the paint. To remove rust use either wire wool or abrasive paper (sandpaper).

PREPARING THE PAINT

1 Wipe the lid first to remove any dust. Then prise it off with a wide lever such as the thicker edge of a table knife to avoid damage to the lip.

2 Decant some paint into a clean metal or plastic paint kettle, or small bucket. This is easier to handle than a full container, especially one without a handle.

3 Remove any paint skin from partly used containers. Then strain the paint into the paint kettle through a piece of old stocking or tights (pantyhose), or cheesecloth.

HOLDING THE BRUSH

1 Before using a new brush, work it vigorously backwards and forwards across the palm of the hand to remove any loose bristles. Wash brushes that have been stored for a while.

2 The best control of a small or medium-sized brush is achieved by holding it with the fingers and thumb on the ferrule, rather than on the handle.

3 Wide wall brushes can be tiring to use, and it is usually more comfortable to grip the brush by the handle rather than by the ferrule.

USING A BRUSH

1 To load the brush with paint, dip it into the paint to about a third of the bristle depth. An overloaded brush will cause drips, and paint will run down the brush handle.

2 Tie a length of string or wire across the mouth of the paint kettle between the handle supports, and use it to scrape excess paint from the bristles.

3 Apply the paint to the wood in long, sweeping strokes, brushing the paint out along the grain direction until the brush begins to run dry.

4 Load up the brush with more paint and apply it to the next area. Blend the two together with short, light strokes, again along the grain direction.

5 Repeat this process while working across the area, blending the edges of adjacent areas together with light brushstrokes to avoid leaving a visible join.

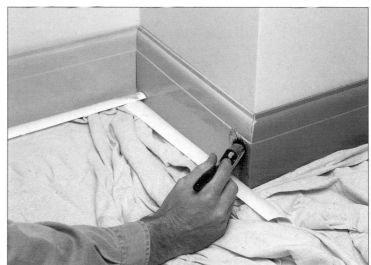

6 At edges and external corners, let the brush run off the edge to avoid a build-up of paint on the corner. Repeat the process for the opposite edge.

USING PAINT ROLLERS AND PADS

Paint rollers are generally used to apply water-based (latex) paints to large, flat areas such as walls and ceilings. Choose a sleeve with a short pile for painting plaster, a medium pile for painting embossed or textured wall coverings, and a long pile for deeply sculpted surfaces such as those created with textured finishes (texture paints). Rollers can also apply solvent-based (oil) paint to flat surfaces such as flush doors, but tend to leave a distinctive 'orange peel' texture rather than the smooth finish left by a paintbrush.

There are some drawbacks with paint rollers: they cannot paint right up to internal corners or wall/ceiling angles, so these need to be painted first with a brush or pad. They can also splash if 'driven' too fast, and the sleeves take a lot of time and effort to clean thoroughly, especially if they have been used for a long period and there is dried paint in the pile. Repeated cleaning eventually causes the sleeve to peel from its core.

People either love or loathe paint pads. They tend to apply less paint per coat than either a brush or a roller, so an additional coat may be needed in some circumstances, but they make it easy to apply paint smoothly and evenly with no risk of brush marks.

USING A ROLLER

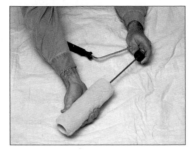

1 Select a sleeve with the required fibre type and pile length, and slide it onto the sprung metal cage until it meets the stop next to the handle.

3 Brush a band of paint about 50 mm (2 in) wide into internal corners and wall/ceiling angles, around doors and windows, and above skirtings (baseboards).

5 Start applying the paint in a series of overlapping diagonal strokes to ensure complete coverage of the surface. Continue until the sleeve runs dry.

2 Decant some paint (previously strained if from an old can) into the roller tray until the paint level just laps up the sloping section.

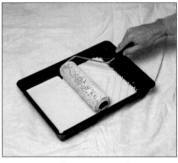

4 Load the roller sleeve with paint by running it down the sloping section into the paint. Then roll it up and down the slope to remove the excess.

6 Reload the sleeve and tackle the next section in the same way. Finish off by blending the areas together, working parallel to corners and edges.

USING A PAINT PAD

1 Pour some paint into the special applicator tray. Then load the pad by running it backwards and forwards over the ridged loading roller.

2 On walls, apply the paint in a series of overlapping parallel bands. Use a small pad or a special edging pad (see step 4) to paint right up to corners or angles.

3 Use smaller pads for painting narrow areas such as mouldings on doors or glazing bars (muntins) on windows. Bush out the paint along the direction of the grain.

4 Special edging pads are designed for painting right up to internal angles, and have small wheels which guide the pad along the adjacent surface as you work.

USING AEROSOL PAINT

Aerosol paints and varnishes are ideal for hard-to-decorate surfaces such as wickerwork. Always follow the maker's instructions when using them.

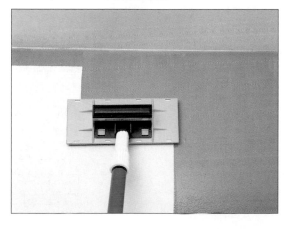

5 Some larger pads can be fitted to an extension pole to make it easier to paint ceilings and high walls. Make sure the pad is attached securely.

PAINTING WALLS AND CEILINGS

Paint is a popular decorative finish for walls and ceilings because it is quick and easy to apply, offers a huge range of colours and is relatively inexpensive compared with rival products such as wall coverings. It can be used over plain plaster, or can be applied over embossed relief wall coverings and textured finishes.

Before starting painting, clear the room and prepare the surfaces. Start by taking down curtains and blinds (drapes and shades). Remove furniture to another room if possible, or else group it in the middle of the room and cover it with clear plastic sheeting. Take down lampshades and pendant light fittings (after turning off the power supply). Unscrew wall-mounted fittings and remove the hardware from doors and windows if they are being repainted at the same time.

Protect surfaces not being repainted, such as wall switches and socket outlets (receptacles), with masking tape. Finally, cover the floor with dust sheets (drop cloths), which will absorb paint splashes; vacuum-clean surfaces such as window sills, picture rails and skirtings (baseboards) where dust can settle, and turn off forced-air heating so that dust is not recirculated into the room.

Access equipment

Normally most of the surfaces to be painted can be reached from a standing or a kneeling position, but for ceilings, the tops of room walls and the upper reaches of stairwells some access equipment is needed. A simple stepladder, ideally with a top platform big enough to support a paint kettle or roller tray, will be adequate for painting walls and ceilings.

Paint walls and ceilings in a series of overlapping bands. Start painting the ceiling next to the window wall so that reflected light on the wet paint shows whether coverage is even. On walls, right-handed people should work from right to left, and left-handed people the other way.

For stairwells, use steps or ladder sections plus secured scaffold boards or the components of a slot-together access tower to set up a work platform that allows you to get to all the surfaces without over-reaching.

Texture paints

These are water-based (latex) paints thickened with added fillers. Once the paint has been applied to the decorating surface, a range of three-dimensional effects can be created using various patterning or texturing techniques. These paints are ideal for covering up surfaces in poor condition. Most are white, but they can be overpainted with ordinary water-based paint for a coloured effect. Avoid using this type of paint in kitchens as the textured surface will over time trap dirt and grease which makes the surface difficult to keep clean.

PAINT COVERAGE

Paint coverage depends on several factors, including the roughness and porosity of the surface to which it is being applied and the thickness of the coating. For example, the first coat of paint will soak into new plaster, so the coverage will be less than is achieved with subsequent coats. Similarly, a textured surface will hold more paint than a smooth one, again reducing the paint coverage.

The figures given here are intended as a rough guide only. Always check the manufacturer's coverage figure on the container, and use that plus the area to be painted to work out how much paint is required.

ESTIMATING QUANTITIES

Paint type	Sq m per litre	Sq ft per gallon
Liquid gloss (oil) paint	16	650
Non-drip gloss paint	13	530
Eggshell	12	490
Matt (flat) water-based (latex) paint	15	610
Silk (satin) water-based paint	14	570
Non-drip water-based paint	12	490
Undercoat	11	450
Wood primer	12	490
Metal primer	10	410
Varnish	15–20	610–820

USING TEXTURE PAINT

1 Start applying the paint to the wall or ceiling surface in a series of overlapping random strokes, recharging the roller or brush at intervals.

2 When an area of about 1 sq m (11 sq ft) is covered, go over the whole area with a series of parallel roller/brush strokes for an even surface texture.

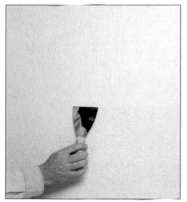

3 Give the textured finish the look of tree bark by drawing a flat-bladed scraper or similar edged tool over the surface to flatten off the high spots.

4 Use a texturing comb to create overlapping swirls, working across the area. Practise the effect on paint applied to a piece of heavy cardboard first.

5 Twist a sponge before pulling it away from the wall surface to create a series of small, overlapping swirls in the paint finish. Rinse the sponge regularly.

6 You can buy patterning roller sleeves in a range of different designs for use with texture paints. This one creates a regular diamond pattern.

7 This patterning sleeve gives a random streaked effect when rolled down the wall. Apply the texture paint with a brush first if using a patterning sleeve.

PAINTING DOORS

The main problem with painting doors – or indeed any woodwork with a large surface area – involves keeping what professional decorators call a *wet edge*. Obviously the door has to be painted bit by bit, and if the edge of one area begins to dry before this is joined up to the next area, the join will show when the paint dries completely.

The secret of success is to work in a sequence, as shown in the accompanying drawings of flush and panelled doors, and to complete the job in one continuous operation, working as fast as reasonably possible.

Before starting to paint a door, wedge it open so there is room to walk through the doorway without touching wet paint, and also so that the hinged edge of the door can be reached easily. Remove handles, locks and other fittings; wedge a length of dowel in the latch hole to make a temporary handle for use until the paint has dried. Slide a dust sheet (drop cloth) underneath the door to catch any drips. Finally, warn everyone else in the house that the door is covered with wet paint, and keep children and pets out of the way in another room or out of doors.

PAINTING FLUSH DOORS

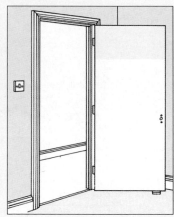

1 Remove the door furniture and wedge the door open. Then divide it up into eight or ten imaginary squares, and start painting at the top of the door by filling in the first square. Brush the paint out towards the door edges so it does not build up on the external angles.

2 Move on to the next block at the top of the door, brushing paint out towards the top and side edges as before. Carefully blend the two areas together with horizontal brushstrokes, then with light vertical laying-off strokes.

3 Continue to work down the door surface block by block, blending the wet edges of adjacent blocks together as they are painted. Always aim to complete a flush door in one session to prevent the joints between blocks showing up as hard lines. Replace the door furniture when the paint is touch-dry.

PAINTING PANELLED DOORS

1 Tackle panelled doors by painting the mouldings (**1**) around the recessed panels first. Take care not to let paint build up in the corners or to stray onto the faces of the cross-rails at this stage. Then paint the recessed panels (**2**).

2 Next, paint the horizontal cross-rails (**3**), brushing lightly inwards towards the painted panel mouldings to leave a sharp paint edge. Feather the paint out thinly where it runs onto the vertical stiles at each end of the rails.

3 Finish the door by painting the vertical centre rail (**4**) and the outer stiles (**5**), again brushing towards the panel mouldings. Where the rail abuts the cross-rails, finish with light brushstrokes parallel to the cross-rails.

PAINTING DOOR EDGES

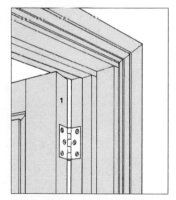

Where the two faces of a door are being painted in two different colours, the convention is to match the colour of the hinged edge to that of the closing face of the door – the one facing the next room – and to paint the leading edge to match the other door face.

1 HINGED EDGE

VARNISHING WOOD

1 On bare wood, use a clean lint-free cloth to wipe the first coat onto the wood, working along the grain direction. This coat acts as a primer/sealer.

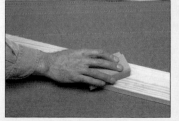

2 Sand the first coat lightly when dry to remove any 'nibs' caused by dust particles settling on the wet varnish, then wipe off the sanding dust.

3 Apply the second and subsequent coats of varnish with a brush, applying it along the grain and linking up adjacent areas with light brush strokes.

PAINTING WINDOWS

Windows are more difficult to paint than doors because they contain so many different surfaces, especially small-paned types criss-crossed with slim glazing bars (muntins). There is also the additional problem of paint straying onto the glass. The ideal is a neat paint line that covers the bedding putty and extends onto the glass surface by about 3 mm ($1/8$ in) to seal the joint and prevent condensation from running down between putty and glass.

With hinged windows, the edges of the casement or top opening light (transom) should be painted to match the colour used on the inside of the window. With double-hung sliding sash windows, the top and bottom edges of each sash and the top, bottom and sides of the frame are all painted to match the inner face of the sashes.

Remove the window hardware before you start painting. On casement windows tap a nail into the bottom edge of the casement and into the lower frame rebate and link them with stiff wire to stop the casement from swinging open or shut.

For best results, sash windows should be removed from their frames before painting. Modern spring-mounted windows are easy to release from their frames. With older cord-operated types, remove the staff beads (window stops) first to free the sashes. Although quite a major task, take the opportunity to renew the sash cords (pulley ropes). This makes it possible to cut the cords to free the window. Some making good and finishing off will have to be done after the window is reassembled.

PAINTING A CASEMENT WINDOW

1 Remove the window furniture from the opening casement and wedge the window open while you work. Tackle the glazing bars (muntins) and edge mouldings first (**1**), then the face of the surrounding casement frame (**2**) and finally the hinged edge of the casement. Paint the other edges from outside.

2 Move on to paint the glazing bars and edge mouldings (**3**) of the fixed casement. Use masking tape or a paint shield to ensure neat, straight edges here and on the opening casement; the paint should overlap the glass by about 3 mm ($1/8$ in). Paint the face of the surrounding casement frame (**4**).

PAINTING A SASH WINDOW

 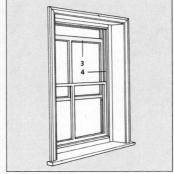

1 To paint sash windows without removing the sashes from their frames, start by raising the bottom (inner) sash and lowering the top (outer) one. Paint the lower half of the top sash (**1**), including its bottom edge, and the exposed parting beads at the top and bottom (**2**) and the exposed sides of the frame itself.

2 When the paint is touch-dry, reverse the sash positions and paint the upper half of the top sash (**3**), including its top edge, and the exposed and unpainted parting beads and frame sides (**4**).

PAINTING AROUND GLASS

3 Paint the outer frame (**5**), then the centre frame member between the opening and fixed casements (**6**). Complete the job by painting the window sill (**7**) and the rebate into which the opening casement closes.

1 Stick masking tape to the glass with its edge 3 mm (¹/₈ in) from the wood. Paint the surrounding wood, removing the tape when the paint is touch-dry.

2 Alternatively, hold a paint shield against the edge of the glazing bar (muntin) or surrounding moulding while painting. Wipe the shield regularly to prevent smears.

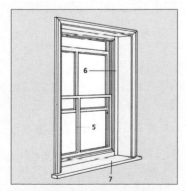

3 Finish off by painting the face and edges of the inner sash (5), the staff beads and any other trim mouldings around the window (6). Finally, paint the window sill (7). Leave the sashes ajar until the paint has dried thoroughly to avoid components sticking.

USING STAIN

Test the stain on an offcut of the same wood, or in an inconspicuous area. If necessary, dilute it. Use a clean lint free cloth to apply stain to bare wood. If the result is too pale, apply further coats when the first is dry. Avoid overlapping parallel bands of stain; the overlap will show up as a darker area when the stain dries.

TIP

To clean up an untidy paint edge on the glass, use a ruler and a very sharp knife to cut a clean edge, and carefully scrape off the excess paint up to the cut line.

SPECIAL PAINT EFFECTS

There is no need to stick to plain colour on painted walls as there is a wide range of special paint effects that will enliven their looks. Some of these effects are purely decorative in their own right; others imitate the appearance of other materials. All can be created with the use of inexpensive tools and materials, and practice and patience will bring highly attractive results.

The special paint effects dealt with here fall into two broad groups: *broken colour* and *imitation*. In the first group a range of different techniques is used to apply a second colour over a different base colour so that the latter still shows through, providing a pleasing two-colour effect. In the second group paint is used to copy the looks of materials such as wood veneers and marble.

For either finish it is essential to prepare the surface of the wall or woodwork thoroughly first (see chart).

Glazes

Most special effects are applied as a tinted glaze which is semi-transparent and allows the underlying base colour to show through. Water-based glazes are made from water-based (latex) paint diluted with water or a proprietary emulsion glaze until the required level of translucency has been achieved. Use coloured paints or tint white paint to the required shade with artists' acrylics. Water-based glazes produce a thinner, more open, coat of colour and they dry extremely quickly, which means they are not suitable for the more complex special paint effects.

Scumble is the main component of solvent-based (oil) glazes and is generally diluted with a mixture of 1 part linseed oil to 2 parts white spirit (paint thinner). However, the proportions can be varied: a higher proportion of scumble will increase the definition of the effect and will retard the drying time; more linseed oil produces a smoother texture; white spirit thins the glaze and speeds up the drying time. Once the glaze has been mixed, pour off a small quantity and add the colour to this, using either eggshell paint or artists' oils. When the correct colour has been mixed, gradually add this to the main quantity of glaze until the required level of transparency is achieved. Solvent-based glazes have a rich, hardwearing

TOOLS AND MATERIALS

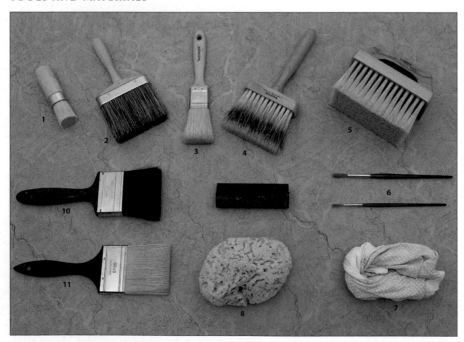

Among the tools and materials needed are a stencilling brush (**1**), a dusting brush (**2**), a small paintbrush (**3**), a softening brush (**4**), a stippling brush (**5**), artists' paintbrushes (**6**), cotton or linen rags (**7**), a natural marine sponge (**8**), a rubber rocker for graining (**9**), a large paintbrush (**10**) and a flat-bristle varnishing brush (**11**).

finish and the slower drying times are particularly suited to special effects.

If working over large areas – more than 2 sq m (22 sq ft) – two people will be needed to achieve the best finish: one to apply the glaze and the other to work it. This is the only way to maintain a wet edge and therefore to avoid noticeable joins between one area of colour and the next.

Stencilling

This is slightly different from the other techniques, since the stencil produces a clearly defined shape. It is very simple to do, and can be used to create effects in more than one colour by using different stencils. Ready-cut stencils can be bought, but it is easy to create designs of your own.

PREPARING SURFACES

The method of preparation varies depending on whether water-based (latex) paints or solvent-based (oil) paints are used for the final effect. Care taken at this early stage will help to ensure a satisfying end result.

Once the preparation is complete, apply the chosen base colour. Use eggshell for a good opaque and non-porous surface if using either a water- or a solvent-based finish and, when dry, rub it down with fine abrasive paper (sandpaper).

Surface	Water-based effect	Solvent-based effect
Bare plaster	Prime with diluted water-based paint	Prime with proprietary primer or PVA adhesive (white glue)
	Apply 1–2 water-based undercoats	Apply 1–2 solvent-based undercoats
Painted plaster	Wash down, repair defects and sand solvent-based finishes	Wash down, repair defects and sand solvent-based finishes
	Apply 1–2 water-based undercoats	Apply 1–2 solvent-based undercoats
Hardboard	Prime with diluted water-based paint	Prime with proprietary primer
	Apply 1–2 water-based undercoats	Apply 1–2 solvent-based undercoats
Bare wood	Apply knotting (shellac) to knots	Apply knotting (shellac) to knots
	Prime with diluted water-based paint	Apply proprietary primer
	Apply 1–2 water-based undercoats	Apply 1–2 solvent-based undercoats
Painted wood	As for Painted plaster	As for Painted plaster
Varnished wood	Strip and prepare as for Bare wood	Strip and prepare as for Bare wood

CUTTING STENCILS

To cut stencils, tracing paper, some special waxed paper for stencils (available from art stores), a pencil, a pin and a scalpel or sharp utility knife are needed. Trace or draw the pattern and enlarge or reduce it on a photocopier, if necessary. Tape the finished trace to the stencil paper and prick through it to mark the design outline on the stencil paper. Join up the prick marks in pencil. Alternatively, transfer the trace onto the stencil using carbon paper. Cut out the design carefully, leaving sufficient ties to bridge the separate areas of the design. Allow a large margin above and below the design so that the stencil is sufficiently strong. Reinforce any tears or accidental cuts with adhesive tape.

1 Affix the stencil to the surface with masking tape, aligning it with a true horizontal pencil guideline. Dip the stencilling brush in the paint and remove the excess on some waste paper. Use a pouncing action to apply the paint to minimize the risk of colour seeping under the stencil and marring the masked-off areas.

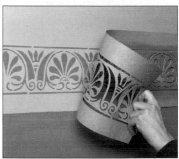

2 When the paint is touch-dry, release the stencil, wipe off the wet paint and reposition it farther along the wall to create the next section of the pattern.

SPECIAL PAINT EFFECTS *(continued)*

Sponging

This technique involves dabbing irregular patches of paint onto the base coat. Two or more different sponged colours can be applied. Note that a natural marine sponge must be used to create this effect; man-made sponges do not work. Soak it in water first until it swells to its full size, then wring it out ready to start applying the paint.

1 After testing the effect on an offcut of board, dip the sponge in the paint and apply light pressure to leave overlapping splodges of colour.

2 Allow the first application to dry, then go over the surface again and add more colour if necessary to deepen the contrast with the base colour.

3 If applying a different second colour, allow the first colour to dry and then use the same technique to apply the new colour over it.

Rag-rolling

Another simple two-colour effect, rag-rolling involves brushing a diluted second colour over the base coat and then using a rolled-up 'sausage' of cloth to remove some of the second colour before it starts to dry.

The technique works best with a base coat of eggshell paint and a top coat of eggshell paint diluted with white spirit (paint thinner). Use lint-free cotton or linen rags and change them frequently before they become soaked with paint.

1 Allow the base coat to dry thoroughly. Then lightly brush on the second diluted colour in bands across the surface, aiming to leave a random pattern of brushstrokes that allows the base colour to show through.

2 Roll the rag sausage across the surface in a continuous motion. Vary the direction for a random effect and touch in small areas by just dabbing with the cloth. Replace the rag regularly.

Stippling

For an attractive mottled appearance, try stippling; apart from being used as a decorative finish in its own right it can also be used to obliterate brush marks in the base coat beneath other broken-colour effects.

The one item of specialist equipment that is needed to create this effect is a stippling brush.

1 Brush the glaze on over the base coat, applying a generous coat. Do not worry about leaving brush marks; the stippling will obliterate them.

2 Hold the stippling brush with the bristle tips parallel with the surface, and simply hit the paint film. Clean paint from the brush regularly, wiping it with a dry cloth.

Colour washing

This is one of the simplest broken-colour effects. Brush on the glaze and then use a dry softening brush or an ordinary wide paintbrush to create a random pattern of brushstrokes that allow the base coat to show through. A further colour can be added.

1 Brush a liberal coat of the glaze over the base coat. The effect of colour washing is enhanced when there is a good contrast between the two paint colours.

2 Draw the softening brush over the glaze in a series of long random strokes in varying directions. Add a further toning colour if desired when this coat has dried.

SPECIAL PAINT EFFECTS *(continued)*

Graining

Graining is a technique that aims to imitate the look of natural wood, especially the more exotic and expensive species. Use a solvent-based (oil) eggshell paint for the base coat, and a solvent-based glaze.

1 Brush the glaze onto the wood surface, leaving the brush marks visible along the direction of the intended wood grain.

2 Then, after a couple of minutes, draw a dry graining brush or an ordinary paintbrush lightly over the glaze to create the actual grain pattern.

3 Use a rubber rocker (above), a graining comb or a bristle grainer to produce the individual grain characteristics of the wood you are copying.

Dragging

Another very simple effect, dragging is created by drawing a dry brush over the glaze in a series of parallel strokes that allow the base colour to show through. Use a normal paintbrush in a width to suit the surface being decorated.

1 Brush a generous coat of glaze over the base coat. Always work parallel to the direction of the grain if applying the effect to wood.

2 Use a dry paintbrush to drag a series of parallel lines in the second colour. Wipe the build-up of paint off the brush at regular intervals with a dry cloth.

Marbling

As its name implies, marbling copies the appearance of marble. It is a relatively difficult technique to master, but the results can be quite spectacular. For a first attempt choose a piece of real marble to copy. For best results work with a solvent-based (oil) glaze, applied over an eggshell base coat. Add the veining details with artists' oils.

1 Either brush out the glaze or apply it with a pad of lint-free cloth. Only a relatively thin coat is needed.

2 Use a dusting brush as here or a stippling brush to stipple the surface of the wet glaze. Add more colour to the glaze mixture, apply selectively to some areas for contrast and stipple the glaze again.

3 Working on the wet glaze, draw in the main areas of veining with an artists' paintbrush and a mixture of glaze and artists' oils. Use different weights of line to create a natural-looking effect.

4 Use the softening brush again to soften the outlines of the veining and to blend it into the background. Wipe the brush regularly to avoid smudges

VARNISHING SPECIAL PAINT EFFECTS

Some special paint effects, especially graining and marbling, should be sealed with a coat of clear varnish once the effect has dried completely. Use satin varnish rather than gloss unless a particularly polished effect is required. When this has dried, burnish the surface with a soft cloth and add a little wax polish to create a realistic surface sheen, if wished.

5 Highlight some areas of the veining by adding more colour or a second colour. Soften the effect again, as in step 4.

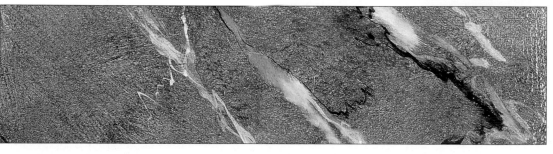

PAPERHANGING

The term 'wall coverings' is used to describe the whole range of decorative materials sold in roll form and designed to be stuck to wall and ceiling surfaces with a strippable adhesive. The range includes an enormous variety of designs, patterns and colourways … almost too many, as any home decorator will testify when confronted by an array of pattern books and trying to decide which covering to select.

The vast majority of wall coverings are either made entirely from paper, or have a plastic or cloth layer bonded to a paper backing so that they can be hung in the same way as all-paper types. The basic technology of paperhanging has changed little over the centuries, even if the products have been subtly altered and improved; people still paper the living room in a way that would be familiar to their grandparents.

The two main developments that have occurred in recent years are the introduction of ready-pasted types which are immersed in a trough of water instead of having paste brushed onto them, and of all-plastic wall coverings which are hung by pasting the wall.

This chapter gives information on the various types of wall covering available and on the tools, materials and other equipment needed to hang or strip them. There is advice on how to go about removing existing wall decorations – other wall coverings, materials such as texture paints, wall panelling and tiles of various types – and on preparing the surface. This is followed by detailed step-by-step instructions on how to hang a new wall covering on walls and ceilings, and on how to cope with awkward areas such as door and window openings, arches and stairwells.

Opposite: There is virtually no limit to the versatility of modern wall coverings. This complementary match of broken colour and simple stripes is linked by a striking multicoloured border at dado (chair) rail level.

TYPES OF WALL COVERING

Wall coverings fall into two basic groups: those with a printed design or a surface material which is decorative in its own right, and those with a surface texture or embossing which are designed to be painted over once they have been hung.

Printed wallpaper is exactly that – paper with a coloured design printed on it. It may also be embossed along the lines of the design, or may have a distinctive surface texture added during manufacture. Cheaper types may be awkward to hang, tearing easily or stretching so as to make accurate pattern matching difficult. More expensive types, especially hand-printed ones, are better in this respect, but care must still be taken when hanging them to keep paste off the face of the paper. The strongest printed wallpapers are called *duplex papers*, and are made by bonding two layers of paper together during the manufacturing process. Most printed papers can be wiped with a damp cloth if they become stained, but it is wise to check whether this is the case when selecting this type of wall covering. All are easy to strip, making them a good choice if you like to redecorate regularly.

Washable wallpaper is a printed wallpaper which has a thin clear plastic coating applied over the design during manufacture to render it water and stain resistant. As with printed types, the surface may be embossed or textured. Washable wallpapers are also widely available in ready-pasted form. The plastic surface will withstand gentle washing and sponging with a mild detergent, but not prolonged scrubbing or the use of abrasive cleaners. Choose them for rooms where they will be subject to moderate wear, or for steamy conditions such as are

Above: Contrasting wall coverings can help to change the proportions of a room. Here a darker wall covering helps lower the ceiling.

Left: Stencil borders with the design printed on a clear self- adhesive backing allow the wall covering beneath to show through – the perfect solution for unwilling stencillers.

Left: In bathrooms, vinyl wall coverings resist steam and splashes well and are easy to wipe clean. Foamed types offer excellent imitations of materials such as ceramic tiles.

Tougher still are the *foamed vinyl wall coverings*, which have a surface layer aerated with tiny bubbles to produce a slightly cushioned feel. The surface may be heavily textured or embossed to imitate materials such as ceramic tiles and wood grains, and is warm to the touch thanks to the insulating effect of the air bubbles – a fact that makes such a covering a good choice for rooms which are prone to mild condensation. Because of their bulk, they are

Below: Many collections of wall coverings feature colour-coordinated borders and fabrics to enable rooms to be given the most stylish of colour treatments.

found in kitchens and bathrooms. Their main drawback is that they are difficult to remove because the plastic coating stops water penetrating and softening the paste unless it is thoroughly scored first; a steam wallpaper stripper is advisable.

Vinyl wall coverings consist of a plastic film onto which the design is printed, laminated to a paper backing. Again, the surface may also be textured or embossed, or may have a metallic appearance – the so-called *vinyl foils*. The result is a wall covering that is much tougher than a washable type; if properly hung it can be scrubbed to remove stains and marks, although care must be taken not to lift the seams by oversoaking the surface. Vinyl wall coverings are widely available in ready-pasted form, and are extremely easy to strip since the plastic layer can be peeled off dry, leaving the paper backing on the wall. They are the ideal choice for walls that will be scuffed or brushed against – in halls and landings or on staircases, for example – and also for children's rooms, kitchens and bathrooms. They are, however, more expensive than most printed or washable wall coverings, so it is just as well that they can be expected to provide excellent wear.

TYPES OF WALL COVERING *(continued)*

sometimes sold in shorter rolls than other wall coverings.

Flock wall coverings are either printed papers or vinyls with parts of the design having a raised pile – of fine wool or silk fibres on paper types and of synthetic fibres on vinyls – that closely resembles velvet. Paper types are quite delicate and must be hung with care, but vinyl flocks are extremely tough and hardwearing.

Yet another printed wall covering is made from *foamed polythene* (polyethylene) with no paper backing, and is intended to be hung by pasting the wall and then brushing the covering into position direct from the roll – the material is very light compared to paper-backed types. The surface can be washed, but is relatively fragile and will not withstand repeated scuffing or knocks. The material can be simply dry-stripped from walls and ceilings, like the plastic surface layer of a vinyl wall covering.

An alternative to a printed surface design is a texture. This can be achieved with a paper-backed *fabric* wall covering. The commonest is hessian (burlap), but there are also

materials such as silk, tweed, wool strands, grasscloth and linen, offering a range of softly tinted or boldly coloured wall finishes. Apart from hessian, they are comparatively expensive. They can also be difficult to hang and remove, and so are best used for decorating or highlighting small and relatively well-protected areas such as alcoves. They can be vacuum-cleaned to remove surface dust, and small marks can be washed gently or lifted with special fabric cleaners.

The other kind of textured wall covering is intended for overpainting. These materials are generally known as *relief wall coverings* or 'whites'. The cheapest is *woodchip paper*, also known as oatmeal or ingrain, which has small chips of wood sandwiched at random between a heavy backing paper and a thinner surface layer. The wood chips may be fine or coarse, and the effect after painting is often likened to thinly-spread porridge.

Vinyls are also made as relief wall coverings, with a plain white aerated plastic surface layer that is moulded during manufacture into a range of random or repeating patterns.

Left: High-relief wall coverings are extremely durable and are ideal for decorating walls below dado (chair) rail level in busy hallways.

Other relief wall coverings are embossed to produce a random or regular surface pattern. Those with a relatively low relief design are generally two-layer duplex papers which are embossed while the adhesive bonding the two layers is still wet; this helps to retain the relief during hanging. Those with more pronounced embossing are made from stronger paper containing cotton fibres rather than wood, and are also embossed wet.

All the relief wall coverings can be painted with water-based (latex) or solvent-based (oil) paints. A steam wallpaper stripper will be needed to remove them.

There is one further type of wall covering: lining (liner) paper. As its name suggests, this is a plain paper used for lining wall surfaces in poor condition or having uneven or zero porosity before a decorative wall covering is hung. It comes in various weights, from 55 g/sq m (360 lb) up to 90 g/sq m (600 lb), and in two grades, white and extra-white. The latter can also be used as an economy wall covering, and is hung in the usual way and then overpainted.

Opposite: Self-adhesive borders can be used to add decorative detail to any room. Here they highlight the cornice (crown molding) and form wall panels.

Below: Borders can be used round door openings, beneath decorative features such as plate rails, and even as an unusual embellishment for panelled doors.

Above: Low-relief wallcoverings are the ideal cover-up for less-than-perfect walls, and are available in a wide range of random and regular designs.

Above: A three-dimensional frieze is an unusual way of filling in above a picture rail. The embossed panels are butt-jointed to form a continuous strip.

PAPERHANGING TOOLS AND EQUIPMENT

As for painting, there are two distinct groups of tools, equipment and materials to deal with wall coverings.

Stripping tools

The basic technique for removing an old wall covering is to soften the paste used to stick it to the wall so that it can be scraped off and discarded. To strip porous materials such as ordinary printed paper and the backing paper left behind after dry-stripping vinyl wall covering, use a bucket of water and a sponge or a garden spray gun to apply the water, dust sheets (drop cloths) to protect floor coverings, and a broad-bladed scraping knife to remove the softened paper.

To remove wall coverings with a water-resistant plastic or painted surface, it is necessary to pierce the surface film and so allow the water to penetrate. This can be done with a serrated wallpaper scraper or preferably a toothed roller or wheels, which is rolled backwards and forwards over the surface to create hundreds of little perforations. The water will take longer to penetrate this type of wall covering.

Stripping can be speeded up dramatically on coated wall coverings (and also on paper-backed fabrics and texture paints) by using a steam stripper. This consists of a perforated steaming plate and a water reservoir heated by electricity or bottled gas. Steam penetrates the surface far more quickly than water does, enabling the covering to be stripped quickly and effectively.

Paperhanging tools

There are four separate operations involved in hanging a new wall covering: cutting to length, pasting, hanging and trimming.

For cutting, the tools are a retractable steel tape measure, a pencil and a pair of scissors (or a sharp utility knife and a steel straightedge).

For pasting the wall covering, there should be a bucket in which to mix the paste (unless using ready-mixed tub paste), plus a stirrer and a brush with which to apply the paste. A 100 mm (4 in) wide paintbrush is satisfactory, but a special pasting brush can be bought.

As far as choosing the correct paste is concerned, follow the instructions for the wall covering concerned. In particular, remember that a paste containing a fungicide should be used for washable and vinyl coverings, to prevent mould from growing in the paste as it slowly dries under the impervious covering. A special overlap adhesive will be needed for lap joints in internal and external corners when using washables or vinyls.

PASTING TABLES

A flat surface is needed to lay the paper on while it is being pasted. It is best to use a proper pasting table. This is a lightweight folding table covered in hardboard or plywood on a softwood frame, and is usually about 1.8 m (6 ft) long and just wider than a standard roll of wall covering. If you cannot buy, borrow or hire a pasting table, one can be improvised by cutting a standard sheet of plywood or chipboard (particle board) down to the same width and supporting it on trestles or sawhorses.

SEAM ROLLERS

For smooth wall coverings, a tool called a seam roller can be used to make sure that the seams are well bonded to the wall. Do not use a seam roller on textured or embossed wall coverings, though, as it will flatten the embossing.

When hanging a ready-pasted wall covering, the table, bucket and brush can be dispensed with. All that is needed is a plastic soaking trough in which to immerse the rolled-up lengths of wall covering.

Before starting hanging, a plumb bob and line are needed to mark a true vertical line on the wall against which to hang the first length.

Most wall coverings are applied with a special soft-bristled paperhanging brush. These are generally between 190 and 250 mm (7½ to 10 in) wide, and have a slim handle. The soft bristles help to make the wall covering follow the contours of the wall surface behind, and also eliminate undue hand contact with the face of the covering, which might mark it.

A sponge can be used instead of a brush for hanging washables or vinyls, especially if they are ready-pasted, since here the sponge helps mop water from the surface of the wall covering as well as smoothing it into place.

The final stage is trimming, and the best tool for this is a special pair of paperhangers' scissors. These have blades up to 300 mm (12 in) long for making long, straight cuts.

For papering walls a stepladder is needed which should be tall enough to enable the ceiling to be easily touched. For papering ceilings, set up a proper platform across the width of the room at a comfortable height, using scaffold boards or staging on trestles or other low supports to ensure complete stability. Do not step from chair to chair or set up similar makeshift arrangements.

Displayed on a fold-up pasting table are a soaking trough (1), rubber gloves (2), sponge (3), pencil (4), sharp utility knife (5), paperhangers' scissors (6), plumb bob and line (7), retractable steel tape measure (8), steel straightedge (9), paste bucket (10), pasting brush (11), packet of ready-mixed paste (12), seam roller (13) and paperhanging brush (14). A spirit level (15) can do double duty in checking verticals and as a straightedge.

PREPARING FOR PAPERHANGING

Unrestricted access is a must for paperhanging. If working on just the walls, move all the furniture to the centre of the room and cover it with dust sheets (drop cloths). When tackling the ceiling too, it is best to remove all the furniture completely if there is space to store it elsewhere in the house; otherwise group it at one end of the room so that most of the ceiling can be done, and then move it to the other end to complete the job.

Next, take down curtains and blinds (drapes and shades) and remove wall-mounted or ceiling-mounted tracks. Turn off the electricity supply at the mains, then disconnect and remove wall or ceiling light fittings as necessary, covering the bare wire ends thoroughly with insulating tape before restoring the power supply to the rest of the house. In the USA, ceiling roses, wall switch plates and socket outlets can be unscrewed and removed without

disconnecting the wall receptacles or switches. Isolate, drain, disconnect and remove radiators, and unscrew their wall brackets. Call in a professional electrician or plumber for these jobs if unsure of how to do them safely.

Lift down pictures, and remove other wall-mounted fittings such as shelves and display units. To make it easy to relocate the screw holes afterwards, push a matchstick (wooden match) into each one (see Tip).

CHOOSING THE STARTING POINT

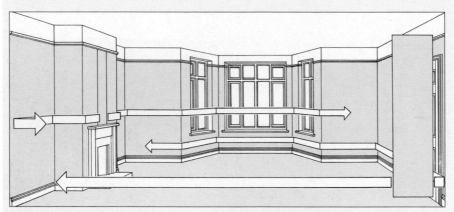

Above: Start paperhanging at the centre of a chimney breast (fireplace projection) if the wall covering has a large, dominant pattern. Otherwise start next to the door so the inevitable pattern break can be disguised above it.

Right: Work outwards from the centre of a dormer window so the design is centred on the window recess.

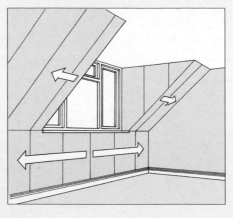

ESTIMATING WALL COVERINGS (WALLS)

Height	Distance around room																	
	9m 30ft	10m 33ft	12m 40ft	13m 42ft	14m 46ft	15m 50ft	16m 52ft	17m 56ft	19m 62ft	20m 66ft	21m 69ft	22m 72ft	23m 75ft	25m 82ft	26m 85ft	27m 88ft	28m 92ft	30m 98ft
2.15–2.30 m/7–7½ ft	4	5	5	6	6	7	7	8	8	9	9	10	10	11	12	12	13	13
2.30–2.45 m/7½–8 ft	5	5	6	6	7	7	8	8	9	9	10	10	11	11	12	13	13	14
2.45–2.60 m/8–8½ ft	5	5	6	7	7	8	9	9	10	10	11	12	12	13	14	14	15	15
2.60–2.75 m/8½–9 ft	5	5	6	7	7	8	9	9	10	10	11	12	12	13	14	14	15	15
2.75–2.90 m/9–9½ ft	6	6	7	7	8	9	9	10	10	11	12	12	13	14	14	15	15	16
2.90–3.05 m/9½–10 ft	6	6	7	8	8	9	10	10	11	12	12	13	14	14	15	16	16	17
3.05–3.20 m/10–10½ ft	6	7	8	8	9	10	10	11	12	13	13	14	15	16	16	17	18	19

Numbers are based on a standard roll size of 10.05 m (33 ft) long and 520 mm (20½ in) wide. The measurement around the room includes all windows and doorway.

If the walls and ceiling are at present painted, they need washing down to remove dirt, grease, smoke stains and the like. If they are decorated with another wall covering, this will have to be removed and any defects in the surface put right. Finally, they need sizing – treating with a diluted coat of wallpaper adhesive to even out the porosity of the surface and to help to improve the 'slip' of the pasted wall covering during hanging.

Measuring up

The next job is to estimate how many rolls of wall covering will be needed to decorate the room. If using a material that comes in standard-sized rolls, simply measure the room dimensions and refer to the charts given here for the number of rolls needed to cover the walls and ceiling. They allow for a typical door and window area; fewer rolls are needed for a room with large picture windows or wide door openings. If using a paper-backed cloth covering which comes in a nonstandard width, measure up each wall, and ask the supplier to estimate what length of material you will need; such materials

are too expensive to waste. Wall coverings in the USA vary in width and length but are usually available in rolls sized to cover a specified area, allowing for trimming.

Buying wall coverings

Wall coverings are made in batches, with a number printed on the label, and it is important to check that there are

sufficient rolls with the same batch number; colours may not match exactly between batches.

When hanging a wall covering with a particularly large pattern repeat, wastage is often unusually high and it may be wise to purchase one or two extra rolls, over and above the numbers given in the charts. Most suppliers will take back unopened rolls.

ESTIMATING WALL COVERINGS (CEILINGS)

Distance around room		No of
m	ft	rolls
10	33	2
11	36	2
12	40	2
13	42	3
14	46	3
15	50	4
16	52	4
17	56	4
18	59	5
19	62	5
20	66	5
21	69	6
22	72	7
23	75	7

TIP

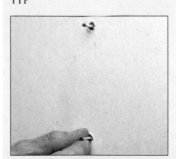

Insert a matchstick (wooden match) in each hole left when unscrewing wall-mounted fixtures and fittings that will be replaced later. It will burst through the wall covering as this is applied and make it easy to find the screw holes.

STRIPPING OLD WALL COVERINGS

In the days when ordinary printed wall coverings were all that were usually on sale, it was common practice to paper over existing wallpaper, often to the point where four or five successive layers would accumulate. This is no longer considered acceptable (and will not work at all over today's washable and vinyl wall coverings), and it is always best to strip all old coverings before hanging new ones. Even if the old material looks sound, hanging a newly-pasted wall covering over it may cause it to lift from the wall, creating ugly bubbles that are impossible to disguise. This also applies to the backing paper that is left on the wall after dry-stripping a vinyl wall covering; there is no guarantee that it is perfectly bonded to the wall, and so hanging another wall covering over it could give very poor results.

Once the room is cleared and dust sheets (drop cloths) are spread over the floor and any remaining furniture, the next step is to identify what type of wall covering is to be removed. An ordinary printed paper will absorb water splashed on it immediately; other types will not. To tell washables from vinyls, pick and lift a corner and try to strip the wall covering dry. The printed plastic layer of a vinyl wall covering will peel off dry, but the surface of a washable paper will not come off in the same way unless it is a duplex paper made in two layers. With paper-backed fabric wall coverings, it is often possible to peel the fabric away from its paper backing; try it before turning to other more complicated methods of removal.

1 To strip printed wallpapers, wet the surface with a sponge or a garden spray gun. Wait for the water to penetrate, and repeat if necessary.

2 Using a stiff wallpaper scraper – not a filling knife (putty knife) – start scraping the old paper from the wall at a seam. Wet it again while working if necessary.

3 Turn off the power before stripping around switches and other fittings, then loosen the faceplate screws to strip the wallpaper behind them.

4 After removing the bulk of the old wallpaper, go back over the wall surface and remove any remaining 'nibs' of paper with sponge/spray gun and scraper.

5 To strip a washable wallpaper, start by scoring the plastic coating with a serrated scraper or toothed roller to allow the water to penetrate, then soak and scrape as before.

6 For quicker results, use a steam stripper to remove washable papers. Press the steaming plate to the next area while stripping the area just steamed.

STRIPPING VINYLS

1 Strip vinyl wall coverings by lifting a corner to separate the vinyl layer from the paper backing. Strip it off by pulling it away from the wall surface.

2 Always soak and remove the plain backing paper left on the wall after stripping a vinyl. It may well not be a sound lining for a new wall covering.

REMOVING OTHER OLD FINISHES

If the wall or ceiling to be given a new covering is painted or wallpapered, preparing the surface for its new finish is quite straightforward. However, if it was previously covered with materials such as texture paint, ceramic or polystyrene tiles or wall panelling, more work will be needed to remove the old finishes and return the surface to its original condition.

Textured finishes are tackled in different ways, depending on their type. Texture paints are basically thick water-based (latex) paints, normally used to create relatively low-relief effects, and can be removed with specially formulated paint removers. Some textured effects formed with a powder or ready-mixed compound are best removed with a steam wallpaper stripper, which softens the compound so that it can be scraped from the wall.

Never attempt to sand off a textured finish. There are two reasons. The first is that it will create huge quantities of very fine dust; the second is that older versions of this product contained asbestos fibres as a filler, and any action that might release these into the atmosphere as inhalable dust must be avoided at all costs.

For tiles and wall panelling, complete removal or a cover-up with plasterboard (gypsum board) are the two options available. The former will leave a surface in need of considerable renovation, while the latter will cause a slight loss of space within the room, as well as some complications at door and window openings.

REMOVING TEXTURED FINISHES

1 Strip texture paint by brushing on a generous coat of a proprietary texture paint remover. Stipple it well into the paint and leave it to penetrate.

2 When the paint has softened, scrape it off with a broad-bladed scraper. Wear gloves, and also safety goggles if working on a ceiling.

3 Once the bulk of the coating is removed, use wire wool dipped in the paint remover to strip off any remaining flecks of paint.

4 Remove powder-based or ready-mixed types using a steam stripper, which will soften the finish. Never try to sand off this type of finish.

REMOVING CERAMIC TILES

1 On a completely tiled wall, use a hammer to crack a tile and create a starting point for the stripping. On partly tiled walls, start at the tile edge.

2 Use a broad bolster (stonecutter's) chisel and a club (spalling) hammer to chip the old tiles off the wall. Have the wall replastered afterwards rather than trying to patch the surface up.

REMOVING POLYSTYRENE TILES

1 Lever the tiles away from the ceiling with a scraper. If they were fixed with a continuous coat of adhesive, consider covering the tiles with heavy lining paper as a temporary measure. For the best finish, fit a new plasterboard (gypsum board) ceiling, nailing through the tile layer into the joists.

2 If the tiles were fixed in place with blobs of adhesive, use a heat gun to soften the old adhesive so it can be removed with a broad-bladed scraper.

REMOVING WALL PANELLING

1 The last board to be fixed will have been nailed to the fixing grounds through its face. Use a nail punch to drive the nails in and free the board.

2 The other boards will have been secret-nailed through their tongues. Use a crowbar (wrecking bar) to prise them away from their grounds.

3 Finally, prise the grounds off the wall, and use a claw hammer or crowbar with some protective packing to lever the fixing nails out of the wall.

PREPARING SURFACES FOR COVERING

Once the previous wall and ceiling decorations have been removed the next task is to restore any defects in the surfaces to be covered, and then to prepare them so that they present the perfect substrate for successful paperhanging.

The first step is to put down some heavy-duty plastic sheeting on the floor to catch splashes, and then to wash down the bare wall and ceiling surfaces thoroughly with strong household detergent or sugar soap (all-purpose cleaner), working from the bottom up on walls, and then to rinse them off with clean water, working this time from top to bottom on walls. Turn off the electricity supply first in case water gets into light switches and socket outlets (receptacles). Leave the surfaces to dry out thoroughly.

Next, repair defects such as cracks, holes and other surface damage which may have been concealed by the previous decorations, or even caused by their removal.

Finally, treat the wall and ceiling surfaces with a coat of size or diluted wallpaper paste, and leave this to dry before starting paperhanging. Size seals porous plaster, providing a surface with even absorption, and also makes it easier to slide the pasted lengths of wall covering into position on the wall.

PREPARING WALLS AND CEILINGS

1 Wash wall surfaces down with sugar soap (all-purpose cleaner) or detergent, working from the bottom up, then rinse them with clean water, working from the top down.

2 Wash ceilings with a floor mop or squeegee, after disconnecting and removing light fittings. Again, rinse off with clean water.

3 Fill cracks, holes and other defects in the wall and ceiling surfaces as appropriate, leave the filler to harden and then sand the repair down flush.

4 Apply a coat of size or diluted wallpaper paste to wall and ceiling surfaces that are to be papered, and leave them to dry before starting paperhanging.

CROSS-LINING

If the wall surface is in poor condition, has been previously decorated with gloss paint or is being decorated with a thin fabric wall covering, it is best to hang lining (liner) paper first. This is usually hung horizontally rather than vertically, with butt joints between lengths and with ends and edges trimmed just short of adjacent ceiling and wall surfaces. Use the same type of paste for the lining paper as for the subsequent wall covering.

MEASURING AND CUTTING TO LENGTH

1 For quick and easy calculations, mark the whole length of the pasting table at 300 mm (12 In) Intervals with a pencil and metal straightedge.

2 Measure the length of wall covering needed for the drop, including trim allowances, and mark this on the paper. Cut the first piece to length.

PASTING WALL COVERINGS

1 Face the light to make it easy to spot any unpasted areas – they look dull, not shiny. Apply a generous band of paste down the centre of the length.

2 Align one edge of the wall covering with the edge of the pasting table, then brush the paste out towards that edge from the centre band.

3 Draw the length across to the other edge of the table, and apply paste out to that edge too. Check that there are no dry or thinly pasted areas.

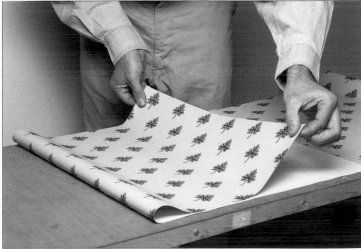

4 Continue pasting until the end of the table is reached. Then lift the pasted end of the wall covering and fold it over on itself, pasted side to pasted side.

5 Slide the paper along the table so the folded section hangs down. Paste the rest of the length and fold the other end over on itself as before.

HANGING THE FIRST LENGTHS

The first length of wall covering must be hung correctly if the decoration of the rest of the room is to go according to plan. Therefore the first thing to do is to decide on exactly where this is to be hung. The usual starting point is close to the door, just less than the wall covering's width away from the frame, so that the inevitable pattern discontinuity that will occur on returning to the starting point can be concealed on the short join above the door. If using a wall covering with a large design motif in a room which has a chimney breast (fireplace projection) it is preferable to start paperhanging on the chimney breast itself so that the design can be centred on it. When papering only part of a room, the starting point should be just less than the width of the wall covering from one corner of the room, to allow the edge of the covering to be trimmed accurately into the corner angle.

Next, use a roll of wall covering as a yardstick and mark off successive widths round the room walls with a pencil to check that there will not be any joins on external corners such as the sides of window reveals. If these occur, move the starting point along by about 50 mm (2 in) and recheck the join positions all round.

Finally, mark a true vertical line on the wall at the chosen starting point, using a pencil and a plumb bob and line. Failure to do this could result in the pattern running seriously out of true as successive lengths are hung.

1 At the chosen starting point, use a plumb bob and line to mark a vertical line on the wall surface. Join up the pencil marks with a straightedge.

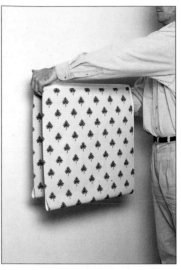

2 Fetch the first length of pasted wall covering after leaving it to soak for the time recommended on the label. Carry it draped over the arm.

6 Peel the end of the length away from the wall so the excess can be trimmed with scissors. Brush the end back into place. Repeat at the bottom.

3 Unfold the upper flap and press the top edge of the length against the wall. Slide it across the wall until the edge lines up with the marked line.

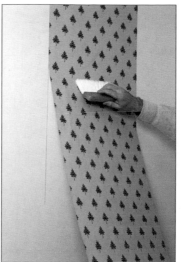

4 Use a paperhanging brush (or a sponge for washables and vinyls) to smooth the wall covering into place. Work from the middle out towards the edges.

5 Use a pencil or the curved back of paperhanging scissors blades to mark the trimming line at ceiling level. Do the same at floor level.

7 Hang the next drop with the lengths exactly edge to edge. Brush the wall covering into the wall/ceiling angle and into the internal angle.

8 On flat wall coverings, run a seam roller down the join to ensure that it sticks securely. Never use a seam roller on embossed or relief wall coverings.

TIP

If a seam refuses to lie flat because it was inadequately pasted and has begun to dry out, brush a little extra paste underneath it and roll it again.

PAPERHANGING AROUND CORNERS

In a perfect world, rooms would have corners that were truly square and truly vertical, and it would be possible to hang wall covering all around the room in a continuous operation, simply turning the lengths that ran into the room corners straight onto the adjoining walls. In reality, corners are seldom square or true, and if the covering was hung in this way, lengths would be vertical on the first wall but could be running well off the vertical by the time they returned to the starting point. The effect can be visually disastrous, with vertical pattern elements clearly out of alignment at corners and horizontal pattern features sloping relative to the ceiling or skirting (baseboard).

The way to avoid these problems is to complete each wall with a cut-down strip that only just turns onto the next wall, to conceal the join in the corner angle. Then hang the remainder of the strip with its machine-cut edge against a newly drawn vertical line on the second wall, so that its other edge can be trimmed to follow the internal angle precisely. Any slight pattern discontinuity that results will not be noticeable except to the closest scrutiny, and the remaining lengths on the second wall will be hung truly vertically. A similar process is used when paperhanging around external corners, as at window reveals and on chimney breasts (fireplace projections).

PAPERING INTERNAL CORNERS

1 Hang the last full length before the corner of the room, then measure the distance to the corner from the edge of the length and add about 12 mm (1/2 in).

2 Use a pencil and straightedge to mark a strip of the required width, measured from the relevant edge (here, the left one), and cut it from the length.

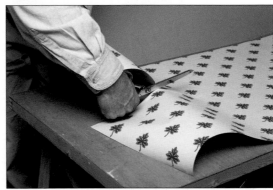

3 Paste the strip and hang it in the usual way, allowing the hand-cut edge to lap onto the adjoining wall. Trim the top and bottom edges as usual.

4 Brush the tongue into the internal angle. If it will not lie flat because the corner is out of true, make small release cuts in the edge and brush it flat.

5 Measure the width of the remaining strip, subtract 12 mm (¹/₂ in) and mark a fresh vertical line on the adjoining wall at this distance from the corner.

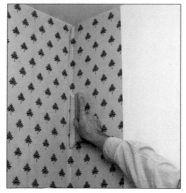

6 Hang the strip to the marked line, brushing the wall covering into the angle so it just turns onto the surface of the first wall.

7 Use the back of the scissors blades to mark the line of the corner on the wall covering, then cut along the line and smooth the cut edge back into the angle. Use special overlap adhesive when using washables and vinyls on all lap joints.

PAPERING EXTERNAL CORNERS

1 Plan the starting point so that lengths turn external corners by about 25 mm (1 in). Brush the paper onto the next wall, making small cuts so it lies flat.

2 Carefully tear off a narrow strip of the wall covering along the turned edge to leave a 'feathered' edge that will not show through the next length.

3 Mark a vertical line on the next wall surface at a distance from the corner equal to the width of the wall covering plus about 6 mm (¼ in).

4 Hang the next full length to the marked line, with its other edge overlapping the feathered edge of the strip turned from the previous wall.

5 Brush this length into position, trim it at top and bottom as before, and run a seam roller down the overlap. (Do not use a seam roller on embossed or textured wall coverings as it will flatten the design). Again, use a special overlap adhesive with washables and vinyls.

PAPERHANGING AROUND DOORS AND WINDOWS

Paperhanging on flat, uninterrupted walls is quite straightforward, calling only for the basic positioning and trimming techniques. Turning corners is only slightly more difficult. The trouble is that rooms also contain doors, windows and wall-mounted fittings and fixtures such as light switches and socket outlets (receptacles). Paperhanging around these obstacles can be tricky, but there are procedures for dealing with them.

Doors and window frames fitted flush with the internal wall surface present few problems; all that is necessary is to trim the wall covering so it finishes flush with the edge of the architrave (trim) or casing. Where the window or door is recessed, some careful patching-in of extra pieces is needed to cover all the surfaces of the reveal. It is also important to select the starting point to avoid joins between lengths falling on the external corners of such reveals; always check this point before beginning paperhanging, and adjust the starting point by about 50 mm (2 in) if it will occur.

Paperhanging round electrical fittings (fixtures) is not so difficult. The idea is to make diagonal cuts over the faceplate, cut away most of the resulting triangular tongues and tuck what is left behind the loosened faceplate. Always turn the power supply to the accessory off first. Do not do this with vinyl foils, which can conduct electricity; instead, simply trim the covering flush with the edges of the accessory faceplate. In the USA wall plates and socket outlets can be removed separately without disconnecting the wall receptacles or switches, which makes the task much simpler.

PAPERING AROUND FLUSH DOORS AND WINDOWS

1 On reaching a flush door or window frame, hang the previous length as normal. Then hang the next length to overlap the door or window frame.

2 Cut away the unwanted wall covering to within about 25 mm (1 in) of the edge of the architrave (trim) or window casing, and discard the waste strip.

3 Press the covering against the frame so that its corner is visible, and make a diagonal cut from the waste edge of the paper to the mark.

4 Use the paperhanging brush to press the tongues of paper well into the angles between the wall and the door architrave or window casing.

5 Peel back the tongues carefully and cut along the marked lines with paperhanging scissors. Then brush the trimmed edges back into position.

PAPERING AROUND FLUSH DOORS AND WINDOWS

1 On reaching a recessed door or window frame, hang the previous length as normal. Then hang the next length, allowing it to overlap the recess.

2 Make a horizontal cut into the overlapping edge level with the underside of the reveal to allow the central portion of the length to cover the side wall.

PAPERING AROUND ELECTRICAL FITTINGS (FIXTURES)

Make diagonal cuts towards the corners, trim off the triangles and tuck the edges behind the loosened faceplate. The power must be turned off first.

3 On recessed windows, make a similar cut lower down the length, level with the top surface of the window sill. Then trim it to fit round the end of the sill.

4 Cut a patch to fit on the underside of the reveal, big enough to turn onto adjoining wall and frame surfaces. Press it well into the internal angles.

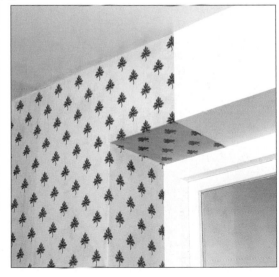

5 Tear along the edges of the patch that will be covered when the piece above the reveal and the tongue covering its side wall are brushed into place.

6 Trim the edges of the patch and tongue to meet the frame neatly. Then hang full widths when the other side of the reveal is reached, and repeat steps 1–6.

PAPERING STAIRWELLS

Paperhanging in stairwells is no different in principle from work in any other room. However, the job is made more difficult by the need to handle longer lengths of wall covering, and also because access to the higher reaches of the stairwell walls can be awkward. It is a job that requires careful planning, and is best tackled with the assistance of a second person.

First of all, work out the starting point. It is best to hang the longest drop – the one that reaches from landing ceiling to hall floor – first of all. Mark

its position and check that other joins will not fall awkwardly round the rest of the stairwell, especially if it has a window opening onto it. Adjust the starting point if necessary.

The next thing to do is to work out how to gain access to the various wall surfaces involved without obstructing passage up and down the stairwell or blocking off the walls themselves. On a straight flight it may be possible to use components from a hired slot-together scaffold tower to make a suitable working platform. On flights with

quarter or half-landings it will probably be necessary to tailor-make an assembly of ladder sections, stepladders, homemade supports and scaffold boards; two typical arrangements are shown in the illustrations. Nail scrap wood to stair treads to locate ladder feet securely, and lock scaffold boards together by drilling holes through them where they overlap and dropping a bolt through the holes (no need for a nut). Note that ladders or steps shown resting against wall surfaces will have to be repositioned as the work progresses.

ACCESS EQUIPMENT FOR STAIRWELLS

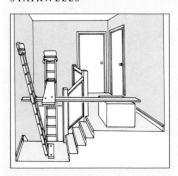

Use a selection of ladders, steps, scaffold boards and homemade supports to construct a platform that allows access to all the wall surfaces being decorated without obstructing movement on the stairs themselves.

STARTING POINT

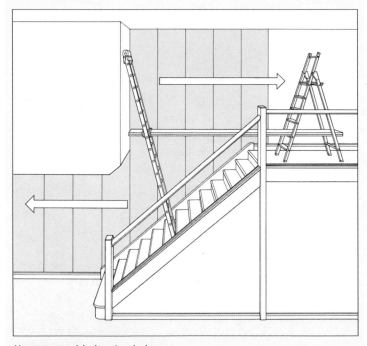

Aim to start work by hanging the longest drop first. Then work along the stairwell walls in sequence, turning corners and tackling obstacles as for other rooms.

1 Fold up long lengths of wall covering concertina-fashion with the top end of the length uppermost, and carry them to the stairs supported over the arm.

2 Get a helper to support the folds of wall covering while positioning the top end of the length on the stairwell wall against a vertical line.

3 When measuring lengths that will meet a dado (chair) rail or skirting (baseboard) at an angle, remember to measure the longer edge of the length.

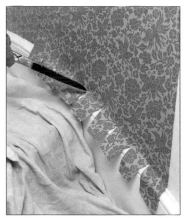

4 Where the bottom edge of the length meets a shaped skirting, make small release cuts in the edge and trim it to follow the curve.

PAPERING AROUND OBSTACLES

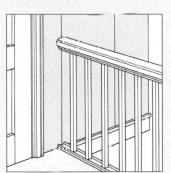

Where the end of a handrail fits flush with the wall, cut the lower part of the length into two strips so their edges can be trimmed around the rail and joined edge to edge beneath it. Use a similar technique to fit the wall covering around a flush newel post.

PAPERING CEILINGS

Many people regard the papering of ceilings with horror. In reality they are easier to deal with than walls because they are flat, do not have any awkward angles (except in rooms with sloping ceiling and dormer windows), and have few obstacles attached to them apart from the occasional light fitting (fixture), which can in any case usually be removed quite easily.

The only thing that takes getting used to when papering ceilings is working on an upside-down surface, but the basic technique is no different from working on walls. The wall covering is simply positioned, brushed into place and then trimmed where it meets adjoining surfaces.

The most important thing to plan carefully is access equipment that will allow a complete length to be hung across the room. Nothing is more dangerous than attempting to step from chair to chair; proper access is a must. The best solution is to use scaffold boards or lengths of staging, supported by stepladders, trestles or homemade supports to create a flat, level walkway spanning the room from wall to wall at a height that allows the ceiling to be reached comfortably. It will take only a few seconds to reposition after hanging each length, ready for the next.

This is also a job where an additional pair of hands will be a big help, at least before gaining the knack of supporting a concertina of pasted wall covering with one hand while brushing it into position with the other. This can be done only with practice.

The first length should be hung to a guideline on the ceiling. The best way of marking this is with a chalked line, held against the ceiling at both ends and snapped against it. Use red chalk for a white ceiling.

1 Paste the wall covering in the usual way, but fold it up concertina-fashion with the starting end of the length folded over on itself.

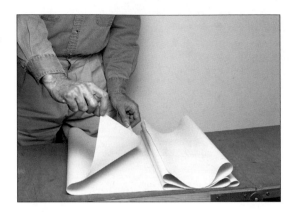

ACCESS EQUIPMENT FOR CEILINGS

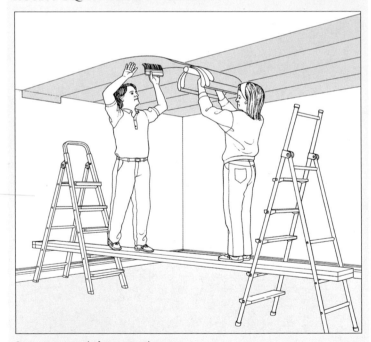

Set up an access platform across the room, using scaffold boards supported on staging or stepladders, to create a walkway at a height that allows the ceiling to be comfortably reached.

2 Hang the first length to a chalked line just less than the width of the wall covering from the side wall. Support the folds on a spare roll of wall covering.

PAPERING ARCHES

The shape of an arch makes it impossible to get a pattern match along the curved join. It is best to choose a wall covering with a small design motif and a random pattern, to use different but complementary designs for the face walls and the arch surface, or to use lining (liner) paper inside the arch and paint it a plain colour.

To paper an arched recess, cover the face and back walls first, turning cut tongues of wall covering onto the arched surface. Then cover the arch surface as described below.

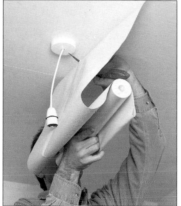

3 Trim the overlaps at the ends and along the side wall. Then hang the second length in the same way, butted up against the edge of the first length.

4 On meeting a pendant light fitting (fixture) pierce the wall covering over its centre and make a series of radial cuts outwards from the pierced point.

To paper a through archway, hang the wall covering on the two face walls and trim out the waste to leave an overlap of about 25 mm (1 in) all around. Make cuts in the edge so that the tongues can be turned onto the arch surface. Then cut a strip of wall covering a fraction narrower than the width of the arch surface and long enough to cover it in one piece, and brush this into place. Work from the bottom of one side upwards to the top of the arch, and then down the other side. Always use special overlap adhesive with washables and vinyls.

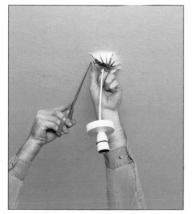

5 With the power turned off at the mains, unscrew the cover and trim the tongues off flush with the base of the fitting. Replace the cover to conceal the cut ends.

6 Where the ceiling runs into an alcove, cut the wall covering in line with the side wall of the recess and brush it into place. Trim off the waste section.

OTHER PAPERHANGING TECHNIQUES

Apart from the traditional method of pasting the wall covering on a pasting table and then hanging it on the wall, two other techniques may sometimes be needed. The first is hanging ready-pasted wall coverings, which are growing in popularity, while the second is hanging speciality wall coverings.

Hanging ready-pasted wall coverings could not be easier. The back of the wall covering – usually a washable or vinyl type, for obvious reasons – is coated during manufacture with an even layer of dried paste. To activate this, simply cut the length that is needed, roll it up with the top of the length on the outside of the roll, and immerse it in water. Special soaking troughs are sold by most wall covering suppliers, and are intended to be placed next to the skirting (baseboard) beneath the point where the length is to be hung. The trough is filled with cold (not hot) water, the length is immersed and drawn upwards onto the wall so that excess water drains back into the trough. It is then hung and trimmed in the usual way.

Many speciality wall coverings are designed to be hung by pasting the wall, not the wall covering. Some also have untrimmed edges, which need to be cut after overlapping adjoining lengths. The technique is, however, quite straightforward.

HANGING READY-PASTED WALL COVERINGS

1 Place the trough next to the wall, fill it with cold water and immerse the rolled-up length of paper in it, top end outermost, for the recommended time.

2 At the end of the recommended soaking time, grasp the top end of the length and draw it upwards so that the excess water runs off it back into the trough.

3 Slide the top of the length into position on the wall, aligning it with a marked line or butting it up against its neighbour. Do not step in the trough.

4 Use a sponge rather than a paperhanging brush to smooth the length into place on the wall. This helps to absorb excess water from the surface.

HANGING SPECIALITY WALL COVERINGS

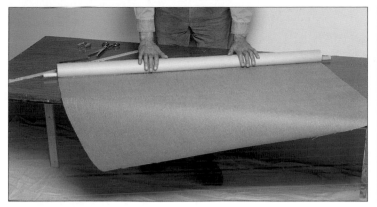

1 Cut the wall covering to the length required, including a trim allowance, and roll it up face inwards around a broom handle or similar object.

2 Apply the recommended paste (usually a thick ready-mixed type) to the wall, and then unroll the wall covering onto the wet paste against a marked line.

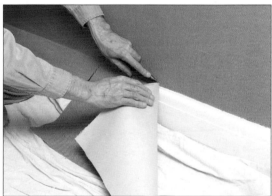

3 Run a clean, dry paint roller backwards and forwards over the surface of the wall covering to bond it firmly to the wall.

4 Use a sharp utility knife – and a straightedge if needed – to trim the wall covering where it meets the ceiling and the skirting (baseboard).

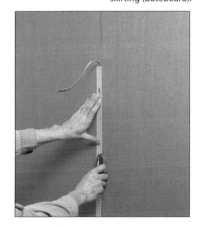

5 To create neat joins, overlap adjoining lengths slightly and then cut through both layers with a sharp utility knife run along a straightedge.

6 Peel away the two waste strips and smooth the cut edges neatly back into place. Run a seam roller along the seam to ensure a good bond.

PUTTING UP FRIEZES AND BORDERS

Friezes and borders are narrow strips of printed paper or vinyl wall covering sold in rolls, and often come in colours and designs that complement wall coverings and fabrics manufactured by the same firm. A frieze is usually applied as a horizontal band running around the room, and can be positioned at ceiling level or next to a picture rail or dado (chair) rail. Borders, on the other hand, are used either to frame features of the room such as a door or window opening, or to create decorative panels on wall or ceiling surfaces – perhaps to frame a group of pictures, for example. They come in a range of widths.

Friezes and borders are available in plain and self-adhesive versions. The former is pasted in the same way as an ordinary wall covering, so this type is ideal for use on walls that have been painted or decorated with a plain printed wallpaper. If a border or frieze is to go over a washable or vinyl wall covering, use a special overlap adhesive or choose a self-adhesive type since ordinary wallpaper paste will not stick to the surface of the covering. Simply cut these to length, then peel off the backing paper bit by bit while positioning the length on the wall.

APPLYING A FRIEZE

1 Decide on the precise position of the frieze or border, then measure the distance from a nearby feature such as a ceiling or door frame.

2 Use a spirit level and pencil to draw true horizontal and vertical guidelines on the wall or ceiling surface at the marked position.

3 Cut the frieze or border to length and carefully apply paste to the length. Fold the paper up concertina fashion while working along the length.

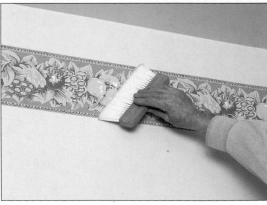

4 Offer the free end of the concertina up to the marked line and brush it into place. It will help to have an assistant when hanging long lengths.

TIP

To gauge the effect a frieze or border will have, and to decide on the best position for it, stick lengths to the wall surface with masking tape before fixing them up permanently.

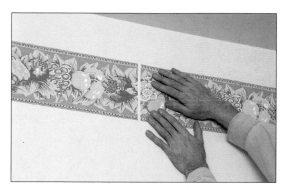

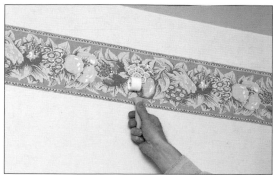

5 Join successive lengths end to end when starting a new roll. If the pattern does not match, overlap the ends so it does and cut through both layers.

6 Finally, check that all horizontal edges and vertical joints are well bonded to the wall by running over them with a seam roller. Remove excess paste.

APPLYING A BORDER

1 Put up the individual lengths of a border in the same way as a frieze. To form corners, overlap the lengths at right angles and cut through both layers at 45°.

2 Peel away the two waste sections and press the neatly mitred ends back into place. Adjust their positions if necessary to get a perfect joint.

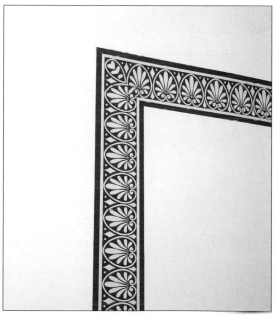

3 The finished corner joint shows how accurate alignment and careful cutting result in a neat joint with the pattern meeting along the mitred cuts.

TILING

Tiles have a long pedigree in the interior decoration business. Faience (glazed earthenware) plaques have been found in Cretan buildings dating from around 1800 BC, and a tradition of ceramic wall and floor decoration was established soon after this farther east in Syria and Persia (now Iran). Mosaic wall and floor decorations, incorporating stone (usually marble), glass and ceramic tesserae, were also a major feature of Roman interiors. The technique spread to North Africa and thence to Spain, and the Renaissance soon led to widespread use of decorative tiling all over Europe.

Probably the most important centre of ceramic tile making in Europe was Holland, where the creation of individually handpainted tiles in a unique blue-grey colour soon made Delft famous in the early seventeenth century. From there, the use of tiles spread rapidly, and it was not long before mass production was introduced. The end product is the familiar ceramic tile we use today. The manufacturing and printing technology may have changed, and the adhesives and grouts used may have improved, but the result would be familiar to a seventeenth-century Dutchman.

The twentieth century has brought new kinds of tile, notably vinyl, lino and cork tiles which owe their existence to advances in plastics and resins technology. They offer a combination of properties that make them useful alternatives to ceramics in a wide range of situations, and are generally much less expensive.

This chapter concentrates on working with ceramic wall tiles, since they are the most popular of the types available. A wide range of situations is dealt with, from splashbacks to whole walls, including information on working around obstacles such as door and window openings and on creating special effects with tiled borders and feature panels. There are also sections on using other types of wall tiles, and on tiling floors.

Opposite: Wall tiles have never been available in such a profusion of styles and designs, ranging from highly glazed plain types to more rustic versions with matt or textured surfaces and patterns that look as though they have been handpainted.

TYPES OF WALL AND FLOOR TILES

Ceramic tiles provide the most durable of all finishes in the home, whether for walls, floors or worktops, and there has never been a bigger choice of colours, designs, shapes and sizes. The main drawback with tiles is that they are comparatively expensive, so it is important to make the right choice of tiles at the start, and to make sure that they are expertly fixed in place.

Vinyl, lino and cork floor tiles offer an alternative floor finish to ceramics, and offer the same advantages of ease of laying small units combined with a surface finish that is warmer to the touch and also less noisy underfoot than ceramic tiles.

Ceramic tiles for walls

In today's homes, the surfaces that are tiled more often than any other are walls, especially in rooms such as kitchens and bathrooms where a hardwearing, water-resistant and easy-to-clean decorative finish is required. Often the tiling protects only the most vulnerable areas such as splashbacks above wash basins and shower cubicles; but sometimes the whole room is tiled from floor to ceiling.

Tiles used for wall decoration are generally fairly thin, measuring from 4 to 6 mm (3/16 to 1/4 in) thick, although some imported tiles (especially the larger sizes) may be rather thicker than

Above: One of the most striking tiling effects is the feature panel (**top**), a group of tiles that builds up into a complete picture and looks particularly effective when framed with a border. Tiles set at 45° and interspersed with triangular cut tiles (**above**) can also add interest to the finished design.

Left: Many tile ranges include a variety of plain and patterned field tiles, teamed up with a complementary border tile, allowing the home decorator complete freedom to decide on the final design.

Right: Encaustic tiles are still made today using traditional materials and techniques. Unlike ordinary tiles, the pattern runs through the tile to form a very hardwearing decorative surface, ideal for hallways.

this. The commonest kinds are square, measuring 108 mm (4^1/4 in) or 150 mm (6 in) across, but rectangular tiles measuring 200 × 100 mm (8 × 4 in) and 200 × 150 mm (8 × 6 in) are becoming more popular.

Tile designs change with fashions in interior design, and current demand seems to be mainly for large areas of neutral or small-patterned tiles interspersed with individual motif tiles on a matching background. Plain tiles, often with a simple border frame, are also popular, as are tiles which create a frieze effect when laid alongside one another. Some sets of tiles build up into larger designs (known as feature panels), which can look quite striking when surrounded by an area of plain tiling. Some tile ranges still include what are known as *insert tiles* – tiles carrying moulded bathroom accessories

Above: Highly glazed tiles can make an unusual and durable surface for counter tops, but the grout lines need scrupulous cleaning to keep them hygienic.

such as soap dishes and toilet roll holders, though these are not as common or as popular as they were.

The surface of ceramic wall tiles is no longer always highly glazed, as it traditionally was. There are now semi-matt finishes, often with a slight surface texture that softens the somewhat harsh glare of a high-gloss surface.

Tile edges have changed over the years too. Once special round-edged tiles were used for the exposed edges of tiled areas, and plain ones with unglazed square edges (known as *field tiles*) elsewhere. Nowadays tiles are either the universal type or the standard square-edged variety. The former have angled edges so that when butted together they leave a gap for the grouting, which fills the spaces between them. The latter, as their name suggests, have square edges and so must be positioned with the aid of spacers.

Both types usually have two adjacent edges glazed so they can be used as perimeter tiles, and sometimes all four edges are glazed.

Tiles for floors and worktops

Although less widely used than wall tiles, ceramic floor tiles are a popular choice for heavy traffic areas such as porches and hallways. They are generally thicker and harder-fired than wall tiles, to enable them to stand up to heavy wear without cracking. Again, a wide range of plain colours, simple textures and more elaborate designs is available. Common sizes are 150 mm (6 in) and 200 mm (8 in) squares and 200 × 100 mm (8 × 4 in) rectangles; hexagons are also available in plain colours, and a popular variation is a plain octagonal tile which is laid with small square coloured or decorated inserts at the intersections.

TYPES OF WALL AND FLOOR TILES *(continued)*

Quarry tiles are unglazed ceramic floor tiles with a brown, buff or reddish colour, and are a popular choice for hallways, conservatories and country-style kitchens. They are usually laid in a mortar bed, and after the joints have been grouted the tiles must be sealed with boiled linseed oil or a recommended proprietary sealer. Common sizes are 100 mm (4 in) and 150 mm (6 in) square. Special shaped tiles are also available for forming upstands at floor edges.

Terracotta tiles look similar to quarry tiles but are larger, and are fired at lower temperatures and so are more porous. They are sealed in the same way as quarry tiles. Squares, ranging in size between 200 and 400 mm (8 and 16 in), and rectangles are the commonest shapes, but octagons with small square infill tiles are also popular.

Mosaics

Mosaics are just tiny tiles – usually plain in colour, sometimes with a pattern –

Above: Handmade terracotta tiles exhibit a subtle variety of shade and colour, but need sealing to keep them clean.

Right: Ceramic tiles provide a durable and waterproof floor surface for bathrooms. Here dark blue square coloured corner inserts set off the dazzling white octagonal tiles.

Below: Mosaic tiles are once more regaining the popularity they enjoyed in times past, but laying them is definitely a labour of love.

Modern lino tiles, made from natural materials rather than the plastic resins used in vinyl tiles, offer far better performance than traditional linoleum. They come in a range of bright and subtle colours and interesting patterns, often with pre-cut borders.

All these types generally come in 300 mm (12 in) squares, although larger squares and rectangles are available in some of the more expensive ranges. They are generally sold in packs of nine, covering roughly 1 sq yd (0.84 sq m), although many kinds are often available singly.

Above: Cork is the warmest of tiled floor coverings underfoot, and when sealed is good-looking and durable too.

Above: The more expensive types of vinyl floor tile offer superb imitations of other materials such as ceramic, wood, marble and terrazzo finishes.

which are sold made up in sheets on an open-weave cloth backing. These sheets are laid like larger tiles in a bed of adhesive, and all the gaps including those on the surface of the sheet are grouted afterwards. Square mosaics are the most common, but roundels, hexagons and other interlocking shapes are also available. Sheets are usually square and 300 mm (12 in) across, and are often sold in packs of five or ten. The best way of estimating quantities is to work out the area to be covered and to divide that by the coverage figure given on the pack to work out how many packs to buy. Note that wall and floor types are of different thicknesses, as with ordinary ceramic tiles.

Cork, vinyl and lino tiles

Cork tiles come in a small range of colours and textures. Their surface feels warm and relatively soft underfoot, and they also give some worthwhile heat and sound insulation – particularly useful in bathrooms, kitchens, halls and even children's bedrooms. The cheapest types have to be sealed to protect the surface after they have been laid, but the more expensive vinyl-coated floor types can be walked on as soon as they have been stuck down. They need little more than an occasional wash and polish to keep them in good condition. However, even the best cork floor tiles are prone to damage from sharp heels and heavy furniture, for example.

Vinyl tiles come in a very wide range of plain and patterned types, and generally resist wear better than cork, so they can be used on floors subject to fairly heavy wear. However, they are a little less gentle on the feet. Some of the more expensive types give very passable imitations of luxury floor coverings such as marble and terrazzo. Most are made in self-adhesive form and very little maintenance is needed once they have been laid.

TILING TOOLS AND EQUIPMENT

Tools for ceramic tiles

For almost any ceramic tiling job, large or small, the following are needed: tile adhesive; a notched adhesive spreader; some tile spacers; lengths of tile edge trim (optional); grout plus a flexible spreader; a steel tape measure; some lengths of 38 × 12 mm (1½ × ½ in) softwood battening (furring strips), plus masonry pins and a hammer for supporting the tiles on large wall areas; a spirit level; a tile cutter; a tile saw; a tile file; a piece of dowel for shaping the grout lines; a pencil and felt-tip pen; some sponges and cloths for wiping and polishing. Some silicone sealant or mastic (caulking) may also be needed for waterproofing joints where tiling abuts baths, basins and shower trays.

Tile cutters range from the basic – an angled cutting tip attached to a handle – to elaborate cutting jigs that guarantee perfectly accurate cuts every time. A tile saw is useful for making shaped cutouts to fit around obstacles such as pipework, and a tile file helps to smooth cut edges.

Both adhesive and grout for wall tiling are now usually sold ready-mixed in plastic tubs complete with a notched plastic spreader. For areas that will get the occasional splash or may suffer from condensation, a water-resistant adhesive and grout is perfectly adequate, but for surfaces such as shower cubicles which will have to withstand prolonged wetting it is essential to use both waterproof adhesive and waterproof grout. Always use waterproof grout on tiled worktops; ordinary grout will harbour germs.

Grout is generally white, but coloured grout is on sale and will make a feature of the grout lines (an effect that looks best with plain or fairly neutral patterned tiles).

TILING TOOLS, MATERIALS AND EQUIPMENT

These include a tile saw (**1**), adhesive (**2**), a polishing cloth (**3**), a spirit level (**4**), tile edge nippers (**5**), a tile cutter/snapper (**6**) or a tiling jig (**7**), a tile scriber (**8**), a tile cutter with width and angle jig (**9**), a heavy duty tile cutter (**10**), tile files (**11**) or a tile edge sander with abrasive strips (**12**), masking tape (**13**), masonry nails (**14**), a hammer (**15**), a homemade tile gauge (**16**), a retractable steel measure (**17**), a pencil (**18**), adhesive spreaders (**19** and **27**), a grout finisher (**20**) or dowel (**21**), tile edging trim (**22**), small and large tile spacers (**23**), a grout remover (**24**), a grout spreader (**25**), grout (**26**) and battens (furring strips) (**28**).

Ceramic floor tile adhesive is widely available in powder form as well as ready-mixed. It is best always to use a waterproof type (plus waterproof grout), even in theoretically dry areas.

Adhesive and grout are both sold in a range of sizes, sometimes labelled by weight, sometimes by volume; always check the coverage specified by the manufacturer on the packaging when buying, so as not to overbuy or run out halfway through the job.

Tools for cork, vinyl and lino tiles
Only a few simple tools are needed to lay cork and vinyl tiles, but, except for the self-adhesive type, special tile adhesive is required. This is sold ready-mixed in tubs, and usually comes complete with a notched spreader.

Special water-based adhesive is the type to choose for both cork and lino tiles; solvent-based contact adhesives were formerly the first choice, but their fumes are extremely unpleasant and also dangerously inflammable, and they are no longer recommended. For vinyl-coated cork tiles a special vinyl acrylic adhesive is needed. For vinyl tiles, an emulsion-type latex flooring adhesive is the best choice.

For unsealed cork tiles a sealer is required. Ordinary polyurethane varnish, as used for furniture, will do; there are also special floor sealers. Three coats will be needed.

Tools are simply a tape measure, a sharp utility knife and a steel straightedge for marking and cutting border tiles. A proprietary profile gauge with sliding steel or plastic needles makes it easy to cut tiles to fit round awkward obstacles such as architraves (trims) and pipework. But it is just as effective, and less costly, to cut a template from card or paper.

SETTING OUT TILED AREAS

The best way to practise tiling skills is to begin by covering just a small area such as a washbasin splashback, where setting out the tiles so that they are centred on the area concerned is a simple job and there is very little tile cutting to do.

For a larger area – a whole wall, or perhaps even a complete room – exactly the same techniques are used. The big difference is the sheer scale of the job, which makes the preliminary setting-out by far the most important part. The problem is that walls are seldom blank surfaces, and there may be a number of obstacles to tile around. Care must be taken to get the best fit around them with these inflexible tile squares, without needing to cut impossibly thin slivers to fill in gaps.

The most important thing to do is to plan precisely where the whole tiles will fall. On a flat, uninterrupted wall this is quite easy; simply find the centre line of the wall and plan the tiling to start from there. However, there will probably be obstacles such as window reveals, door openings and built-in furniture in the room, all competing to be the centre of attention, and it will be necessary to work out the best 'centre point' while all the time trying to avoid having very thin cut tile borders and edges.

It is best to use a device called a *tiling gauge* – a batten (furring strip) marked out in tile widths – to work this out. The gauge is easy to make from a straight piece of timber about 1.2 m (4 ft) long, marked off with pencil lines to match the size of the tile. Use this to ensure that the tiles will be centred accurately on major features such as window reveals, with a border of cut tiles of equal width at the end of each row or column of tiles.

The next stage is the actual setting-out. With large areas of tiling, two things are vitally important. First, the tile rows must be exactly horizontal; if they are not, errors will accumulate as the tiles extend across the wall, throwing the verticals out of alignment with disastrous results. When tiling right around a room, inaccurate levels mean that rows do not match up at the start and finish point. Second, the tiles need some support while the adhesive sets; without it, they may slump down the wall.

The solution is to fix a line of battens across the wall – or right around the room – just above the level of the skirting (baseboard), securing them with partly-driven masonry nails so that they can be removed later when the adhesive has set. The precise level will be dictated by setting-out with the tiling gauge, but will usually be between half and three-quarters of a tile width above the skirting. Do not rely on this being level; it may not be. Draw the line out in pencil first, using the spirit level, and then pin the battens up and check the level again. If everything is straight, it is time to start tiling.

TILING AROUND A DOOR

1 If the door is close to the room corner, start with whole tiles next to the frame. Use a vertical tile guide if the architrave (trim) is not truly vertical.

2 Tile the whole of the main wall area, adding cut tiles next to the room corner and at ceiling level. Remove the tile supports when the adhesive has set.

3 Fit a tile support above the door in line with the tile rows, and another between it and the other room corner, just above skirting (baseboard) level.

TILING AROUND A WINDOW

1 For tiling a wall with a window opening, first decide on where to centre the tiling. On a wall with one window, centre the tiling on a line drawn through its centre.

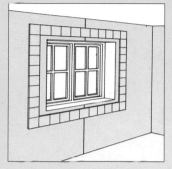

2 If there are two window openings on a wall, centre the tiles on a line drawn through the centre of each window, provided an exact number of whole tiles will fit between them.

3 Otherwise, centre the tiling on a line drawn midway between the windows. Always work across and up the wall, placing whole tiles up to window-sill level, then up the wall at either side of the window. Then, fit a tile support above the opening to support whole tiles there.

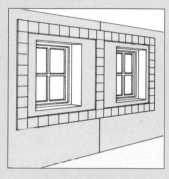

4 Remove the support strips and cut tiles to fit on the face wall at each side and across the top of the window. To tile a window reveal, place whole tiles so they overlap the edges of the tiles on the wall face. Then fill in between these and the frame with cut tiles.

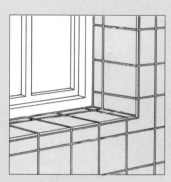

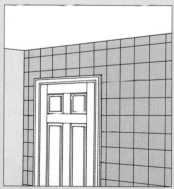

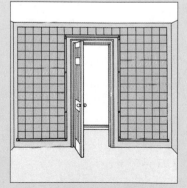

4 Carry on placing whole tiles above the door opening, filling in with cut tiles at the room corner and at ceiling level as in step 2.

5 Remove the tile support above the door opening and fill in all around it with cut and whole tiles as required. Grout the tiles when the adhesive has set.

6 If the door opening is near or at the centre of the room wall, centre the tiling on it and fix tile supports and guide battens (furring strips) as required.

PREPARING THE WALL FOR TILING

The wall surface should be clean and dry. It is possible to tile over painted plaster or plasterboard (gypsum board), but old wall coverings should be removed and brick walls must be rendered. Note that modern tile adhesives allow tiling over existing tiles, so there is no need to remove these if they are securely bonded to the wall surface. There is also no need to fill minor cracks or holes; the tile adhesive will bridge these as it is applied to the wall surface.

When estimating quantities, first select the tile size. Then set out the area to be tiled on the wall and use the setting-out marks to count how many tiles are needed in each horizontal row and each vertical column. Count cut tiles as whole tiles, and then multiply the two figures together to reach the total required. Always add a further 5 per cent to the total to allow for breakages and miscalculations.

MAKING AND USING A TILING GAUGE

1 Use a pencil and one of the chosen tiles to mark up a length of wood for use as a tiling gauge. Allow for the width of tile spacers if using them.

2 Hold the tiling gauge horizontally against the wall to see how many tiles each row will take, and also to centre the tiling on a wall feature or window opening.

3 Similarly, hold the gauge vertically to assess how many tiles will fill each column, and where best to position any cut tiles that may be needed.

MARKING OUT A SPLASHBACK

1 When tiling a small area with rows of whole tiles, use the tiling gauge to mark the extent of the tiled area on the wall. Here each row will have five tiles.

2 Next, use a spirit level to mark a true horizontal base line above which the first row of whole tiles will be fixed. Cut tiles will fit below it.

3 Then use the spirit level again to complete a grid of horizontal and vertical guidelines on the wall surface, ready for a tile support to be fixed.

FITTING TILE SUPPORTS

1 Use masonry pins (tacks) to fix the support to the wall, aligned with the guide line. Drive the pins in only part of the way so that they can be removed later.

2 When tiling large areas or whole walls, pin a vertical guide batten (furring strip) to the wall as well to help keep the tile columns truly vertical.

POSITIONING CUT TILES FOR PANELS

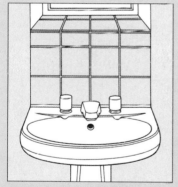

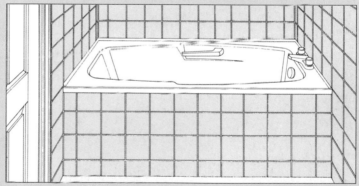

Above: If the height of a tiled splashback is determined by a feature such as a mirror or window, position a row of cut tiles along the top of the panel.

Above: If the width of the tiling is defined, as with a bath panel, always position cut tiles of equal size at either side.

ESTIMATING QUANTITIES		
Tile size	No/sq m	No/sq yd
106 × 106 mm (4¼ × 4¼ in)	86	71
200 × 100 mm (8 × 4 in)	48	41
150 × 150 mm (6 × 6 in)	43	36

TILING PLAIN WALLS

Once all the necessary setting-out work has been done, the actual technique of fixing tiles to walls is quite simple: spread the adhesive and press the tiles into place. However, there must be an adhesive bed of even thickness to ensure that neighbouring tiles sit flush with one another. To obtain this, use a toothed spreader (usually supplied with the tile adhesive; buy one otherwise). Scoop some adhesive from the tub with the spreader, and draw it across the wall with the teeth pressed hard against the plaster to leave ridges of a standard height on the wall. Apply enough adhesive to fix about ten or twelve tiles at a time.

Bed the tiles into the adhesive with a pressing and twisting motion, aligning the first tile with the vertical guideline or batten (furring strip). If using tile spacers, press one into the adhesive next to the top corner of the first tile, and place the second one in the row. Carry on placing spacers and tiles until the end of the row is reached.

Add subsequent rows in the same way until all the whole tiles are in place. It is now time to tackle any cut tiles that are needed at the ends of the rows, and along the base of the tiled area beneath the horizontal tile support. Remove this, and the tile spacers, only when the adhesive has set; allow 24 hours.

FIXING WHOLE TILES

1 Use a notched spreader to scoop some adhesive from the tub and spread it on the wall. Press the teeth against the wall to leave ridges of even height.

2 Place the first tile on the tile support, with its side edge against the pencilled guideline or vertical guide batten (furring strip) as appropriate.

3 Add a tile spacer against the tile corner and place the second tile. Add more tiles to complete the row, then build up succeeding rows in the same way.

CUTTING TILES

1 Use a pencil-type tile cutter and a straightedge to make straight cuts. Measure and mark the tile width needed and score a line across the glaze.

2 Place a nail or matchstick (wooden match) under the scored line at each side of the tile, and break it with downward hand pressure on each half of the tile.

USING A TILE-CUTTING JIG

1 For making angled cuts as well as straight ones, a tile-cutting jig is invaluable. To set it up, first fix the side fence to the angle required.

2 Then draw the slide-mounted cutting point across the tile while holding it firmly in place with the other hand. Take care to score the tile only once.

3 Finally snap the tile along the scored line by holding the tile against the guide bars and lowering the cutter handle with its tip under the tile.

COMPLETING THE WALL

1 Measure, mark and cut the sections of tile needed to complete each row of tiling. Spread a little adhesive over their backs and press them into place.

2 When tiling adjacent walls, place all the cut pieces on the first wall. Repeat the operation on the second wall, overlapping the original cut pieces.

3 When tiling external corners, always set out the tiles so that whole tiles meet on the corner. Overlap the tiles as shown.

3 Use a cutting guide or tiling jig if preferred, especially for cutting narrow strips. This type holds the tile securely and also guides the tile cutter accurately.

4 The traditional way of making a cutout in a tile is to score its outline on the tile and then to gradually nibble away the waste material with pincers.

5 An alternative is to use a special abrasive-coated tile saw. This is indispensable for making internal cutouts to fit around pipes, for example.

FINISHING OFF TILED AREAS

When all the tiles are in place, including any cut tiles that are required, it is time to tackle the final stage of the job – filling in the joint lines between the tiles with grout. This can be bought in powder form or ready-mixed; the latter is more convenient to use, but a little more expensive. Use a flexible spreader (usually supplied with the grout) to force it into the gaps, a damp sponge or cloth to remove excess grout from the face of the tiles, and a short length of wooden dowel or similar material to smooth the grout lines. A clean, dry cloth is needed to polish the tiles afterwards.

Alternative edging techniques

Most ceramic wall tiles have two glazed edges, making it possible to finish off an area of tiling or an external corner with a glazed edge exposed. However, there are alternative ways of finishing off tiling. It can be edged with wooden mouldings or plastic trim strips.

Wooden mouldings can be bedded into the tile adhesive on walls; to edge worktops they can be pinned (tacked) or screwed to the worktop edge.

Plastic edge and corner mouldings (nosings) have a perforated flange which is bedded in the tile adhesive before the tiles are placed. These mouldings come in a range of pastel and bright primary colours to complement or contrast with the tiling.

GROUTING THE TILES

1 Apply the grout to the tile joints by drawing the loaded spreader across them at right angles to the joint lines. Scrape off excess grout and reuse it.

2 Use a damp sponge or cloth to wipe the surface of the tiles before the grout dries out. Rinse it out in clean water from time to time.

3 Then use a short length of wooden dowel or a similar implement to smooth the grout lines to a gently concave cross section.

4 Allow the grout to harden completely, then polish the tiles with a dry cloth to remove any slight remaining bloom and leave them clean and shiny.

USING EDGE TRIMS

1 Bed plastic edge or corner trim into the adhesive, then position the tiles so that they fit flush against the curved edge of the trim strip.

2 As an alternative to plastic, use wooden mouldings bedded in the tile adhesive. Here an L-shaped moulding forms a neat external corner trim.

3 When tiling over existing tiles, some way of disguising the double thickness along exposed edges will be needed. A quadrant (quarter-round) moulding is ideal.

4 Wood can be used to edge a tiled counter top. Start by attaching the moulding to the edge of the worktop so it will fit flush with the tiled surface.

5 Spread the tile adhesive and bed the tiles in place, checking that they lie level with the top edge of the moulding and flush with each other.

6 Plug the counterbored screw holes by gluing in short lengths of dowel and chiselling them off flush with the moulding. Finally, grout the tile joints.

DECORATIVE TILE EFFECTS

The preceding pages have dealt with tiling walls in the technical sense of planning the layout and fixing the tiles. However, tiles are more than just wall covering units; they come in a range of sizes and designs which can also be used creatively in a variety of ways.

The first involves finishing off a part-tiled wall with a band of narrow tiles in a colour or design that complements or contrasts with the main tiled area, to form a decorative border. These tiles are available in lengths that match standard tile widths, and are usually 50–75 mm (2–3 in) wide. They are cut and fixed just like any other tile.

The second method is to incorporate a group of patterned tiles as a feature panel within a larger area of plain tiling. The group may just be contrasting patterned tiles, or may be a multi-tile motif – a group of four, six or more tiles that fit together to form one large design when they are fixed in position. Tile manufacturers offer a range of mass-produced designs you can choose from, or a motif panel can be commissioned from a specialist tile supplier. Plan the motif's position on the wall carefully, and build it in the usual way as tiling progresses.

CREATING A DECORATIVE PANEL

 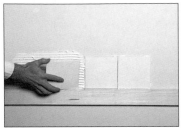

1 Start by making up a tiling gauge to suit the tiles you are working with, and use it to mark the position of the first row of tiles on the wall surface.

2 Put up a support batten (furring strip) if necessary, then spread some tile adhesive on the wall, and place any plain tiles that will be below the decorative panel.

3 Start placing the first tiles that will form the decorative panel. Here the tiles are being laid at an angle of 45°, so half tiles are placed first.

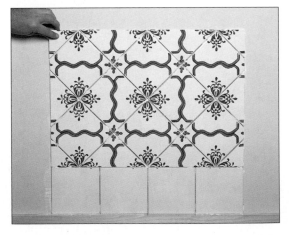

4 Continue adding whole and half tiles to build up the pattern, checking as you work that the edges of the panel are truly horizontal and vertical.

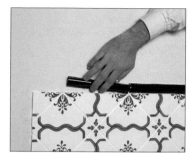

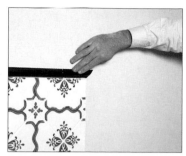

5 Here the panel is being surrounded by slim border tiles. Add whole tiles to the top of the panel first, working from the centre line outwards.

6 At the corners of the panel, fit an over-long horizontal tile and hold another vertically over it so you can mark a 45° cutting line on each tile.

7 Make the 45° cuts on the end of each corner tile, then bed the horizontal tile in place. Check that the cut end is precisely aligned with the panel corner.

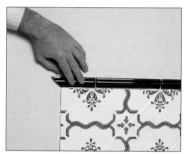

8 Repeat the process at the other end of the horizontal section of the border. Both end pieces should be the same length, as the border is centred.

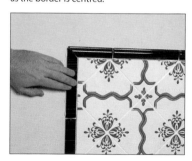

9 Fit the border tiles up each side of the decorative panel, then mark the position of the mitre cut on the last tiles, cut them and fit them in place.

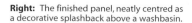

Right: The finished panel, neatly centred as a decorative splashback above a washbasin.

USING MOSAICS AND CORK TILES

Small mosaic tiles are an attractive alternative to square or rectangular tiles, especially for small areas of tiling where their size will look particularly appropriate. Modern mosaic tiles come in a range of shapes and sizes, from simple squares and roundels to interlocking shapes such as hexagons. They are generally sold in sheets backed with an open-mesh cloth that holds the individual mosaic pieces at the correct spacing and greatly speeds up the installation process, since the entire sheet is stuck to the wall in one go. If cut pieces are needed to fill in the perimeter of the tiled area, simply cut individual mosaic tiles from the sheet with scissors, trim them to size with a tile cutter and position them one by one. Mosaic tiles are fixed and grouted with ordinary tiling products.

One other type of wall tile is popular as a wall covering. Cork tiles are made by compressing the bark of the cork tree into blocks, and then slicing them up into squares – 300 mm (12 in) is the commonest size – or rectangles. They come in a range of natural shades, and may also be stained or printed with surface designs during manufacture. They are stuck to the wall surface with a special water-based contact adhesive, and since they are virtually impossible to remove once placed, they should be regarded as a long-term decorative option and their use carefully planned beforehand.

USING MOSAIC TILES

1 Start by putting up a horizontal tile support and a vertical tiling guide, as for ordinary tiling. Then apply an area of tile adhesive to the wall.

2 Position the first sheet of mosaic tiles on the wall, in the angle between the tiling support and the tiling guide, and press it firmly into place.

USING CORK TILES

1 To ensure that the tile rows and columns build up correctly, draw horizontal and vertical pencil guidelines on the wall. Place the first tile.

2 If border tiles are to be cut, hold a whole tile over the last whole tile fixed, butt another against the frame and mark its edge on the tile underneath it.

TIP

If using cork tiles on walls, change the faceplate screws on light switches and socket outlets (receptacles) for longer ones; the originals will be too short to reach the lugs in the mounting box.

3 After positioning several sheets, use a mallet and a piece of plywood to tamp the mosaics down evenly. Use a towel or a thin carpet offcut as a cushion. Ensure the grouting spaces between each sheet are equal.

4 To fill in the perimeter of the area, snip individual mosaic tiles from the sheet, cut them to the size required and bed them in the adhesive.

5 Spread grout over the tiled area, working it well into the gaps between the individual mosaics. Wipe off excess grout, and polish the surface when dry.

3 Place the marked tile on a board and cut it with a sharp utility knife. The exposed part of the sandwiched tile in step 2 will fit the border gap precisely.

4 Fit the cut piece of border tile in place on the wall. Shave or sand its cut edge down a fraction if it is a tight fit. Cut and fit others in the same way.

5 To fit a tile around an obstacle such as a light switch, make a paper or card template and test its fit before cutting the actual tile.

6 Run a rolling pin or a length of broom handle over the completed surface to ensure that all the tiles are well bonded to the wall.

SETTING OUT TILED FLOORS

Like tiled walls, tiled floors need careful setting-out if the end result is to look neat and professional. This is especially important with glazed ceramic and quarry tiles and also patterned vinyl and lino tiles, but matters rather less with plain vinyl or cork tiles where the finished effect is of uniform colour and the joints between the tiles are practically invisible.

Fortunately the necessary setting-out is much easier with floor tiles than wall tiles, since the tiles can be dry-laid on the floor surface and moved around until a starting point is found that gives the best arrangement, with cut border tiles of approximately equal size all around the perimeter of the room.

In a regular-shaped room, start by finding the actual centre point of the floor, by linking the midpoints of opposite pairs of walls with string lines. In an irregularly-shaped room, place string lines as shown in the illustration so that they avoid obstructions, and then link the midpoints of opposite pairs of strings to find the room's centre. Now dry-lay rows of tiles out towards the walls in each direction, remembering to allow for the joint thickness if appropriate, to see how many whole tiles will fit in and to check whether this starting point results in over-narrow border tiles or awkward cuts against obstacles. Move the rows slightly to improve the fit if necessary, then chalk the string lines and snap them against the floor surface to mark the starting point.

Left: Quarry and terracotta tiles provide a durable and attractive floor covering and are especially suited to kitchens and conservatories. To ensure that the tiles are correctly aligned with equal borders around the perimeter of the room, it is essential to follow the correct setting-out procedures.

1 In a regular-shaped room, find the room's centre by linking the midpoints of opposite pairs of walls with string lines.

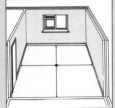

2 In an irregularly shaped room, use string lines that avoid obstacles, and link the midpoints of these as shown to find the centre point.

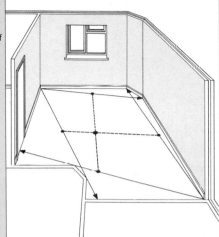

3 To ensure that tiles will be laid square to the door threshold if the walls are out of square, place a string line at right angles to it across the room to the opposite wall.

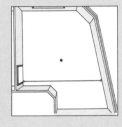

4 Place a second string line at right angles to the first so that it passes through the room's centre point.

5 Place a third string line at right angles to the second, again passing through the centre point, to complete the laying guide.

6 Dry-lay rows of tiles out from the centre of the room towards the walls, allowing for the joint width as appropriate to check the width of the border tiles and the fit around any obstacles.

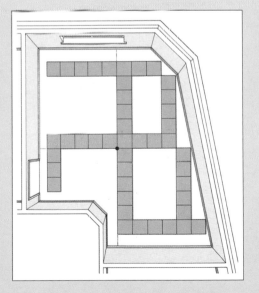

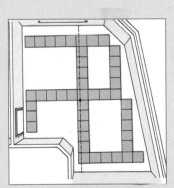

7 Adjust the string lines to get the best possible fit, chalk them and snap them against the floor to mark the laying guidelines.

LAYING CERAMIC FLOOR TILES

Both glazed ceramic and quarry tiles can be laid directly over a concrete floor, as long as it is sound and dry. They can also be laid on a suspended timber floor if it is strong enough to support the not inconsiderable extra weight (check this with a building surveyor). In this case cover the floorboards with exterior-grade plywood, screwed down or secured with annular nails (spiral flooring nails) to prevent it from lifting; this will provide a stable, level base for the tiles.

Glazed ceramic floor tiles are laid with specially formulated adhesive, which should be a waterproof type in bathrooms and a flexible type if tiling on a suspended floor. Quarry and terracotta tiles are laid on mortar over a solid concrete floor, and in thick-bed tile adhesive over plywood.

Old floor coverings should be lifted before laying ceramic or quarry tiles, but if a solid floor is covered with well-bonded vinyl or cork tiles, these can be left in place and tiled over, using tile adhesive. First remove any wax polish used on them.

Set out the floor as described previously, but transfer the starting point to the corner of the room farthest from the door once the setting-out has been completed.

TIP

Remember to take off and shorten room doors before laying floor tiles, and remove enough to allow the door to clear both the plywood underlay and the new tiles.

LAYING CERAMIC FLOOR TILES

1 Pin tiling guides to the floor in the corner of the room at right angles to each other, then spread some adhesive on the floor with a notched-edge trowel.

2 Place the first tile in the angle between the tiling guides, butting it tightly against them and pressing it down firmly into the adhesive bed.

3 As the tiles are laid, use tile spacers to ensure an even gap between them. Use a straightedge to check that all the tiles are horizontal and level.

4 To cut border tiles, lay a whole tile over the last whole tile laid, butt another against the skirting (baseboard) and mark its edge on the tile underneath.

5 Cut the tile and use the exposed part of the sandwiched tile in step 4 to fill the gap along the border. Use the offcut to fill the next border gap if it is wider than it.

6 Use a squeegee to spread grout over the tiles and fill all the joint lines. Wipe excess adhesive from the surface of the tiles with a damp cloth.

7 Use a piece of dowel or a similar rounded implement to smooth the grout lines. Then polish the tile surface with a clean, dry cloth.

LAYING QUARRY TILES

1 Add a third tiling guide to form a bay four tiles wide. Put down a thin mortar bed and place the first row of tiles, using a tiling gauge to space them.

2 Complete four rows of four tiles, then check that they are level. Tamp down any that are proud and lift and rebed any that are lying low.

3 Complete the first bay, then remove the third tiling guide and reposition it another four tile widths away. Fill the second bay with mortar and tamp it down.

4 Complete the second bay in the same way as the first. Continue in this fashion across the room until all the whole tiles have been laid.

5 If installing a tiled upstand, place this next, aligning individual units with the floor tiling. Then cut and fit the border tiles.

6 Mix up a fairly dry mortar mix and use a stiff-bristled brush to work it well into the joints between the tiles. Brush away excess mortar while working.

LAYING VINYL, LINO AND CORK FLOOR TILES

Vinyl, lino and cork floor tiles are available in both plain and self-adhesive types. Cork tiles may be unsealed or vinyl-coated. For plain vinyl tiles an emulsion-type latex flooring adhesive is used, while plain cork tiles and lino tiles are best stuck with a water-based contact adhesive; solvent-based types give off fumes that are most unpleasant and are also dangerously flammable. For vinyl-coated cork tiles, use a special vinyl acrylic adhesive.

Since these tiles are comparatively thin, any unevenness in the subfloor will show through the tiles. Cover timber floors with a hardboard underlay first. Concrete floors may need localized repairs or treatment with a self-smoothing compound to give them a smooth finish.

If laying patterned tiles, set the floor out carefully. With plain tiles, setting-out may not appear to be so important, but nevertheless the floor should still be set out carefully to ensure that the tile rows run out at right angles from the room door.

1 If using self-adhesive tiles, simply peel the backing paper off and place the tile in position on the subfloor against the marked guidelines.

2 Align self-adhesive tiles carefully with their neighbours before sticking them down; the adhesive grabs positively and repositioning may be difficult.

3 If using non-adhesive tiles, spread the appropriate type of adhesive on the subfloor, using a notched spreader to ensure an even thickness.

4 After placing an area of tiles, use a smooth block of wood to work along the joints. This will ensure that they are all well bedded in the adhesive.

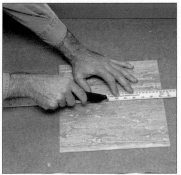

5 To cut border tiles, lay a whole tile over the last whole tile laid, butt another against the skirting (baseboard) and mark its edge on the tile underneath.

6 Place the marked tile on a board and cut it with a sharp utility knife. The exposed part of the sandwiched tile in step 5 will fit the border gap perfectly.

7 Fit the cut piece of border tile in place. Trim its edge slightly if it is a tight fit. Mark, cut and fit the other border tiles in exactly the same way.

8 To cut a tile at an external corner, lay a whole tile over the last whole tile in one adjacent row, butt another against the wall and draw along its edge.

9 Move the sandwiched tile to the other side of the corner, again butt the second whole tile against the wall and mark its edge on the sandwiched tile.

10 Use the utility knife to cut out the square waste section along the marked lines, and offer up the L-shaped border tile to check its fit before fixing it.

SEALING CORK TILES

When laying unsealed cork tiles, take care not to get adhesive on the faces of the tiles, and seal the surface with three coats of polyurethane varnish or a proprietary cork sealer to protect the surface from dirt and moisture. If access to the room is necessary while the floor is being sealed, do half the floor one day and the other half the next day.

LAYING FLOOR COVERINGS

The wide range of floor coverings includes carpets, sheet vinyl, and decorative wood panels and strips.

Carpets laid loose have been used on floors for millennia, but it is only a few decades ago that wall-to-wall fitted carpeting became widely popular. Traditional woven carpets made from natural fibres have been challenged by carpets made from synthetic fibres and by alternative methods of manufacture. There is now a huge choice of colours and patterns in types to suit all locations and wear conditions, available in various widths.

Sheet vinyl floor coverings come in a huge range of colours and patterns, and may also have a surface embossed along the lines of the design to give plausible imitations of other floor coverings such as tiles, marble, wood and cork. Some more expensive types have a cushioned underside formed by incorporating small air bubbles during manufacture, which makes them warmer and softer underfoot than their solid counterparts.

There are two main types of wooden floor covering, wood-block, sometimes called wood mosaic, and wood-strip. The former consists of small slivers of wood (usually a hardwood) laid in groups and stuck to strong cloth to form wooden 'tiles', while the latter is just what its name implies: narrow hardwood planks laid over an existing floor.

Opposite: Fitted carpet is still the most popular choice for living rooms, and the combination of hardwearing fibres and stunning designs now available makes it possible to complement and enhance any style of interior.

TYPES OF FLOOR COVERING

Below: Plain – or almost plain – carpets are the key to simple yet sophisticated colour schemes. Neutral tones, here softly textured with a twist pile, can be off-set with the subtlest of colour contrasts.

When choosing new floor coverings, remember that there is more to it than simply ordering wall-to-wall carpet throughout, and mistakes can be expensive. Floor coverings have to withstand a great deal of wear and tear in certain areas of the average home, especially if there are children or animals in the family, so choosing what to put where is very important.

There is a wide choice of materials on the market, and laying them is well within the capability of most people. Shopping for floor coverings has never been easier either. All the major do-it-yourself suppliers stock a huge range of materials – plus all the tools and accessories needed to lay them. If they do not stock exactly what is required, there are also specialist flooring and carpet suppliers.

Carpets

Carpets consist of fibre tufts or loops woven or stuck to a durable backing. *Woven* carpets are generally the most expensive. Modern types are made by either the Axminster or the Wilton method, which differ in technical details but both produce a durable product which can be patterned or plain. *Tufted* carpets are made by stitching tufts of fibre into a woven backing, where they are secured by attaching a second backing under the first with adhesive. Some of the less expensive types have a foam underlay bonded directly to the backing; others require a separate underlay.

A wide range of fibre types is used in carpet construction today, including wool, nylon, acrylic, polypropylene and viscose rayon. Fibre blends can improve carpet performance; a mixture of 80 per cent wool and 20 per cent nylon is particularly popular for providing a combination of warmth, resilience, wear, low flammability and resistance to soiling.

Pile length and density affect the carpet's performance as well as its looks, and most carpets are classified to indicate the sort of wear they can be expected to withstand. The pile can be *cut*, often to different lengths, giving a sculptured effect; *looped* (shag), that is, uncut and left long; *corded*, which means uncut and pulled tight to the backing; or *twisted*, which gives a tufty effect. A dense pile wears better than a loosely woven one which can be parted to reveal the backing.

Carpet widths are described as *broadloom*, more than 1.8 m (6 ft) wide; or *body* (stair carpet), usually up to 900 mm (3 ft) wide. The former are intended for large areas, the latter for corridors and stairs. Broadloom carpet is available in various imperial and metric widths.

Carpet tiles

These are small squares of carpet of various types, designed to be loose-laid.

Cheaper tiles resemble cord and felt carpets, while more expensive ones may have a short or long cut pile. Common sizes are 300, 450, 500 and 600 mm (12, 18, 20 and 24 in) square.

Sheet vinyl flooring

This is a relatively thin material which provides a smooth, hygienic and easy-to-clean floor covering that is widely used in rooms such as kitchens, bathrooms and hallways. It is made from layers of plastic resins, with a clear wear layer protecting the printed design and frequently with an air cushion layer between this and the backing for extra comfort and warmth underfoot. It is fairly flexible and easy to cut for an exact fit; it is generally loose-laid, with double-sided adhesive tape used only at seams and edges.

Sheet linoleum (lino) is also becoming popular again for domestic use, and is available in some stylish designs and colourways with optional contrasting border designs. Lino is more difficult for the amateur to lay,

TYPES OF FLOOR COVERING *(continued)*

however, being heavier, less flexible and harder to cut than sheet vinyl.

Vinyl flooring is available in a wide range of designs, including realistic imitations of ceramic tiles, wood, cork and stone. It is sold by the linear metre (or yard) from rolls 2, 3 or 4 m (6 ft 6 in, 10 ft or 13 ft) wide; the larger width enables seamfree floors to be laid in most medium-sized rooms.

Above: Modern sheet linoleum has taken on a new lease of life, offering a range of sophisticated colourways teamed with stylish borders that are perfect for kitchens, utility rooms and hallways.

Left: Sealed cork flooring offers a unique combination of warmth and resilience underfoot, coupled with an easy-clean surface that looks attractive too.

Below: Solid wood-strip flooring, shown here in beech, provides a luxury floor covering that looks stunning and will also last a lifetime.

Wood floor coverings

These come in two main forms: as square wood-block panels made up of individual fingers of wood stuck to a cloth or felt backing for ease of handling and laying; or as wood-strip flooring – interlocking planks, often of veneer on a plywood backing. They are laid over the existing floor surface; most are tongued-and-grooved, so only occasional nailing or clipping is required to hold them in place.

Wood-block panels are usually 300 or 450 mm (12 or 18 in) square, while planks are generally 75 or 100 mm (3 or 4 in) wide and come in a range of lengths to allow the end joints to be staggered from one row to the next.

Left: Wood is an excellent choice for entrance halls too, where a durable yet good-looking floor surface is essential.

are extremely hardwearing kitchen carpets available, with a specially treated short nylon pile that is easy to keep clean, and also water-resistant bathroom carpets that give a touch of luxury underfoot without turning into a swamp at bathtime.

Leisure areas – living rooms, dining rooms and bedrooms – are commonly carpeted wall to wall. Do not be tempted to skimp on quality in living rooms, which get the most wear and tend to develop distinct traffic routes. However, it is reasonable to choose light-duty types for bedrooms.

Alternatives to carpets depend simply on taste in home decor. Options include sanded and sealed floorboards teamed with scatter rugs, or a parquet perimeter to a fine specimen carpet. Sheet vinyl or cork tiles may also be worth considering for children's rooms.

Room-by-room choices

In principle it is possible to lay any floor covering in any room of a home. However, custom and the practicalities of life tend to divide the home into three broad areas.

Access areas such as halls, landings and stairs need a floor covering that is able to cope with heavy traffic and muddy shoes. Ideal choices for hallways are materials with a water-repellent and easy-clean surface – for example, sheet vinyl, vinyl tiles, a wood-strip or wood-block floor, sanded and sealed floorboards, or glazed ceramic or quarry tiles. For stairs, where safety is paramount, the best material to choose is a heavy-duty carpet with a short pile, which can also be used on landings.

Work areas such as kitchens and bathrooms also need durable floor coverings that are easy to clean and, especially in the case of bathrooms, water-resistant as well. Sheet vinyl is a popular choice for both rooms, but tiles of various types can also provide an excellent surface – sealed cork, with its warm feel underfoot, is particularly suitable in bathrooms. However, if carpet is preferred for these rooms there

Below: Sanded floorboards can be further enhanced with a delicate stencilled border design. Always seal floorboards with several coats of good quality varnish for a hard-wearing finish.

FLOORING TOOLS AND EQUIPMENT

For laying *carpet* the basic essentials are a tape measure and a sharp utility knife with a good supply of extra blades for cutting and trimming the carpet to fit. As an alternative, special carpet shears can be used.

For a *woven carpet* a carpet stretcher is invaluable. This is a device with a horizontal pad of metal spikes at one end which is locked into the carpet, and a cushioned pad at the other end which is nudged with the knee to stretch the carpet into place. It is probably best to hire this relatively expensive tool, which will not be needed very often.

Also needed are some carpet gripper strips to hold the carpet in position around the perimeter of the room. Gripper strips are thin strips of plywood fitted with angled nails that grip the underside of the carpet, and they are themselves nailed to the floor about 10 mm (3/8 in) from the skirting (baseboard) all around the room. The edge of the carpet is then tucked down into the gap, usually with a carpet fitter's bolster. A wide brick bolster (stonecutter's) chisel may be used instead, as long as it is clean.

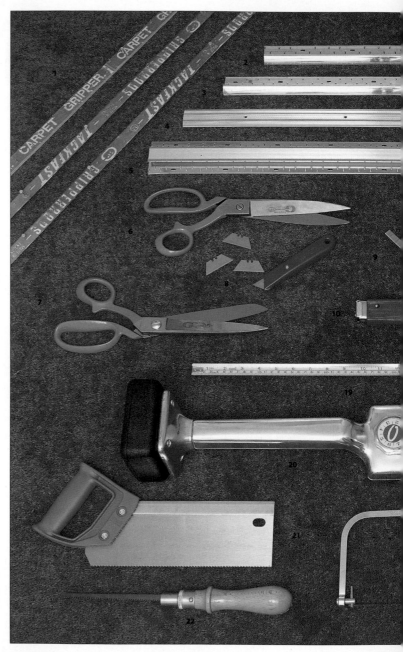

A range of tools for laying carpet, vinyl and wooden floorings include: gripper rods (**1**), a single-sided brass threshold (saddle) strip (**2**), an aluminium carpet-to-vinyl strip (**3**), a threshold cover strip (**4**), a carpet-to-carpet strip (**5**), right-handed (**6**) or left-handed (**7**) carpet shears, a carpet knife with spare blades (**8**), staples (**9**) and a staple hammer (**10**), a recess scriber (**11**), a tack hammer (**12**), a carpet fitter's bolster (**13**), dividers (**14**), an adjustable straightedge (**15**), hessian (burlap) carpet tape (**16**), liquid adhesive (**17**), double-sided tape (**18**), a retractable steel tape measure (**19**), a carpet stretcher (**20**), a tenon saw (**21**), a pad saw (**22**), a coping saw (**23**) and an electric jigsaw (saber saw) (**24**).

Foam-backed carpet does not need gripper strips. It may be stapled to the floor with a staple gun, or stuck down with double-sided adhesive tape. For both woven and foam-backed types, adhesive seaming tape may also be needed to join sections of carpet together and threshold (saddle) strips to neatly finish the carpeted edge off at door openings.

For laying sheet vinyl, again a tape measure and a sharp utility knife are needed. A long steel straightedge will also be invaluable. For bonding the lengths to the floor along edges and seams, use either double-sided tape or bands of liquid adhesive, spread with a toothed spreader. Lastly, a pair of compasses or a scribing block and pencil, plus a shape tracer, are needed to transfer onto the sheet the outlines of the various floor-level obstacles around the edge of the room.

For laying wood-block and wood-strip floor coverings, the requirements are general woodworking tools, some adhesive and a spreader for wood-block floors, and pins (tacks) or fixing clips for wood-strip floors, plus varnish or sealer if laying an unsealed type.

UNDERLAYS

Lining paper or cloth underlay is recommended for foam-backed carpets as it prevents the foam from sticking to the floor surface. For woven carpets use either a foam or felt underlay: they are available in various grades and should be matched to the carpet being laid. Heavy-duty underlays are recommended for heavy wear areas such as hallways, or where extra insulation is required.

PREPARING WOOD FLOORS

Securing loose boards

For suspended wood floors – boards laid over floor joists – start by lifting the old floor covering and checking that all the boards are securely fixed to their joists, and that they are reasonably flat and level. Loose boards will creak annoyingly when walked on, and raised edges or pronounced warping may show as lines through the new floor covering.

Use either cut nails or large ovalheaded nails to secure loose boards. When driving them near known pipe or cable runs, take care not to pierce them; it is best to drive the new nails as close to existing nail positions as possible for safety.

Laying hardboard

Covering the existing boards with a hardboard underlay is an alternative to floor sanding as a way of ensuring a smooth, flat surface ideal for thin sheet floor coverings. Lay the boards in rows with the joints staggered from row to row, and pin them down with hardboard pins driven in at 150 mm

(6 in) spacings. Lay separate strips above known pipe runs.

If preparing to lay glazed ceramic or quarry tiles on a suspended wood floor, put down exterior-grade plywood.

Sanding floors

Where old floorboards are very uneven, or it is planned to leave them exposed but they are badly stained and marked, hire a floor sanding machine. This resembles a cylinder (reel) lawnmower, with a drum to which sheets of abrasive paper are fitted. A bag at the rear collects the sawdust; however, always wear a face mask when sanding floors. Also hire a smaller disc or belt sander for finishing off the room edges.

If necessary, drive any visible nail heads below the surface. Start sanding with coarse abrasive paper, running the machine at 45° to the board direction, then use medium and fine paper in turn with the machine running parallel to the boards. Use the disc or belt sander to tackle the perimeter of the room where the large sander cannot reach.

SECURING FLOORBOARDS

1 Drive in any nails that have lifted due to warping or twisting of the floorboards, and then recess their heads slightly using a nail punch.

2 If nails will not hold the floorboard flat against the joist, drill pilot and clearance holes and use wood screws to secure the board firmly In place.

TIP

When sanding floorboards, always raise the drum at the end of each pass to prevent the abrasives from damaging the boards while the machine is stationary.

LAYING HARDBOARD

1 If hardboard sheets are used as an underlay for a new floor covering, start by punching in any raised nail heads all over the floor.

2 Nail the hardboard sheets to the floorboards at 150 mm (6 in) intervals along the edges and also 300 mm (12 in) apart across the face of each sheet.

SANDING FLOORBOARDS

1 Use a floor sander to smooth and strip old floorboards. Drape the flex (cord) over one shoulder and raise the drum before starting the machine up.

2 Run the machine at 45° to the board direction to start with, first in one direction and then in the other at right angles to the original passes.

3 Then switch to a medium-grade abrasive and run the sander back and forth parallel with the board direction. Finish off with fine-grade abrasive.

4 Use a smaller disc or belt sander to strip areas close to the skirtings (baseboards) and door thresholds, where the larger drum sander cannot reach.

5 Use a scraper to remove paint or varnish from inaccessible areas such as around pipework, then sand the stripped wood smooth by hand.

PREPARING SOLID FLOORS

Ground floors of solid concrete are prone to two main problems: cracking or potholing of the surface, and rising damp caused by a failure in the damp-proof membrane within the floor structure. Cracks and depressions may show through new floor coverings, especially thinner types such as sheet vinyl, while dampness will encourage mould growth beneath the covering.

Relatively narrow cracks can be patched with a repair mortar of 1 part cement to 3 parts sand, or an exterior-quality masonry filler.

If the floor surface is uneven or pitted, it can be covered with a thin layer of self-smoothing compound. There are two types available; both are powders and are mixed with either water or with a special latex emulsion. The mixture is made up in a bucket and poured onto the floor surface, trowelling it out to a thickness of about 3 mm (1/8 in). The liquid finds its own level and dries to give a hard, smooth surface which can be walked on in about 1 hour. Leave it to dry for 24 hours before laying a floor covering over it.

An alternative approach is to cover the concrete with a floating floor of chipboard (particle board), if raising the floor level will not cause problems at door thresholds. The boards can be laid directly on the concrete over heavy-duty polythene (polyethylene) sheeting, which acts as a vapour barrier. If additional insulation is required, put down polystyrene boards first and then lay the new flooring over them.

Treat damp floors immediately with one or two coats of a proprietary damp-proofing liquid.

LAYING A SELF-SMOOTHING COMPOUND

1 Start by sweeping the floor clear of dust and debris. Then scrub away any patches of grease from the surface with strong detergent solution.

2 Key the surface of vinyl floor tiles by sanding it before laying the compound. Wipe away the dust with a damp cloth.

3 If the concrete surface is very dusty or appears unduly porous, seal it by brushing on a generous coat of diluted PVA adhesive (white general-purpose adhesive).

4 Mix up the self-smoothing compound in a bucket, following the manufacturer's instructions carefully to ensure that the mix is the right consistency and free from lumps.

5 Starting in the corner farthest from the room door, pour the compound out onto the floor surface to cover an area of about 1 sq m (11 sq ft).

6 Use a plasterer's trowel to smooth the compound out to a thickness of about 3 mm (1/8 in). Mix, pour and level further batches as required.

LAYING A CHIPBOARD FLOOR

1 You can level and insulate a concrete floor by laying a floating floor of chipboard (particle board) over it. Put down heavy-duty polythene (polyethylene) sheets first.

2 Tape the sheet to the walls; it will be hidden behind the new skirting (baseboard) later. Then butt-joint 25 mm (1 in) polystyrene insulation boards.

3 Cover the insulation with tongued-and-grooved flooring-grade boards. Use cut pieces as necessary, and add a tapered threshold (saddle) strip at the door.

REMOVING OLD FLOOR COVERINGS

Generally speaking, old floor coverings should always be lifted before laying new ones. This also provides an opportunity to inspect the floor itself and to carry out any repairs that may be necessary. However, there are some situations where it may not be practical or necessary to lift an existing floor covering – for example, where vinyl tiles have been laid over a concrete floor and they are firmly stuck to it. Stripping such a large area will be an extremely time-consuming job unless a professional floor tile stripping machine is hired.

1 The backing of old foam-backed carpets may remain stuck to the floor surface. Brush it up, and also remove any remaining staples or seaming tape.

2 To lift vinyl tiles or sheet vinyl that has been stuck along edges and seams, use a heat gun to soften the adhesive and quickly pull up the flooring.

3 If vinyl or cork tiles have been stuck onto a hardboard underlay, lift a few tiles to expose the board edges and then lever the boards up in one piece.

4 Lift wood-block or wood-strip floors if they are damaged or show signs of lifting. Otherwise cover them by pinning on a hardboard overlay.

PAINTING AND VARNISHING FLOORS

Rather than being replaced, floors can simply be brightened up with paint or varnish. This is not only economical, but can create some effects that an off-the-shelf material cannot provide. This technique can be used directly on both solid and wooden floors as long as the surface is in good condition. If it is not, cover floorboards with a hardboard overlay, or treat solid floors with a self-smoothing compound.

Concrete floors can be given a smooth, washable and durable finish by using special floor paint. Make sure the surface is clean, dry and free from oil or grease. Then apply the first coat thinned with white spirit (paint thinner) to act as a sealer, and add two further full-strength coats.

Varnishing bare floorboards, especially after they have been stripped with a floor sander, can create a stunning floor that will contrast beautifully with loose-laid rugs. A stain can be applied before the varnish if wanted. Simply prepare the floor in the same way as any other indoor woodwork, repairing any major surface defects and checking that nail heads are well punched down. If using stain, apply sparingly with a cloth along the grain direction and leave it to dry. Apply three coats of clear varnish to seal the surface. Alternatively, use a coloured sealer to do both jobs with one product. Paint can also be used if it is preferred to hide the grain of the wood.

Stencils or other patterns can be applied either direct to the boards or to a hardboard overlay. A tiled effect can be created by putting down hardboard squares that have been decorated with a special paint effect such as marbling. At least three coats of varnish should be applied over any painted effect, or it will soon wear away.

PAINTING CONCRETE FLOORS
Seal and decorate concrete floors in areas such as utility rooms by applying a proprietary floor paint with a paint roller on an extension pole.

STAIN EFFECTS
Stain and varnish new or stripped floorboards after sanding them smooth and filling any defects. Use a cardboard mask if applying more than one shade.

STENCIL DESIGNS
Effects such as stencils can be applied to a stained or painted floor. Mark out the line of the pattern on the floor and stencil on the design.

1 **PAINTING HARDBOARD** Cover poor-quality floorboards with hardboard, laid with the smooth side uppermost, then paint on the chosen design. Use a strip of wood as a guide.

2 Alternatively, use masking tape to outline the design, apply the paint, and remove the tape when the paint is just touch-dry.

3 With any painted effect, allow the paint to dry hard, then seal the floor surface with three coats of clear varnish or floor sealer.

Above: Here plain floorboards have been enhanced with a two-colour painted diamond design, an effect that tones well with the simple painted decor.

LAYING FOAM-BACKED CARPET

Laying traditional woven carpet can be difficult for the amateur, because it has to be correctly tensioned across the room by using gripper strips and a carpet stretcher if it is to wear well. Because of the cost of such carpet, it may be considered best to leave the job to professionals. However, there is no reason why the do-it-yourselfer should not get some practice by laying less expensive foam-backed carpet in, for example, a spare bedroom. It is possible to disguise any slight inaccuracies that creep into the cutting and fitting process more easily here than with smooth sheet floor coverings such as vinyl, so the job is a good introduction to the general technique of laying roll floor coverings.

Start by putting down a paper or cloth underlay on the floor, taping the joins and stapling the underlay down so that it cannot creep as work continues. Unroll the carpet across the room, with the excess lapping up the walls. Roughly trim the excess all around the room, leaving 50 mm (2 in) for final trimming. Make small cuts at external corners such as around chimney breasts (fireplace projections), and let the tongues fall back into alcoves, then trim off the waste across the face of the chimney breast. Next, press the carpet into internal corners and mark the corner point with a finger. Make cuts to remove the triangle of carpet from the internal angle. Finally, trim the perimeter with a knife drawn along the angle between skirting (baseboard) and wall, and secure the edges with double-sided adhesive tape. Fit a threshold (saddle) strip across door openings.

1 Before laying a foam-backed carpet, put down a paper or cloth underlay to keep the foam from sticking to the floor. Tape joins and staple it in place.

2 Put double-sided adhesive tape all around the perimeter of the room, then unroll the carpet and position it so that it laps up the room walls.

3 Butt the edge of the carpet up against the longest straight wall in the room. Peel the backing paper off the tape and bed the edge into place.

4 Work the carpet across the floor to the opposite wall to ensure that it is lying flat. Then trim that edge against the skirting (baseboard) and tape it down too.

5 Make cuts at internal and external corners in order to bed the carpet onto the tape. Trim excess carpet by drawing a knife along the angle. Take care not to over-trim.

6 Use adhesive seaming tape to join pieces of carpet together where necessary in particularly large rooms. Pressure from a wallpaper seam roller ensures a good bond.

LAYING CARPET TILES

Carpet tiles are among the simplest floor coverings to lay, because they are highly tolerant of any slight inaccuracy in cutting to fit. The cheapest types are usually plain in colour and have a very short pile or a corded appearance, while more expensive tiles may have a longer pile and are available in patterns as well as plain colours. Most are designed to be loose-laid, with just the edges and door thresholds (saddles) secured with bands of adhesive or double-sided tape. This makes it easy to lift individual tiles for cleaning or to even out wear.

Most carpet tiles are marked on the back with an arrow to indicate the pile direction. Align these for a plain effect, or lay them at right angles to create a chequerboard effect. When satisfied with the layout, lift perimeter tiles and put down double-sided tape all around the room. Peel the backing paper off the top of the tape and press the tiles into place. Finish doorways with a threshold (saddle) strip.

CUTTING CARPET TILES

1 Cut carpet tiles from the back on a cutting board, using a sharp utility knife and a steel straightedge, after measuring the size of the cut tile required and marking the tile back.

2 After cutting cleanly through the backing, separate the two halves and lay the cut tile in place. Trim any frayed pile off with scissors.

LAYING WOVEN CARPET

The laying and trimming technique used for laying woven carpets is broadly similar to that described for foam-backed carpets, with two main exceptions: the edges are secured on toothed gripper strips instead of by double-sided adhesive tape, and the carpet must be tensioned across the room to ensure that it wears evenly and cannot ruck up in use.

Start by nailing the gripper strips to the floor all around the room, using a hardboard or cardboard spacer to set them about 10 mm (³/8 in) away from the skirtings (baseboards). Then put down a good-quality foam underlay, paper side up, cutting it to fit just inside the gripper strips. Tape any joins and staple the underlay to the floor at regular intervals.

Now unroll the carpet, trim it roughly and make small diagonal cuts at internal and external corners. Use a carpet fitter's bolster or a clean brick bolster (stonecutter's chisel) to press one edge of the carpet down onto the gripper strips, then trim off excess carpet and use the bolster to tuck the carpet edge into the gap between the strips and the wall.

Use the carpet stretcher to tension the carpet along the adjacent walls and across the room, hooking it onto the gripper strips as each section is stretched. Trim the other walls too, and finally fit the carpet neatly into the doorway, securing it with a threshold (saddle) strip.

1 Nail gripper strips all around the perimeter of the room, using a spacer to set them slightly away from the skirting (baseboard).

2 Lay underlay, trimmed to butt up to the gripper strips. Tape pieces together as necessary, then staple the underlay to the floor at intervals.

3 Unroll the carpet and trim it roughly all around. Then make cuts at external corners so that tongues of carpet will fit around them.

4 Press one edge of the carpet onto the gripper strips with a carpet fitter's bolster to ensure that the angled teeth grip the carpet backing securely.

5 Cut off the excess carpet along this edge by running a sharp utility knife along the angle between the gripper strip and the skirting, as shown.

6 Use the blade of the bolster to tuck the trimmed edge of the carpet into the angle between strip and the skirting. Then tension the carpet along adjacent walls.

7 Make release cuts at internal corners too, then trim the waste along the other walls of the room as before and tuck the cut edges into the perimeter gap.

8 At door frames and similar obstacles, trim the carpet to follow the contours of the obstacle as closely as possible, and press it onto the gripper strip.

STRETCHING CARPET

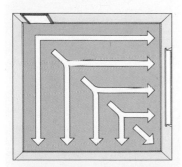

Stretch a carpet along two adjacent walls of the room, hooking it onto the gripper strips. Then stretch it across the room first in one direction, then in the other.

9 Complete the installation by fitting a door threshold (saddle) strip. Different types are available for linking carpet to carpet and carpet to smooth floor coverings.

LAYING STAIR CARPET

The technique of carpeting a flight of stairs is similar in principle to that used for carpeting a room, with gripper strips being used to hold the carpet to the treads. The job is easiest on a straight flight, but it is not too difficult to cope with winding flights or projecting bullnose steps because cuts can be made across the carpet at any point on the flight and the joins hidden neatly at the back of the tread.

Start by nailing on the gripper strips just above the bottom edge of each riser and just in front of the rear edge of each tread. The space between them should be about the same as the thickness of a single fold of the carpet. Instead of two lengths of the normal plywood-based strip, special one-piece L-section metal grippers can be used here. Add short lengths of ordinary gripper strip to the sides of the treads, the thickness of the carpet away from the sides of the flight. Next, cut pieces of underlay to cover each tread and the face of the riser below, and fix them in position with a staple gun or carpet tacks.

Start laying the carpet at the top of the flight. If the same carpet is being used on the landing, this should be brought over the edge of the top step and down the face of the first riser. Therefore the top edge of the stair carpet should be tucked into the gripper strips at the bottom of the first riser. Trim the edges of the carpet on the first tread, then on the next riser, and tuck them in before locking the fold of carpet into the gripper strips at the back of the next tread with a carpet fitter's bolster. Continue in this way to the bottom of the flight, where the stair carpet finishes at the base of the first riser whether or not the floor below uses the same carpet.

1 Cut lengths of gripper strip to fit across the width of the flight, and nail them in position at the foot of each riser and also at the back of each tread.

2 Next, cut and fit a short length of gripper strip to the side of each tread. Position them just less than the carpet thickness away from the sides of the flight.

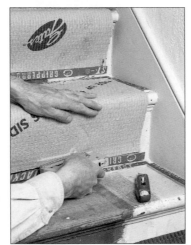

3 Cut pieces of underlay to fit between each tread/riser angle, and staple or tack them in place so they fit smoothly over the nosing at the front of the tread.

4 As an alternative to using two lengths of plywood gripper strip in the tread/riser angle, fit a one-piece L-section metal strip there instead.

5 Start fitting the carpet at the top of the flight, trimming each tread and riser in turn and then forcing a fold of carpet into the angled gripper strips.

6 On an open-string staircase, either trim the carpet to fit around each baluster or fold over the edge and tack it to fit against the baluster as shown here.

7 On winder (curved) stairs, cut a piece of carpet to cover each tread and the riser beneath it. Align it so that the weave is at right angles to the riser.

8 Secure each piece of carpet to the gripper strip at the rear of the tread first, then stretch it over the tread and down to the next gripper strip.

9 Trim off the waste from the bottom edge of the riser, then repeat the cutting and fitting sequence for any other winder steps on the flight.

10 If the flight finishes with a projecting bullnose step, trim and tack the carpet to the riser as shown and cover the riser with a separate strip.

ALTERNATIVE FIXINGS

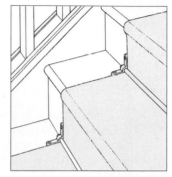

1 When fitting a stair runner rather than a full-width carpet, paint or stain the stair treads and anchor the carpet with stair rods.

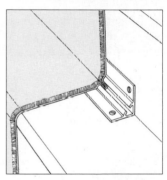

2 If you are using foam-backed carpet on your stairs, fit special gripper strips for foam-backed carpet into the angles between treads and risers.

LAYING SHEET VINYL

Sheet vinyl flooring can be difficult to lay because it is wide and comparatively stiff to handle, and edge cutting must be done accurately if gaps are not to be noticeable against skirtings (baseboards). Lengths of quadrant beading (a base shoe) can be pinned (tacked) around the perimeter of the room to disguise any serious mistakes.

Most rooms contain at least one long straight wall, and it is often easiest to butt one edge of the vinyl up against this first of all. Use a block of wood and a pencil to scribe the wall profile onto the vinyl and cut along this line for a perfect fit. Alternatively, simply press the vinyl into the angle between wall and floor and cut along it with the knife held at a 45° angle. Then press the ends of the length neatly against the walls at right angles to the first wall, make small diagonal cuts at internal and external angles, and trim the edges to fit there. Finally stick down the edges and any seams with double-sided adhesive tape. Finish off doorways with proprietary threshold (saddle) strips.

1 Unless the wall is perfectly straight, make a cut at the corner and trim the adjacent edges of the sheet with a sharp knife along the angle of wall and floor.

2 At door architraves (trims), make cuts into the edge of the sheet down to floor level so the sheet will lie flat, and trim off the tongues.

3 Use a similar technique for trimming the sheet around larger obstacles such as washbasin pedestals.

4 To join sheet vinyl edge to edge, overlap the two sheets so that the pattern matches and cut through both layers against a steel straightedge. Discard the waste strips.

5 Place a strip of double-sided tape underneath the joint line, peel off the backing paper and press the two cut edges firmly down onto the tape.

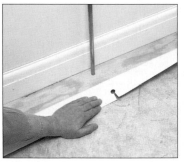

6 To fit the sheet around plumbing pipework, make a cut into it at the pipe position and then trim out a circle of the material to fit around it.

7 At door openings, fit a threshold (saddle) strip to anchor the edge of the sheet. Here an existing strip has been prised up and is being hammered down again.

Below: Sheet vinyl flooring is ideal for kitchens with its easy-to-clean surface. The cushioned types also offer extra warmth and softness underfoot.

MAKING TEMPLATES FOR SHEET VINYL

Where sheet vinyl flooring is being laid around unusually shaped obstacles such as washbasin pedestals and piping, the best way of getting an accurate fit is to make a template of the obstacle so that its shape can be transferred onto the vinyl. Use taped-together sheets of paper cut to roughly the outline of the room and the obstacle. Tape the template to the floor, and use a block of wood and a pencil (or a pair of compasses) to draw a line on the template parallel with the outline of the obstacle.

Next, transfer the template to the vinyl, and use the same block of wood or compass setting to scribe lines back onto the vinyl itself. These lines will accurately represent the shape of the room and the obstacle. Cut along them and remove the waste, then stick down edges and seams as before.

1 Use a block and pencil to scribe the wall outline onto the paper.

2 Tape the template over the sheet vinyl and use the same block with a pencil to scribe a copy of the room outline back onto the vinyl.

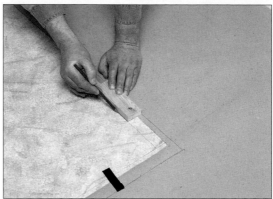

3 Use the same scribing technique as in step 1 to draw the outline of obstacles such as washbasin pedestals onto the paper template.

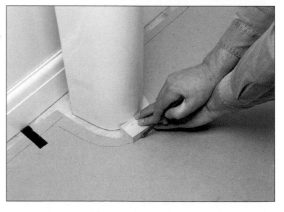

PREPARING THE TEMPLATE

To make a cutting template for a room full of obstacles, such as a bathroom, tape sheets of paper together with their edges about 50 mm (2 in) from the room walls all around. Tear in from the edges to fit the template around the obstacles as shown, ready for the outline of the room and the obstacles to be scribed onto the template.

4 Repeat step 2 to scribe the outline of the obstacle onto the vinyl. Fix the pencil to the block with tape or a rubber band if that makes it easier to use.

5 Using a sharp utility knife, cut carefully around the outline of the obstacle. Make a cut into the waste area, test the cutout for fit, and trim it slightly if necessary.

6 To make cutouts around pipes, use a slim block and a pencil to scribe the pipe position onto the template as four lines at right angles to each other.

7 Place the template over the vinyl at the pipe position, and use the same block and pencil to mark the cutout on the vinyl as a small square.

8 Use compasses or a pipe offcut to draw a circle inside the square, then cut carefully round the circle and cut into the waste area from the edge.

LAYING WOOD MOSAIC FLOORING

The least expensive way of getting a decorative timber floor finish is by laying mosaic floor tiles, which are square tiles made up from a number of small fingers of decorative hardwood mounted on a cloth or felt backing sheet. This acts as an underlay as well as bonding the fingers together; the result is a sheet that will bend along the joint lines, and so can be easily cut to size if required. Alternatively, the fingers may be wired or stuck together to produce a rigid tile. In either case, tiles are generally either 300 mm (12 in) or 450 mm (18 in) square.

The fingers themselves may be solid wood or veneer on a cheaper softwood backing, and are usually arranged in a basketweave pattern; however, other patterns are also available. A wide range of wood types is used, including mahogany, teak, oak, iroko and merbau. Some tiles are supplied sealed, while others have to be varnished or sealed after being laid.

Laying wood-block floor tiles is a comparatively straightforward job, similar to any other floor tiling project in terms of preparation and setting-out. Store the panels unpacked in the room where they will be laid for at least seven days, to allow them to acclimatize to indoor temperature and humidity levels. This will help to reduce shrinkage or expansion after the tiles are laid. However, an expansion gap should always be left around the perimeter of the room.

1 Find the starting point in the same way as for other kinds of tile. Mark tiling guidelines on the floor and spread some adhesive in the first quarter.

2 Align the first tile carefully with the tiling guidelines and press it firmly down into the adhesive. Bed it down with a hammer and a wood offcut.

3 Lay the next panel in the same way, butting it up against its neighbour. Wipe off any adhesive from the tile faces immediately.

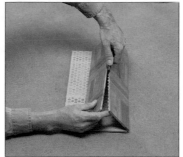

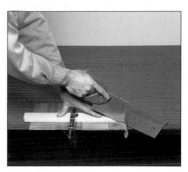

4 To cut edge pieces, lay a whole tile over the last whole tile laid and butt another on top against the skirting (baseboard). Draw along its edge on the middle tile.

5 The tile can be bent along the main joint lines, and then sections can be separated by cutting through the backing fabric with a sharp utility knife.

6 More complicated cuts running across the fingers of wood can be made with a tenon saw, using very light pressure to avoid splitting or tearing the thin strips.

7 At door architraves (trims) and other similar obstacles, make a paper template or use a proprietary shape tracer to mark the tile. Cut the outline with a coping saw.

8 Cover the cut edges of the tiles by pinning lengths of quadrant beading (a base shoe) to the skirtings. Alternatively, use cork expansion strips along the edges.

9 On new work, do not fix the skirtings until the flooring has been laid. They will then hide the expansion gap.

10 Sweep and dust unsealed panels, then apply two or three coats of clear varnish or floor sealer, sanding the surface lightly between coats.

ACCESS HATCHES

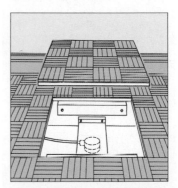

If there is a need for access to electrical fittings or pipe runs below the floor, make small hatches so that a whole tile plus the hatch cover can be lifted if necessary. Screw the tile and cover down onto the base floor with wood screws.

LAYING WOOD-STRIP FLOORING

Wood-strip flooring is available in two main types: as solid planks, and as laminated strips (rather like plywood) with a decorative surface veneer. Lengths range from as little as 400 mm (16 in) up to 1800 mm (6 ft), and widths from 70 mm (2³/4 in) up to around 200 mm (8 in). Solid planks are usually about 15 mm (⁵/8 in) thick; laminated types are a little thinner.

Both types are generally tongued-and-grooved on their long edges for easy fitting. Some are designed to be fixed to a wooden subfloor by secret nailing; others are loose-laid, using ingenious metal clips to hold adjacent strips together.

A wide range of wood varieties is available in each type. Laminated types are generally pre-finished; solid types may also be, but some need sealing once they have been laid.

All the hard work involved in putting down wood-strip flooring lies in the preparation; the actual laying, like so many decorating jobs, is simple and proceeds gratifyingly quickly.

Always unpack the strips and leave them in the room where they will be laid for about a week to acclimatize to the temperature and humidity levels in the home. This will help to avoid buckling due to expansion, or shrinkage due to contraction, when laid.

If the manufacturer recommends the use of a special underlay – which may be polythene (polyethylene) sheeting, glass fibre matting or foam – put this down next, and tape or staple the joins together so they do not ruck up while the floor is laid.

1 Make sure that the subfloor is clean, dry and level. Then unroll the special cushioned underlay across the floor, taping one end to keep it in place.

2 Prepare all the lengths of board by hammering the special metal joint clips into the groove on the underside of the boards, next to the tongued edge.

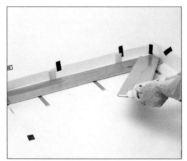

3 Lay the first length, clips outwards, against the wall, using spacers to create an expansion gap next to the wall. Glue the ends of butt-jointed lengths.

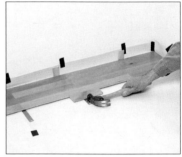

4 Position the second row of boards, tapping them together with a hammer and an offcut so the clips on the first row engage in the groove of the second.

5 The last board is fitted without clips. Cut it to width, allowing for the spacers as in step 3, and apply adhesive along its grooved edge.

6 Insert some protective packing against the wall before levering the strip into place. Tamp it down level with a hammer and protect the floor with a board offcut.

7 Replace skirtings (baseboards) or pin (tack) on lengths of quadrant beading (a base shoe) to hide the expansion gap. Weight the board down so it fits tightly against the floor.

8 To fit a board around a pipe, mark its position and drill a suitably sized hole. Then cut out a tapered wedge which can be glued back after fitting the board.

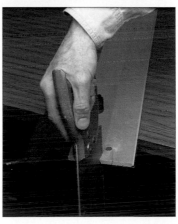

Above: Hardwearing and elegant, wood-strip flooring is a practical choice for living rooms, especially if teamed with scatter rugs.

FEATURES AND FITTINGS

A bare room with its areas of flat and featureless plasterwork is a blank canvas which can be embellished in many different ways. Paint and wall coverings obviously play their part, but there is also a wide range of other features which can be added to the room to give it its own personality. Some are purely decorative, but the majority are practical as well.

In the purely decorative department come features such as cornices (crown moldings) which run around the angle between wall and ceiling, friezes and panel mouldings used to frame door and window openings or groups of pictures, and even such things as recessed ornamental niches for displaying treasures.

In the more practical group come wooden mouldings fitted to protect the fragile plaster surfaces. These include skirtings (baseboards) fitted around the walls at floor level, architraves (trims) around flush door and window openings, and dado (chair) rails to prevent furniture – especially chairs – from damaging the walls. Picture rails belong in this group too, allowing pictures and mirrors to be hung anywhere without having to make new fixings.

On a larger scale are add-on features such as wall panelling, which can be fixed to wall and ceiling surfaces as an alternative to more usual wall coverings, and replacement doors and ornamental fire surrounds. The last of these can set off a chimney breast (fireplace projection) to excellent effect even if the fireplace is not in use.

The scheme is completed with the right choice of fittings – handles, catches and so on – for the doors and windows, and also with the selection of hardware to support curtains and drapes, whether this is an unobtrusive track or a more decorative pole. There is a huge range of products to choose from in all of these categories.

Opposite: The decoration of wall, ceiling and floor surfaces sets the tone for any colour scheme, but it is the fixtures and fittings – the extra touches such as decorative mouldings, door and window furniture, even pictures and mirrors – that give a room its individual look.

WHAT TO ADD TO A ROOM

The walls and ceilings of your rooms can be enhanced in many ways: for example, with decorative wood or plaster mouldings, fire surrounds, wall panelling, replacement doors, new door and window furniture, and curtain (drapery) tracks and poles. Pictures and mirrors provide the finishing touches.

Plaster mouldings

Perhaps the simplest type of ornamental plasterwork is the panel moulding. This is a relatively narrow and shallow decorative strip used, as its name suggests, to outline areas on walls or ceilings which will be treated in a different way to the rest of the room, especially as a way of highlighting pictures, mirrors or alcoves.

Panel mouldings are made in a wide range of profiles, from plain fluted and reeded effects to more elaborate versions such as egg-and-dart, flower-and-husk, Roman vine and Greek key. They are made in standard lengths which vary according to the complexity of the design, and these are simply butt-jointed to make up the panel size required. Corners can be mitred to create square and rectangular panels, or can be formed with matching corner blocks or special re-entrant curves.

Cornices (crown moldings)

Cornices have always been one of the most impressive decorative plaster features. They were originally used externally in classical architecture at

Above: Ornamental plasterwork, such as cornices (crown moldings) and corbels supporting delicate arches, add a flourish to any decor, especially in period homes.

Left: Decorative mouldings are very much in vogue as a means of breaking up large expanses of wall and displaying picture groups. The choice of paint colours is important in balancing the different, defined areas of wall.

Left: Open fires, whether real or gas-powered, need a fire surround to frame them. Softwood mouldings with marble inserts look particularly effective.

Below: Even the simplest colour schemes gain a three-dimensional element from the use of wall panelling and mouldings.

the edges of roofs, but were soon also used inside on the perimeter of ceilings. As with panel mouldings, a huge range of profiles is available, from authentic Greek and Roman forms through eighteenth-and nineteenth-century styles, and featuring such classic motifs as acanthus, dentil, swag-and-drop and egg-and-dart. Wall and ceiling projections range from a delicate 32 mm (1¼ in) for single ogee (or cyma) types up to the massive 400 × 100 mm (16 × 4 in) of an ornate Adam-style frieze. Cornices are made in standard lengths, usually 2 or 3 metres or yards. Corners are formed by cutting mitres with a tenon or fine-toothed panel saw.

Plain concave mouldings – known as coving – are also available, made either as a paper-faced moulding with a plaster core, or machined from wood.

Ceiling roses

A ceiling rose is the perfect complement to a room with a cornice

(crown molding) or ceiling panelling. It is a circular or elliptical moulding which can be used with or without a pendant light at its centre. A wide range of patterns is available, from classic designs to plainer modern versions. Sizes start at around 300 mm (12 in) in diameter and range up to a massive 1.5 × 1.2 m (5 × 4 ft) for the largest decorative ovals.

Wooden mouldings

The term 'moulding' is really a misnomer, better applied to decorative plasterwork which is, literally, moulded into shape. Timber mouldings are machined with shaped cutters and routers, to produce a wide range of cross sections.

Most everyday mouldings are machined either from softwood or from

Left: In high-ceilinged rooms, deeper skirtings (baseboards) and cornices (crown moldings) can help to make the ceiling appear lower. They can be picked out with contrasting shades of paint or matched to the wall colour.

WHAT TO ADD TO A ROOM *(continued)*

a cheap hardwood. As a general guideline, the larger mouldings – architraves (door and window trims), skirtings (baseboards) and the like – are cut from softwood, while mouldings with smaller and more intricate profiles are made from hardwood. Mouldings can be given a coloured finish, or other woods can be imitated, by staining and varnishing them.

Skirtings (baseboards)
These boards are fitted to plastered walls at ground level to protect the plaster surface from damage by careless feet or furniture – and incidentally to allow floor cleaning implements to be used right up to the floor edge without wetting or marking the walls. Until recently, the fashion was for fairly low, plain skirtings with either a pencil-

Below: Panelled doors can be made part of an overall colour scheme by highlighting the panel surrounds to match the other decorative mouldings in the room and to complement furnishing fabrics.

rounded or splayed-and-rounded cross section; these were usually painted. However, in many new homes there is now a switch back to deeper, more ornate skirtings with traditional profiles, often stained and varnished.

Architraves (trims)
These perform a similar job to skirtings (baseboards), being fitted around flush door and window openings to create a decorative and protective border. They are available in styles to match both plain and ornate skirtings, and are either run down to floor level, with the skirting abutting their outer edges, or rest on a small floor-level plinth block.

Dado (chair) and picture rails
These are horizontal mouldings fixed to wall surfaces, the former about 900 mm (3 ft) from the floor and the latter a short way below ceiling level. They were both popular until the 1930s, and are now making a comeback.

The dado rail was designed to protect the plaster from damage by the backs of chairs, and also provided a natural break in the wall's colour scheme. Traditionally the area below the rail – the whole surface was known as the dado (wainscot) – was panelled or finished in a relief wall covering, while that above it was papered or painted.

The picture rail allowed pictures to be hung – and moved about – at will, and also provided a visual break in rooms with high ceilings.

Left: Dado (chair) rails allow the use of different but complementary wall coverings above and below the rail. Picture-frame mouldings in a similar style and finish integrate the decorating scheme.

Left: Cornices (crown moldings) and picture rails do not have to be the shrinking violets in a colour scheme. Here they contrast vividly with the two complementary wall coverings. Picture rails provide an attractive and traditional way of hanging pictures suspended on chains and S-hooks.

Below: Window dressing adds the finishing touch to any room. Here an attractive festoon blind is suspended from a wooden pole.

Bottom: Wood panelling below dado (chair) rail level is a durable alternative to wall coverings. The natural divide can be highlighted with attractive stencil borders.

Curtain (drapery) tracks and poles

One last fixture that deserves some attention is the hardware that supports the curtains (drapes). Curtain tracks and poles may be wall- or ceiling-mounted, and can be made of metal, wood or plastic in a range of styles and finishes. The simplest types of curtain track are slim and unobtrusive; more complex versions include cords or motor drives to move the curtains. Ornamental poles are a distinctive feature in their own right.

Wall panelling

This is formed by fixing tongued-and-grooved or overlapping 'shiplap' boards to wall surfaces. It is often used between the skirting (baseboard) and dado (chair) rail, but floor to ceiling panelling is another option. It can also be fixed to ceiling surfaces, and can be painted or stained and varnished, as wished, once installed.

Doors and windows

Replacing room doors is one way of giving a room a dramatic facelift, especially if the existing doors are out of keeping with the look of the room. There is a huge range of panelled and glazed doors now available, and installing one may be as simple as removing the old door and hanging the new door in its place.

New doors deserve new fittings, and again there is a wide range of handles, knobs and latches to choose from, including various metallic finishes, wood, plastic and even glass and ceramics. The same applies to windows. Changing these is a bigger job than replacing a door, but simply fitting new stays and catches can give an old window frame a new lease of life.

PUTTING UP A CORNICE

Three types of decorative cornice (crown molding) are commonly used in today's homes. The first is coving, a relative of sheet plasterboard (gypsum board), which consists of a concave hollow-backed plaster core sheathed in a strong paper envelope. It is fixed in place with adhesive. The second is the moulded cornice, made either from traditional fibrous plaster or from modern foamed plastics to imitate the ornate decorative cornices often found in older buildings. This comes in a range of profiles, and plaster types must generally be secured in place with screws because of their weight. Plastic types are stuck in position with adhesive. The third type is a machined wooden trim with a similar profile to plasterboard cornice, and is either nailed direct to the wall framing or to a nailing strip or batten (furring strip) in the angle of the wall and ceiling.

Apart from its decorative appearance in framing the ceiling, a cornice can also help to conceal unsightly cracks which often open up around the ceiling perimeter as the ceiling expands and contracts with changes in temperature and humidity, or the building settles.

FITTING A CORNICE

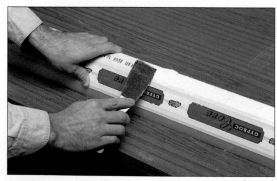

1 Hold a length of cornice (crown molding) squarely in the wall/ceiling angle and draw out two parallel pencil guidelines on the wall and ceiling surfaces.

2 Remove any old wall coverings from between the guidelines by dry-scraping them. Cross-hatch painted or bare plaster to key the surface.

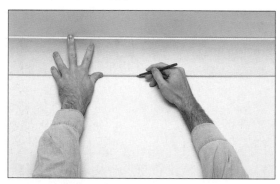

3 Either mix up powder adhesive or use a ready-mixed type. With plasterboard (gypsum board) or plastic types, butter adhesive onto both edges of the rear of the cornice.

4 Press the length into place between the guidelines, supporting it if necessary with partly-driven masonry nails. These are removed once the adhesive has set. Cut any mitres first.

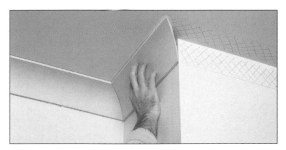

5 Fit the adjacent corner piece next. Here the next section also incorporates an external mitre; measure and cut this carefully before fitting the length.

6 Complete the external corner with a further length of cornice, butting the cut ends closely together and ensuring that the length fits between the lines.

7 Fill any slight gaps at external and internal angles with a little cellulose filler (spackle), applied with a filling knife (putty knife) to leave a crisp, clean joint. Sand the filler smooth once hardened.

8 Before the adhesive sets hard, use a damp sponge to remove any excess from wall and ceiling surfaces and also to smooth over the filled joints.

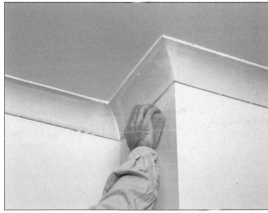

CUTTING A CORNICE

1 Make up a large mitre block big enough to hold the cornice (crown molding), and use this and a tenon saw to make accurate 45° cuts for internal and external corners.

2 Some cornice manufacturers supply a paper template which enables cutting lines to be marked accurately for internal and external corners.

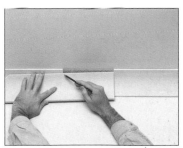

3 When using cut pieces to complete a wall, mark off the length required directly, square a line across the cornice with a pencil and cut it to length.

PUTTING UP A DADO RAIL

A dado (chair) rail is a flat-backed wooden moulding that runs around the room about one-third of the way up from the floor. Its primary purpose is to protect the wall surfaces from damage caused by furniture – especially chair backs – knocking against them. Once fitted, it can be painted, varnished or stained to complement or contrast with the room's colour scheme. It also serves as a visual break in the surface of the wall, since different treatments can be used above and below the rail – wallpaper above, for example, and wood panelling below. The rail can be nailed to wood-framed walls after using a stud finder to locate the vertical members of the frame. On masonry walls, do not use masonry nails, as the rail may need to be removed in the future; use screws and wall plugs instead.

A picture rail is, as its name implies, used to support pictures. It is fixed to the wall a short distance below the ceiling, and has a curved upper edge designed to accept S-shaped picture hooks, from which the pictures hang on wire, cord or chain. Since large pictures (and also large mirrors) can be heavy, the rail must be securely fixed – with screws rather than nails. As with dado rails, a picture rail can be decorated to complement or contrast with the wall covering. Its presence also allows the ceiling decoration to be carried down to rail level, a useful trick for making a high ceiling appear lower.

1 Start by deciding on the precise height at which to fix the rail, and draw a horizontal line around the room with a spirit level and pencil.

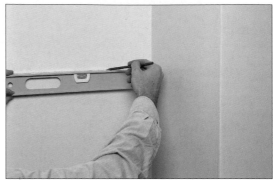

2 Alternatively, use a chalked string line pinned to the wall to mark the horizontal guideline on each wall of the room in turn.

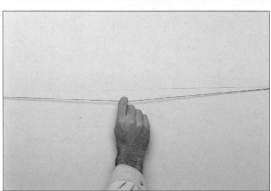

3 Drill clearance and countersink holes in the moulding at roughly 600 mm (2 ft) intervals. Alternatively, counter-bore holes for wooden plugs instead.

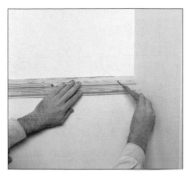

4 Hold the first length of rail up to the guideline and use a bradawl or similar tool to mark the fixing positions on the wall through the screw holes.

5 On masonry walls, drill holes for wall plugs. On wood-framed walls, use cavity fixings or locate the studs so that nails can go directly into them.

Drive the first screw at one end of the length, then the next at the other end before driving intermediate screws. This keeps the rail exactly on line.

6

MAKING ANGLED JOINS

1 If planning to fit a dado (chair) rail down a staircase, draw guidelines parallel with the flight on the staircase wall and mark the two meeting rails.

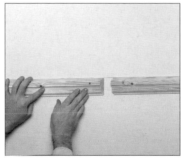

7 If lengths need joining along the length of a wall, make 45° mitre cuts on the mating ends so that any shrinkage which occurs will not open up a visible gap.

8 Always use butt joints at internal angles. Scribe the rail profile onto the rear face of the length that will go on the second wall.

2 Cut the ends of the two rail sections so that they will form a neat joint line; it should exactly bisect the angle between the two sections.

9 Cut carefully along the marked line with a coping saw, then fit the cut end so it butts tightly against the face of the dado rail on the first wall.

10 Use mitred joints at external corners, cutting at just under 45° so that there is no chance of an ugly gap at the corner.

USING DECORATIVE MOULDINGS

Panel mouldings, made in fibrous plaster, plastic or resin compound, can be used to form a range of decorative panels on wall and ceiling surfaces. These can frame features such as a group of pictures, a large mirror, or simply an area decorated in a different way to bring visual contrast to the wall or ceiling surface. Panels can also be used in conjunction with a dado (chair) rail of a matching moulding, decorating the wall below the rail in the same way as the wall surface within the panels, to help make high walls appear lower than they really are.

Panels can be joined with simple mitred joints at the corners or with matching corner pieces which come in a range of styles, from ornate square corner blocks to elegant re-entrant quadrant (quarter-round) shapes.

It is a good idea to plan the shape, size and effect a panel will have by simply forming its outline on the wall or ceiling surface with masking tape. Reposition the tape as necessary until the proportions look right, then mark up, cut and fit the mouldings.

Other moulded embellishments that can be added with the minimum of effort include corbels, which give arches and mantel shelves some visible if non-structural support, and decorative niches which appear to be recessed into the wall surface.

Moulded plaster or foamed plastic ceiling roses can be bought in styles to match the more decorative cornice (crown molding) styles. These can be used to great effect either on their own or in conjunction with pendant light fittings. The heavier plaster types must be screwed to ceiling joists, but light plaster and plastic ones can simply be stuck in place.

USING PANEL MOULDINGS

1 Once the size, shape and position of the panel are fixed, use a spirit level and pencil to mark the panel outline on the wall surface.

3 Press the moulding into place on the wall, aligning it carefully with the pencil lines. If necessary, part-drive thin pins (tacks) through it for extra support.

5 Square the cutting line across the back of the moulding and saw through it carefully with a fine-toothed tenon saw. Sand the cut end smooth.

2 Spread the adhesive smoothly onto the back of the moulding with a flexible filling knife (putty knife). Remove excess adhesive along the edges.

4 Before fitting the corner pieces, check that the patterns will match at the joints. Mark the overlap and cut down the moulding if necessary.

6 Cut and fix all the horizontal and vertical components first, working to the guidelines, then position and align the corner pieces to complete the panel.

FITTING A NICHE

1 To fit an ornamental niche, spread a generous bed of adhesive all around the perimeter of the flat back, and add one or two blobs in the centre.

2 Press the niche into place on the wall, checking that it is truly vertical with a spirit level. Provide some temporary support if necessary.

3 Use a damp sponge to remove any adhesive that has been squeezed out around the perimeter of the niche. Do not disturb the niche while doing this.

Above Right: The niche installed, with its clever proportions making the recess appear deeper than it really is. Leave the adhesive to harden completely before putting anything on display.

CEILING ROSES

To add a ceiling rose, mark its position carefully, then apply adhesive to its rear face and press it into place. Wipe off excess adhesive. Heavy plaster types should be screwed to ceiling joists for security and the screw holes filled.

REPLACING TRIM MOULDINGS

Trim mouldings are both practical and decorative. They are used as skirtings (baseboards) to protect wall surfaces at floor level from accidental damage, and around door and window openings as architraves (trims) which frame the opening and disguise the joint between the frame and the wall surface. Both can be plain or ornate, and can be painted, stained or varnished. They may need replacing if they are damaged or simply look unfashionable.

Skirtings are often fixed directly to masonry walls with large cut nails in older homes, or with masonry nails in more recent ones. Alternatively, they may be nailed to rough timber fixing blocks or grounds (furrings) which are themselves nailed to the masonry. Boards fixed to blocks are much easier to remove than those nailed direct to the wall, since both cut and masonry nails can have a ferocious grip. In the latter situation it is often easier to

punch the nails through the boards and into the walls than to try to prise them out. Boards on wood-framed walls are simply nailed to the frame, and so are easy to remove.

Architraves are pinned (tacked) in place to the edges of the door or window frame. It is an easy job to prise the trims away with a bolster (stonecutter's) chisel without causing undue damage to the frame or the surrounding wall surface.

REPLACING SKIRTINGS

1 To replace a small area of damaged skirting (baseboard), prise it away from the wall slightly, wedge it and use a tenon saw and mitre box to cut out a section.

2 Nail small support blocks behind the cut ends of the board, using masonry nails on solid walls, and then nail the cut ends to the support blocks.

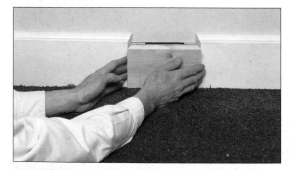

3 Cut a piece of replacement board to fit, with its ends mitred to match the cutout section. Use plain wood if the skirting profile cannot be matched.

4 Nail the replacement board to the support blocks. If using plain wood, pin (tack) on decorative mouldings to build up a close match to the existing board.

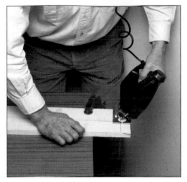

5 When replacing whole lengths, use mitre joints at external corners. Fix the first length, then mark the inside of the mitre on the back of the next board.

6 Cut the mitre joints with a power saw with an adjustable sole plate. Set the cutting angle to just under 45° to ensure that the joint will fit well.

7 At internal corners, fit the first length right into the corner. Then scribe its profile onto the second board; cut this with a coping saw, and fit it.

REPLACING ARCHITRAVES

1 Prise off the old mouldings. They should come away easily. If necessary, lever against a block to avoid damaging the surface of the wall.

2 Hold an upright against the frame so that the inside of the mitre joint can be marked on it. Repeat for the other upright.

3 Cut the end of the moulding, using a mitre block or box. Alternatively, mark the line across the moulding with a protractor or combination square.

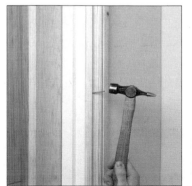

4 Fix the uprights to the frame by driving in nails at 300 mm (12 in) intervals. Recess the heads with a nail punch and fill the holes later.

5 Hold the top piece above the two uprights to mark the position for the mitre cut at each end. Make the cuts as before and test the piece for fit.

6 Nail the top piece to the frame, checking that the mitre joints are accurately aligned. Then drive a nail through each corner to secure the joint.

CREATING FIRE SURROUNDS

For those who are bored with the minimalist look of a simple hole-in-the-wall fireplace, a traditional fire surround and mantelshelf is just the thing. Complete fire surrounds are made in various types of wood or stone (and sometimes in a combination of the two), but they are relatively expensive and may not be precisely what is wanted. But it is possible to create the ideal effect, and save money into the bargain, by creating a custom-built surround from off-the-shelf planed timber (dressed lumber) and a range of decorative mouldings.

This simple design illustrates the basic principles of creating a tailor-made surround. Start by deciding on the overall height and width, and mark this on the wall around the fireplace opening. Then screw a series of vertical and horizontal support strips to the wall to act as fixing grounds for the various components of the surround.

The surround shown here is made from wood measuring 150 × 25 mm (6 × 1 in) and 50 × 25 mm (2 × 1 in). The mantelshelf and the crosspiece below it are full width, while the vertical side members are cut down in width by the wood's thickness (see step 2). This means that the angled joint between the sides and the crosspiece is not 45°, although it appears so in the pictures (see steps 7 and 8).

The completed surround can be finished with paint, stain or varnish; or it could be given a special paint effect such as marbling or graining.

1 Start by deciding on the precise size and location of the surround. Mark this on the face of the chimney breast (fireplace projection), using a spirit level.

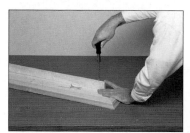

2 Mark the wood thickness on the face of the two uprights. Cut them down in width, using a power saw with a fence or a clamped-on guide.

4 Screw a length of 50 × 25 mm (2 × 1 in) wood on edge to the underside of the mantelshelf. Its length is the width of the surround minus twice the width of the wood.

5 **Right** Fix the support strips. The side strip spacing matches the width of the uprights. The cross strip is placed to match the width of the crosspiece.

3 Make up the mantelshelf by nailing lengths of 50 × 25 mm (2 × 1 in) wood to its underside and then pinning on scotia (cove) mouldings as shown.

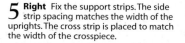

6 Fix the mantelshelf in place with screws as shown. Check that the cross strip spacing is correct by holding the crosspiece against the two strips.

7 Lay an upright and the crosspiece at right angles to each other, and set a sliding bevel to the angle of the corner mitre. Cut the mitres as required.

8 Cut the uprights to length and screw both uprights to the supports. Then fix the crosspiece in place, checking that the mitres are a close fit.

9 Cut a corner block to match the dimensions of the uprights and crosspiece. Nail it in place as shown and then punch in the nail heads.

10 Make up each pedestal by nailing the full-width facing piece to a short length of 50 × 25 mm (2 × 1 in) wood. Support the facing piece with an offcut.

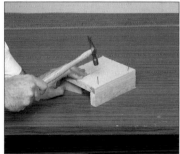

11 Nail the pedestals in place and punch in the nail heads. Complete the surround by nailing two mitred lengths of scotia moulding as shown.

Above: The fire surround in position. Add decorative wood mouldings to the uprights, crosspiece and/or corner blocks and plinths, if wished. The surround can be painted or stained and varnished to complement the decor.

PANELLING A ROOM

Wood has many attractions as a surface covering for walls and ceilings – apart from its price. The natural variety of the wood grain can look highly attractive when varnished or stained, and the material both looks and feels warm and welcoming.

The commonest types of wood used are softwoods, but if money is no object hardwoods can be used instead. The individual planks should have tongued-and-grooved edges; square-edged boards will shrink slightly once installed, and unsightly gaps will open up between the boards as a result.

When estimating how much wood will be needed, remember to use the width of the exposed face, not the overall board width. To avoid visible butt joints between lengths, order lengths that are long enough to reach from floor to ceiling (or across the room if cladding a ceiling surface). When the wood arrives, stack it in the room where it will be installed for several days to allow it to dry out and acclimatize to the ambient temperature and humidity; this will minimize any subsequent shrinkage or expansion.

Nail 50 × 25 mm (2 × 1 in) support strips to the walls about 600 mm (2 ft) apart to provide a true fixing ground for the panel boards. These will run horizontally for vertical boards and vice versa. Add extra support strips at ceiling level, and at floor level if removing and repositioning the existing skirting (baseboard). Otherwise leave it to serve as the base support strip, and fit a new skirting when all the panelling is in place.

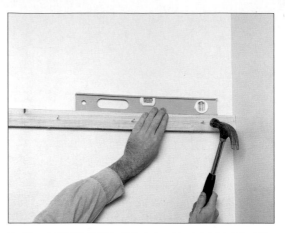

1 Tap fixing nails into each support strip at about 300 mm (12 in) intervals and hold the strip to the wall. Check that it is level and drive in the nails.

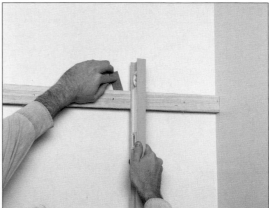

2 If the walls are uneven or out of true, insert slim packing pieces between the strips and the wall to keep the faces of the strips vertical.

3 Scribe the wall outline onto the face of the first board by holding its grooved edge against the wall and running a block and pencil down it as shown.

4 Fix the boards to the support strips by interlocking their tongued-and-grooved edges and then driving nails through the exposed tongue of each board.

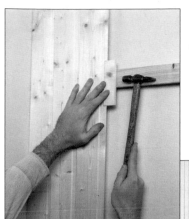

5 When fixing subsequent boards, close up the joints by tapping the board edge with a hammer. Use an offcut of wood to protect the board edge.

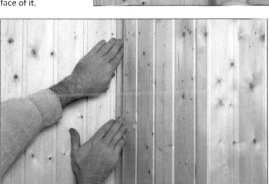

6 Saw or plane the final board down to the required width and 'spring' the last two boards into place. Secure the last board by nailing through the face of it.

7 Neaten internal corners by pinning or gluing a length of scotia (cove) moulding into the angle. Use this at ceiling level too.

8 Butt-join the two boards that form an external corner, and then conceal the joint with a length of birdsmouth (corner bead) moulding.

DEALING WITH OBSTACLES

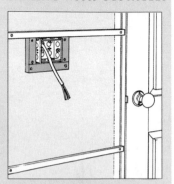

1 To fit panelling round a flush socket outlet (receptacle), replace the old flush mounting box with a surface-mounted one and then fix battens (furring strips) round the box to support the edges of the panelling.

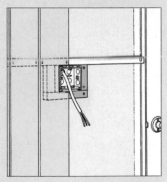

2 Cut boards to length as necessary to fit beneath projecting window sills, and make cutouts in individual boards so they will fit neatly round socket outlets.

HANGING A NEW DOOR

Fitting new internal doors can go a long way towards giving the home a completely new look. A new door may be fitted for purely cosmetic reasons – because the existing one is out of style with the room's decor – or because the old one is warped or damaged. Whatever the reason, there is a huge selection of replacement doors available, made from hardwood or softwood in styles ranging from plain flush doors to highly ornate ones with solid or glazed panels. Glazed doors are ideal for admitting extra light to dark rooms or passageways, but national building regulations or local building code requirements must be followed in the choice of glass – reinforced (safety) glass may be required if there is any danger of an accident.

When replacing a door, it is generally advisable to fit new hardware – hinges and latches especially. Door handles and knobs can be removed and replaced if they must match others in the room. In countries where wood-frame construction is the norm, pre-hung doors complete with frame and architrave (trim) are widely available. To fit them, all that is necessary is to set the unit in the opening, using wood shims to get it plumb, and then nail it into position ready for the trim mouldings to be attached. The door is even pre-bored to accept the new lock or latch.

1 Remove the old door and use it as a guide to marking the hinge positions on the edge of the new door. Square the lines across it with a try square.

2 Set a marking gauge to match the width of the hinge, and scribe a line parallel to the door edge between those made in step 1.

3 Use a chisel and mallet to cut into the door along the marked lines and then to chop out a shallow recess to match the thickness of the hinge leaf.

4 Hold the hinge in position in the recess, and mark the positions of all the screw holes on the door edge with a pencil or bradawl.

5 Drill pilot holes into the door edge at each of the marks. Check that they are at right angles to the door edge. If not, the screws will be crooked.

6 Screw the hinge to the door with matching screws. Drive them fully home and check that the screw heads sit square and flush in the countersinks.

DOOR SIZES

Doors are made in a range of standard sizes. If the old door is a standard size, buying the correct replacement is simple; but if it is not, a door in the next largest size will need to be sawn or planed down as required. Bear this in mind when deciding on the style of door. Panelled doors can be reduced in size more easily (and by more) than flush ones. However, doors cannot be cut down excessively or they come apart: do not cut away the tenon joints in the corners, nor remove too much of the edge wood on a flush door.

7 If re-using the old hinge recesses, screw the door to the frame using screws one size up from the originals. If cutting new recesses, hold the door in the opening and mark the hinge positions.

8 Square lines across the frame at the marks, then measure the width of the hinge leaf and mark the width of the recess required on the frame.

9 Cut along the marked lines with a sharp chisel, then carefully cut out the recess to the required depth. Take care not to let the chisel slip.

10 Prop the door back in position and mark the hinge screw positions. Drill pilot holes, then drive in the screws to secure the hinges to the frame.

TIP

If the door binds on the hinge side and will not close properly, the hinge recesses are too deep. Unscrew the hinges and insert cardboard packing pieces.

DOOR AND WINDOW HARDWARE

Door and window fittings can be ornamental as well as practical and secure. The simplest type of door catch is a spring-loaded ball which is recessed into the door edge. The ball engages in a recess in the door frame as the door is pushed closed, and retracts as the door is pulled open.

A more positive action is provided by a mortise latch; this is also recessed into the door edge and has a projecting bolt which is flat on one face and curved on the other. As the door is pushed shut, the curved face hits the striking plate on the door frame and pushes the bolt back into the latch body. When the door is fully closed the bolt springs out into the recess in the striking plate, with its flat face providing a positive latching action. Turning the door handle rotates a spindle, withdrawing the bolt from the striking plate and allowing the door to open again. A mortise lock combines the same latch mechanism with a lockable bolt.

The commonest items of hardware used on hinged windows are a rotating cockspur handle that is used simply to fasten the window, and a casement stay which props it open in one of several different positions. On sliding sash windows, the basic hardware is a catch that locks the two sashes together when they are closed.

TIP

If fitting lockable window catches and stays, do not leave the keys in the locks in case they fall out as the window is opened and closed. Instead, hang them on a pin driven into the window frame. This also ensures that they are readily available if the window has to be opened in an emergency.

FITTING A MORTISE LATCH

1 To fit a mortise latch to a new door, use the latch body to mark the mortise position on the door edge, in line with the centre rail or lock block.

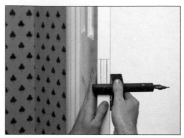

2 Set a mortise gauge to a setting just wider than the thickness of the latch body, and scribe the outline of the mortise centred on the door edge.

3 Use a flat wood bit in a power drill to make a series of holes between the guidelines, a little deeper than the length of the latch body.

4 Chop out the waste with a chisel and mallet, then pare down the sides of the mortise and clean out the recess. Try the latch for fit in the mortise.

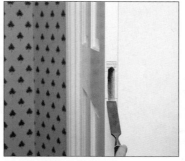

5 Draw around the latch faceplate on the edge of the door, then cut around the lines with a chisel and make a series of parallel cuts across the grain.

6 Carefully chisel out the waste wood between the marked guidelines, taking care not to let the chisel slip and cut beyond the ends of the recess.

7 Hold the latch body against the face of the door in line with the mortise and with its faceplate flush with the door edge. Mark the spindle position.

8 Clamp a piece of scrap wood to the other side of the door. Drill a hole big enough to accept the spindle through the door into the scrap wood.

9 Slide the latch into place in its mortise and make pilot holes through the faceplate with a bradawl. Then drive in the faceplate fixing screws.

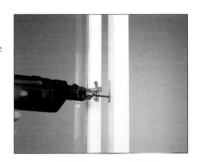

10 Insert the spindle and fit a handle onto each end of it. Check that the spindle rotates freely, then screw both the handles to the door.

11 Close the door in order to mark where the latch bolt meets the frame. Then chisel out the recesses for the bolt and striking plate, and screw on the plate.

FITTING A WINDOW HANDLE AND STAY

1 Decide where the cockspur handle should go on the casement and make pilot holes through it with a bradawl. Then screw the handle to the casement.

2 Fit the striking plate to the frame so the cockspur will engage in it. Drill out the frame to a depth of about 20 mm ($^3/_4$ in) through the slot in the plate.

3 Fit the casement stay by screwing its baseplate to the bottom rail of the casement about one-third of the way along from the hinged edge.

4 Open the window to find the right position for the pins on the frame. Attach the pins, then fit the stay rest on the casement rail.

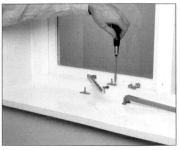

FITTING CURTAIN TRACKS AND POLES

There are many different methods of hanging curtains and drapes, ranging from simple rings on a wooden pole to complex tracks which are often cord-operated and which may even be motor-driven. Poles may be wood or metal, while tracks are either metal or plastic. Some are designed to be unobtrusive, others to be a definite design feature. The choice depends on the style of decor, and also to some extent on the curtains themselves, since some heading styles work better with one type than another. Choose the curtain style first, then check with the supplier to see which track styles will work best.

Fixing curtain track can be tricky on a masonry wall. The top of the window opening may be bridged by a reinforced concrete or a galvanized steel beam, concealed behind the plaster. The problem lies in making firm fixings into this beam, since drilling concrete at a precise spot to take a wall plug and screw can be difficult, and a cavity fixing such as a spring toggle is needed for a steel beam. It is often easier either to fit the track above the beam, or to put up a wood support strip first and then attach the track to that. If the worst comes to the worst, a ceiling-mounted track could be used instead. Fixing track to wood-framed walls, by contrast, could not be easier. The brackets can be fixed anywhere on the wooden beam over the opening.

PUTTING UP A CURTAIN POLE

1 Draw a pencil guideline on the wall, and mark the bracket positions along it. Attach the bracket bases after drilling and/or plugging the holes.

2 Slot in the bracket extensions and tighten the locking screws. Slide in the pole, fit the rings and finial, and screw through the brackets into the pole.

PUTTING UP A ROLLER BLIND

Roller blinds (shades), as their name implies, consist of a length of material – usually fabric – wound onto a roller that is mounted in brackets close to the window. They can be used instead of curtains and drapes for a simple, uncluttered effect, or in conjunction with them – for example if extra shade is required in sunny windows.

1 Screw the roller brackets to the frame close to the top corners, with the fixing flanges facing inwards so there is room to use a screwdriver.

2 Cut the roller and fabric to the required width, and insert the pin caps at each end to match the brackets – one is round, the other rectangular.

3 Hang the roller on its brackets, then pull it down to check the tension. If it will not retract, lift off the ratchet end, roll up the blind and replace it.

PUTTING UP CURTAIN TRACK

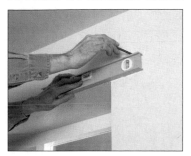

1 Decide at what level to fit the track, and use a pencil and spirit level to draw a guideline on the wall surface. Extend the line at the sides.

2 Drill holes for wall plugs in masonry walls, or make pilot holes in wood-framed ones, at the spacings recommended in the instructions. Fit the brackets.

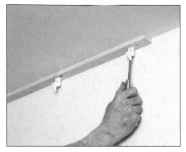

3 If a ceiling-mounted track is needed, locate the joist or joists and screw a support strip into place. Then attach the track brackets to the support strip.

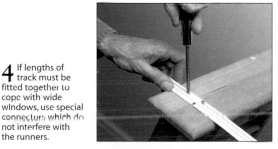

4 If lengths of track must be fitted together to cope with wide windows, use special connectors which do not interfere with the runners.

5 Mount the track on the brackets. Here this is done by rotating a locking cam via a small lever; on other types there is a locking screw.

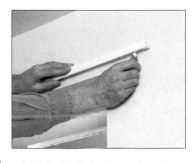

6 Fit the curtain hooks to the heading tape, then clip the hooks to the track. Some types have hooks on the track already; simply hook on the curtains.

TIP

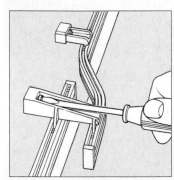

If a curtain overlap is required, form an S-bend on one length of track so that it overlaps the track behind. Clip the special extension bracket to the tracks and screw the bracket to the wall.

HANGING PICTURES AND MIRRORS

However beautifully walls are decorated, they will still look rather featureless unless they are brightened up by hanging some pictures, and perhaps a mirror or too as well. Apart from their obvious function, mirrors can make a room seem brighter by reflecting light from the window.

For hanging pictures there is a choice of using individual supports for each picture, or hanging them from a picture rail. Individual supports range from small plastic or metal picture hooks, which are simply nailed to the wall, to heavy-duty fixings attached with screws – and wall plugs on masonry walls. The choice depends solely on the weight of the picture. Use single-pin picture hooks for pictures with a slimline frame up to around 600 mm (2 ft) in either dimension, and a two-pin hook for anything of similar size in a heavy frame. Use two hooks, one at each side of the frame, for pictures up to about 900 mm (3 ft) across, and switch to a screw-in hook for anything larger. With picture rails, the standard S-shaped hooks will support reasonable weights.

Mirrors can be hung like pictures as long as the fixing is strong enough to take the weight. Otherwise they can be secured directly to the wall with special mirror clips. If they have pre-drilled holes at the corners they can be fixed with screws – ideally, mirror screws with special domes or clip-on covers (rosette fastenings).

MIRROR FIXINGS

1 Mirrors can be fixed with pre-drilled holes, using screws plus special washers and spacers that cushion the mirror and allow air circulation.

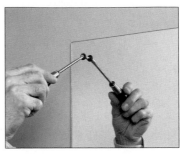

2 Mark and drill the fixing holes, then thread the screw through the washer, the mirror and the rear spacer before driving the screw. Do not overtighten it.

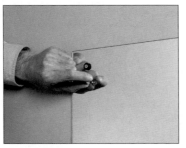

3 The screw head should just start to compress the washer. Cover it with a screw-on dome (rosette fastening) if using mirror screws, or with a plastic cover.

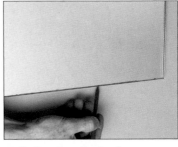

4 If using mirror clips, first draw a guideline on the wall where the bottom of the mirror will go, and fit the fixed bottom clips at each end.

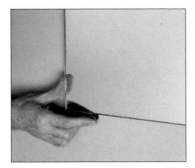

5 Set the bottom edge of the mirror in the bottom clips, checking that it is truly level, and mark the wall to indicate where its top edge will be.

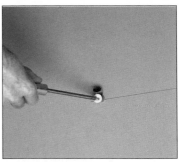

6 Screw the slotted top clips to the wall so their top edges are just above the line. Raise them, set the mirror in place, and press the top clips down.

For a more attractive finish, choose special screws with screw-on domes (rosette fastenings) for fixing mirrors.

PICTURE FIXINGS

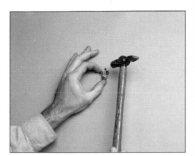

1 Traditional brass picture hooks come in one-pin and two-pin versions. The holes in the hook guide the pin in at an angle to the wall for a firmer fixing.

2 Small plastic picture hooks have three or four short pins to help locate the hook, and are secured by a longer pin driven through the centre hole.

3 A picture rail allows pictures to be hung in any position and at any height. Simply place the hook over the rail and hang the picture wire over it.

SOFT FURNISHINGS

Most items of soft furnishing are expensive to buy ready-made but they can be made just as successfully at home and much more cheaply. Curtains and drapes, cushion covers, bed linen and table linen require the minimum of sewing skills and little equipment beyond a sewing machine and iron.

The choice of fabric plays a major part in setting the style of a room, creating accents of colour to enliven a neutral decor or providing a means of coordinating different elements effectively in a room. Colour is an important consideration when furnishing a room – light shades tend to open it out, while dark and vivid shades tend to enclose it. Many people tend to play safe by choosing neutral or pastel shades which, although easy to live with, can look rather boring and impersonal.

Making soft furnishings at home is the perfect way to experiment with colour and make a visual statement. Most items require a few metres (yards) of fabric at the most. A good point to bear in mind when selecting fabric is that there are no hard-and-fast rules, apart from trying not to mix too many different colours and patterns

in one setting. Most good stores will supply swatches of furnishing fabrics without charge for colour matching at home.

Another consideration is that the chosen fabric should be suitable for the intended purpose – for example, heavyweight cloths will make up into good curtains and cushion covers but will be too stiff and unyielding to make a successful tablecloth or bed valance. A lot of these details are primarily common sense but, when in doubt, be guided by the sales assistant's specialist knowledge.

This section contains information about the types of fabric and curtain heading tapes, tools and equipment required as well as comprehensive instructions showing how to make a variety of soft furnishings from lined curtains to tablemats. When making any of the projects in this section, read through the instructions carefully before starting, especially those which refer to calculating the amount of fabric required. Finally, make sure each stage is understood before starting to cut out the fabric.

Opposite: Soft furnishings in stunning fabric designs can transform a room. Curtains and drapes, tie-backs, piped and frilled scatter cushions and stylish box cushions for benches and window seats are just some of the projects featured in this section.

1   2   3   4

TYPES OF FABRIC

Fabrics are made from different types of fibres which can be used singly or in combinations of two, three or more. The fibres can be natural, such as cotton, wool and linen, or man-made, such as acrylic and acetate. Fabric is formed by weaving, knitting or netting threads made from these fibres. When selecting fabrics for different items of soft furnishing, always choose the appropriate weight and a suitable fibre composition.

Cotton is the most common type of fabric, often with small amounts of synthetic fibres added for strength and to improve the crease-resistance of the finished item. Linen is extremely strong, although expensive and inclined to crease badly; the addition of both cotton for economy and synthetics to help prevent creasing is usual. Both

cotton and linen shrink when laundered and this should be taken into account when estimating the amounts required. Some furnishing fabrics are pre-shrunk during manufacture and this point should always be checked when purchasing.

Man-made fibres have different properties, depending on their composition, but the majority resist creases and shrinking. Their most common use for soft furnishings, apart from being added to cotton and linen blends, is for making easy-care nets and sheer curtains (drapes) which are lightweight, launder well and keep their colour through countless washes.

BROCADE
Cotton, cotton/synthetic blend or acetate with a woven self-pattern

created by areas of different weaves. Used for making formal curtains and drapes and cushion covers.

CALICO
Inexpensive, medium-weight woven cotton either dyed or printed, also sold unbleached. Used for curtains and blinds (shades), in particular.

CHINTZ
Glazed, medium-weight furnishing cotton, traditionally printed with patterns of roses and other flowers, birds and animals.

DAMASK
Similar to brocade, but with a satin weave giving a flatter finish. Made in cotton, cotton/synthetic blends and linen and used for tablecloths and napkins.

DOWN-PROOF CAMBRIC
Medium-weight plain cotton fabric

10   11   12   13

5   6   7   8   9

Here are just some of the myriad fabrics available for soft furnishings; checked (**1**), plain (**2**) and striped (**3**) in a multitude of different colourways; glazed cotton chintz (**4** and **5**); sateen in cotton/synthetic mix (**6**); printed cotton (**7** and **8**); and calico (**9**). Other choices include: synthetic weaves (**10**); brocade (**11**); velvet (**12**); jacquard weave (**13**); linen union (**14**); damask (**15** and **16**); silk (**17**); and synthetic taffeta (**18**).

specially treated to prevent feathers and down from working their way through the weave. Used for making feather cushion pads and pillows.

GINGHAM
Checked fabric woven from cotton or cotton/polyester blends often used to make soft furnishings for kitchens.

HAND-WOVEN FABRIC
Heavyweight or medium-weight cotton with an irregular, rather rough weave used for curtains, cushion covers and bedspreads.

LACE
An openwork cotton or synthetic fabric, usually with a strong pattern applied to a mesh background, used for curtains, tablecloths and bedspreads.

LAWN
A light, delicate cotton, often with a woven stripe pattern.

LINEN UNION
Hardwearing, heavyweight fabric made from linen with some added cotton suitable for curtains and upholstery. Often printed with floral designs.

MADRAS
Hand-woven pure cotton originating from Madras, India. Usually dyed in brilliant colours, often with a woven pattern of checks, plaids and stripes.

POPLIN
A lightweight or medium-weight cotton either plain or printed.

PVC
Sturdy cotton treated with a wipe-clean plastic coating (polyvinylchloride). Used for kitchen tablecloths.

SATEEN
Cotton or cotton/synthetic fabric with a slight sheen. Curtain lining is usually lightweight cotton sateen.

SHEETING
Extra-wide fabric for making bed linen, usually woven from 50 per cent cotton and 50 per cent polyester or other man-made fibre so it is easy-care.

TICKING
Heavy woven cloth with narrow stripes. Originally used for covering pillows, mattresses and bolsters but today used as a decorative fabric in its own right.

VELVET
Heavy fabric made from cotton or cotton/synthetic blends with a cut pile used for formal curtains and cushion covers. Corduroy (needlecord) is similar, but here the cut pile forms regular ridges down the cloth.

VOILE
Light, semi-transparent cotton or synthetic fabric used for sheer curtains and bed drapes.

14   15   16   17   18

TOOLS AND EQUIPMENT FOR SOFT FURNISHINGS

The most expensive piece of equipment needed for making soft furnishings is a sewing machine. Although a modern swing-needle machine is preferable because of its zigzag stitching, an ordinary straight stitch machine, either hand or electric, is perfectly adequate. Always work a small piece of practice stitching on a fabric sample before starting a project, adjusting the stitch length and tension as necessary. Fit a new needle whenever necessary; machine needles become blunt very quickly, especially when sewing on synthetic blends, and a blunt needle can cause uneven stitches and puckering. Have the machine serviced by a professional repairer at regular intervals and put it away after each sewing session to prevent it from becoming covered with dust.

A steam iron is also essential. Choose a fairly heavyweight one and keep the sole plate spotlessly clean at all times. Fill the iron with distilled water (available from a pharmacy or motor accessory shop) when using the steam facility to avoid limescale forming inside the water reservoir and clogging the steam jets. A sturdy ironing board with a well-padded surface or slip-on cover is also needed.

Sewing needles come in various shapes and sizes; choose a type of needle which feels comfortable when stitching. As a general guide, *betweens*

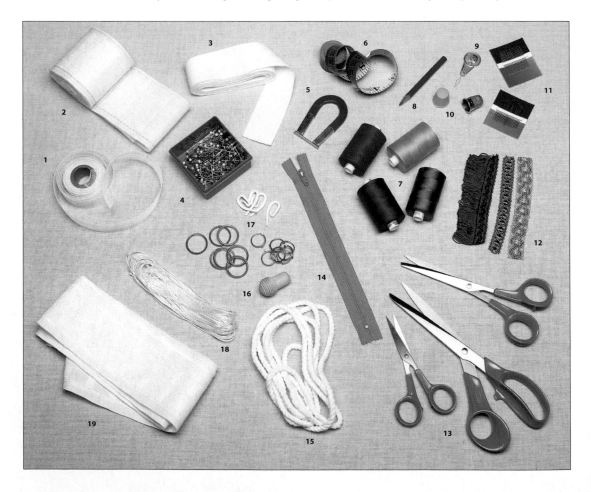

Right: Choose fabrics from a wide range of plain, woven and printed patterns, accessorizing with ribbons, cords and braid in complementary or contrasting colours.

are short needles, *sharps* are slightly longer and used when tacking (basting) or gathering, *straws* or *milliner's needles* are very long and useful when sewing through several layers of fabric.

STORING EQUIPMENT

Try to keep the necessary equipment in good order, clean and tidily stored so it is always easy to find immediately. A plastic tool box with divided trays is useful for this purpose.

Fabric, threads and trimmings should be stored in a cool, dust-free place. Keep offcuts of fabric in self-seal plastic bags with the appropriate threads and label the bags with the date and the name of the project. This is useful in case the stitching needs to be repaired or a patch added to conceal a damaged area.

TOOLS AND EQUIPMENT

Opposite: This selection of useful sewing aids includes: looped vertical tape for Austrian and Roman blinds (shades) (**1**), curtain (drapery) heading tape (**2 & 19**), woven curtain tape (**3**), pins (**4**), magnet (**5**), tape measure (**6**), sewing threads (**7**), dressmaker's pencil (**8**), needle threader (**9**), thimbles (**10**), sewing needles (**11**), furnishing braid and fringe (**12**), three sizes of scissors (**13**), zip fastener (**14**), piping cord (**15**), toggle for blind or curtain pull cords (**16**), curtain rings and hooks (**17**) and blind cord (**18**).

There are different types of needle threader available and these can be helpful when using fine, hard-to-thread needles. Whether or not a thimble is used when hand sewing is largely a matter of personal preference, but using one will protect the fingers.

Glass-headed pins are easy to see and handle. If the ordinary type of pin is preferred, choose a brand which is stainless and rustproof to avoid marking the fabric. Store pins in a dry place. A small horseshoe magnet is useful to retrieve pins and needles from the floor after a sewing session.

There are several types of sewing threads for both hand and machine use. Use mercerized cotton thread when sewing pure cotton and linen; core-spun thread (thread with a coating of cotton around a polyester core) for general purpose stitching; spun polyester thread on synthetic fabrics. Use tacking thread for tacking in preference to sewing thread as it breaks easily and tacking stitches can be removed without damaging the fabric.

Good quality scissors are a real investment as they will cut accurately and stay sharp longer than cheaper ones. Drop-forged scissors are heavy, but the blades can be sharpened repeatedly over many years while the lightweight type with plastic handles are very comfortable to use. Buy a large pair with 28 cm (11 in) blades for cutting out fabric, a medium-sized pair with 10 to 12.5 cm (4 to 5 in) blades for trimming seams and cutting small pieces of fabric and a small pair of needlework scissors for unpicking or snipping thread ends.

Choose a fibreglass tape measure marked with both metric and imperial measurements as fabric and plastic tape measures will eventually stretch and become inaccurate. A wooden metre ruler (yard stick) is also useful. A dressmaker's pencil is more convenient for marking fabric than tailor's chalk as it can be sharpened to a fine point. Choose white or yellow for marking dark fabrics and blue for light ones.

NOTE

The metric and imperial measurements quoted in the following projects are not exact equivalents. Always follow just one set of measures, either centimetres or inches, to ensure perfect results. Note also that contrasting thread has been used for the stitching for clarity only; it is normal to match the colour of the thread with the dominant shade of the furnishing fabric.

CURTAIN AND DRAPERY HEADINGS

Curtains and drapes can remain drawn across a window at all times, serving either as a purely decorative feature in the room, or a means of disguising a less than desirable outlook. In other rooms, curtains will need to be pulled back during the day to let in light and air and then be drawn across the window at night to provide privacy and keep out the evening chill. Curtains can be made in a variety of fabrics and styles, but they all need some means of attaching them to a pole or rail fixed above the window.

There is a wide range of ready-made heading tapes available in the stores which will help to create a number of different window treatments, giving effects from a narrow ruched band (standard tape) to an intricately pleated border (smocked tape). The tapes are stitched along the top of the fabric, usually with two parallel rows of stitching, then the fabric is gathered or pleated by means of integral cords in the tape. A series of pockets suspends the curtain from rings or hooks attached to the curtain (drapery) track or pole.

The choice of heading tape is largely a matter of personal preference, but keep in mind that the weight of the curtain fabric should be suitable for the style to be created – a very fluid, lightweight cloth, for example, is not suitable for forming cartridge pleats as this requires a more substantial fabric. With all these tapes, follow the manufacturer's instructions to calculate the exact amount of fabric required and how to stitch the tapes in position.

Above: An elegant metal pole with ornate finials enhances a curtain with a smart triple pleated heading.

STANDARD TAPE

Suitable for all types of fabric, standard tape produces a narrow, ruched band at the top of the curtain (drape). This type is particularly useful for unlined curtains in the kitchen or bathroom. Between 1 1/2 and 2 times the track width of fabric will be needed.

HEAVYWEIGHT PENCIL PLEAT TAPE

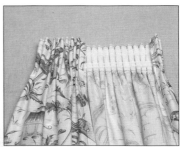

Pencil pleat tapes are probably the most popular type available, especially for floor-length curtains. Use this tape to create narrow, regular pleats on heavy fabrics. Between 2 1/4 and 2 1/2 times the track width of fabric will be needed with this heading.

Right: Make a dramatic feature of floor length curtains by adding contrasting bows and a deep border. The wooden pole blends well with other woodwork features.

OTHER TYPES OF HEADINGS

In addition to other tapes specifically designed for making valances and attaching separate curtain (drapery) linings, one of the most useful types is the lightweight curtain tape for use with net, lace, voile and other semi-transparent fabrics. This type of tape will gather the cloth evenly, but is light enough not to show through sheer fabric and make a heavy distracting line across the curtain top.

Lightweight tapes are made from synthetic materials, so be careful to set the iron at a moderate temperature when giving the curtains a final press before hanging them.

MEDIUM-WEIGHT PENCIL PLEAT TAPE

Similar to the heavyweight version, this tape is narrower and ideal for medium weight printed and woven cottons. Between 2 1/4 and 2 1/2 times the track width of fabric will be needed.

TRIPLE PLEAT TAPE

This type of tape creates elegant, fanned pinch pleats in groups of three at intervals across the curtain. Double the track width of fabric will be needed, plus special triple pleat hooks to hold the fanned pleats in position when the curtain is hanging.

CARTRIDGE PLEAT TAPE

Cartridge tape creates formal, cylindrical pleats spaced at regular intervals across the curtain. Use a medium-weight or heavyweight fabric to show the pleats to best effect. Double the track width of fabric will be needed.

BOX PLEAT TAPE

Crisply tailored box pleats are simple to achieve with this tape, which is suitable for curtains, valances and dressing table drapes. About 2 1/2 times the track width of fabric will be needed.

GOBLET TAPE

A stylish effect creating neat, goblet-shaped pleats. This tape requires three rows of stitching instead of the usual two rows and about 2 1/2 times the track width in fabric. This tape can also be used to make valances.

SMOCKED TAPE

This creates an unusual smocked effect, once strictly the preserve of the professional curtain-maker. This tape requires four rows of stitching instead of the usual two rows and about 2 1/2 times the track width in cloth. This tape can also be used to make valances.

LINED CURTAINS AND DRAPES

Curtains are the largest item of soft furnishing to make and although they may appear difficult, they in fact require only the minimum of sewing skills. The secret of successful curtain-making lies in accurate measuring, estimating and cutting out. Choose one of the curtain heading tapes illustrated on the previous two pages, depending on the required effect and the weight of the fabric, and always consult the manufacturer's instructions when stitching the tape in position.

Lined curtains are suitable for most windows, but for the kitchen and bathroom unlined ones may be preferable, as these are easier to launder. To make unlined curtains, simply omit the lining steps shown below and turn and stitch a narrow double hem along the side edges before attaching the heading tape.

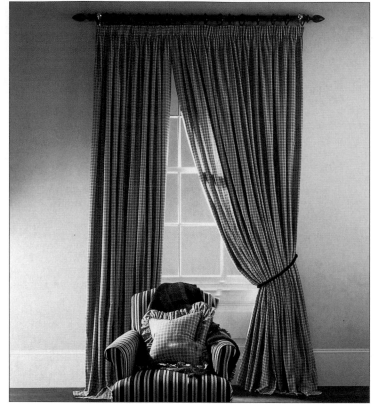

Right: Lined curtains and drapes are heavier and hang well, with the lining also acting as a barrier to sunlight, preventing fabric colours from fading.

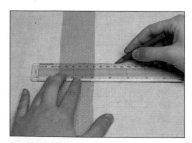

1 Place the lining on the fabric chosen for the curtain (drape) with the right sides together and the lower raw edges aligning. Mark the centre point of the curtain on both the fabric and the lining, using a dressmaker's pencil.

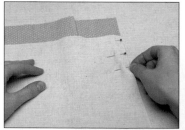

2 With the right sides of the fabric and lining still facing, pin them together along the side edges taking care that the lower edges of both the fabric and lining are still aligned. At the top of the curtain, the lining should be 4 cm (1 1/2 in) shorter than the fabric.

3 Mark the finished length of the curtain and the sewing line for the hem on the lining with a dressmaker's pencil, taking into account the 15 cm (6 in) hem allowance. Stitch along the side edges 1 cm (3/8 in) from the raw edge, stitching from the top of the lining to about 10 cm (4 in) from the hem sewing line.

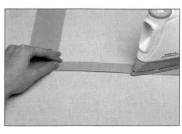

4 Turn to the right side. Press the side edges making sure that the fabric pulls over to the wrong side by 2.5 cm (1 in). Matching the marked points at the top of both fabric and lining, fold 4 cm (1¹/₂ in) of fabric over onto the wrong side and press in place.

5 Tucking under the raw edges, pin the heading tape in position just below the top of the fabric. Following the manufacturer's instructions, machine stitch the tape to the curtain, taking care to stitch each long side in the same direction to avoid puckering.

CURTAIN AND DRAPE STYLES

Floor length curtains can add the illusion of height to square windows. Accentuate the effect by holding the curtains back at window sill level with tie-backs.

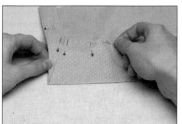

6 Fold over a double 7.5 cm (3 in) hem along the lower edge of the fabric and press in place. If using heavyweight fabric, fold the corners over to form a mitre, trimming away the surplus cloth. Tack (baste) along the hem.

7 Turn up and pin a double hem along the lower edge of the lining so the hem edge will hang about 2 cm (³/₄ in) above the finished fabric hem. Trim away any surplus lining and tack along the hem.

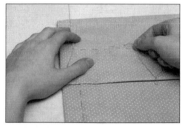

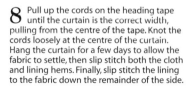

8 Pull up the cords on the heading tape until the curtain is the correct width, pulling from the centre of the tape. Knot the cords loosely at the centre of the curtain. Hang the curtain for a few days to allow the fabric to settle, then slip stitch both the cloth and lining hems. Finally, slip stitch the lining to the fabric down the remainder of the side.

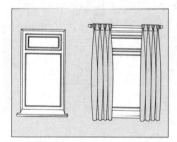

To add width to a narrow window, extend the curtain (drapery) track or pole at each side so that, when pulled back, the curtains do not obscure the window or block out light.

CALCULATING FABRIC REQUIREMENTS

To calculate the amount of fabric and lining required, follow these guidelines.

To calculate the *width*, multiply the width of the curtain (drapery) track or pole by the amount of fullness needed for the chosen heading tape (usually between 1¹/₂ and 2¹/₂ times the width of the window) and allow 3.5 cm (1³/₈ in) for each side hem. Divide the curtain width required by the width of the fabric, rounding up as necessary. Allow 3 cm (1¹/₄ in) for each join that is necessary.

To calculate the *length*, measure downwards from the track or pole to the required curtain length, then add on 4 cm (1¹/₂ in) to accommodate the heading tape and 15 cm (6 in) for the bottom hem.

To calculate the *total* amount of fabric required, multiply the length by the number of widths needed.

Almost the same amount of *lining* as curtain fabric is needed, with just 5 cm (2 in) less in the width and 4 cm (1¹/₂ in) less in the length.

LIGHTWEIGHT CURTAINS AND DRAPES

Lightweight curtains can be made from fine cottons and sheer fabrics, such as net, lace and voile. Shears are used to make curtains for windows where privacy is needed from the outside world, but light is still required to filter through into the room. This type of curtain is often used as a permanent feature, together with heavier, lined curtains which are drawn at night. Lightweight

cotton curtains also add a decorative touch to windows and glazed doors and cupboards.

A simple method is shown in the first set of steps, where the curtain is supported with lengths of curtain wire threaded through casings at the top and bottom. The wires are held in place by small hooks attached to the top and bottom of the window or door frame. The other two treatments are less

formal and the curtains can be drawn back where permanent privacy is not essential. These styles look best hung from a narrow wooden or brass pole.

The curtain with ribbon bows is softly gathered and is suitable for floor-length curtains made about 1 m (39 in) longer than usual to allow the fabric to settle into graceful folds when it reaches the floor. The eyelet heading requires less fabric as the curtain is not gathered.

CURTAINS AND DRAPES ON WIRES

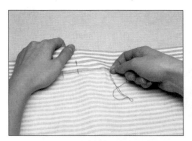

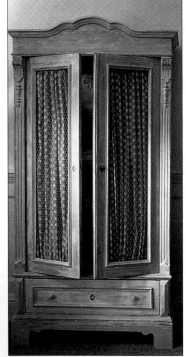

1 Cut out the fabric, allowing 2 or 3 times the window width and 2 cm (3/4 in) for each side hem, 6.5 cm (2 1/2 in) for the top hem and 6.5 cm (2 1/2 in) for the bottom one. Turn, pin and machine stitch double 1 cm (3/8 in) side hems. Along the top of the fabric, turn under 1 cm (3/8 in) and press. Turn under a further 5.5 cm (2 1/4 in), pin and tack (baste) in place. Repeat to make the bottom hem.

2 Measure 3 cm (1 1/4 in) from the outer fold along the top of the curtain (drape) and mark the point with a pin. Machine stitch along the hem from this point, parallel with the folded edge. Repeat along the bottom hem.

3 Machine stitch 5 mm (3/8 in) from the inner fold along the top hem to complete the top casing. Repeat along the bottom hem to make the second casing. (A plain hem instead of a casing can be used at the bottom of the curtain, if wished.)

4 Thread a piece of curtain wire through the top casing and another piece through the bottom casing (if using). The screw eyes at either end of the wires are held in place with small hooks screwed into the window frame in the required positions.

Above: Lightweight curtains gathered on wires at the top and bottom of the doors enhance a country-style cupboard (closet) as well as hiding its contents.

EYELET HEADING

 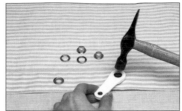 

1 Cut out the fabric, allowing 2.5 cm (1 in) for each side hem, 6.5 cm (2 1/2 in) for the top hem and 5 cm (2 in) for the bottom one. Turn, pin and machine stitch double side and bottom hems. Along the top of the fabric, turn under 1 cm (3/8 in) and press. Turn under a further 5.5 cm (2¹/4 in), pin and tack (baste) in place. Machine stitch 5 mm (¹/4 in) from the inner and outer folds.

2 Mark the positions for the eyelets on the wrong side of the hem approximately 10 cm (4 in) apart using a sharp pencil. Position the hem over a scrap piece of thick cardboard or wood and, following the manufacturer's instructions carefully, use the eyelet tool and a hammer to make a hole in the fabric at one of the pencil marks.

3 Following the manufacturer's instructions, assemble both parts of the eyelet around the hole. Position the other end of the eyelet tool over the top and hit sharply with the hammer. Repeat steps 2 and 3 until all the eyelets are attached. Attach the curtain (drapes) to the pole by looping thick piping cord through the eyelets and over the pole.

BOW HEADING

1 Cut out the fabric in the same way as an ordinary unlined curtain (drape), allowing extra on the length if floor-length folds are required. Turn the side and bottom hems in the same way, then attach a suitable heading tape along the top of the curtain.

2 Divide the top of the curtain into 15–20 cm (6–8 in) sections and mark with a pin on the right side. (It may be necessary to adjust the size of the sections slightly to suit the width of the curtain, but make sure that the ribbons will be evenly spaced.)
Cut 2 cm (3/4 in) wide satin ribbon into 1 m (39 in) lengths, fold in half and mark the centre with a pin. Stitch a ribbon to the curtain at every marked position. Pull up the cords until the curtains are the correct width, then attach to the pole by tying the ribbons in a reef knot over the pole. Tie the ends into bows and trim.

Left: The light and airy feel of this bedroom is in part due to the lightweight cotton curtains, held in place with ribbon bows, which allow the sunlight to filter into the room.

WORKING WITH SHEERS

When working with sheers, try to avoid joining fabric widths as this can look unattractive. Instead, make separate curtains or drapes and hang them together on the same wire or curtain pole.

Take care when pressing sheer fabrics as many contain a high proportion of synthetic fibres which melt when in contact with high heat. Test by pressing a spare piece of fabric with the iron set to 'low' or 'synthetics' and then adjust the temperature as required.

PELMETS AND TIE-BACKS

Fabric-covered pelmets (valances) are quick and simple to make with a special PVC material which is self-adhesive on one side and lined with velour on the other. The adhesive is covered with backing paper, which is printed with ready-to-cut pelmet patterns to suit most styles of decoration. Attach the finished pelmet to a batten (furring strip) with the returns secured to the wall above the curtain (drapery) track with angle irons. The batten should be 5 cm (2 in) longer than the curtain track at each side of the window.

Plain shaped tie-backs are made with the help of buckram shapes coated with a special iron-on adhesive. The buckram is available in kit form, pre-cut in several sizes to suit the width of the curtains. Tie-backs are attached to the wall with rings and hooks. Experiment with the position of the hooks, before fixing, to assess the most pleasing effect.

Left: A fabric-covered pelmet (valance) provides the perfect finishing touch to this window treatment and echoes the shape of the wallpaper border.

PELMET

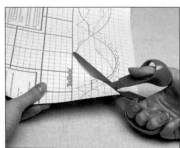

1 Measure the batten (furring strip) and the returns. Cut out the PVC pelmet (valance) material to this length, taking care to centre the chosen pattern. Cut out the shaped edge of the pelmet material along the correct line for the required shape. Cut out a piece of fabric about 3 cm (1¼ in) larger all around than the pelmet material.

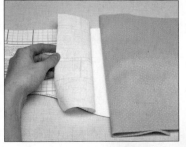

2 Lift the backing paper at the centre of the pelmet material, cut across and peel back a small amount on either side. Matching the centre of the fabric with the centre of the pelmet material, press the fabric onto the exposed adhesive. Keeping the fabric taut, peel away the backing and smooth the fabric onto the adhesive using the palm of the hand.

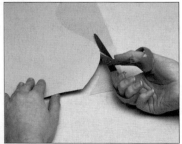

3 Turn the pelmet material so the velour backing is facing upwards. Using a sharp pair of scissors, cut the surplus fabric away around the edge of the pelmet material.

PELMET STYLES

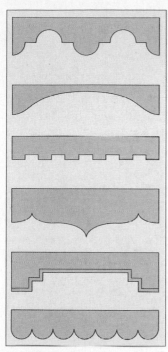

Pelmet (valance) styles can be plain or fancy, scalloped or stepped. Choose a style to suit the chosen fabric and the general decor of the room. Always make the shape perfectly symmetrical.

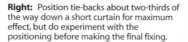

4 For a neat finish, glue a length of braid around the edge of the pelmet using a suitable craft adhesive. Attach strips of touch-and-close fastener to the batten with staples or tacks – use the hooked part only as the velour backing of the pelmet material acts as the looped part of the fastener. Press the finished pelmet in position on the batten.

SHAPED TIE-BACK

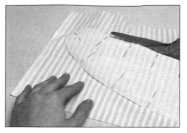

1 To make the back of the tie-back, pin the buckram shape onto the fabric and cut out around the edge of the shape. Lay this on the wrong side of the fabric to make the front and mark a line on the fabric with a dressmaker's pencil 1.5 cm (1/2 in) outside the buckram shape all around. Cut out the larger front piece.

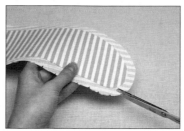

3 Snip into the edge of the surplus fabric all around the tie-back. This will help the fabric to lie neatly without puckering when it is turned over to the wrong side.

TIE-BACK VARIATIONS

It is easy to vary the look of plain tie-backs by adding a narrow frill or by binding the edge with a bias strip of contrasting fabric.

A strip of wide, fancy ribbon or braid makes an unusual tie-back – simply apply iron-on interfacing on the wrong side to stiffen the ribbon and cover the back with a strip of lining fabric. Turn the raw edges under, and slip stitch together around the edge.

Right: Position tie-backs about two-thirds of the way down a short curtain for maximum effect, but do experiment with the positioning before making the final fixing.

2 Sandwich the buckram between the front and back pieces (wrong sides together) and press with a hot dry iron to secure all the layers together, taking care not to scorch the fabric.

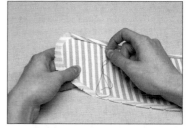

4 Fold the surplus fabric over to the wrong side of the tie-back and turn under the raw snipped edge. Using matching sewing thread, stitch the folded edge neatly in place taking care that the stitches do not go through onto the right side of the tie-back. Stitch a brass ring onto each end of the tie-back.

BLINDS AND SHADES

Blinds are becoming a popular alternative window dressing to a pair of curtains (drapes). The two styles described here, although made using very similar techniques, create very different effects – choose the softly ruched Austrian blind for a pretty, feminine window treatment and the smartly pleated Roman blind for a room with a modern decor.

Use a light- or medium-weight fabric to make an Austrian blind – anything from lightweight voile or sheer to standard cotton curtain fabric is fine. Heavy brocades and handwoven cottons are unsuitable as they are much too thick to drape well. A special type of track is needed to hang and mount the blind; known as Austrian blind track, it is now widely available.

Roman blinds, on the other hand, benefit from being made in a reasonably substantial fabric and can be lined to add body to the horizontal pleats and also to retain the warmth of a room. A batten (furring strip) and angle irons will be needed to mount the blind to the top of the window. Use strips of touch-and-close fastener to hold the blind in place on the batten.

ROMAN BLIND

1 Cut out the fabric. Turn, pin and stitch double 1.5 cm (1/2 in) side hems. Turn, pin and stitch a double 2.5 cm (1 in) hem along the top of the fabric. Press all the hems flat.

2 Pin and stitch a strip of Roman blind tape close to the side edge, turning under 1 cm (3/8 in) at the top to neaten. Stitch another strip along the remaining edge, then attach further strips at regular intervals across the blind, about 25–30 cm (10–12 in) apart.

3 At the bottom of the blind, turn over 1 cm (3/8 in) and press, then turn over a further 5 cm (2 in) to enclose the ends of the tape. Pin and stitch the hem close to the inner fold, leaving the sides open.

4 Stitch narrow tucks across the width of the blind to correspond with alternate rows of loops or rings on the tape. Make the first tuck level with the second row of loops or rings from the bottom of the blind. To make the tucks, fold the fabric with the wrong sides facing and stitch 3 mm (1/8 in) from the fold.

Left: Tailored Roman blinds (shades) are the perfect answer for windows and decors which demand a simple treatment.

AUSTRIAN BLIND

1 Cut out the fabric. Turn, pin, tack (baste) and stitch double 2 cm (3/4 in) side hems. Turn, pin, tack and stitch a double 2 cm (3/4 in) hem along the bottom of the fabric. Press all the hems.

2 Fold the fabric, right sides together, vertically like a concertina at approximately 60 cm (24 in) evenly spaced intervals and press thoroughly. The resulting folds mark the positions of the vertical tapes.

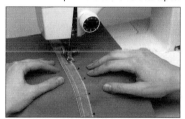

3 Pin and stitch a strip of Austrian blind tape close to one of the side hems, turning under 1 cm (3/8 in) at the bottom to neaten. Stitch another strip along the remaining side hem, then attach further strips vertically at regular intervals across the blind, aligning one edge of the tape with the pressed folds.

4 Turn 2 cm (3/4 in) over at the top of the blind and press. Pin the heading tape in position, folding under the raw edges, and stitch in place.

CALCULATING FABRIC REQUIREMENTS

Austrian blind

To calculate the *length*, measure the window drop and add 11 cm (2 1/4 in) for hem allowances.

For the *width*, measure the width of the window and multiply by 2 to 2 1/2 depending on the type of heading tape used. Add 8 cm (3 in) for side hems.

For the two types of *tape*, enough heading tape to extend across the width of the fabric is needed, plus extra for turnings. Sufficient strips of Austrian blind tape to position at 60 cm (24 in) intervals across the width of the blind are also needed. Each strip should be the length of the blind plus 1 cm (3/8 in); make sure there is a loop or ring 1 cm (3/8 in) up from the bottom of each strip so they will line up across the blind.

Roman blind

To calculate the *length*, measure the window drop, add 14 cm (4 1/2 in) for hem allowances and a little extra for the horizontal tucks.

For the *width*, measure the window and add 6 cm (2 in) for side hems.

For the *tape*, sufficient strips of Roman blind tape to position at 25–30 cm (10–12 in) intervals across the width of the blind are needed. Each strip should be the length of the blind plus 1 cm (3/8 in); make sure there is a loop or ring 1 cm (3/8 in) up from the bottom of each strip so they will match across the blind.

TO MOUNT A ROMAN BLIND

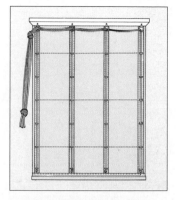

Attach the blind (shade) to the top of the batten with touch-and-close fastener. Cut each length of cord twice the length of the blind plus the distance of the right hand edge. Lay the blind on a flat surface and thread each cord through the loops in the tape. Knot each length securely on the bottom loop and thread the other end through the corresponding screw eyes on the batten, ending with all the cord ends on the right-hand side of the blind. Knot the cords together at the top, cut the ends off level and knot again.

Austrian blinds are mounted in much the same way, with the cords threaded through rings attached to the track.

Left: Austrian blinds (shades), although made in much the same way as Roman blinds, offer a totally different window treatment – pretty, feminine and very decorative.

SQUARE AND ROUND CUSHION COVERS

Cushions add comfort and a stylish touch to most rooms. Newly covered cushions are a relatively inexpensive way of enlivening a monotone colour scheme as they require little fabric compared to curtains (drapes) or blinds (shades). Simple shapes like squares and circles show off strong colours and patterns to best advantage and both shapes can be decorated with frills or piping or both combined.

Both types of cushion shown on this page have a zip inserted in the back seam – a neater method than making the opening in a side seam. Although a zip is the most convenient method of fastening a cushion cover, making it easy to remove for laundering, the opening may be closed with a row of slip stitches which need to be replaced whenever the cover is removed.

SQUARE CUSHION COVER

1 Measure the cushion pad, adding 1.5 cm (1/2 in) all around for ease, plus 1.5 cm (1/2 in) for seam allowances. Do not forget to allow an extra 3 cm (1 in) for the centre back seam. Cut out the front and two back pieces. Pin and stitch the centre back seam 1.5 cm (1/2 in) from the raw edges, making sure to leave an opening to accommodate the zip fastener. Press the seam open.

Below: Frills and piping in matching or contrasting fabric add a special touch to round and square cushion covers.

2 Pin and tack (baste) the zip in position along the opening, as shown, allowing the fabric to meet centrally over the zip teeth. Machine stitch the zip in place using a zip foot on the machine.

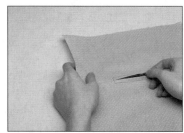

3 Press the seam allowances around the zip. Open the zip, making sure the fabric does not catch in the teeth and the ends are stitched securely. With the zip still open, place the front and back pieces together so that the right sides are facing.

4 Pin and machine stitch twice around the edge about 1.5 cm (1/2 in) from the raw edge. Clip the surplus fabric away close to the stitching at the corners to reduce the bulk. Press the seams and turn the cover to the right side through the zipped opening. Press the seams, insert the cushion pad and close the zip.

FRILLS

To make a frill, a piece of fabric is needed which is twice the depth of the finished frill plus 3 cm (1¹/4 in), and between 1¹/2 and 2 times the outside measurement of the cover. You may need to join several strips together to achieve the right length.

Right: Choose sumptuous fabrics for cushion covers to complement curtains and wall coverings for a harmonious decorating scheme.

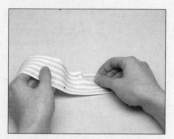

1 Join the ends of the strips together with a flat seam. Fold the strip in half lengthways with the wrong sides facing. Make one or two rows of running stitches along the raw edges of the strip, taking the stitches through both layers and leaving a long end of thread at one end of each row.

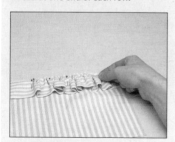

2 Gather the frill by pulling up the long threads until the frill is the right size to fit around the cushion front. Wind the long threads around a pin to secure them and even out the gather with the fingers.
   To add a frill to either a square or round cushion, align the raw edge of the frill with the raw edge of the front cover, right sides together. Tack and sew the frill in place, then continue making up the cover in the usual way.

ROUND CUSHION COVER

1 Measure the diameter of the cushion pad and add 1.5 cm (¹/2 in) all around for ease, plus 1.5 cm (¹/2 in) for seam allowances. Make a paper pattern to this size using dressmaker's pattern paper. Pin onto the fabric and cut out one piece for the front of the cover.

2 Rule a line across the paper pattern to mark the position of the back seam. The line should measure approximately 12.5 cm (5 in) longer than the zip. Cut the paper pattern in two along this line.

3 Pin both pattern pieces onto the fabric and cut out, remembering to allow an extra 1.5 cm (¹/2 in) for the seam allowance on the straight edge of each piece.

4 Pin and stitch the back seam, making sure to leave an opening which is long enough to accommodate the zip fastener. Finish off the cover in the same way as the square cover.

BOX AND BOLSTER CUSHIONS

Box cushion covers are often made to fit a particular chair or window seat as they can accommodate a thick cushion pad or piece of foam block. The covers should look neatly tailored and are best made in a crisp, cotton furnishing fabric. The seams can be enhanced with piping made from matching or contrasting fabric – plain piping looks particularly effective with patterned cushion fabric. Always pre-shrink cotton piping cord by washing it in hot water before use.

Circular bolster cushions look attractive on most types of furniture and make a good visual contrast against the more usual rectangular cushions. This shape of cushion works particularly well with striped, check and tartan cloth, especially when a contrasting tassel, ribbon bow or pompon is used as a trim.

BOX CUSHION

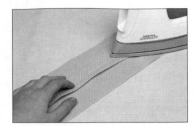

1 Cut out the fabric. Cut the back gusset in half lengthways and place together with the right sides facing. Pin and stitch the seam 1.5 cm (1/2 in) from the raw edges, leaving an opening for the zip. Press the seam open.

2 Pin and tack the zip in position along the opening, as shown, allowing fabric to meet centrally over the zip teeth. Stitch the zip in place using a zip foot on the machine.

3 With the right sides facing, join the four gusset pieces together along the short ends, taking a 1.5 cm (1/2 in) seam allowance and leaving 1.5 cm (1/2 in) unstitched at each end of the seams. Press the seams open.

4 With the right sides facing, pin and stitch the top edge of one gusset section to one edge of the top cover piece taking a 1.5 cm (1/2 in) seam allowance. At the gusset seam, leave the needle in the fabric, raise the machine foot and pivot the fabric so the next section of gusset aligns with the next side of the top cover piece. Continue pinning and stitching each section around the top in this way. Open the zip, then repeat the procedure to attach the bottom cover piece to the remaining side of the gusset. Trim away the surplus cloth at the corners and then turn the cover right side out through the zip opening.

FRENCH SEAMS

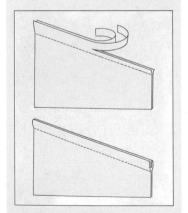

A French seam encloses the raw edges of fabric and prevents them fraying. It is worked in two stages: first stitch with the pieces wrong sides facing (**TOP**). Trim down the raw edges close to the first row of stitching. Then stitch with the right sides facing (**ABOVE**).

Below: A box cushion adds comfort and style to an attractive bench. The seams have been piped in a contrasting fabric to accentuate the boxy shape.

BOLSTER CUSHION

1 Cut out the fabric. Pin and stitch the length of the bolster cover with a French seam (see illustrations). Turn the resulting tube right side out and press the seam.

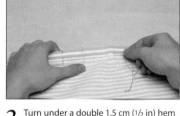

2 Turn under a double 1.5 cm (½ in) hem at each end of the tube. Pin and tack (baste) in place using a contrasting coloured thread so the stitches are easy to detect.

3 Machine stitch along the hems, keeping the stitching close to the inner folds. Remove the tacking stitches and press thoroughly.

Above: Gathered bolsters contrast well with the more usual rectangular cushion shapes.

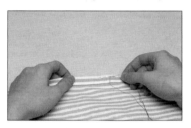

4 Using double thread run a row of gathering stitches along each end of the tube, close to the outer fold of the hem and leaving a long thread end. Insert the bolster pad in the tube, then tighten the gathering threads to close the cover. Secure the thread ends, then cover the small hole left at each end by attaching a furnishing tassel, ribbon bow or a covered button.

CALCULATING FABRIC REQUIREMENTS

Box cushion

Measure the length and width of the top of the pad and add 1.5 cm (½ in) all around for seam allowances. Two pieces of fabric this size are needed, one for the top and one for the bottom of the cover. The gusset is made from four pieces of fabric joined together. Measure the depth and width of the pad and add 1.5 cm (½ in) all around for seam allowances. Cut out three pieces of fabric to this size. Add an extra 3 cm (1 in) to the depth of the fourth piece for the zip seam in the back gusset.

Bolster cushion

To calculate the *length*, measure the bolster from the centre point of one end, along the length and around to the centre point of the opposite end, adding a total of 6 cm (2 in) for hem allowances.

To calculate the *width*, measure the circumference of the pad and add 3 cm (1 in) for seam allowances.

PIPING

1 Fold a piece of fabric in half diagonally and press the fold. Open out the fabric and using a ruler and pencil, mark out strips parallel to the fold about 4–5 cm (1½–2 in) apart, depending on the thickness of the piping cord. Cut out the strips.

2 Join the strips together with a flat seam to make the required length. Place the piping cord along the centre of the strip, fold it over with wrong sides facing and pin together. Tack (baste) and stitch close to the cord.

3 Lay the covered cord on the right side of the fabric with raw edges aligning and tack in place. Cover with a second piece of fabric, right side downwards and raw edges matching. Stitch the layers together along the seamline using a zip foot on the machine. Remove the tacking stitches.

TABLECLOTHS

Both square and round tablecloths are quick to make. For practical uses choose a washable fabric, either plain or patterned, in a shade which matches or coordinates with the general colour scheme of the room as well as any favourite tableware.

Cotton and synthetic blends are easy to sew, require practically no ironing and so make a good choice for everyday tablecloths in the kitchen or dining room. Plain, heavy cotton and linen look better for more formal occasions, but they require more hard work to keep them looking good over the years. Always treat stains on table linen immediately and launder as soon afterwards as possible.

SQUARE TABLECLOTH

1 Measure the sides of the table top, adding twice the required drop from the edge of the table and 3 cm (1 in) all around for hem allowances. Cut out the fabric. Turn and press a double 1.5 cm (1/2 in) hem around the sides.

Below: Choose a pretty printed fabric to make a covering for a rectangular kitchen or occasional table.

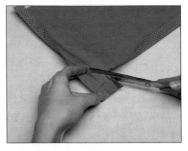

2 Unfold both hems and cut across each corner diagonally, as shown, within 5 mm (1/4 in) of the corner point at the inner fold.

3 Pin the diagonal edges together, with the right sides facing, and stitch a narrow seam 5 mm (1/4 in) from the raw edge. Stitch from the inner corner point and make the seam 1.5 cm (1/2 in) long. Press each seam and turn the corners out to the right side.

4 Re-fold the double hem along the pressed lines. The diagonal seams at each corner make a neat mitre. Pin, tack (baste) and stitch around the edge of the tablecloth, close to the inner fold. Press the hem.

Right: Cover a round occasional table with a floor-length plain undercloth, then top it with a small square cloth made of coordinating fabric.

JOINING FABRIC

When joining fabric to make either a square or round tablecloth, avoid making a seam down the centre as this can look rather unsightly. Instead, cut out two pieces of fabric to the correct width and use one as the central panel. Cut the second piece in half lengthways and join to either side of the panel, matching the pattern if necessary. Use an ordinary flat seam and neaten the raw edges.

ROUND TABLECLOTH

1 Measure the diameter of the table top and add twice the depth of the drop plus 3 cm (1 in) for hem allowances. Make a pattern from dressmaker's pattern paper using a pencil tied to a piece of string measuring half your final measurement. Hold one end of the string down on the paper, pull the string taut and draw a quarter circle on the paper with the pencil. Cut out the pattern.

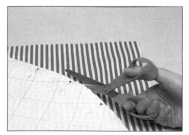

2 Fold the fabric into four and pin on the quarter circle pattern, aligning the folded edges of the fabric with the straight edges of the paper. Cut out using dressmaker's scissors.

3 Stitch around the outside of the fabric 1.5 cm (½ in) from the raw edge. This line of stitching marks the hem edge. Press the edge over onto the wrong side of the fabric along the stitched line without stretching the fabric.

4 Carefully turn under the raw edge to make a double hem, then pin and tack (baste) the hem in place. Stitch around the edge of the tablecloth close to the inner fold of the hem. Press the hem well.

TABLEMATS AND NAPKINS

Tablemats and napkins make the perfect table setting for an informal meal. They are simple to make and can be a good way of using offcuts and remnants of fabric.

Tablemats can be made from plain or patterned fabric and are most effective when machine quilted with a layer of wadding (batting) sandwiched between the top and bottom pieces of fabric. The layers help to protect the table surface beneath the plates. Bind the edges with matching or contrasting fabric or ready-made bias binding. Alternatively, choose ready-quilted fabric and follow the instructions for binding given here to finish the edges.

Napkins are simply a hemmed piece of fabric, usually square and made in a cloth which coordinates with the tablemats or a tablecloth. Give some thought to the practical purpose of napkins and always make them from fabric which is washable. Polyester and cotton blends are a popular choice for informal napkins, but nothing beats the look of pure linen for a formal occasion.

TABLEMAT

1 Decide on the size of the tablemat and cut out two pieces of fabric. Along the short edge of one piece, mark evenly spaced points 2.5 cm (1 in) apart using a ruler and a sharp pencil. Join the points to make lines running across the fabric.

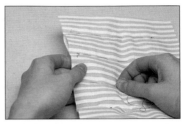

2 Cut a piece of wadding (batting) to the same size as the fabric and sandwich it between the two fabric pieces, with the wrong sides together and the marked piece on top. Pin together carefully, then work rows of tacking (basting) between alternate pencil lines.

3 Lengthen the stitch on the sewing machine slightly, then work parallel rows of machine stitching over the pencil lines using a matching or contrasting thread. Round off the corners by drawing around a cup or small plate, then trim away the surplus fabric.

4 Cut out and join the bias strips until the strip of binding is long enough to go around the edge of the tablemat. Fold the strip so that the raw edges meet in the middle and press. Open out one folded edge of the binding and pin it around the tablemat with the right sides facing and raw edges aligning. Neatly fold back the raw edges where the binding meets. Stitch along the crease of the binding.

5 Fold over the binding to the wrong side of the tablemat. Pin and stitch the binding in place by hand as shown. Turn the tablemat to the right side and strengthen the edge by working one row of machine stitching around the edge close to the inside fold of the binding.

SIZES AND FABRIC REQUIREMENTS

Tablemats

To decide on a suitable size for tablemats, first arrange a place setting with two sizes of plate plus cutlery (flatware) and measure the area these cover. The side plate and glass can be placed on the table at the edge of the mat, if preferred.

Traditionally, rectangular tablemats measure approximately 20 × 30 cm (8 × 12 in), but they can be larger – up to 30 × 45 cm (12 × 18 in). Having decided on the finished size of the tablemats, allow at least 5 cm (2 in)

extra all around for working the quilting. Always trim the surplus fabric away after completing the machine quilting but before beginning to bind the edges.

Napkins

Napkins are usually square and vary in size from small napkins of 30 cm (12 in) square for tea or coffee parties to large ones measuring 60 cm (24 in) for formal occasions. However, a good all-purpose size for napkins is 40 cm (16 in) square.

Right: For a heavily-quilted tablemat, work two sets of parallel quilting lines across the fabric to make diamond shapes, then bind the edges with plain fabric.

NAPKIN

Cut out the fabric to the required size. Fold and press a double 5 mm (1/4 in) hem all around the edge, taking care to fold the corners over neatly. Pin, tack (baste) and stitch the hem close to the inner fold.

Below: Make a feature of a linen napkin by adding a bow of narrow ribbon and dainty fresh flowerhead.

BIAS STRIPS

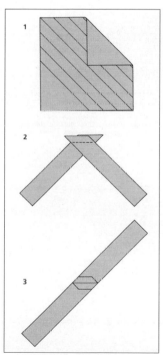

To make bias strips, mark out parallel lines the required distance apart on the cross of the fabric using a ruler and pencil (**1**). Cut out along the lines, then join the strips together with narrow seams until you have the required length (**2**). Press the seams open (**3**).

BED LINEN

Be imaginative in choosing colour
schemes and pattern combinations for
bed linen. A matching duvet cover and
valance looks stylish, particularly when
the fabric coordinates with the curtains
or drapes and other bedroom furnishings.

The duvet cover is simply a large bag
made from two pieces of fabric joined
together around the four sides, with an
opening left in the bottom edge to
allow the duvet to be inserted. Close
the opening with either touch-and-
close fastener or press stud tape. The
valance fits over the bed base,
underneath the mattress, and has a frill
around three sides reaching right down
to floor level.

Right: A matching gathered valance finishes
off this arrangement perfectly. Lace edging
around the pillows and duvet cover adds a
feminine touch.

DUVET COVER

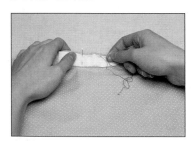

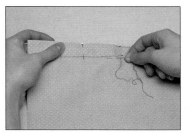

1 Measure the length of the duvet, usually
200 cm (78 in), and add 7 cm (2 ³/₄ in) for
hem and seam allowances. Measure the
width and add 4 cm (1 ¹/₂ in) for seam
allowances. Cut out two pieces of fabric. Turn
and stitch a double 2.5 cm (1 in) hem along
the bottom of each piece. Cut a length of
touch-and-close fastener 3 cm (1 ¹/₄ in)
longer than the desired opening, separate
the strips and pin one to the right side of the
hem on each piece. Machine stitch in place
around the edge of each strip.

2 Place the two fabric pieces with right
sides together so the fastener strips close.
Tack (baste) along the bottom hem from 3
cm (1 ¹/₄ in) inside the strip of fastener and
up to each corner.

3 Machine stitch through both layers at
right angles to the hem 3 cm (1 ¹/₄ in)
inside the fastener strip to enclose the raw
edges. Pivot the fabric and continue
stitching along the tacked line to the edge of
the fabric. Repeat at the other corner.

VALANCE

1 Measure the mattress top and add 3.5 cm (1 1/2 in) to the length and 3 cm (1 in) to the width. Cut out one piece of fabric to this size for the panel. Round off the two bottom corners of the panel by drawing around a plate and cutting around the curves.

2 For the frill, sufficient pieces of fabric wide enough to reach from the top of the bed base to the floor, plus 6.5 cm (2 1/2 in), are needed to make a long strip four times the mattress length plus twice the mattress width. Join the strips with French seams (see Duvet Cover, step 4) and press. Turn a double 2.5 cm (1 in) hem along the lower edge of the frill. Pin, tack (baste) and stitch as shown.

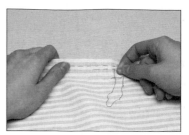

3 Divide the frill into six equal sections and mark with pins along the top edge. Work two rows of gathering stitches between the pins, leaving long thread ends.

CHOOSING FABRIC FOR BED LINEN

The best choice for bed linen is specially woven sheeting either in pure cotton or a polyester and cotton blend. Although pure cotton is cooler in summer, synthetic blends do have the advantage of needing little or no ironing. Sheeting is very wide, so joins are not necessary, and it is available in a large range of pastel and strong colours, both plain and patterned.

4 Divide the sides and bottom edge of the panel into six equal sections and mark with pins. Pull up the gathering stitches in each frill section until it fits the corresponding panel section. Pin each section in place with the right sides of the fabric facing.

Stitch the frill in place 1.5 cm (1/2 in) from the raw edge. Stitch again close to the first line of stitching and neaten the raw edges by machine zigzagging over them. Press the seam allowance towards the panel. Turn a double 1 cm (1/2 in) hem along the remaining raw edges of both the frill and panel. Pin and stitch.

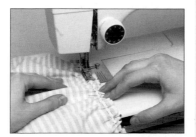

Right Crisply checked pillowcases and duvet cover accentuate the light and airy feel of a country style bedroom.

4 Turn so that the wrong sides are facing. Make a French seam around the remaining three sides, as follows. Pin and stitch 5 mm (1/4 in) from the raw edge. Trim the seam close to the stitching, then open the fastener and turn the cover so that the right sides are facing. Stitch around the three sides again to enclose the raw edges and complete the seam. Turn the cover to the right side.

STORAGE

Finding suitable storage space around the house for all the personal and household belongings every family accumulates can be quite a challenge. One difficulty is making a sensible compromise between tidiness and accessibility; it is no good having a place for everything if that means spending hours each day laboriously taking things out and putting them back again.

The solution is to tailor-make storage to suit its purpose. Some things need a temporary resting place where they remain readily accessible. Others need long-term storage, perhaps being retrieved and used only occasionally. And there is a third storage category, that of display – simply to show things off.

In a typical home, possessions are stored in one of three main ways: on shelves, in cupboards (closets) or in drawers. These may be combined in a variety of storage or display units, and the amount of each type of space that is required will vary from house to house. For example, the avid bookworm will have miles of shelves, while the clothes horse will need more wardrobe space.

The storage that is needed can be provided in one of two ways. One is to buy or make pieces of freestanding furniture that match the required storage function. The other is to use raw materials such as wood and manufactured boards plus the appropriate hardware to create built-in storage space – arrays of shelving, cupboards in alcoves and so on. The former is the best solution for those who value furniture more than function, since the pieces can be moved from one house to another. However, built-in storage is generally more effective in providing the most space for the least money, since the house walls can often be used as part of the structure. The following pages look at some of the storage options available.

Opposite: Shelving is an indispensable requirement when it comes to providing storage and display space around the house. It can be freestanding, wall-hung or built in to corners and alcoves, and can be tailor-made to suit its task or adjustable for maximum flexibility.

INCREASING STORAGE SPACE

Apart from obvious places such as kitchen units (cabinets) and bedroom wardrobes, there are many places in the main rooms of the house where items can be stored. This can be done without spoiling the look of the room. Properly planned storage space can be not only practical and capacious, but positively elegant.

The kitchen

Storage is a serious business here, and what is needed and how it is provided depends on what kind of kitchen it is and how it is used. The fully fitted kitchen is still popular, because it packs the most storage into the least space, although there is now a discernible movement back to farmhouse-style kitchens with freestanding rather than built-in furniture. This is suitable only for people who are either very tidy and well organized or, on the other hand, happy to live in chaos. The style of such kitchens restricts the amount of storage space they can offer at the expense of the look of the room, so for those who have a lot of kitchen utensils and like to keep large stocks of food, a fitted kitchen is a better idea. However, there is one big advantage with freestanding furniture: it can be taken along when moving house.

In deciding what is wanted, analyze storage needs thoroughly. Think about food, cooking utensils and small appliances for a start; all need a place close to cooking and food preparation areas. Move on to items like china, cutlery and glassware; do they need to

Below: No corner is too small to provide either some useful extra storage space or an attractive display of kitchenware.

Above: If the fully fitted kitchen does not appeal, a central food preparation area can restore the period kitchen look and provide useful storage space too.

Left: Fitted kitchen storage units (cabinets) offer much more than a home for provisions and pots and pans. Tailor-made units can now store and display everything from wine bottles to the family china.

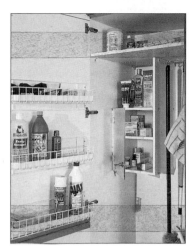

Above: Use can be made of every inch of cupboard (closet) space by adding internal shelves and fitting racks on door backs.

Above: Pull-out baskets are often more accessible than traditional shelving in kitchen base units (cabinets).

Right: Shelf support strips make it easy to put up single shelves or shelving groups wherever they are needed. The shelves are securely gripped along their rear edges and can be easily repositioned.

be in the kitchen at all, or would the dining room be a better place to keep them? Then consider non-culinary items – things like cleaning materials, table linen and so on – and make sure there is enough space for them.

Remember that ceiling-height cupboards (closets) are always a better bet than ones that finish just above head height, even if some small steps or a box are needed to reach them. It is best to use the top shelves for storing seldom-used items.

Always aim to make the best possible use of cupboard space. Fit extra shelves where necessary, use wire baskets for ventilated storage, hang small racks on the backs of cupboard doors and use swing-out carousels to gain access to corner cupboards.

If there is a separate laundry room, it is often easier to split cooking and non-cooking storage needs by moving all home laundry and cleaning equipment out of the kitchen

altogether. Such a room can also act as a useful back porch if it has access to the garden.

The living room

Here storage needs are likely to be firmly leisure-oriented. There has to be room for books, records, tapes, compact discs and videotapes, not to mention display space for ornaments and other treasures. The choice is again between freestanding and built-in furniture, and is a much freer one than in the kitchen

STORAGE IN THE HALLWAY

Simple hooks and an umbrella stand are the bare minimum, but consider having an enclosed cupboard (closet) that is built-in rather than freestanding. It is simple to borrow some porch or hall floor space to create a suitable enclosure. If it is fitted with a door to match others leading to the rest of the house, it will then blend in perfectly. Make sure it is ventilated so that damp clothes can dry.

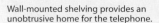

Wall-mounted shelving provides an unobtrusive home for the telephone.

INCREASING STORAGE SPACE *(continued)*

Below: Alcoves are the perfect site for built-in shelving for books or display and storage cupboards for music cassettes and discs, videos, hi-fi equipment and the like.

While planning living-room storage, pay particular attention to working requirements for power points (receptacles), especially if you have a lot of hi-fi equipment, and for any concealed lighting in the unit.

The dining room

Here storage needs relate mainly to providing places for china, glassware and cutlery – especially any that is kept for special occasions. Think too about storage for table mats, cloths and other table accessories. There may also be a need for somewhere to store small appliances such as toasters, coffee makers and hotplates. Once again, the choice is between built-in storage units and freestanding furniture; this is largely a matter of taste.

The bedrooms

Now take a look at storage requirements upstairs, starting with the bedrooms. Here the main need is for space to store clothes, and this is one area where built-in (and ideally, walk-in) storage is the perfect solution. Space can often be poached between

because here looks are as important as performance.

Built-in furniture can make optimum use of alcoves and other recesses. A more radical option is a complete wall of storage units which could incorporate space for home

entertainment equipment, as well as features such as a drinks cupboard. This also offers the opportunity to include a home office – some desk space, plus somewhere to file all the essential paperwork which every family generates.

USING THE ROOF SPACE

Except in older houses, the roof space is usually cluttered with all the woodwork that makes up a modern trussed-rafter roof and is of little use for storage. However, it is still worth boarding over the area immediately around the access hatch so that luggage, boxes and the like can be put there. If the roof construction permits, however, there is a chance to create almost unlimited storage capacity for everything from hobby materials to the summer's fruit crop. Fit a proper fixed ladder for safe and easy access.

Right: A high-level plate rack is a traditional way of storing and showing off the best china. It can be used to display other treasures too.

Left: Built-in furniture is becoming increasingly popular in bedrooms as a way of maximizing the use of precious space.

Below: A beautifully tiled bathroom is further enhanced with an attractive vanity unit, which can offer valuable storage space for toiletries.

bedrooms by forming a deep partition wall, accessible from one or both rooms; this can actually save money in the long run, as there is no furniture to buy. An alternative if overall upstairs floor space permits is to create a separate dressing room, at least for the master bedroom.

Bedrooms built under the roof slope offer an unparalleled opportunity to make use of the space behind the room walls by creating fully lined eaves cupboards (closets). These are

Above: Clothes organizers offer the maximum storage flexibility when space is limited, especially in built-in wardrobes.

WORKSHOP STORAGE

An area where some storage space is certainly needed is the workshop, whether this is a spare room, an area at the back of the garage or a separate building. The basic need is for shelf space, to take everything from cans of paint to garden products, and also some form of tool storage to keep everything in order.

Freestanding utility shelving is the ideal way of providing sturdy and compact garage or workshop storage.

particularly useful for long-term storage of items such as luggage which may be needed only occasionally, as well as providing a home for toys and games in children's rooms.

Do not just restrict bedroom storage to clothes and bedlinen, though. There is no reason why it should not also allow for books, ornaments, or even a small portable television.

The bathroom

Finally, look at the bathroom. Here requirements are likely to be relatively low-key – somewhere to keep toiletries and cleaning materials, for example. It is not a good idea to store towels and the like in a potentially damp and steamy atmosphere. The choice is likely to be between a floor-standing vanity unit and some wall-hung cupboards (cabinets), although if space permits some thought might be given to the growing number of fully fitted bathroom furniture ranges.

Where space is very limited, use might be made of 'hidden' space such as that behind a removable bath panel to store small items such as children's bath toys.

FITTING FIXED SHELVING

Wall-mounted shelving is one of two basic types – fixed or adjustable. With fixed shelving, each shelf is supported independently of others using two or more shelf brackets, which are fixed to the wall and to the underside of the shelf itself. With adjustable shelving, the shelves are carried on brackets, studs or tongues which are slotted or clipped into vertical support strips screwed to the wall.

Fixed brackets are ideal for putting up a single shelf – over a radiator, for example – although they can equally well be used to support several shelves. They come in many styles, shapes and colours. Metal brackets are the most usual, but wooden ones in various finishes are also available.

Shelves can be of natural wood or manufactured boards. Ready-made shelves can be bought from do-it-yourself stores; they are usually made of veneered or plastic-coated chipboard (particle board). The latter traditionally have either a white or imitation woodgrain finish, but subtle pastel shades and bold primary colours are becoming more widely available. Otherwise shelves can be cut from full-sized boards: chipboard, plywood, MDF (medium-density fibreboard) and blockboard are all suitable.

SHELF SUPPORT STRIP

This is an ingenious support for single shelves. It consists of a specially shaped channel which is screwed to the wall at the required position; then the shelf is simply knocked into place with a soft-faced mallet. The channel grips the shelf securely, and can support surprisingly heavy loads. Various sizes are available.

USING SHELF BRACKETS

1 Select the correct bracket spacing, then attach the shorter arm of each bracket to the underside of the shelf, flush with the rear edge.

2 Fix the shelf to the wall with a screw driven through one bracket, then check that it is horizontal and mark all the remaining screw positions.

3 Let the shelf swing downwards on its first fixing screw, then drill the other holes. Insert plugs for masonry wall fixings if needed.

4 Swing the shelf back up into position and drive in the remaining fixing screws. Tighten them fully so the screw heads pull the brackets against the wall.

USING SHELF SUPPORT STRIPS

1 Hold the support strip against the wall at the desired level, and mark the position of the central screw hole. Drill the hole and attach the strip.

2 Place a spirit level on top of the strip. Swivel the strip until it is precisely level, and mark the positions of the remaining screw holes.

3 Swivel the strip out of the way and drill the other holes. Then secure it with the remaining screws and slot the shelf into place.

4 Small shelf support blocks are also available for mounting small display shelves. The shelf is clamped in place by tightening a locking screw underneath.

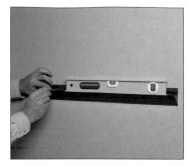

Right: Individual brackets can be used to mount more than one shelf, as long as there is no need to change the shelf spacing in the future.

FITTING ADJUSTABLE SHELVING

There are many different patterns of adjustable shelving on the market, with uprights and brackets usually of metal but occasionally of wood. All operate on broadly the same principle. Start by deciding on the position and spacing of the uprights; this will depend on what sort of shelf material is used, what load it will carry and what is to be stored there. Then hang the uprights on the wall, making sure that they are perfectly vertical and set level with each other. Finally, clip in the brackets and fit the shelves.

Adjustable shelves may also be wanted inside a storage unit. There are two options. The first involves drilling a series of carefully aligned holes in each side of the unit, then inserting small plastic or metal shelf support studs. The second uses what is known as bookcase strip – a metal moulding with slots into which small pegs or tongues are fitted to support the shelves. Two strips are needed at each side of the unit.

PUTTING UP ADJUSTABLE SHELVES

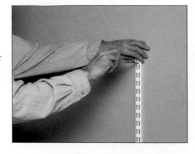
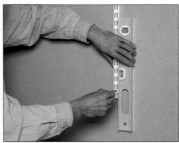

1 Decide where to position the shelves, then fix the first upright to the wall by driving a screw through the topmost hole. Do not tighten it fully.

2 Hold a spirit level alongside the upright and pivot it until the upright is vertical. Mark the position of all the other fixing holes on the wall.

3 Swing the upright aside and drill the rest of the holes. Fit wall plugs for masonry wall fixings if needed, and drive in the remaining screws.

PLANNING SHELVES

Think of how to make best use of the new storage area. It is a good idea to make a rough sketch of the plans, in order to take account of things like the height of books or record sleeves, or the clearance that ornaments or photographs will require. Aim to keep everyday items within easy reach – in practice, between about 750 mm (2 ft 6 in) and 1.5 m (5 ft) above the floor. Position deep shelves near the bottom so that it is easy to see and reach the back. Allow 25–50 mm (1–2 in) of clearance on top of the height of objects to be stored, so that they are easy to take down and put back.

Think about weight too. If the shelves will store heavy objects, the shelving material must be chosen with care, since thin shelves will sag if heavily laden unless they are well supported. With 12 mm ($1/2$ in) chipboard (particle board) and readymade veneered or melamine-faced shelves, space brackets at 450 mm (18 in) for heavy loads or 600 mm (2 ft) for light loads. With 19 mm ($3/4$ in) chipboard or 12 mm ($1/2$ in) plywood, increase the spacing to 600 mm (2 ft) and 750 mm (2 ft 6 in) respectively. For 19 mm ($3/4$ in) plywood, blockboard, MDF (medium-density fibreboard) or natural wood, the bracket spacing can be 750 mm (2 ft 6 in) for heavy loads, 900 mm (3 ft) for light ones.

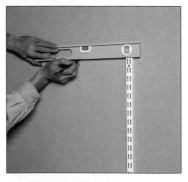

4 Use a spirit level to make a mark on the wall, level with the top of the first upright and at the required distance from it. Fix the second upright there.

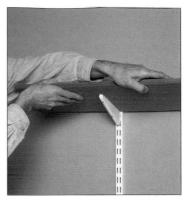

5 Mark the upright positions on the rear edge of each shelf. Align the back of each bracket with the edge of the shelf and with the mark, and screw it on.

6 If the shelves are to fit flush against the wall, cut notches at the upright positions to fit around them and then attach the brackets as shown.

7 Position all the shelf brackets. Simply insert their tongues into the slots in the uprights. The weight of the shelf will lock them in place. Adjust the shelf spacings as necessary.

USING BOOKCASE STRIP

1 Mark the positions of the top ends of the strips to ensure that they are level, then mark the screw positions to a true vertical and screw on the strips.

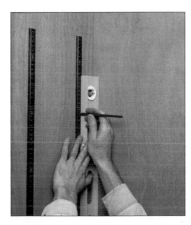

2 Insert pairs of pegs into the strip at each shelf position, checking that their lugs are properly engaged in the slots. Then lift the shelf into place.

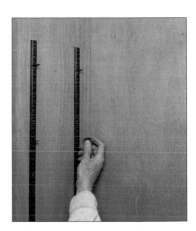

USING SHELF SUPPORTS

1 Use a simple pre-drilled jig to make the holes for the shelf supports in the sides of the unit. A depth stop avoids drilling too deep.

2 Drill two sets of holes in each side of the unit, with the top of the jig held against the top of the unit to guarantee alignment. Insert the supports.

FREESTANDING SHELVING

Freestanding shelf units have several advantages over wall-mounted or built-in ones. They can easily be moved if the room layout is changed. They can be moved away from the wall to allow painting or papering. They can even be taken along when moving house. However, they have drawbacks too. Some manufactured shelving and display units are rather flimsy, and may twist out of square or sag if they are heavily loaded. In general, better results come from building units from stronger materials such as natural wood and plywood. The other problem is getting them to stand upright against the wall; skirtings (baseboards) prevent

standard units from being pushed back flush with the wall surface, and carpet gripper strips make them lean forwards slightly. The answer is to design the side supports on the cantilever principle with just one point of contact with the floor, as far as possible from the wall, so that the unit presses more firmly against the wall as the load on the shelves is increased.

Since a shelf unit is basically a box with internal dividers, it can be constructed in several different ways, using simple butt joints or more complicated housings. Perhaps the best compromise between strength and ease of construction is to use glued butt

joints reinforced with hardwood dowels, which give the joints the extra rigidity they need in a unit of this sort.

Start by deciding on the dimensions of the unit, then select materials to suit the likely loading the shelves will have to support. Mark up and cut matching groups of components to length in batches to ensure that they are all precisely the same size. Pre-drill all the dowel holes, using a drill stand and depth stop for holes in the board faces and a dowelling jig for those in the board ends. Insert the dowels and make up the joints. A thin plywood or hardboard backing panel can be nailed on to give the unit extra rigidity.

1 Clamp groups of identical components together. Mark them to length and cut them in one operation to ensure that they are all the same length.

2 Mark the positions of the shelf dowel holes on the unit sides, ensuring that they match. Drill them all to the required depth, using a drill stand if possible.

3 Use a dowelling jig to drill the dowel holes in the shelf ends. This ensures that the holes are correctly positioned and centred, and are drilled straight.

4 Glue the dowels and tap them into the holes in the shelf ends. Check that they all project by the same amount, and cut down any that are overlong.

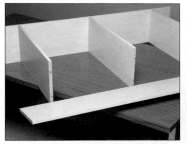

5 Assemble the unit by gluing one end of each of the three shelves and joining them to one of the side panels. Then glue the other ends and add the second side panel.

6 Cut a hardboard or plywood backing panel. Check that it is perfectly square, then pin it to the back of the unit.

Below: Freestanding shelves combined with cupboards (cabinets) and an office area offer valuable storage potential. The natural wood finish harmonizes with the decor and handsome beech wood-strip flooring.

FITTING SHELVES IN ALCOVES

Alcoves beside chimney breasts (fireplace projections) or other obstructions make a perfect site for shelves, since the back and side walls can be used as supports. Although it is easy to use fixed shelf brackets or an adjustable shelving system to support shelves here, it is cheaper to fix slim wood or metal support strips directly to the alcove walls and rest the shelves on these.

If using wooden supports, cut their front ends at an angle so that they are less noticeable when the shelves are fitted. Paint them the same colour as the walls (or to tone with the wall covering) to make them even less obtrusive. If using L-shaped metal strips for the supports, choose a size that matches the shelf thickness so they are almost invisible once the shelves have been fitted.

The actual job is quite simple. Mark the shelf level on the alcove walls, cut the supports to the required lengths and screw them to the walls. Then cut your shelf to size and slip it into place, resting on the supports. It can be nailed, screwed or glued in place for extra stability. The only difficult part is in making the shelf a good fit, since the alcove walls may not be truly square. Accurate measuring of the alcove width at front and back, plus some careful scribing of the rear edge of the shelf, will ensure good results.

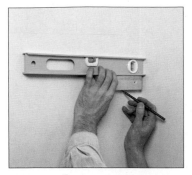

1 Decide on the shelf positions, then use a spirit level to mark the position of the first shelf support on one alcove wall.

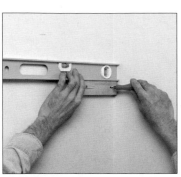

2 Drill clearance and countersink holes in the supports, and use the first one to mark the fixing hole positions on the wall. Drill the holes and fix this support.

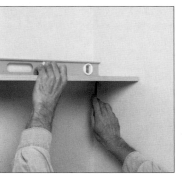

3 Rest a shelf on the first support, get it level and mark the shelf position on the opposite wall of the alcove. Then prepare the second shelf support.

4 Screw the second support in place after using it as in step 2 to mark the positions of the fixing holes on the wall. Check again that it is level.

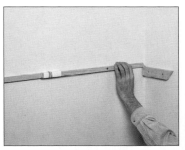

5 Make up a set of pinch rods from scrap wood, held together as shown with a rubber band. Extend the rods to span the rear wall of the alcove.

6 Lift the rods out carefully without disturbing their positions and lay them on the rear edge of the shelf. Mark the width of the alcove on it.

Right: Alcove shelving can be put to practical or decorative use. Here, painted shelves form a focal point in the room for the display of wooden boxes and wicker baskets.

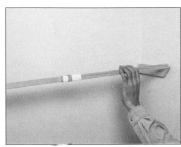

7 Repeat the operation in step 5 to measure the width at the point where the front edge of the shelf will be, then transfer the measurement to the shelf.

8 Cut the shelf to width and lay it on the supports. If the fit is poor against the back wall, use a block and pencil to scribe the wall outline on it.

9 Saw carefully along the scribed line with a power jigsaw (saber saw). Sand the cut edge smooth and then fit the shelf back in position.

MAKING CABINETS

Freestanding storage units consist simply of a basic box, fitted out internally as required. For example, these can include one or more shelves, vertical dividers, hanging rails, drawers and doors. All this applies to units as diverse in scale as a small hi-fi cabinet and a large double wardrobe. A pair of boxes can be placed under a counter top to create a desk or dressing table.

Units will probably be made from manufactured boards. It is difficult to get natural wood wider than about 225 mm (9 in), which rather restricts its scope; it is also more expensive. The most popular material for making box furniture is chipboard (particle board), especially the veneered and melamine-faced varieties which are sold in planks and boards of various sizes with the long edges (and sometimes the ends) already veneered or faced. Its main

disadvantage as a constructional board is its weakness – it will sag under its own weight across spans of more than about 900 mm (3 ft).

Stronger alternatives are plywood, MDF (medium-density fibreboard) and blockboard. Blockboard is the strongest – a 19 mm (3/4 in) thick board can be used unsupported over spans twice as great as for chipboard. Sheets of blockboard sold as door blanks usually have the long edges faced.

Plywood offers the best of both worlds – it is almost as strong as blockboard, and has edges that can be neatly finished. It is also available in thicknesses from 4 mm (just over 1/8 in) up to 19 mm (3/4 in), so there should be a perfect match for any application.

MDF is a popular choice for box furniture as well as shelves as it cuts beautifully without the need for

finishing sawn edges. It is a medium-strength material and its very smooth surface finish can be painted, varnished or stained, as wished. Available in 2440 × 1220 mm (8 × 4 ft) sheets and in thicknesses ranging from 6 to 25 mm (1/4 to 1 in), MDF falls into the medium price range.

Those who are inexperienced in using power tools to make rebates and housing joints will be making up boxes using glued butt joints, nailed or screwed for extra strength. These are adequate for small items, but will need reinforcing on larger pieces. The ideal way of doing this is with hardwood dowels. It is advisable to use dowels for chipboard, in which nails and even screws will not hold well. Alternatives, for light loads only, are special chipboard screws, or ordinary screws set in glued-in fibre wall plugs.

MAKING BUTT JOINTS

1 To make a box, take measurements and start by cutting the components to size. Use a circular saw or a jigsaw (saber saw) to ensure clean, square edges.

2 While cutting the various components, label each piece in pencil and mark both halves of each joint with matching letters to avoid mix-ups during assembly.

3 To make a straightforward glued butt joint, spread woodworking adhesive along the edge of one component. Assemble the joint and clamp it to keep it square.

4 Reinforce a glued joint with nails driven in so they pass into the centre of the panel underneath. Use a damp cloth to remove any excess adhesive.

5 Screwed joints are stronger than nailed ones. Place the edge component against the face component and mark its position on the latter.

6 Mark the screw positions carefully, especially if the joint is a T-joint rather than a corner. Double-check all measurements from nearby edges.

7 Drill clearance holes through the face component, then pilot holes in the edge component. Countersink the clearance holes and drive in chipboard (particle board) screws.

USING DOWELS

1 Draw a pencil line along the centre of the joint position, then align the two components and mark corresponding dowel hole positions on both pieces.

2 Drill the dowel holes in the face component, using a depth stop to avoid drilling too deep. Use a dowelling jig to drill holes in board edges.

3 Insert glued dowels in the holes in the edge component, then glue this to the face component. Add glue along the joint line too for extra strength.

4 A back panel will give any box extra strength, and also helps to resist skewing. Cut the panel fractionally under size and then nail it in place.

FIXING DOORS AND DRAWERS

Adding doors and drawers to a basic storage box will turn it into a cupboard (cabinet) or a chest. Doors can be hung on any one of the many types of hinge available, but two of the most versatile are the *flush hinge* and the *concealed hinge*. The former has one leaf fitting into a cutout in the other, and so can be surface-mounted to the door edge and the frame, without the need to cut recesses.

The concealed hinge is a little more complex to fit – the hinge body sits in a round hole bored in the rear face of the door, while the hinge arm is attached to a surface-mounted baseplate fitted to the side of the cabinet carcass – but it can be adjusted after fitting to ensure perfect alignment on multi-door installations, as in kitchens.

When it comes to adding drawers to your cabinets, the simplest solution is to use plastic drawer kits. These consist of moulded sections that interlock to form the sides and back of the drawer, special corner blocks to allow a drawer front of any chosen material to be attached, and a base (usually of a piece of enamelled hardboard). The drawer sides are grooved to fit over plastic runners that are screwed to the cabinet sides. The sides, back and base can be cut down to size if necessary.

FITTING FLUSH HINGES

1 Mark the hinge position on the door edge, then make pilot holes and screw the smaller flap to the door. Check that the hinge knuckle faces the right way.

2 Hold the door in position against the cabinet carcass, and mark the hinge position on it. Mark the screw holes too, and drill pilot holes for the screws.

3 Reposition the door and attach the larger hinge leaf to the carcass. Check the door alignment carefully, then attach the other hinge in the same way.

FITTING A CONCEALED HINGE

1 Mark the centre line of the hinge baseplate on the side wall of the cabinet, then lay the door flat against the carcass and extend the line onto it.

2 Use a power drill with an end mill, held in a drill stand, to cut the recess for the hinge body to the required depth in the rear face of the door.

3 Press the hinge body into the recess, check that the arm is at right angles to the door edge, and make pilot holes for the fixing screws. Drive these in.

MAKING UP A DRAWER KIT

1 Cut the sides and back to size if necessary, then stick the side and back sections together, using the clips and adhesive provided in the kit.

2 Cut the base down in size too if the drawer size was altered. Then slide the panel into place in the grooves in the side and back sections.

3 Screw the two corner joint blocks to the inner face of the drawer front, stick on the drawer base support channel, and glue the front to the sides.

4 Hold the drawer within the cabinet to mark the position of its side grooves on the side walls. Then attach the plastic drawer runners.

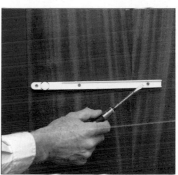

4 Next, attach the baseplates to the side wall of the cabinet, centred on the guidelines drawn earlier. Check that they are fitted the right way around.

5 Hold the door against the cabinet, slot the hinge arm over the screw on the baseplate, and tighten it to lock the hinge arm in place.

TIP

Make in-out adjustments to the door by loosening the mounting screw and repositioning the door. Make side-to-side adjustments using the smaller screw.

FITTING A BUILT-IN WARDROBE

The walls of a room can be used to create larger storage spaces for a wardrobe (closet), for example. These can range from filling in an alcove, through a unit in the corner of a room, to one running right across the room to the opposite wall. If the room has a central chimney breast (fireplace projection) with an alcove at either side, both alcoves can be used for storage and the chimney breast can be concealed with a dummy door.

In each case, the most important part is a frame to support the doors; these can be conventionally hinged or suspended from ceiling-mounted track. Remember that hinged doors allow unlimited access but need floor space in front of them so they can be opened easily. Sliding doors do not need this floor space, but they do have the minor disadvantage that access to the interior is sometimes restricted – when one door is open, it blocks access to the next section. Sliding doors can also catch on things such as suitcases inside the unit.

Such a flexible structure affords an opportunity to plan storage needs precisely. Start by selecting the depth needed to allow clothes to hang freely on hanging rails, then work out what width should be given to hanging space and what to shelving, drawers or basket space for storing other items of clothing. The space at the top level is suitable for storing seldom-used items. Shoe racks can be added at floor level.

Doors can either be made into a feature of the room, or else painted or covered to blend unobtrusively with the room's colour scheme. Large flat-surfaced doors become almost invisible if decorated with a wall covering.

FITTING SLIDING DOORS TO STORAGE UNITS

1 Decide on the unit depth required, then locate the positions of the ceiling joists and screw a track support strip to them. Use packing to level it.

2 Next, screw the top track to the support strip, making sure that it is fitted parallel with the strip. Leave a gap next to the wall for the side upright.

6 Realign the side upright with the positioning marks made earlier, and screw it to the wall. Repeat the process at the other side of the opening.

8 Hang the doors by engaging the hanger wheels on the track as shown and then lowering the door to the vertical position. Finally, fit the floor guides.

7 Cut the doors to size if necessary, allowing for clearances or overlaps as required in the door gear instructions, and then fit the door hangers.

3 Hold the length of wood that will form the side frame uprights against the wall, and mark on it the profile of the skirting (baseboard) on it.

4 Use a coping saw or power jigsaw (saber saw) to cut away the waste wood from the foot of the upright, then test it for fit against the wall.

5 Use a spirit level to check that the side upright is vertical, then mark its position on the wall and drill the necessary clearance and fixing holes.

9 Conceal the track and door hangers by pinning (tacking) a decorative moulding to the track support batten. Some tracks come complete with a metal pelmet strip.

10 Finish off the installation by pinning slim wooden mouldings to the front edges of the side uprights. These hide any slight gaps when the doors are closed.

FITTING A CLOTHES ORGANIZER

In both freestanding and built-in wardrobes (closets), best use of the interior space can be made by creating tailor-made hanging and shelving sections. Clothes organizers of this kind can be professionally made to measure, but in fact they can be constructed from the simplest of materials, at a great saving in cost. A wardrobe up to 2.4 m (8 ft) wide can be 'organized' with just four standard lengths of veneered or plastic-coated chipboard (particle board), a length of clothes pole and some 75 × 25 mm (3 × 1 in) wood to act as shelf supports.

Start by marking up and cutting out the components. All are 300 mm (12 in) wide. There are two uprights 1930 mm (6 ft 4 in) long, two shelves long enough to span the wardrobe or alcove, and six small shelves 300 mm (12 in) square. Sand all the cut edges.

Next, cut two sets of shelf supports to fit the back and side walls of the wardrobe or alcove. Nail or screw the first supports in place so that their top edges are 2140 mm (7 ft) above the floor. Add the second set 1930 mm (6 ft 4 in) above the floor. Then make up the central shelf unit, using the two uprights and the six small shelves and spacing these to suit the storage requirements. Notch the top rear corners of the unit so that they will fit around the lower shelf support, and stand it in place. Add the lower shelf first, then the upper one, and complete the unit by adding upper (and, if desired, lower) hanging rails at each side of the central unit.

1 Start by fixing the upper set of shelf supports to the sides and back of the wardrobe or alcove, with their top edges 2140 mm (7 ft) above floor level.

2 Add the lower set of shelf supports with their top edges 1930 mm (6 ft 4 in) above floor level. Check that they are all horizontal with a spirit level.

5 Cut down the shelves and uprights to the length required with the circular saw. Then cut the six small squares for the central shelf unit.

6 Make up the central shelf unit by gluing and nailing or screwing the shelves into place between the uprights. Space the shelves as required.

3 Next, mark up and cut the components to width, using a circular saw with a fence or a guide strip clamped across it to keep the cuts perfectly straight.

4 Mark the height of the uprights and the length of the shelves required on the components. Square a cutting line across them, using a try square.

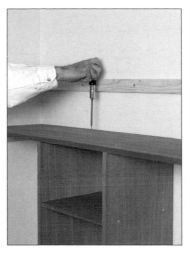

7 Stand the unit against the back of the wardrobe or alcove. Mark the position of the lower shelf supports on it. Cut notches to fit the supports.

8 Reposition the central shelf unit, then lay the lower shelf on its supports. Nail or screw down through it into the supports and the shelf unit.

9 Fit hangers to support the clothes rail beneath the lower shelf. Add a second lower rail if wished. Complete the unit by adding the top shelf.

MAKING UTILITY SHELVING

Storage space in workshops, garages, basements and attics is best provided by building simple but sturdy shelves from inexpensive materials. Use wood that is sawn, not planed (dressed), for the framework, and cut the shelves from scrap plywood. Damaged boards and offcuts are often available cheaply from timber merchants (lumberyards).

The shelving units shown here are made from 50 mm (2 in) square wood, with shelves of 19 mm (3/4 in) plywood. The only other materials needed are some scraps of 9 mm (3/8 in) thick plywood for the small triangular braces that help to stiffen the structure.

Start by working out how big the unit is to be. Uprights should be spaced about 760 mm (2 ft 6 in) apart so that the shelves will not sag; they can reach right up to ceiling level if desired. Match the depth of the unit to what is to be stored and to the amount of space available. Remember that it can be difficult reaching things at the back of deep shelves. After measuring up and estimating how many uprights and shelves are needed, buy all the materials and start work.

Make the uprights like a ladder, with glued and nailed butt joints reinforced with plywood triangles measuring about 100 mm (4 in) along the edges forming the right angle. Space the horizontals to suit storage requirements and cut plywood shelves to fit.

Stand the uprights against the wall at the appropriate spacing and screw them to the wall – either into the wall studs, or into wall plugs or masonry anchors if it is solid masonry. Then cut the shelves to length; each 'rung' of the ladder will support two shelves except at the ends of the run, so cut the latter to span between the centres of the rungs. Notch the shelf corners so that they fit around the uprights and are locked in place.

1 Start by deciding on the height the uprights should be, and on how many 'ladders' are needed. Cut them all to length with a power saw.

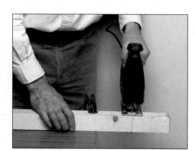

2 Make up the ladders by gluing and nailing the rungs between pairs of uprights. Reinforce the joints by gluing and screwing on plywood triangles.

3 Stand the assembled ladders against the wall, check that they are truly vertical, and screw them to the wall – into wooden studs or masonry anchors.

4 Cut as many plywood shelves as are needed so they span between the centre lines of the rungs; notch the corners so they will fit neatly around the uprights.

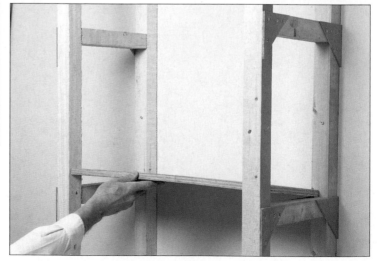

MAKING A TOOL CABINET

This tool storage rack is basically a wall-mounted backing board of 19 mm (³/₄ in) thick plywood. Tools are hung on various supports, as shown in the illustration. These are located in, and slide along, horizontal channels formed by pinning 38 mm (1 ¹/₂ in) wide strips of 12 mm (¹/₂ in) plywood to the backing panel and then pinning 75 × 19 mm (3 × ³/₄ in) softwood strips to the plywood. Make the trays for small tools from 12 mm (¹/₂ in) plywood, and use hardwood dowel pegs or old wire coat hangers to make support hooks for larger tools. Slide the back plate of each support into its channel at the sides of the rack, and move them along to where they are needed.

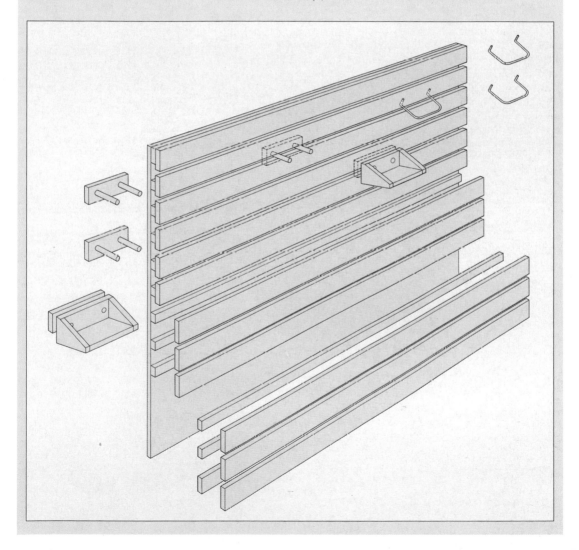

MAKING A GARAGE STORAGE WALL

The garage is a favourite place to store all manner of things, including tools and materials for do-it-yourself, gardening and car maintenance. Unless these are kept under control, they will spill over until there is no room for the car. The solution is to build a shallow full-height storage unit along either the side or the end wall of the garage, tailor-made to suit whatever will be stored there.

The design concept of the storage wall is quite simple, and is based around creating bays offering different storage facilities. One can have floor-to-ceiling shelves, another a drawer system using plastic washing-up bowls (washbowls) sliding on wooden support strips. The next bay can offer full-height open storage for stepladders and scaffold boards, and another wider one provides space to store sheet materials neatly on edge beneath a wall-mounted rack for hanging up things such as a portable workbench or a set of car ramps. Simply select whatever types of bay are needed, and arrange them in any order.

The structure is based on ladder frames fixed to the wall to support shelves, drawers and whatever else is required. The frame is made mainly from 50 mm (2 in) square sawn softwood, with 75 × 25 mm (3 × 1 in) wood for the shelves and the slatted hanging rack. The hinged section drops down to allow sheets of plywood and the like to be placed on edge behind it, and is held shut with a simple hasp and staple at each side. The wall-mounted rack allows heavy items to be hung out of the way yet readily to hand on metal S-hooks.

1 Start by securing the uprights to the garage wall to form the various bays. Check that each is vertical before fixing it in place.

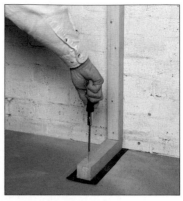

2 Set sole plates on something damp-proof (here sheet vinyl flooring), and screw them down into wall plugs in holes drilled in the garage floor.

3 Simply nail components together as required to form the frames making up each bay. Add horizontals to support shelves or plastic bowl drawers.

4 To make up the drop-down flap for the sheet materials storage bay, hinge the two front uprights to their baseplates and add a cross rail.

5 To make up the wall rack, nail on the slats, using an offcut as a spacer. Make the shelves in the same way, nailing the slats to 50 × 25 mm (2 × 1 in) bearers.

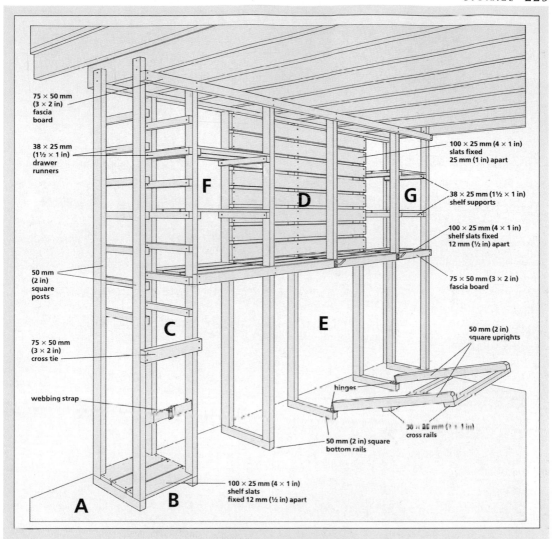

75 × 50 mm (3 × 2 in) fascia board

38 × 25 mm (1½ × 1 in) drawer runners

50 mm (2 in) square posts

75 × 50 mm (3 × 2 in) cross tie

webbing strap

100 × 25 mm (4 × 1 in) slats fixed 25 mm (1 in) apart

38 × 25 mm (1½ × 1 in) shelf supports

100 × 25 mm (4 × 1 in) shelf slats fixed 12 mm (½ in) apart

75 × 50 mm (3 × 2 in) fascia board

50 mm (2 in) square uprights

hinges

38 × 25 mm (2 × 1 in) cross rails

50 mm (2 in) square bottom rails

100 × 25 mm (4 × 1 in) shelf slats fixed 12 mm (½ in) apart

A B C D E F G

The garage storage wall offers a variety of options. Bay A is a full-height space ideal for storing stepladders and lengths of wood and mouldings, copper or plastic pipe and the like.

Bay B provides a raised platform for sacks of cement or garden fertilizer, which must be kept clear of the floor in case of damp; a sturdy webbing strap keeps them in place.

Bay C, above the platform, has a series of parallel runners supporting plastic baskets, which slide in and out like drawers and provide storage for a host of small and easily lost items.

Bay D has a slatted back on which large items such as car ramps or a portable workbench can be hung on wire hooks.

Bay E provides a wide compartment designed for storing sheet materials – boards, plastic laminates, etc. – on edge and clear of the damp floor. A simple fold-down front frame prevents the sheets from falling forward and can be quickly released when necessary.

Bays F and G complete the structure, offering full-depth shelf storage space for items like paint, garden chemicals and car lubricants.

MAINTENANCE
AND REPAIRS

Creating a well-appointed home is a thoroughly satisfying leisure activity pursued by millions of householders. Unfortunately, being creative is not the whole story; houses, like anything else, develop faults from time to time and need some attention to keep them in good working order. This final chapter looks at some of the everyday maintenance and repair problems which may occur in the home, and also explains how to use the right products – adhesives, mastics, fillers, repair tapes and fixing devices – to get good results.

It also deals with a subject that is of increasing importance to householders everywhere: energy conservation and the efficient use of energy resources. Many homes, especially older ones, are very inefficient; they cost a lot to heat, and leak like sieves so that much of the heat supplied is completely wasted. However, creating a well insulated and draughtproofed house is not the complete answer. Activities such as cooking, bathing and washing clothes create large amounts of water vapour, and if this accumulates in a poorly ventilated building, condensation will result. This can be more than just a nuisance, causing steamed-up windows and mouldy patches on walls and ceilings. It can actually damage the house structure and can also be bad for the health of the building's occupants. Getting the right balance of heat input, insulation and controlled ventilation is the solution. The last part of the chapter explains how to achieve it in the home.

Opposite: Keeping track of running repairs and updating insulation and ventilation needs are necessary tasks for the homeowner. Shown here, from left to right and top to bottom: applying flashing tape; fixing insulation tape around doorways; removing window beads; repairing wallpaper blisters; sealing cracks with mastic; laying roof insulation; insulating sash windows; insulating pipework; and repairing stairs.

MAKING FIRM FIXINGS

Before making fixings into solid masonry, make a couple of test drillings to find out whether the wall is built of brick or lightweight blocks. If brick is identified from red or yellow bore dust, use ordinary plastic wall plugs; but if grey dust suggests lightweight blocks it is better to use a proprietary block plug which is fatter and has larger 'wings' to grip the softer material. In either case the screw must be long enough to penetrate at least 38 mm ($1^1/_2$ in) into the masonry behind the plaster, so use screws at least 62 mm ($2^1/_2$ in) long. Increase this to 75 mm (3 in) for fixings that will carry heavy loads. Screw gauge 8 will be adequate for normal loads; increase this to gauge 10 for 75 mm (3 in) screws. Make sure, too, that the screw and wall plug sizes are compatible, and take care to drill the holes at right angles to the wall surface, deep enough to accept the screw length.

Making fixings to stud (dry) walls poses different fixing problems. Cavity fixing devices such as spring or gravity toggles and cavity anchors can be used only for fixings that will carry the lightest loads. For any other use, the fixing must be made either to a horizontal nogging (cross bridging) fixed between adjacent studs – difficult to fit except during construction of the wall framework – or directly to the vertical studs themselves. These will have to be located with an electronic stud finder or, less satisfactorily, by tapping and test drilling – they are usually at 400 mm (16 in) or 600 mm (24 in) centres. Make sure that pilot holes are drilled into the centre of the stud, not near its edge, since this could result in a weak fixing. Use screws 50 mm (2 in) long for medium loads, 75 mm (3 in) long for heavy ones.

MAKING FIXINGS IN MASONRY

1 Mark where the fixing is to go and use a masonry drill sized to match the wall plug. Wind some tape around the drill bit to act as a depth guide.

2 If the drill has an adjustable depth stop attachment, use it instead of the tape flag to set the drilling depth. Drill until the stop touches the wall surface.

MAKING FIXINGS IN PLASTERBOARD

1 If the fixing must be between joists or studs rather than into them, drill a clearance hole for the fixing device through the plasterboard (gypsum board).

2 Push a cavity anchor into the hole so it can expand against the back of the board, and drive in the screw. With toggles, thread the screw through the object first.

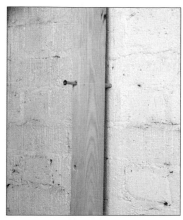

3 Choose a wall plug sized to match the screw being used, and push it into the hole until its rim is flush with the wall. Tap it with a hammer if necessary.

4 Thread the screw through a clearance hole drilled in the object being fixed, insert it in the mouth of the wall plug and drive it home.

5 Alternatively, use long-sleeved frame plugs. Drill holes through the wood and into the wall, insert the plug and tighten the screw to make the fixing.

MAKING FIXINGS INTO STUDS

1 Use an electronic stud finder to locate the stud or ceiling joist positions. It works by detecting the nails which secure the plasterboard (gypsum board).

2 When the stud or joist positions are marked, drill clearance holes in the object to be fixed at matching centres. Check these for accuracy.

3 Drill pilot holes through the board surface and into the stud or joist. Make sure that the drill bit is at right angles to the surface.

4 Insert screws in all the clearance holes, then offer up the object, align it with the pre-drilled holes and drive the screws home.

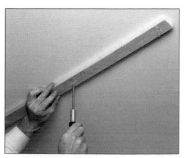

ADHESIVES, MASTICS AND REPAIR TAPES

There is a huge range of adhesives available nowadays. Their labelling is now generally much clearer than it was a few years ago, so finding the right product is considerably easier than it used to be. Here is a guide to the types that are likely to be needed for most repair jobs.

General-purpose adhesives

These are clear solvent-based adhesives which will stick paper and cardboard, wood, leather and a few types of plastic such as solid polystyrene and ABS. They are used straight from the tube. Check the instructions carefully; some recommend applying the adhesive to both surfaces, others to just one. Whichever method is used, hold or clamp the repair for a while; the adhesive takes some time after assembly to gain full strength. The joint is generally not heat-resistant and may not be water-resistant either. Adhesive can be removed from fingers, or anywhere else it gets by mistake, with cellulose thinner, acetone or nail varnish remover – but the last will attack gloss paint, french polish, some varnishes, and any plastic that the adhesive will stick.

Adhesives for wood

The most widely used type of adhesive for general woodwork is PVA *woodworking adhesive*, often referred to as 'white glue'. It will bond softwood, hardwood and all manufactured boards, and is colourless when dry; spills can be wiped away with a damp cloth before the adhesive sets. The joint must be clamped until the adhesive hardens – for a couple of hours at least – to get the best results. Exposure to damp will weaken the adhesive and cause failure. If such exposure is likely, be sure to use one of the cross-linking versions which give a high degree of water resistance.

Adhesives for laminates

Plastic laminates, flexible sheet materials such as foam and leather, and vinyl or cork floor tiles are stuck in place with a *contact adhesive*. This is spread on both surfaces and is allowed to become touch-dry before the two are pressed together. The resulting bond is instant, and cannot normally be repositioned; but some kinds offer a degree of slip – they are often called *thixotropic adhesives*. Contact adhesive is also moderately heatproof and water-resistant.

Most contact adhesives are solvent-based, and the fumes are both inflammable and noxious to inhale, so work with good ventilation and no naked lights. Clean up spills with the manufacturer's own solvent, cellulose thinner, acetone or nail varnish remover. Water-based contact adhesives are also available, and these are much safer and more pleasant to use; spills can be removed while still wet with a damp cloth.

Adhesives for plastics

Some plastics are very difficult to stick with adhesives. Two which cannot be stuck by any means are polythene (polyethylene) and polypropylene, the bendy plastics used for such things are washing-up bowls (wash bowls) and buckets; they must be fused by heat. Flexible PVC – used for seat covers, sunbeds and beach balls, for example – can be stuck with special *vinyl repair adhesive*. Polystyrene cement or general-purpose adhesive will mend rigid polystyrene – used for some kitchen and bathroom accessories – and the similar but tougher ABS. Do not use it for expanded polystyrene ceiling tiles or coving (crown molding), though, as

SILICONE MASTIC Use silicone mastic to seal around bathroom fittings. Push the nozzle along the gap so it leaves a neat concave finish to the mastic bead.

ACRYLIC MASTIC Use acrylic mastic indoors and frame sealant outdoors to seal gaps between wood and masonry where a rigid filler would tend to crack and fall out.

REPAIR TAPE Use repair tapes to make temporary repairs to cracked glass, or to waterproof glazing bars on glass roofs. Simply press the tape into place.

the adhesive will eat these away. Always use a special adhesive paste made for the purpose.

For other plastics, experiment with epoxy resin adhesives, two-part acrylics or cyanoacrylates (see right).

Mastics and repair tapes

Mastic is a permanently flexible adhesive filler that is used to seal joints indoors and outdoors. The material comes in cartridges, and is usually extruded by using a hand-held gun. The resulting bead of mastic is simply piped into place, and may be smoothed out with a wet finger or a filling knife (putty knife) if necessary. Various types are available: *acrylic* types are used as a general-purpose decorating filler indoors; *silicone* types are best for such jobs as waterproofing joints around bathroom and kitchen fittings; and *frame sealants* are designed for filling and sealing gaps around window and door frames.

Repair tapes of various types are used to make temporary repairs to things such as cracked glass, leaky glazing bars and porous flashings. As with mastics, choose the type appropriate to the task in hand.

Adhesives for glass, china and metal

Three types of adhesive can be used for repairing these materials. Each has advantages and disadvantages.

Epoxy resin adhesives are two-part products, prepared by mixing equal quantities of resin and hardener, and generally applied to both surfaces. Quick-setting types set hard in a few minutes, others take about half an hour, with full bond strength developing more slowly. Once set, the bond is heat- and waterproof, and the adhesive will fill gaps; however, it does leave a noticeable glue line, and this may darken with time. Clean up spills with white spirit (paint thinner) or methylated spirit (wood alcohol), and trim off dried adhesive with a sharp utility knife.

Cyanoacrylate adhesives, also known as superglues, are liquids which are applied sparingly to just one surface. The resulting glue line is very thin, so they are ideal for repairing china and glass, but apart from the newer gel types the adhesive has negligible gap-filling properties so the parts must be a good fit. With most brands, the joint is not waterproof, but some are specially

formulated for repairing items that will have to be washed or must hold liquids. Avoid skin contact when using this type of adhesive; if fingers, or anything else, get stuck together, instantly immerse them in hot soapy water and gently peel the stuck areas apart. Some manufacturers supply a special release agent with the adhesive. Always keep glues away from children, but especially this type.

Two-part acrylic adhesives are not mixed directly; instead adhesive is applied to one surface and hardener to the other, and the two brought together to form the bond. This sticks immediately, and reaches full strength in a few hours. The adhesive has good heat resistance and is fairly waterproof, but does not fill gaps very well. Wipe up spills with a dry cloth or use methylated spirits. Alternatively, trim off dried adhesive with a sharp knife.

Speciality adhesives

The shelves of a do-it-yourself store will also contain all kinds of special-purpose adhesives, clearly labelled as to their use. These include *wallpaper paste*, *ceramic tile adhesive* and *coving (crown molding) adhesive*.

1 FLASHING TAPE Use flashing tape to seal porous felt or metal flashings. Start by brushing on a coat of special primer; use an old paintbrush and wear protective gloves.

2 Unroll the flashing tape, peel off the release paper and press the strip into position over the band of primer, bedding it well into the roof/wall angle.

3 To ensure that the tape bonds well to the wall and roof surfaces, run a wallpaper seam roller firmly along both edges of the strip.

CURING DOOR PROBLEMS

A well fitted door should have a long and trouble-free life. If it does misbehave, the problem is generally the door binding against its frame and, in extreme cases, failing to shut properly. There is likely to be one of three causes: a build-up of paint on the door and frame surfaces after years of repainting, expansion due to atmospheric conditions – the door sticks in damp weather as moisture causes it to swell slightly, but it shrinks and closes freely in dry weather – and hinge faults caused either by wear and tear or bad fitting.

Where a paint build-up is to blame, the remedy is quite simple; strip off the old paint from the door edge back to bare wood, and repaint from scratch.

If atmospheric conditions are to blame, the solution is to plane down the door edges slightly to increase the clearance between door and frame. The door will have to be taken off its hinges to do this unless it is only the leading edge that is binding.

Hinge faults that can cause binding include hinge screws standing proud or working loose, and hinge recesses being cut too deep or too shallow. In each case the cure is relatively simple; the biggest problem is often trying to undo the old hinge screws, especially if they have become encrusted with paint over the years. Clean out the slots in the screw heads thoroughly before trying to remove the screws; paint remover is useful for this. Then position the screwdriver in the slot and give the handle a sharp blow with a hammer to help free the grip of the threads in the wood.

1 If the hinge screws show signs of pulling out, remove them, drill out the screw holes and hammer in glued dowels. Then drill new pilot holes.

2 If the door is striking the frame because it has expanded, close it and mark a pencil line on the door face against the edge of the frame.

5 If the door binds on the hinge side of the frame, the hinge recesses may be too deep. Remove the hinge and pin some packing into the recess.

6 Drill fresh pilot holes for the screws through the packing piece, and drive the fixing screws back into place. Make sure their heads fit in the countersinks.

3 Take the door off its hinges, remove the handles and latch mechanism, and plane the leading edge of the door down until the pencil line has disappeared.

4 If the door is binding at the top or bottom, take this opportunity to plane off a little wood there too. Plane inwards from the corners to avoid causing splits.

7 Alternatively, relocate the hinges in a new position. Chisel out the new recesses and refit the hinge.

8 If the hinge recesses are too shallow the hinge leaves will bind and stop the door from closing. Remove the hinges and chisel out the recesses slightly.

CURING WINDOW PROBLEMS

By far the commonest window problem is a cracked or broken pane, caused by a flying object or by the window being allowed to slam. Make a temporary repair to cracked glass with a clear waterproof repair tape – not household adhesive tape – but aim to replace the pane at the earliest opportunity. If the glass is broken, lift out all the loose pieces for safety's sake and make a temporary repair by fixing heavy-duty polythene (polyethylene) sheet or a piece of board over the opening.

When measuring up for the replacement glass, measure all four sides in case the rebate in the frame is not perfectly square, and use the smaller of each pair of figures. Subtract 3 mm (1/8 in) from each one to allow for clearance all around, and note which way the pattern ran if the glass was obscured rather than clear. Take a piece of patterned glass when buying a replacement so as to be sure of getting the correct type.

The other problems that windows suffer from are similar to those affecting doors – paint build-up, expansion or warping. They may also pull out of square if the frame corner joints start to open up, causing the casement to bind in its frame and possibly also cracking the glass. The trouble can be cured by strengthening the frame corners with small L-shaped metal repair plates; cut shallow recesses for them and disguise their presence with filler and a coat or two of paint.

TIP

Always dispose of broken glass safely, by wrapping it in newspaper and then packing it in a box so it cannot injure anyone.

REPLACING BROKEN GLASS

1 When a window breaks, remove all the loose glass immediately for safety's sake. Wear stout gloves to protect hands and dispose of the glass safely.

2 Use an old chisel or a glazier's knife to remove all the old putty from the rebate in the frame. Take care not to cut into the wood while doing this.

3 Use a pair of pincers or pliers to pull out the old glazing sprigs all around the frame. Metal frames have glazing clips; save these and reuse them.

4 Knead some putty with the hands to warm and soften it, then press it into the rebate by extruding it between thumb and forefinger.

5 Set the replacement pane in position against the bedding putty with equal clearance all around, and press it into place around the edges to compress the putty.

6 Secure the pane in the rebate by tapping in glazing sprigs at roughly 300 mm (12 in) intervals. Replace clips in their locating holes in metal frames.

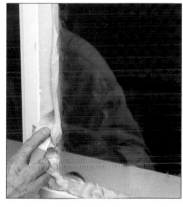

7 Repeat step 4 to extrude a bead of facing putty all around the pane, then neaten it to a 45° bevel by drawing the blade of a putty knife along it.

8 Trim off excess putty from the outside and inside of the pane and leave it to harden for about 14 days before painting over it to disguise and seal the joints.

CURING BINDING CASEMENTS

1 If a build-up of paint is causing the edge of the casement to bind against the frame, strip it back to bare wood. Use chemical strippers; heat may crack the glass.

2 If the frame has swollen because of moisture penetration, plane a little wood off the leading edge. Prime and paint it immediately to keep the wood dry.

3 If the corner joints of a casement show signs of opening up and the frame is pulling out of square, screw on small L-shaped metal repair plates.

PATCHING WALL AND CEILING DAMAGE

Plasterboard (gypsum board) is an immensely versatile material for lining walls and ceilings, since it provides a smooth surface for any finish and has useful sound-deadening and fireproofing properties. The one thing it does not do very well is to resist impacts, and the resulting hole cannot simply be patched with filler because the board's strength has been lost at the point of damage. The solution is either to strengthen the board or to replace a section altogether.

Very small holes can be disguised with self-adhesive scrim tape and cellulose filler (spackle), but holes more than about 50 mm (2 in) across need a more substantial repair. Use an offcut of plasterboard and cut a piece slightly narrower than the hole width and twice as long as its height to use as a patch. Pierce a hole in it, thread a piece of string through, tie one end to a nail and pull this against the face of the patch. Then butter some plaster or filler onto the other face of the patch and push it into the hole, keeping hold of the string with the other hand. Position the patch against the inner face of the plasterboard, pulling on the string to help the filler stick it in place. When it has stuck fast, fill the hole and cut off the string.

For larger holes – a foot through the ceiling, for example – in plasterboard and (in older properties) lath-and-plaster surfaces, the only solution is to cut out the damaged piece and nail on a new section in its place. Supports will need to be fixed around the edges of the opening where the damaged section has been cut out. Then fill the cut edges, apply joint tape to hide them and skim over the patch with a little plaster to complete the repair.

PATCHING SMALL HOLES IN PLASTERBOARD

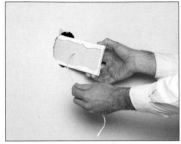

1 Cut a plasterboard (gypsum board) patch slightly longer and narrower than the hole, and thread a length of string with a nail tied on through a hole in its centre.

2 Butter some plaster or filler onto the edges of the patch and feed it end-on into the hole, keeping hold of the string with the other hand.

3 Pull the string to hold the patch against the rear face of the board, then fill the recess with plaster or filler and cut off the string.

4 Complete the repair by applying a skim coat of plaster over the patch. Flick water onto it with a brush and polish it smooth with a float.

PATCHING LARGER HOLES IN PLASTERBOARD

1 If the plasterboard (gypsum board) surface is more extensively damaged, cut through it with a sharp knife back to the adjacent wall studs or ceiling joists.

2 Cut across to the stud or joist centres, then make two vertical cuts down the centre of the stud or joist to free the damaged panel.

3 Cut two strips of wood to fit between the studs/joists, and screw or nail them into place so they will support the edges of the main board and the patch.

4 Cut a plasterboard patch to match the section removed, and nail it into place. Fill and tape the joints and skim plaster over the repair to conceal it.

REPAIRING LATH-AND-PLASTER SURFACES

1 If the wood laths are split or broken, pull them away from the surface. Remove any loose sections of plaster from around the site of the damage.

2 Continue cutting back the old plaster and the laths behind it to expose the studs or ceiling joists at each side of the hole. Square off the edges.

3 Cut a plasterboard patch to fit the hole, and nail it in place. Add two support strips as described for patching plasterboard if the panel is large.

4 Complete the repair by plastering over the patch after filling and taping the cut edges all around. Polish the repair with a steel float.

CURING FLOOR PROBLEMS

Floorboards suffer more from being lifted for access to pipes and cables beneath them than they do from everyday wear and tear. If the floor has nothing worse than the occasional creak, the trouble can generally be cured by lifting floor coverings and then nailing – or better still, screwing – the offending board down again. With a chipboard (particle board) floor, make sure that the boards are nailed to every joist they cross, not just at the edges; if they are not, the boards can bow upwards and will then bang against the joists when walked on.

Before lifting a section of floor to gain access to services below it, look first of all to see whether someone has already cut an access panel. If they have not, it will be necessary to create one. Locate the joist position closest to where access is needed – the flooring nail positions will reveal its whereabouts. Then drill a starter hole and use a jigsaw (saber saw) to make a 45° cut next to the joist. Prise up the cut end and wedge a strip of wood underneath it, then saw through the board over the centre of the next joist to free the section. To replace it, nail

one end to the joist and either skew nail (toe nail) the other angled end to its neighbour or nail a support block to the side of the joist and nail or screw the board end to that.

With concrete floors, the only repair that is likely to be needed is the filling of cracks or small potholes that may be revealed when an old floor covering is lifted. Cut back any loose edges, brush away loose material and fill the cracks with a fine mortar mix. If the floor surface is sound but uneven or out of level, lay a self-smoothing compound over it.

CREATING AN ACCESS PANEL

1 Start by locating an adjacent joist. Drill a starter hole for the saw blade. Cut through the board at 45° next to the joist with a jigsaw (saber saw).

2 Use a bolster (stonecutter's chisel) or a similar broad-bladed levering tool to prise up the cut end of the board and release its fixing nails.

3 Slide a length of scrap wood under the raised end of the board to hold it clear of the floor, and saw through it above the centre of the next joist.

4 To replace the panel, simply lay it back in position. Nail the square-cut end to its joist and skew nail (toe nail) the angled end to the neighbouring board.

5 An alternative way of supporting the cut ends of an access panel is to nail small wood blocks to each side of the adjacent floor joists.

6 The panel can also be screwed down onto the wooden blocks. This will allow easy access without damaging the panel.

REPAIRING A CONCRETE FLOOR

1 If cracks are found in a concrete floor after lifting old floor coverings, use a cold (box) chisel and club (spalling) hammer to undercut the edges of the crack.

2 Brush away all loose material from the crack, then use the crevice nozzle of a vacuum cleaner to remove dust which the brush will not pick up.

3 Dilute some PVA building (white general purpose) adhesive as recommended on the can, and brush it along the surface of the crack to help the repair mortar to bond to it.

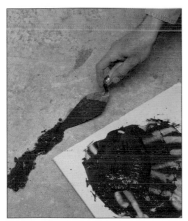

5 If the floor has noticeable potholes in its surface, pack the hole with small pieces of stone or other non-compressible filler.

4 Mix up some quick-setting repair mortar and trowel it into the crack, levelling it flush with the surrounding concrete. Leave it to harden.

6 Patch the pothole with quick-setting mortar, using the edge of the steel float to remove excess mortar so the patch is flush with its surroundings.

CURING STAIRCASE PROBLEMS

A timber staircase consists of a series of evenly spaced horizontal *treads* which form the flight. Most staircases also have vertical *risers* which fill the space between the rear edge of one tread and the front edge of the tread above; these may be nailed in place, or may have tongued edges which slot into grooves in the treads.

The treads are supported at each side by two parallel timbers called *strings*. A *closed-string* staircase has the treads and risers set into grooves cut in the inner faces of the strings, while an *open-string* staircase has the outer string cut in a zigzag fashion so the treads can rest on the cutouts. The inner string – the one against the wall of the stairwell – is always a closed string.

At the open side of a conventional flight, a guard is fitted to run between the top and bottom *newel posts* – the main vertical timbers supporting the flight. This usually consists of a series of closely-spaced *balusters* which are fixed between the top edge of the outer string and the underside of a handrail, but it may be a solid panelled barrier. There may also be a wall-mounted handrail at the other side of the flight, and freestanding flights must obviously have a *balustrade* at each side.

Stairs creak because one of the components has become loose; a footfall then causes the loose part to move against an adjacent component of the flight. A cure is simple if the underside of the flight is accessible, but less straightforward if it is not.

1 If there is no access to the underside of the flight, secure loose or squeaking treads by fixing metal repair brackets to tread and riser.

2 If the underside can be reached, check that the wedges securing the treads and risers to the strings are in place. Hammer them in firmly if they are loose.

3 Glue back any of the support blocks beneath the fronts of the treads if they have fallen off. Fit extra blocks beneath troublesome treads.

4 Drill clearance holes up through the rear edges of each tread, then drive screws up into the bottom edge of the riser above to lock the tread to it.

5 If the tread is found to be split, it must be replaced. Start by prising off the side moulding, then tap the balusters out with a mallet.

6 Insert a knife into the joint along the back of the tread to check if it has been nailed or screwed. If it has, use a hacksaw blade to cut the fixings.

7 Insert a crowbar or similar lever between the string and the tread, and prise it upwards and outwards to free it from the risers above and below it.

8 Use the damaged tread as a template to mark out and cut a replacement. Plane the nosing to shape, and cut notches in one end for the balusters.

9 Glue and clamp support blocks to the rear face of the riser below, and nail another block to the closed string to provide extra support for the tread.

10 Fit the new tread in place and secure it to the support blocks and to the cutout in the open string with screws rather than nails.

11 With the tread securely fixed in position, replace the balusters in their notches and nail the side moulding back on to complete the repair.

REPAIRING WALL COVERINGS

It is a simple matter to repair minor damage to painted walls and ceilings and then to cover it up with a fresh coat of paint. With wall coverings, patching damage or curing paperhanging defects requires a different approach.

The commonest form of damage to a wall covering is an impact that leaves a jagged tear. If the torn part is still attached, brush some paste onto its rear face and press it back into place, rolling it flat with a seam roller.

If the torn part is missing it will be necessary to patch the damage. If there are some offcuts from the original papering job, cut a patch from them. If not, cut and dry-strip a patch from an out-of-sight area behind a piece of furniture to use for the repair. Tear around the edges of the patch, holding it face down, to create a thin 'feathered' edge, then paste it, place it over the damaged area and flatten it with a seam roller. If the paper is a thick two-layer duplex type, try to peel away the backing paper to reduce the thickness of the patch.

Two other common problems, blisters and lifting seams, are the result of inadequate pasting during paperhanging. It is a relatively simple task to slit blisters open and lift dry seams to apply a little fresh paste and stick the covering firmly back to the wall. With fragile printed or flocked wall coverings, take care not to get paste on the surface.

PATCHING DAMAGED WALLPAPER

1 Cut a repair patch from an offcut of the original wall covering, or strip one from behind a piece of furniture. Check that it will cover the damage and match the pattern.

CURING DRY BLISTERS

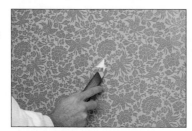

1 If a dry blister appears after wallpapering, use a sharp utility knife to make two cuts through it at right angles.

2 Peel back the triangular tongues formed and apply a little paste to the wall surface and to the back of the tongues. Leave to soak for a few minutes.

3 Press the triangles back into place and run a seam roller along the cuts to bond the paper firmly to the wall and leave an almost invisible repair.

3 **BELOW** Some two-layer duplex papers are too thick to use as a patch. Try to separate the backing paper at a corner of the patch and peel it off.

2 **ABOVE** Carefully tear along the edges of the patch to reduce its thickness and create a thin feathered edge. Check that no backing paper is visible.

4 **BELOW** Paste the back of the patch and place it over the damaged area, aligning the pattern carefully. Then 'iron' it into place with a seam roller.

STICKING DRY SEAMS

1 If a seam has failed to stick flat, lift it with a filling knife (putty knife) and use a slip of abrasive paper to sand off the dried paste behind it.

2 Use the filling knife to hold the edge of the wall covering away from the wall, and brush a little paste onto the back and the wall surface. Leave to soak.

3 Press the seam down flat with a seam roller, then use a sponge or damp cloth to remove any paste that has oozed onto the face of the wall covering.

INSULATION AND VENTILATION

Insulation means saving energy, and that is becoming more and more essential on every level, from the personal to the global. People are increasingly conscious of the importance of environmental issues. One of the greatest contributions that any one household can make is to cut down on unnecessary waste of fossil fuels, and so to reduce the amount of carbon dioxide released into the atmosphere by burning them. This means making more efficient use of energy, and insulation has a big part to play in this. It saves money too.

Insulation is a means of reducing heat transfer from a warm area to a cold one. In temperate countries the outside air temperature is below what most

DRAUGHT EXCLUDERS Special brush draught excluders can be fitted over letter plate openings, as shown, and also to the bottoms of doors to minimize heat loss.

DOUBLE GLAZING Glass is an extremely poor insulator and secondary glazing can cut down on heat loss provided the inner panes are well sealed to their tracks.

people regard as a comfortable level for much of the year, so that heating is needed for long periods and heat is constantly lost to the outside.

All materials conduct heat to a greater or lesser extent. Wood is a good insulator, brick an average one and glass is downright poor, as anyone who has sat next to a window on a cold winter's day will testify.

Except in countries which have very cold winters, proper insulation of homes has until recently been a very low priority, both for housebuilders – who will not pay for something that provides only a hidden benefit unless they have to – and for the legislators who frame the regulations and codes with which builders must comply. At last, however, the tide is turning, and current building rules call for much higher standards of insulation than ever before. They have also recognized that over-insulation can cause condensation, both inside the rooms and within the building's structure.

Unfortunately, this will not help those people living in older properties, many of which were originally built with no thought to their insulation performance at all. Over the years, various attempts will have been made to insulate houses like these, but what was deemed adequate twenty years ago will be well below par for today.

Condensation

Condensation is a big problem in many homes. It can lead to serious health problems and can also cause damage to the structure of the home.

The air always contains a certain amount of moisture – a lot on a humid summer's day, less on a clear winter one. When the air at a particular temperature cannot hold any more

moisture, it is said to have reached saturation point, and this condition is described as a *relative humidity* of 100 per cent.

Air at saturation point is the key to the problem. If that saturated air is cooled, for example by coming into contact with a surface such as a window pane on a chilly day, it can no longer hold so much vapour. The excess moisture vapour in the air condenses into droplets of water, and these are deposited on the cold surface – first as a fine film that mists up the glass but then, as more moisture is deposited, the droplets combine to form rivulets that run down the surface to create pools of water on the window sill. This can ruin decorations and cause window sills and

ROOF INSULATION If the roof of the house is pitched (sloping), blanket insulation can be laid over the loft (attic) floor. This is one of the most cost-effective forms of insulation.

FLOOR INSULATION With suspended floors, the floorboards can be lifted and insulation blanket suspended on netting stapled to the joists. A vapour barrier, such as heavy plastic sheeting, is then laid on top.

COST-EFFECTIVENESS OF INSULATION

Before thinking about individual types of insulation, it is important to understand the concept of cost-effectiveness. Insulation costs money to install, and can bring benefits in two main ways.

It can reduce heating bills, since the home will waste less heat and the same internal temperatures can be maintained without burning so much fuel. The annual saving on the heating bill will therefore 'pay back' the cost of the extra insulation. Also, when replacing a heating system, having better standards of insulation allows a less powerful, and less expensive, boiler

to be used – an indirect saving, but valuable none the less.

Alternatively, the house can be made warmer than before without increasing heating bills. In this case there will be no direct savings, just greater comfort.

The checklist on the right includes various ways of improving the insulation of a home. Each one has a rating that indicates how cost-effective it is. The best will pay for themselves in a year or two, while the least cost-effective (one star) are worth doing only if planning to carry out other major renovation work at the same time.

A hot water cylinder jacket *****
Pay-back period: less than 1 year.
Loft (attic) insulation ****
Pay-back period: 1–2 years.
Reflective radiator foil ****
Pay-back period: 1–2 years.
Draught excluders ***
Pay-back period: 2–3 years.
Flat roof insulation **(*)
Pay-back period: 2–4 years.
Floor insulation **
Pay-back period: 3–5 years.
Cavity wall insulation **
Pay-back period: around 5 years.
Double glazing **(*)
Pay-back period: 5 years or more.
Solid wall insulation *
Pay-back period: over 10 years.

---

frames to rot and rust; it can also cause two further problems, both of which are potentially more serious.

The first is mould. Apart from moisture vapour, the air also contains millions of tiny spores which float around looking for somewhere to live and multiply. The one thing they need is water, and if they find a damp surface in the home they will germinate and grow there quite happily over a wide range of temperatures. The result is the patches of black, brown or dark green mould seen especially around windows, in fitted cupboards (closets) and in the upper corners of rooms which have poor insulation and ventilation and inadequate heating.

The second problem is interstitial condensation. If the materials used to build walls, roofs and other parts of a building allow water vapour to penetrate, and if the air's moisture content is high and the structure's temperature is low, condensation can occur actually inside the structure. Most building materials are porous to some extent, although in a well designed and properly maintained building the absorbed moisture can evaporate harmlessly to the outside. But if it cannot do this the affected part of the structure remains damp; this can then encourage rot to grow on wood,

CONDENSATION Constant condensation ruins paintwork and will eventually cause wooden window frames and sills to rot, unless action is taken to increase ventilation.

MOULD Poor insulation, inadequate ventilation and poor heating levels can, in extreme cases, lead to patches of mould occurring around windows and inside fitted cupboards (closets).

EXTRACTOR FANS To control ventilation in steamy rooms such as kitchens and bathrooms, extractor fans can be fitted. The types linked to humidity detectors are ideal as they activate automatically.

and may also result in frost damage to masonry in cold weather, caused by the water expanding as it freezes. What is more, a damp wall has a lower resistance to the passage of heat than a dry one, and therefore becomes colder and encourages yet more condensation.

WHERE MOISTURE COMES FROM

People themselves are a major source of the moisture in the air inside a building. Breath is moist and sweat evaporates; one person gives off 250 ml (roughly 1/2 pint) of water during eight hours of sleep, and three times as much during an active day.

Domestic activities create even more moisture. Cooking, washing up, bathing, washing and drying clothes and so on can create as much as a further 10 to 12 litres (about 3 gallons) of water a day, and every litre of fuel burnt in a flueless oil or paraffin heater gives off roughly another litre of water vapour. The air in the house is expected to soak up all this extra moisture invisibly. It may not be able to manage unaided. However, a combination of improved insulation and controlled ventilation will go a long way towards eliminating the problem of condensation.

INSULATING ROOFS AND PIPEWORK

In a building with a pitched (sloping) roof, where the loft (attic) space is used only for storage, it is usual to insulate the loft floor, using either blankets of glass fibre or mineral wool, sold by the roll, or else loose-fill material (vermiculite, a lightweight expanded mineral, is the most widely used). Some kinds of loose-fill insulation, usually mineral wool or fireproofed cellulose fibres, can be blown into the loft by specialist contractors.

Blanket materials are generally easier to handle than loose-fill types unless the loft is awkwardly shaped, contains a lot of obstructions or has irregular joist spacings. The rolls are generally 600 mm (24 in) wide to match standard joist spacing, and common thicknesses are 100 mm (4 in) and 150 mm (6 in). Choose the latter unless there is already some thin loft insulation, and ensure that it is laid with eaves baffles to allow adequate ventilation of the loft. It is essential to wear protective clothing when handling glass fibre insulation. Wear a face mask, gloves and cover any exposed skin with suitable clothing.

Apart from being awkward to handle, loose-fill materials have another drawback. To be as effective as blanket types, they need laying to a greater depth – usually at least an extra 25 mm (1 in). With few ceiling joists being deeper than about 150 mm (6 in), there is nothing to contain the insulation and allow for maintenance access unless strips of wood are fixed along the top edge of every joist.

When the loft floor is completely insulated, remember to insulate any water tanks and pipework within the loft, since they are now at risk of freezing. For this reason, do not lay insulation under water tanks.

LAYING ROOF INSULATION

1 Clear all stored items from the loft (attic) area, then put down a sturdy kneeling board and use a heavy-duty vacuum cleaner to remove dust and debris.

2 Always put on gloves and a face mask and wear long sleeves to handle the insulation. Unroll it between the joists, leaving the eaves clear for ventilation.

3 Butt-join the ends of successive lengths of blanket. To cut the material to length, either use long-bladed scissors or simply tear it.

 6 RIGHT The same insulation material will lag water storage tanks too, as long as the tank has a lid. Simply wrap the blanket around the tank and tie it on.

4 ABOVE While working across the loft, make sure that any electrical cables are lifted clear of the insulation so they cannot overheat.

5 ABOVE Insulate the upper surface of the loft hatch by wrapping a piece of blanket in plastic sheeting and then stapling this to the hatch door.

INSULATING PIPEWORK

1 The quickest and easiest way of insulating pipework is to slip on lengths of foam pipe insulation, which is slit lengthways.

2 To make neat joins in the insulation at corners, cut the ends at 45°, using a mitre box and a carving knife or hacksaw blade. Tape the corner joint.

3 Make a V-shaped cutout in the insulation at tee joints, then cut an arrow shape on the end of the insulation which will cover the branch pipe.

4 As with butt and corner joints, use PVC tape to secure the sections of insulation together and prevent them from slipping out of position.

5 Pipe bandage can be used instead of foam insulation. Wrap it around the pipe in a spiral, with successive turns just overlapping.

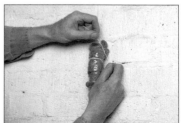

6 Tie the insulation bandage in place at the end of each length, or where the pipe passes through a wall. Simply tear the material to length as necessary.

INSULATING MASONRY WALLS AND FLOORS

House walls are the most massive part of the whole building and absorb a lot of heat, which is why a cold house takes so long to warm up. This heat can be retained by insulating the walls in one of two ways.

The traditional cavity wall consists of two 'leaves' of masonry with a gap, usually of 50 mm (2 in), between them. Their insulation performance can be improved by filling the cavity with insulating material. This is done by specialist installers who pump treated fibres, pellets or insulating foam into the cavity through holes drilled in the wall's outer leaf.

For solid walls, the most economical solution is to dry-line them on the inside with insulating plasterboard (gypsum board), fixed directly to the wall with panel adhesive or nailed to a supporting framework of treated wood strips. Alternatively ordinary plasterboard sheets can be used, with insulation blanket or boards placed between the support strips and covered with a polythene (polyethylene) vapour barrier.

For wood-framed walls, the best alternative is to remove the interior finish, install insulation batts and then cover these with a vapour barrier, such as polythene sheeting.

Insulating floors

Few people think of ground floors when considering insulation, yet a surprisingly large amount of heat can be lost through both solid and suspended wood floors.

With suspended timber floors insulation can be fixed between the joists after lifting the floorboards. One method is to cut strips of rigid expanded polystyrene and rest them on nails driven into the sides of the joists. Another is to suspend lengths of insulation blanket between them, supported on garden netting stapled to the joists. The insulation is then covered with a vapour barrier.

With direct-to-ground concrete floors (slab on grade), the commonest method of insulation involves lining the floor with polythene sheeting and placing sheets of rigid polystyrene directly on the floor surface and then putting down tongued-and-grooved chipboard (particle board) flooring over them.

INSULATING SOLID WALLS

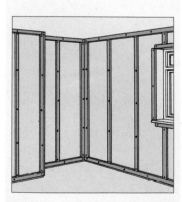

Fix a framework of 50 × 25 mm (2 × 1 in) softwood strips to the walls with masonry nails to support the edges and centres of the insulating boards.

1 Mark cutting lines on the board surface in pencil, then cut along the line with the insulation facing downwards using a fine-toothed saw.

2 To make cutouts for light switch boxes and similar obstacles, mark their positions and cut them out with a padsaw.

3 Fix the boards by positioning them against the support framework so that adjacent boards meet over a strip, and nail them in place.

INSULATING WOODEN FLOORS

1 To insulate beneath a wooden floor, lift all the floorboards. Then drape lengths of garden netting loosely over the joists and staple them in place.

2 Lay loft insulation blanket or wall insulation batts in the 'hammocks' between the joists. If the netting sags, pull it up a little and staple it again.

3 To prevent moisture from the house condensing within the insulation, cover it with a vapour barrier of heavy-duty polythene (polyethylene) sheeting.

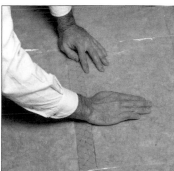

4 Re-lay the floorboards by nailing them to the joists. Take this opportunity to close up any joints between the boards for a neat finish.

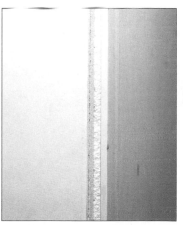

4 At external corners, remove a strip of the polystyrene insulation as wide as the board thickness so the edges of the plasterboard (gypsum board) can meet in a butt joint.

5 Arrange the boards at external corners so that a paper-covered board edge overlaps one that has its plaster core exposed.

6 Use a simple lever and fulcrum to raise the boards to touch the room ceiling as they are fixed. A skirting (baseboard) will cover the gap at floor level.

DOUBLE GLAZING

The glass in windows is the least efficient part of the house at keeping heat in, and the only way of cutting this heat loss while still being able to see out is to add another layer of glass. Double glazing can be done in two ways: existing single panes of glass can be replaced with special double-glazed panes called *sealed units*, or a second pane can be installed inside the existing one – so-called *secondary glazing*.

Secondary glazing is the only practical course of action unless the existing windows are being completely replaced. There are dozens of types available for do-it-yourself installation, providing hinged and sliding inner panes that blend in well with most types of window; similar systems are also available from professional installers. The panes are either fixed to the window frame itself, or else fit within the window reveal on special track. An effective but flimsy alternative is clear acetate or PVC film fixed to the inside of the frame with double-sided tape.

Apart from reducing heat losses through the windows, double glazing eliminates 'cold spots' in the room next to the windows. It also helps to reduce noise penetration from outside as long as the inner panes are kept closed. It will reduce condensation too, but only if the inner panes are well sealed to their track to stop warm moist air getting into the air gap between them and the window itself. Lastly, lockable types will give a measure of additional security; burglars may tackle one pane of glass, but many will flinch at two.

As far as external doors are concerned, solid doors offer better insulation than glazed ones, so go for this type if planning a replacement. If a glazed panel is a must, choose one with a sealed double glazing unit using safety glass. Heat loss through any external door can be reduced by building a porch outside it, to create an airlock between the house and the outside world.

FITTING SLIDING UNITS

1 Measure the height and width of the window reveal at each side. If the figures differ, work from the smaller measurements for height and width.

2 Cut the track sections to length with a fine-toothed saw and sand the cut ends smooth. Make cutouts as the instructions dictate to form the corners.

3 Offer up the side track sections and screw them in place. Use thin packing to get them truly vertical if the walls are out of square.

4 Next, secure the top track section in place. Screw it directly to a wooden lintel or pre-drill holes in concrete ones and insert wall plugs first.

FITTING THIN-FILM DOUBLE GLAZING

1 Start by sticking lengths of double-sided adhesive tape to the window frame, about 12 mm (¹/₂ in) in from the surrounding masonry.

2 Press the film onto the tape, pulling it as taut as possible. Then play hot air from a hair-drier over it to tighten it up and pull out any wrinkles.

3 When the film is even and wrinkle-free, trim off the excess film all the way around the window with a sharp utility knife.

5 When positioning the bottom track on the window sill, use a straightedge and a spirit level to check that it is perfectly aligned with the top track.

6 Measure up for the glass as directed in the kit manufacturer's instructions, and order the glass. Fit cut lengths of glazing gasket to the edges of each pane.

7 Fit the first pane into the track by inserting its top edge in the top channel, and then lowering its bottom edge. Repeat the procedure for the other pane.

DRAUGHTPROOFING

Ill fitting windows and doors are a major source of heat loss, as well as causing cold draughts. Fitting efficient draught stripping around them will reduce the losses and cut down the draughts, and is a simple job to carry out. Modern self-adhesive foams are much more efficient and longer-lasting than older types, and are ideal for windows, while doors and sash windows are best draughtproofed with pin-on (tack-on) plastic or sprung metal strips

or types containing a compressible rubber seal. Special draught excluders are available for door thresholds (saddles), and can be fitted to the door bottom or across the threshold. There are even excluders designed to fit over letter plate openings.

Remember that draughtproofing a home will close off many 'unofficial' sources of ventilation, turning it into a well sealed box. Fuel-burning appliances such as boilers and room

heaters must have an adequate source of fresh air to burn safely, so it is wise to ask a fuel supplier to check that there is adequate ventilation in rooms containing such appliances. Often a ventilator in a window pane will solve the problem. Efficient draughtproofing may also increase condensation, especially in kitchens and bathrooms. This can be prevented by providing controlled ventilation in these rooms with an extractor fan.

DRAUGHTPROOFING DOORS

1 The simplest type of door-bottom draught excluder is a brush seal mounted in a wood or plastic strip. Simply cut it to length and screw it on to the foot of the door.

2 Alternatively, fit a threshold (saddle) strip. Cut the metal bar to length and screw it to the sill, then fit the compressible rubber sealing strip in the channel.

3 Draughtproof a letter plate opening by screwing on a special brush seal. Check that it does not foul the letter plate flap if this opens inwards.

4 Draughtproof the sides and top of the door frame by pinning (tacking) on lengths of plastic or sprung metal sealing strip. Pin the edge farthest from the door stop bead.

5 Alternatively, stick lengths of self-adhesive foam excluder to the stop bead against which the door closes. At the hinge side, stick it to the frame.

6 A third option is to use lengths of self-adhesive brush strip excluder. These three types can also be used for draughtproofing hinged casement windows.

DRAUGHTPROOFING SASH WINDOWS

1 To fit sprung metal strip excluder to a sliding sash window, first prise off the staff bead (window stop) that holds the inner sash in position, and swing it out.

2 Measure the length of strip needed to fit the height of the window, and cut it to length with scissors. Beware the sharp edges of the metal.

3 Pin (tack) the strip to the side of the frame so it will press against the edge of the sliding sash. Pin it through the edge facing towards the room.

4 Use the special wheeled springing tool provided with the excluder to make a small groove in the strip, causing it to spring outwards.

5 Pin a strip along the inner face of the top sash meeting rail (mullion), and 'spring' it so it presses against the outer face of the bottom sash rail.

6 Draughtproof the bottom edge of the lower sash and the top edge of the upper one by sticking on lengths of self-adhesive foam excluder.

PROVIDING CONTROLLABLE VENTILATION

In every house stale, moist air must be removed and replaced with fresh air from outside. This happens not only in an obvious way when a window is opened or an extractor fan switched on, but all the time. For example, air passes up chimney flues, or finds a way out through the inevitable small gaps in the house structure.

Unless power ventilated, most modern houses have very little chance of such ventilation because improved standards of insulation and draughtproofing have made them much more airtight than formerly. Of course

this reduces heating bills and keeps the house's occupants warm and comfortable, as long as they do not create too much moisture for the air to hold. If they do, condensation will be the inevitable result, and extra ventilation will be needed.

This reduction in natural ventilation not only causes trouble within the house, it can also affect its structure. Two particular problem areas are roof spaces and under-floor voids. To prevent it, more ventilation must be provided via ridge and eaves-level vents in roofs, and airbricks in walls.

For ventilating rooms, what is needed is some controllable means of getting rid of excess moist air without wasting too much valuable heat. In habitually steamy rooms such as kitchens and bathrooms, an extractor fan is the best solution. It will extract the moist air quickly, and will also help to get rid of unwanted smells. In other rooms, fitting small 'trickle' ventilators at the top of window frames and putting in extra airbricks will often supply enough ventilation to allow the moist air to disperse before condensation becomes a problem.

FITTING AN EXTRACTOR FAN

1 Decide on the fan position, then mark the outline of the ducting on the wall outside. Drill holes right through the wall to mark it on the inside too.

2 Drill a series of closely spaced holes through the wall from inside, working within the guide holes drilled from outside. Repeat on the wall outside.

3 Chop out the brickwork with a wide bolster (stonecutter's chisel) and club (spalling) hammer, again working from inside and outside the house.

4 Use ducting for a cooker hood. Line the hole with a short length of pipe, then use connectors as required to connect the hood to the outlet.

5 Wall-mounted fans usually need a round hole. Cut it out, line it with a short length of sleeving and make good around it inside and outside the house.

6 Fit the fan into the sleeving, ready for its electrical supply to be connected. Fit a cover grille to the outside end of the ducting.

SAFE VENTILATION

There are two very important points to remember concerning ventilation. Firstly, many fuel-burning appliances need an adequate supply of fresh air to work efficiently and safely, so rooms where they are sited must contain provision for this if they are well sealed against natural draughts. Secondly, disused flues must be ventilated at top and bottom; if they are not, condensation can occur within the flue, which may show up as damp patches on the internal chimney walls.

FITTING EXTRA AIRBRICKS

1 Airbricks are the same size as one, two or three bricks. To fit one, start by drilling a series of closely spaced holes through the wall.

2 Then use a club (spalling) hammer and a wide bolster (stonecutter's chisel) to cut out the brickwork. With solid walls, drill holes right through and work from inside too.

3 Fit a cavity liner if the wall is of cavity construction, then trowel a bed of fairly wet mortar onto the bottom of the opening.

4 Butter mortar onto the top of the airbrick and slide it into the opening. Push mortar into the gaps at the sides and pack it down well.

5 Use drier mortar to point neatly all around the airbrick. Inside, make good the wall with plaster and cover the opening with a ventilator grille.

6 As an alternative to a terracotta airbrick, fit a two-part plastic type. The sleeves interlock to line the hole as the two parts are pushed together.

7 Slide the outer section into place, and point around it. Then slide the inner section into place from inside the house, and fit its cover grille.

PART TWO

INSTANT MAKEOVERS

INTRODUCTION

An instant makeover on windows, walls and floors can help you create a home that is unique in style and completely personal. This section of the book shows you how to achieve unusual and innovative design effects with the minimum of labour and materials, and at little cost – but with maximum ingenuity!

Curtains (drapes) can be totally transformed by the judicious use of ribbons, lace, beads, shells and even fishing nets. Walls take on a totally new look with the help of everyday items such as string, brown wrapping paper, or an eye-catching blanket. Floors,

too, can be enlivened by stencilling or
painting, or with unusual rugs and mats.
Each project lists the tools and materials that
are needed, and full colour step-by-step photographs
show you exactly how to do each stage.

Furniture and soft furnishings are given a new lease of life with
imaginative accessories, trimmings and images. Experiment with
different fabrics, such as chintz, muslin (cheesecloth),
mosquito netting, gingham or tartan. Even natural
materials such as grass beach mats, twigs and branches
can be used to good effect.
Chairs can be dressed up for

special occasions with silk, fresh flowers,
or stylish Nova suede – or you can make
your own chair with cardboard – using a
template – which children will
particularly enjoy.

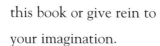

Lighting has a huge impact on the overall atmosphere
and style of a room, and here you will find ideas for every occasion, be it
uplighters, an old-fashioned wire chandelier, standard lamp or stained-glass
bulb. Even the simplest items – containers – can be given a touch of individual style
with paint, varnish, paper, string, paper clips, or whatever is available. In fact there is
nothing in your home that couldn't benefit from an instant makeover – use the ideas in
this book or give rein to
your imagination.

W I N D O W S

Basement, balcony, or bedsit – whatever the style of your home and whatever you're looking to achieve, you'll to find something here to revolutionize your windows. So, if you thought it was all just plastic curtain hooks and tracks, read on! All you have to do is invest in a staple gun and some inexpensive fittings and fixings, and follow our simple step-by-step instructions to show you exactly how to make your windows the fabulous focal point of each room. You will never look in curtain (drape) departments again once you have been shown our instant window makeovers and realize how easy it is to create stunning and dramatic effects.

The ideas in this book will carry you away from traditional methods and old-fashioned styles towards the freshness and freedom of experimental window dressing. Many of our projects were inspired by looking at familiar materials in a new light, such

as using grass beach mats for blinds (shades) or tartan wool rugs for an imposing curtain. There are all kinds of materials that can make the leap from their everyday practical uses to highly original ones. This chapter contains projects to suit every taste and every budget including quick stylish ideas for tie-backs, hanging treatments and colour schemes and simple effects created by draping, typing, stapling, buttoning, hanging, clipping and glueing all kinds of fabrics. You will probably come up with your own ideas and variations on our themes, too.

So, armed with these innovative ideas, take a fresh look at the windows around your home and have lots of fun transforming them to reflect your personality. The real beauty of our quick and inexpensive window dressing creations is that, if you happen to change your mind at a later date, you can simply come up with another one!

Opposite. /(/(// drape at the window can be all it takes to lift a newly decorated room and make it feel more homely.

EGYPTIAN DREAM

A PAIR OF COTTON SHEETS makes the most wonderful drape and all the seams are perfectly finished. The bigger the sheets, the more luxurious and elegant the window will look – drapes should always be generous. Wooden clothes pegs (pins) can be wedged into a piece of old wooden floorboarding or driftwood – if you drill the holes at an angle, the fixing will be stronger as well as more decorative.

YOU WILL NEED

scissors

cotton tape, 2.5m (2½yd)

2 flat king-size cotton sheets

needle and white sewing thread

drill

length of floorboarding or driftwood, window width plus 15cm (6in) either side

6 old-fashioned wooden clothes pegs (pins)

spirit level

wall plugs (plastic anchors) and screws

screwdriver

1 With scissors, cut the cotton tape into six strips of equal length.

2 Divide the width of each sheet top by three and use the divisions as points to attach the tapes. Fold each tape in half and use small stitches to sew them to the top of the sheet.

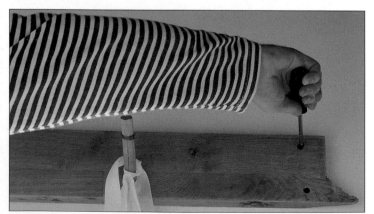

3 Drill six holes at equal distances along the floorboarding and wedge in the pegs (pins). Drill a hole either end of the floorboarding and screw it into the wall, using a spirit level to check it is straight, and appropriate fixings to secure it.

4 Tie the tapes securely and neatly to the pegs and arrange the drapes.

POT-POURRI

THIS IS AN EXTREMELY QUICK and effective way to trim the top edge of a loop-headed curtain (drape). Tie ribbons round the loops and hang a selection of decorations from them. Here we have used pieces of pot-pourri but you could also use odd earrings, bells, tin stars, buttons and so on. If you have a pinch-pleated or a simple gathered curtain heading, a small bow or knot with ribbon hanging down would look effective.

YOU WILL NEED

tape measure

1cm (½in) wide hessian (burlap)
or linen

ribbon or tape

dressmaker's scissors

needle and matching sewing
thread (optional)

pot-pourri

glue gun and glue sticks

1 Decide the appropriate length or lengths of ribbon or tape needed in relation to the drop of the curtain (drape), so they look in proportion.

2 Cut the ribbon or tape to length and cut the ends at an angle, so they look neat. If you are using a ribbon that frays, hem the ends. Select the pieces of pot-pourri that most complement one another. Using a glue gun, attach the pieces of pot-pourri to the ends of the ribbon or tape.

3 Tie the ribbon or tape to the curtain loops. It is best not to fix them permanently, so you can change the design when you wish and take them off when you wash the curtains.

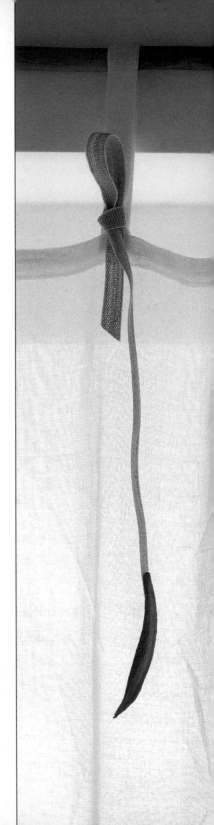

WHITE MISCHIEF

SMALL DETAILS SUCH AS the curtain (drape) clips in this project make the important difference between an obvious and an elegant solution to curtain hanging. The white muslin (cheesecloth) is a generously long piece, folded in half, allowing a drop 1½ times the length of the window – it really is a very simple, yet elegant example of window dressing! Small brass curtain clips fit over the rail and catch the muslin along the fold.

1 Stain the length of dowel by shaking woodstain on to a soft cloth and rubbing the dowel with it until you achieve the effect you want.

2 Drill two holes either side of the window and insert the wall plugs (plastic anchors). Bang in the nails.

3 Clip the muslin (cheesecloth) along the fold, leaving an equal distance between the clips. Thread the rings on to the dowel and place the dowel over the nails.

4 Spread the rings along the dowel so that the muslin falls in even drapes.

5 Knot the front drop of muslin on to the end of the spear and prop this across the window.

SHELL TIE-BACKS

CURTAIN (DRAPE) TIE-BACKS can be made in a tremendously wide range of styles so you can use them to create whatever decorative effect you like. Though we normally think of a simple braid or tassel, tie-backs can be trimmed to make them focal- and talking-points within the room. Here a fishing net was festooned with different types and sizes of shells. You could wire a mass of very small shells on to the net or even edge the curtain with a widely spaced line of matching shells.

YOU WILL NEED

fishing net

shells

fine wire

wire cutters

glue gun and glue sticks
or electric drill, with very
fine drill bit

string (optional)

1 Take the fishing net and arrange it in graceful folds. Gather together a mass of shells and see how they look best when arranged on the net. Cut lengths of fine wire. These can then be glued to the back of the shells so that they can be wired on to the netting.

2 Alternatively, drill holes in the shells. Thread string through the holes for attaching to the net.

3 Fix the shells on the netting. Make another tie-back in the same way. Loop the tie-backs around the curtains and on to the wall.

CRYSTAL TIES

TIE AN EXQUISITE SILK curtain with crystal drops for a really elegant look. The use of a rough hessian (burlap) tassel, bound quite casually and loosely, makes this interesting and unusual. The crystal drops were bought from an antique shop; search around for interesting examples. Failing that, use crystal drops from a bead shop or some coloured stones from a cheap necklace or earrings, all of which will look equally lovely.

YOU WILL NEED

hessian (burlap) tassel tie-back

scissors

crystal chandelier drops

gold beading wire or very fine gold string

wire cutters

1 You need only one tassel tie-back for two curtains. Split the tassel in half, then unravel the rope. Re-bind the tassel to make it look less formal.

2 Thread the crystal drops on to gold wire or fine string to make several lengths of various sizes.

3 Fasten the lengths of crystal drops on to the tie-backs. Some will simply hook on; others should be wired. Loop the tie-backs around the curtains and on to the wall.

BIJOU BOUDOIR

 BALLROOM DANCERS, bad-taste rockers, brides and prima ballerinas all love it – netting has that special star quality that windows sometimes need! You can cut, pleat (tuck), layer, scrunch and bunch it – there is nothing to sew and it is so light that many filmy, glamorous lengths can hang from a single strand of plastic-coated sprung wire. Netting comes in all sorts of colours and the idea from this project could easily be translated into a completely stunning party window in dramatic purple or scarlet and black. Tie the lengths of netting back with feather boas, strings of pearls or even kitsch diamanté dog collars to make the most glamorous window this side of Cannes.

YOU WILL NEED

pliers

4 eyelet hooks

2 lengths of plastic-coated sprung wire, window width

4 m (4 yd) each pink and white netting

scissors

fine wire

feather boa

fake pearl strands

1 Screw in an eyelet hook at the same height either side of the window recess.

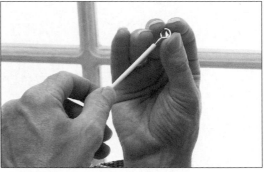

2 Loop the eyelet on the wire through the hooks and stretch the wire taut across the window.

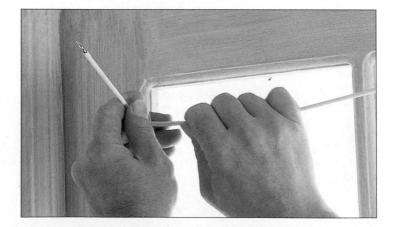

3 Repeat the process, positioning the second wire about 8cm (3in) in front of the first (of course, this distance will be dictated by the depth of your window recess).

4 Cut the netting in half. Feed half the length of the pink netting over the back wire. Set aside the rest of the pink netting.

5 Feed the length of the white netting over the back wire, next to the pink netting. Pull both lengths of netting into shape, making a double layer with each.

6 Hang the other layer of pink netting over the front wire.

7 Cut out a large circle of pink netting to make the pelmet and fold this over the front wire to create a semi-circle.

8 Cut long strips of netting and scrunch them into rosettes. Tuck them between the wires. You will find that the netting is very easy to scrunch into good shapes. Pleat up the semi-circular pelmet, adding folds and creases along the wire as you go. ➤

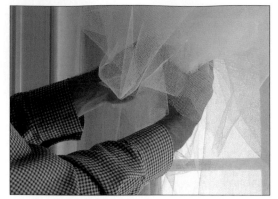

9 Make big white rosettes to go into the corners by scrunching up the white netting. Tuck them into the wire to secure and smooth them out to make a pleasing shape.

10 Twist the fine wire into connecting rings and use them to attach the feather boa along the curve of the netting pelmet.

11 Drape the strands of fake pearls from the centre of the front wire and tie up the ends.

Right: One of the great advantages of netting is that it is easy to handle, and is quite forgiving. If you don't like the first shape you have made, smooth it out and scrunch it up again. These rosettes are simply tucked between the front and back.

RAINBOWS

THIS REALLY MUST BE THE QUICKEST, cheapest and brightest way to deal with a bare kitchen window. It would also work well in a hall or on a small staircase window. All you need to do is buy an insect blind – those door-length, multi-coloured plastic strips. Then screw two cup hooks into the window frame to hold the rail and get your scissors out for a trim! The one in this project is V-shaped, but zig-zags, rippling waves, castellations or even asymmetrical designs are equally possible.

YOU WILL NEED
ruler
pencil
wooden rail
2 cup hooks
door-size insect blind
scissors

1 Place the rail along the top of the window and position the cup hooks so that the strips will hang over the whole width of the window.

2 Measure the windowsill to find the mid-point and make a small mark. This will be used as a guide when trimming the blind.

3 Place the ruler on a slant between the mark and the point you want the side drop to reach. Measure and mark the same point on the other side of the window frame.

4 Hang the insect blind on the rail and position it on the hooks, then hold the ruler up against it, between the two pencil marks. Cut the strips along the top of the ruler.

NO-PROBLEM LINKS

WHAT LENGTHS WILL YOU GO TO for a bargain? If you find the fabric of your dreams in the remnant bin, but it's just that bit too short for your window, it's no longer a problem. Use curtain (drape) rings to connect the different lengths of fabric you have found – you can use as many as you need for the drop. Nobody will ever suspect that the linked effect was anything other than a deliberate design decision.

YOU WILL NEED
drill

spirit level

wall plugs (plastic anchors) and screws

screwdriver

metal curtain (drape) rail and fixings

assorted lengths of remnant fabrics

iron-on hem fix (such as Wundaweb)

iron

needle and matching sewing thread

split curtain rings

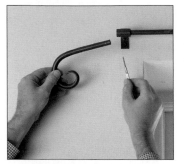

1 Attach the rail fixings above the window. Check with a spirit level before you screw them in. Assemble the curtain (drape) rail and fixings.

2 Hem all the rough edges of the fabric, either with iron-on hem fix or by hand. Sew small split rings along the top edge of the curtain to link into the rail rings. Sew rings in the same positions along the bottom of the first piece of fabric.

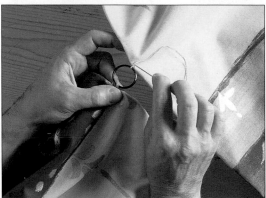

3 Line the curtain up with the next piece of fabric and mark the positions for attaching the rings. Make sure they line up exactly with the first curtain if you have a geometric or striped pattern. Sew the rings to the second piece of fabric along the whole width, then hang in place.

Above: The curtains can be linked with single rings, split rings or interconnecting rings like these.

RIBBONS AND LACE

MAKE THE MOST OF A BEAUTIFUL PIECE of sari fabric or a superb lace panel by displaying it in a window so that the light shines through. A few hand-stitched lengths of ribbon will allow you to tie back the fabric to reveal as much or as little of the window and the view as you like. As the main fabric is very light and translucent, hang a length of white muslin behind it for extra privacy.

YOU WILL NEED

muslin, $1\frac{1}{2}$ × window width

iron-on hem fix
(such as Wundaweb)

iron

white tape

thread

dowel, window width

2 cup hooks

scissors

white or cream linen or
satin ribbon

sari fabric or antique
lace panel

1 Finish the hems on the muslin with iron-on hem fix, then sew lengths of white tape along the top to tie the muslin to the dowel. Screw the hooks into the window frame and hang up the dowel rail. Tie the curtain on to the rail.

2 Cut the ribbon into eight 25cm (10in) lengths and stitch four along the top edge of the sari fabric or lace panel. Stitch the others at intervals along the sides – their positions will depend on the size of the panel and the parts that you want to show off. You can also hide any defects when you tie them up in this way.

3 Tie the top ribbons to the rail using simple bows. Arrange them along the rail so that the fabric drapes over the window in the most appealing way.

4 Tie up sections of the panel using the side ribbons. Experiment with different combinations, standing back from the window to check your adjustments until you are happy.

WIRED-UP WINDOW

THIS IS A QUIRKY PROJECT for people who see the window as a frame to be filled, but not necessarily frilled! A selection of crisp Irish linen tea towels, linen scrim window cloths, dusters and oven gloves are arranged on a wire framework of tracks and hangers for a practical and stylish window treatment in the kitchen. Yachting chandlers sell good wire with all kinds of interesting bits and pieces for fastening and tightening up. Follow the steps here for an explanation on how to use them and to ensure everything connects securely. Look at this window treatment as a movable feast and reposition the key elements every now and again for a new design at no extra cost.

YOU WILL NEED

rigging wire, 2 × window width; 1 × ½ window length, plus 30cm (12in)

fixed rigging wire grips and thimbles

adjustable rigging wire grips and thimbles

hammer

pliers

2 deck eyes with pulleys

2 fixed deck eyes

bradawl

rigging screw (tension adjuster)

connecting rings (key-ring style), various sizes

wire coat hangers

selection of tea towels, dusters, and oven gloves

1 To make the rigging, thread the rigging wire through the fixed wire grip to form a loop with the end.

2 Place the thimble inside the loop and pull the wire tight, so it fits snugly round the thimble. Place it on a hard surface and bang the wire grip closed with a hammer.

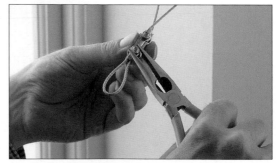

3 Loosen the screw on the adjustable wire grip and thimble and thread the other end of the wire through. Tighten the screw to hold the wire firmly in place.

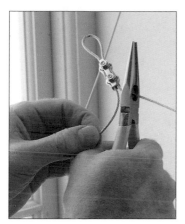

4 Cut off the excess wire at the point where it enters the thimble.

5 Loop the thimble fitting over a deck eye, then hold it in position to the window frame while you use a bradawl to make holes for the screws. Screw the deck eye securely into the window frame.

6 Thread the wire through one of the pulleys and screw this pulley into the window frame opposite the first fixing.

7 Thread the wire through the second pulley and screw this pulley into the window frame halfway down the side of the window.

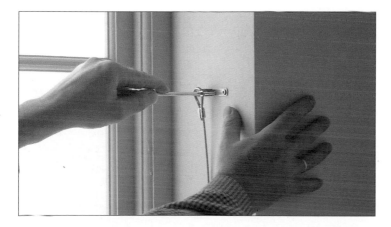

8 Attach a thimble to the end of the shorter length of wire. Loop this through a deck eye and screw it into the frame halfway down the side of the window – opposite the last pulley. ➤

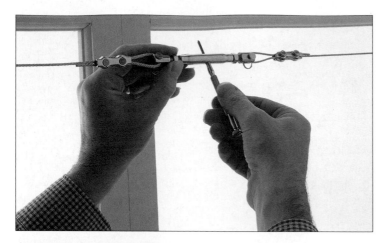

9 Attach an adjustable wire grip so that it can join on to each end of the rigging screw. Because of the nature of a rigging screw, you will be able to make minor adjustments to centralize it, but aim to cut the wire as accurately as possible to begin with. Twist the rigging screw to increase the tension.

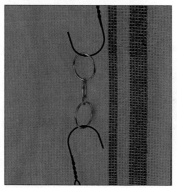

10 To assemble the arrangement, use connecting rings to link the wire coat hangers together.

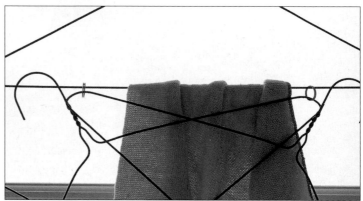

11 You could also make up 'cat's cradle' shapes by interlinking hangers. Always reinforce the links with rings to make them more secure.

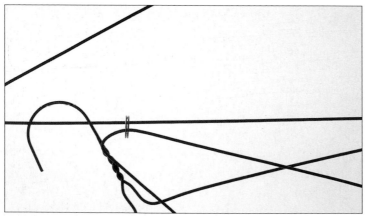

12 To make further variations of the linked coat hangers, experiment with them until you are pleased with the arrangement.

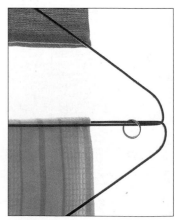

13 Finally, iron the tea towels and fold them over the hangers.

AFRICAN DAYS

KENYAN CLOTHS ARE GORGEOUSLY rich and vibrant. The patterns and colours are bold and brilliant and there is no need to hem, stitch or gather them. Just run a washing line across the window and peg the cloth on to it – use colour co-ordinated clothes pegs (pins) and line to pull this easy and exotic window treatment together. You won't be able to draw this curtain, but keep an extra peg or two handy so you can use them to hold the cloth back and let the sunshine in – even on a rainy day!

YOU WILL NEED

2 cup hooks or eyelets
plastic-coated washing line
multi-coloured plastic pegs (pins)
African cloth panel

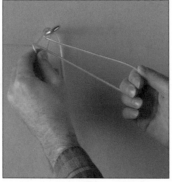

1 Screw the hooks into the wall (or window frame) at an equal distance from the window.

2 Loop the washing line around the hooks and tie a knot.

3 Peg the cloth to the line, gathering it up a bit for the first and last pegs to add weight around the edges.

4 Bundle up the excess line on one side and tie it in a knot. Let this hang down instead of cutting it off.

ROBINSON CRUSOE BLINDS

THIS REALLY MUST BE one of the cheapest, simplest, yet most effective blind (shade) solutions ever: it involves two grass beach mats, three cup hooks, a length of rope and some brass paper fasteners. The beach mats are made with coloured tape binding, and as they are extremely light-weight, they can be rolled up by hand and tied with rope. Measure your window carefully – the mats are available in one width only, so they are not suitable for all types and sizes of window.

YOU WILL NEED
bradawl
3 cup hooks
2 grass beach mats
paper fasteners
rope
scissors

1 Make three holes with a bradawl, one either side and one in the middle of the window recess. Screw in the cup hooks.

2 Make a channel for the rope at the top of the blind by folding over the mat 4cm (1½in) and securing with a row of evenly spaced paper fasteners, pushed through and folded back.

3 Knot the rope on to one of the cup hooks, leaving a tail hanging about a third of the way down the window. Thread the rope through the blind (shade) and pull it tight before knotting it on to the middle hook. Cut the rope the same length as before.

4 Cut a length of rope twice the length of the window drop and knot it in the middle, on to the middle hook. Roll up the blind by hand and tie the two ends of this rope to hold it at the required height. Repeat this process with a second length of rope for the second blind.

ARTIST'S STUDIO

 THIS IS THE IDEAL WAY to cover a large studio window, and as canvas comes in so many sizes, you're bound to find a piece to fit your window. If you have never previously considered the possibility of becoming a painter, then this is a good way to start – curtains (drapes) can also be art! Here, chalks were used to draw on to the canvas and change the flat panel into a boldly gathered backdrop. You could use this idea as your inspiration, or you could flick colours on it in Jackson Pollock style, or simply add a few minimalist squiggles. If your window receives a lot of light, you may want to suspend a builder's dust-sheet (drop cloth) in front of the window. This will provide a lining for the main curtain.

YOU WILL NEED

canvas, 1½ × window width

chalks or acrylic paints and paintbrush

drill

4 chunky garage hooks

screwdriver

metal cleat

rope

double-sided carpet tape

brass eyelets

hammer

1 Draw, paint or print on to the canvas using whatever style or design you have chosen – the bolder the better, as the canvas will cover a large surface area.

2 Fix the garage hooks securely into the wall above the window, spaced at equal intervals.

3 Screw the cleat to the wall, about halfway down the side of the window, then wind one end of the rope around it several times.

4 Take the long end of the rope up and through the hooks along the top.

5 Pull the rope taut and tie it on to the end hook. Then fix the seams and eyelets on to the canvas following the manufacturer's instructions.

6 Thread the rope through the first eyelet from behind, allowing about 16cm (6¼in) between the hook and the eyelet. Then, leaving the same distance again, twist a loop in the rope and put it on the hook.

7 Take the rope down and through the back of the next eyelet, then up and over the back taut rope, which now forms a 'rail' for the rope to rest on.

8 When you reach the end of the curtain, take the rope through the last hook.

9 Take the rope straight down the side of the window and tie it neatly on to the cleat.

➤

10 Cut an extra length of rope and hook it over one of the top centre hooks so that one length falls to the front and the other to the back of the canvas. Gather the canvas up and get hold of both ends of the rope. Tie these together in a knot and leave the ends dangling free.

Above: The knot holding the curtain back from the window allows the light to come through.

Above: Allow plenty of canvas so that it spills generously out on to the floor below the window.

Above: The knotted rope forms an additional decorative element in its own right.

Above: The natural colour of the canvas enhances the subtle colours of the design.

BUTTONED BLANKETS

THESE BLANKETS WERE too brilliant to hide away in the bedroom so they were transformed into an attractive window treatment. They make good draught excluders and are simply rigged up on a couple of towel rails. You need a solid wall as the blankets are weighty. The blankets are doubled over and held together with a row of large safety pins.

YOU WILL NEED

2 chrome towel rails

drill

wall plugs (plastic anchors) and extra-long screws

screwdriver

2 colourful wool blankets

10 large coloured buttons, to contrast with blanket colours

dressmaker's pins or double-sided tape

large safety pins or nappy pins

tailors' chalk

needle and button thread or wool

1 Fix the towel rails to the wall above the window, by drilling holes and inserting wall plugs (plastic anchors). As towel rails are not long enough to cover the whole width, hang them at different heights.

2 Fold both the blankets in half lengthways. Drape them over the curtain (drape) rails, to create a 30cm (12in) pelmet as shown. Take down the blankets. Decide upon the position of the buttons, trying them out by fixing them to the blankets with dressmaker's pins or with double-sided tape.

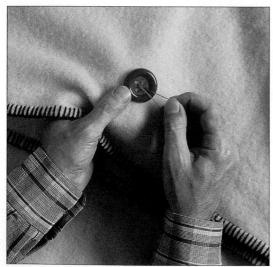

3 Stitch the buttons along the pelmet, just catching the first layer with a few stitches to secure the buttons, but without damaging the blanket.

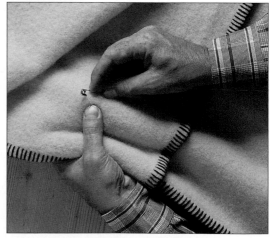

4 Pin a row of safety pins about halfway down the pelmet, on the underside where they won't show. Hang the blankets back in position. Re-pin carefully, so that each safety pin goes through the inside layer of the pelmet, and the outer layer of the curtain.

HULA-HULA

ORDINARY WINDBREAKS used on the beach can be transformed into instant blinds (shades). They come in a range of lengths with poles in pockets to divide the equal sections, just like a Roman blind, but bolder. All you have to do is saw off the extra piece of pole that goes into the sand and hang up the blind on a couple of plumbers' pipe fittings. A wide range of cheerful summer colours is available.

YOU WILL NEED

windbreak, to fit window

scissors

stapler

saw

tape measure

drill

2 wall plugs (plastic anchors)

2 plumbers' pipe fittings

screwdriver

flower garlands, elastic
or rope

string (optional)

1 Hold the windbreak vertically against your window. If the drop is too long, then cut out the nylon mesh and make a new channel for the bottom pole. Fold over a hem, check the pole fits, and staple along the edge.

2 Saw off the excess pole. Measure the window and the top of the blind to find the place for the fixings. Drill holes and insert the wall plugs (plastic anchors) and plumbers' fittings.

3 Hang the blind, then loop the garlands, elastic or rope between the first and last poles. If the garlands are too long, tie them in divisions with string to shorten.

SCOTLAND THE BRAVE

HERE IS THE PERFECT WAY to show off bright tartan wool rugs. Draped and pinned over a wooden rail, they will add a baronial touch to the plainest of windows. Tartan has quite a masculine feel and looks good alongside old leather cases and other "practical" accessories. This window would suit a study or hallway with plain walls, contrasting with the richness and pattern of the tartan. Fix the curtain rail above the window, extending about 30cm (12in) each side.

YOU WILL NEED

wooden curtain rail

spirit level

drill

wall plugs (plastic anchors) and screws

screwdriver

3 different coloured tartan rugs

6 kilt pins

1 Fix the wooden rail according to the pack instructions. Begin on the left with one corner of a rug. Take the corner over from the back and pin it about 30cm (12in) down the rug.

2 Drape the second rug over the rail, also on the left, but arrange it so that the drape is more or less equal at the front and back. Lift it in places and pin it on to the first rug using kilt pins.

3 Drape the third tartan rug along the rest of the pole diagonally so that the fringed edge can be seen hanging down from the right corner. Lift sections of this rug and pin it in drapes by attaching it with kilt pins to the second rug.

4 Stand back and check the effect, then use any remaining pins to hold the rugs in place, making a feature of the fringing and the pins.

MAGIC BEADS

TRANSPARENT BEADS DON'T block out the light or keep out the draughts, but when the sun catches them, they sparkle like jewels, and using them full-length on a small square window can turn a light source into something bright and magical. Beads are available in brilliant, gem-like colours, softly co-ordinated pastels and clear colourless textures and each has its own unique, light-enhancing quality.

YOU WILL NEED

2 wooden battens (furring strips), window width, plus 8–10cm (3–4in) each side

wood glue

hammer

panel pins (brads)

ruler

emulsion (latex) paint: black and white

paintbrush

drill

coloured bead curtain, with fixing strip and screws

screwdriver

wall plugs (plastic anchors) and screws

spirit level

small jewelled drawer knob

1 Stick one edge of a batten (furring strip) to the long edge of the other to form a right angle. Hammer in a few panel pins (brads) to secure it. Divide the length into equal sections and paint them alternately black and white.

2 Drill, then screw through the holes in the bead fixing strip to secure it underneath the pelmet.

3 Drill, insert wall plugs (plastic anchors) and screw the pelmet in place. Use a spirit level to check the position after attaching one side. Hang the lengths of beads, in a pattern or at random, along the fixing strip.

4 Drill a hole, insert a wallplug and screw in the drawer knob in position – level with the base of the window if it is a small one, or halfway down if you have got a larger window.

MAD HATTER

IF YOU HAVE EVER felt like going right over the top with your home decorating, milliner's velvet must be the curtain (drape) choice for you! Milliner's velvet comes in gorgeous colours and it is great to work with. It is backed with paper and folds into the biggest cabbage roses and most luscious drapes imaginable. A window treatment such as this is definitely not for those of a shy and retiring disposition!

YOU WILL NEED

wooden batten (furring strip), window width plus 10cm (4in) either side

spirit level

drill

wall plugs (plastic anchors) and screws

screwdriver

milliner's velvet in dark green and pink

scissors

staple gun

tape measure

2 or more artificial cabbages on wire stems

1 Screw the batten (furring strip) above the window. Cut two pieces of green velvet to length and staple them to the batten in pleats, meeting in the middle.

2 Cut two rectangular pieces of green velvet, roughly 1½ times the width of the window. Bunch them up and staple them across the top. Scrunch the pink velvet into three large roses and staple to the top of the pelmet.

3 Staple the stems of the wire cabbages to the walls on either side of the windows. Roll the curtains (drapes) into twists and tuck behind the cabbages. Pull the cabbages in front of the curtains and staple in place.

HANGING AROUND

MAKE THE PRETTIEST of chandelier-hangings with simple deciduous twigs such as apple or pear branches. Select a few branches with gnarled, interesting shapes and bind them together to make a pleasing structure, then hang the finished chandelier in the centre of a window suspended from a length of gold cord. Trim the branches with eye-catching trinkets such as crystal droplets and tiny pearls, all fixed with the finest of gold twine. This project would also look stunning hanging from a ceiling rose or as a wall decoration.

YOU WILL NEED

2–3 apple or pear tree branches

fine gold wire

scissors

gold cord

crystal droplets

gold beading wire

small pearls

gilded decorations

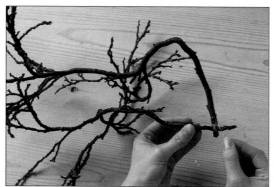

1 Take the branches and move them around until they form a pretty shape. Bind the branches together at the top with fine gold wire.

2 Attach a length of gold cord to hang the branches.

3 Thread crystal droplets on to gold wire. Make short strings of pearls.

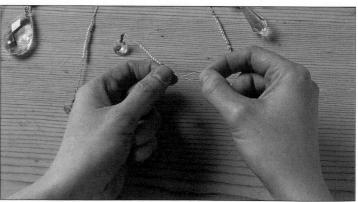

4 Wire the remaining decorations, then twist the wires to make hanging loops. Position the twig chandelier and hang on the jewels.

WALLS AND FLOORS

How often have you looked at your rather tired walls and thought about giving them a lift? How often have you looked at a jaded old carpet and wished you could afford an alternative?

If lack of time and money have stopped you before, we have the answers for you. Packed with really original and innovative ideas – and without a rag roller or stippling brush in sight – these stylish projects for wall and floor decoration will provide creative inspiration at little cost and in next to no time. Our fabulous treatments go far beyond simple paint effects and are totally original: from using photocopies for a graphic black and white effect, draping fabric to disguise an irregular surface, creating mosaics from broken china, or applying solid panels of colour to liven up a neutral space.

Applying simple paper cut-outs, designing your own stencils, hanging fabric – all these projects will provide a rich source of ideas to help you make the most of colours and textures, and are all illustrated with the help of simple, step-by-step photographs.

Floors are expensive to replace, so decisions have to be made carefully. All you need to follow our eye-catching projects is a clean, flat, level surface. If you are working on bare boards, check that they are securely fixed to their joists. Sand boards down with coarse abrasive paper – or hire a sanding machine – before commencing work.

We have up-to-the-minute ideas for every type of floor in your house – laying carpet tiles to resemble a board game, or creating a marbled-effect or stencilled floor.

Opposite: There are lots of ways to treat walls and floors, with geometric patterns, and interesting details that won't put a dent in your pocket.

PARCHMENT PAPER ART

THERE IS SUCH AN INTERESTING VARIETY of textured and coloured papers available from ordinary stationery stores as well as specialist art and craft suppliers that it is easy to find the right basic ingredients to make simple but extremely effective pictures, without being skilled at painting. Choose your colour combination and then make slits in the background paper, through which to weave the contrasting colours. These contrasting papers don't need to be clean-cut; in fact, tearing their edges actually enhances the finished look.

YOU WILL NEED

parchment paper sheets
coloured paper sheets
scrap paper
pencil
metal ruler
craft knife
self-healing cutting mat

1 Decide on the most interesting combination of papers. Use ordinary scrap paper to plan your design first before cutting the parchment.

2 Draw lines on the scrap paper where you want the slits to be.

3 Laying the paper on the cutting mat, cut these slits carefully with the craft knife.

4 Weave paper through the slits. When you are happy with the design, rework using parchment.

COLOURED STRING

THE IDEA OF DECORATING a wall with coloured string wound around tacks might evoke thoughts of nursery-school crafts; but it's surprising what wonderfully graphic patterns and eye-catching designs you can achieve with this simple technique. Set out a grid of tacks on the wall – substitute picture tacks if the wall won't take ordinary ones – and then you are set to create any design you want. Just wind the string around tightly and evenly, either running the decoration across a wall from side to side or using it to make interesting borders.

YOU WILL NEED

spirit level

straight edge

pencil

tacks

tack hammer

emulsion (latex) paint to match
existing wall colour

paintbrush

coloured string

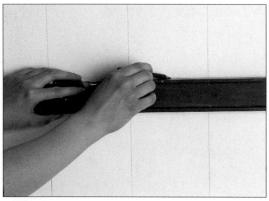

1 Lightly draw a grid on the wall, using the spirit level, straight edge and pencil.

2 Knock in the tacks to the same depth at all the cross points of the grid and all around the outside edges.

3 Paint out the pencil lines with emulsion (latex) paint in the existing wall colour.

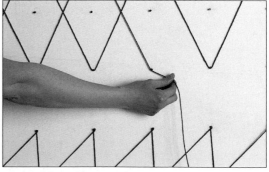

4 Arrange the string. Either buy coloured string or dip plain string in coloured paint to get exactly the colours you want. Wind the string tightly around the tacks, and start and finish with neat loops.

PANELS AND STAMP MOTIF

BRING LARGE AREAS OF DECORATION to a wall with these easy panels. Painting or dragging panels over a base coat quickly gives interest to large expanses of wall. It's a good idea to connect the panel and wall area outside visually with a simple motif. This could be a strong modern shape, wavy lines or even flowers. The colour of the walls and the style of the motif give scope for a wide range of different looks from the same basic treatment and, of course, you can vary the size of the panel to fit the shape and dimensions of the room.

YOU WILL NEED

emulsion (latex) paint in cream, white and black

paint roller

paint-mixing tray

spirit level

straight edge

pencil

masking tape

dragging brush

scrap paper

scissors

high-density foam

glue

craft knife

tape measure

old plate

small roller

1 Give the wall a base coat of cream emulsion (latex) paint. Using the spirit level and straight edge, draw the panels on the wall when it is dry.

2 Mask off the outer edge of the panels with masking tape. Drag white emulsion paint over the base coat.

3 Design the motif on paper. Stick the motif to the foam. With the craft knife, cut out the unwanted areas of the design to leave a raised stamp.

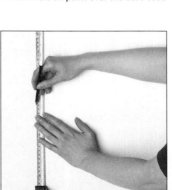

4 Decide on the spacing of the stamps and lightly mark the positions on the wall.

5 Put some black paint on to the plate and evenly coat the small roller. Roll the paint on to the stamp. Stamp the design in the marked positions.

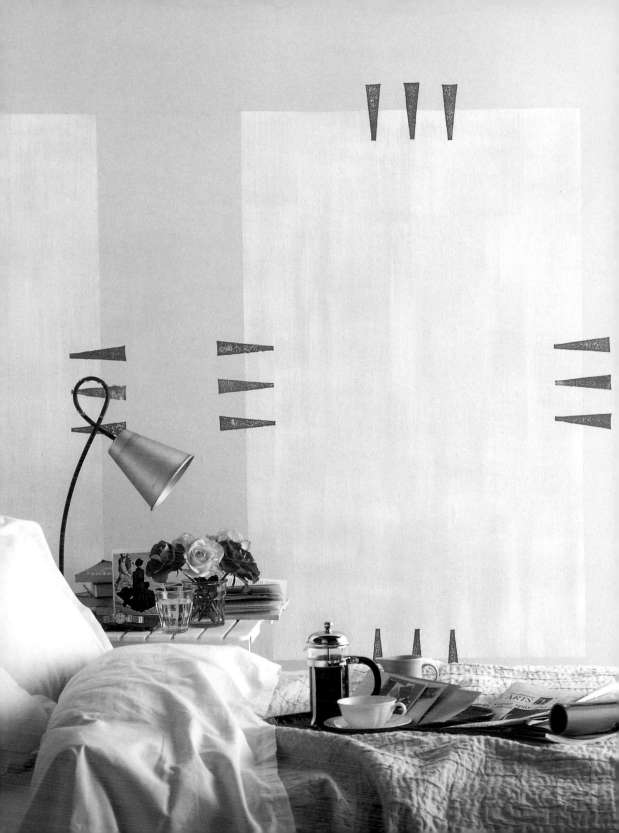

PUNCHED TIN WALL

PUNCHED TIN DESIGNS are surprisingly interesting and effective. They are a traditional technique found in folk-art interiors, but in this context they are often kept to quite small areas. However, there's no reason why punched tin can't be used over a much larger area, where it will look much more dramatic and exciting. You will need to frame the tin in some way, so it makes sense to put it above a dado rail; it could be bordered at the top by a picture rail. Another idea would be to enclose it within mouldings to form a series of matching panels on the wall.

YOU WILL NEED

scrap paper
pencil
thin tin sheet
metal file
long metal ruler
chinagraph pencil
metal punch
tack hammer
wood offcut
drill, with metal and masonry bits
spirit level
straight edge
wall plugs (plastic anchors)
dome-headed screws
screwdriver
clear varnish or lacquer
varnish brush

1 Design and draw the pattern to scale on paper first. Use a metal file to smooth any rough edges on the metal sheet. Draw the pattern to size on the reverse side of the metal sheet using a chinagraph pencil.

2 Practise on a spare scrap of metal to get a feel for how hard you need to punch. Punch out the pattern. Put a piece of wood behind the tin to protect your work surface. Drill holes in the corners of the metal sheet.

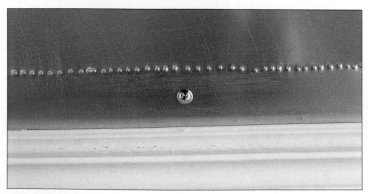

3 Using a spirit level and straight edge, draw accurate horizontal guidelines on the wall to indicate the position of the metal sheet. Drill holes in the wall where the corners will be. Insert wall plugs (plastic anchors) in the holes. Screw the metal sheet securely in position on the wall.

4 Finish with a protective coat of varnish or lacquer.

FABRIC WALL

NO SPECIAL SEWING SKILLS are needed to achieve this dramatic wall treatment. Draping fabric on a wall is a good way to disguise lumps and bumps and add a lot of interest for little effort. When you have a modern fabric design, however, such as this eye-catching blanket, it may not seem appropriate to drape it on the wall in baroque folds. Instead, create a contemporary look by pulling it as taut as possible with coloured string at the corners and middle of the fabric.

YOU WILL NEED

tape measure
fabric or blanket
pencil
drill, with masonry bit
wall plugs (plastic anchors)
screw eyelets
coloured string
matching strong cotton
thread

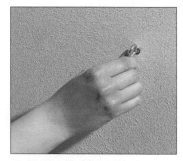

1 Measure the fabric or blanket and mark the positions for the screw eyelets on the wall, bearing in mind that you want the fabric to be pulled taut. Drill and insert wall plugs (plastic anchors) at the pencil marks. Screw the eyelets into the wall.

2 Wrap lengths of string tightly around the corners of the fabric and around a small pinch of fabric in the middle of the two long edges.

3 Feed the strings through the eyelets, pull them tight and secure them by looping the string back on itself and binding it with cotton, for a neat finish.

BROWN PAPER PANELLING

BROWN WRAPPING PAPER has its own characteristic colour and texture, which look quite wonderful on walls. You can buy it on large rolls, which make papering under a dado rail simplicity itself. Here, the brown paper has been combined with gum arabic adhesive tape for an unusual and elegant interpretation of a classic interior look. You could also add a simple skirting (base) board, using 5 × 2.5cm (2 × 1in) timber.

YOU WILL NEED

brown wrapping paper
wallpaper paste
pasting brush
plumb line
pencil
straight edge
paintbrush
gum arabic adhesive
paper roll
spirit level
black beading
glue gun and glue sticks

1 Stick the brown wrapping paper, matt (flat) side inwards, to the wall. Use wallpaper paste, as for wallpaper.

2 Use a plumb line and straight edge to mark vertical guidelines for the stripes on the brown paper. With a paintbrush, wet the wall in a stripe the width of the gum arabic tape and stick the tape down. Make sure you cover up all the guidelines.

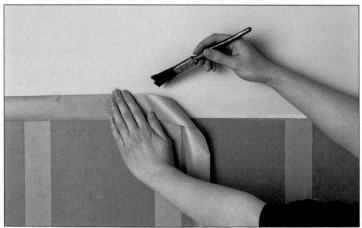

3 Use a spirit level and straight edge to draw a horizontal guideline for the under-dado border. Stick the tape in place in the same way.

4 Attach the beading along the top of the border, using the glue gun.

CORK-STAMPED FLOOR

THIS PRETTY STAMP has been made from seven wine bottle corks. They have been taped together in a daisy shaped bundle and the pattern shapes are cut from the surface of the cork bundle with a scalpel. Dense cork like this is a good material to carve into, being both soft and very smooth. Use the stamp on dust-free sanded wood, or on cork tiles with a dark woodstain. Allow it to stand and soak up the stain for ten minutes then blot it on kitchen paper before you begin printing. Use the paper strips to ensure that the pattern is an even distance from the wall.

YOU WILL NEED

7 wine bottle corks
wood glue or PVA (white) glue
strong adhesive tape
felt-tipped pen
scalpel
2 paper strips of equal width
dark woodstain
bowl
kitchen paper

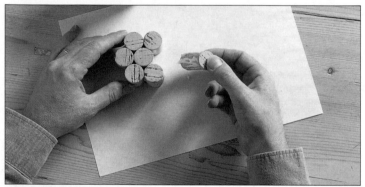

1 Glue the corks in a daisy formation, standing the ends flat on a piece of paper. This will provide a level printing surface. Bind the corks together with strong adhesive tape once the glue has become tacky.

2 Draw the pattern onto the cork surface with a felt-tipped pen. Cut out the background pieces with a scalpel.

3 Start by making one stamp at each corner, placing the paper spacing strips against the skirting (base) boards.

4 Move the strips along the straight skirting (base) board section and stamp a motif halfway between the first two. Stamp a row of evenly spaced motifs between the existing prints. Continue to stamp a border all round the room.

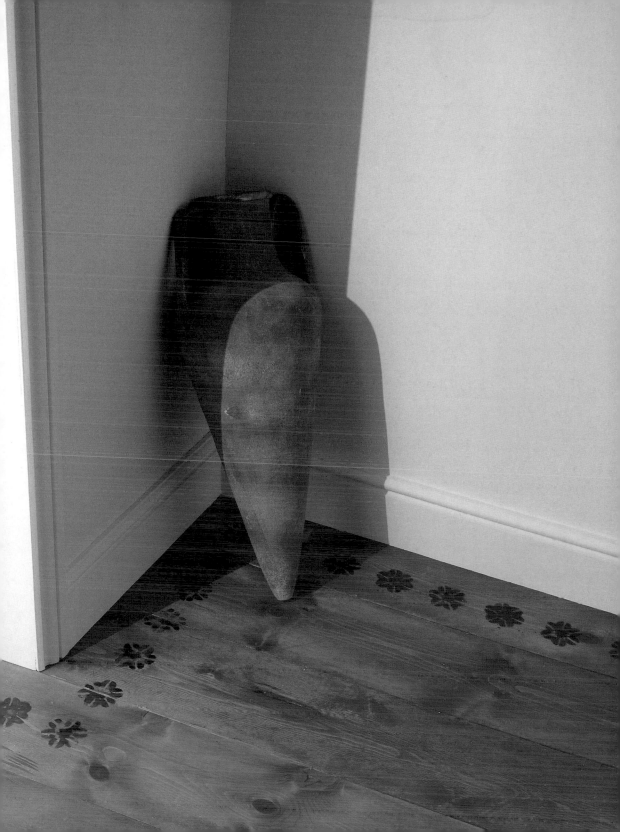

FAKE ANIMAL-SKIN RUG

GIVING A NEW MEANING to the cliché of a baby on a sheepskin rug, this fun idea could be scaled up for a full-size rug. Rather than making a classical bear-, tiger- or lion-skin rug, be more tongue-in-cheek, with shapes such as prehistoric animals or farm animals. Fake furs now come in a range of wonderfully bright colours, so you could take the concept even further from reality; mix up shapes and patterns.

1 Draw a line down the middle of the paper, then draw half the bear shape on one side. Fold in half along the line and cut out the shape.

2 Enlarge the paper pattern to size then pin it to your fur fabric.

3 Cut your shape out and then cut the shape out again from the felt, using pinking shears. Include a 6cm (2½in) allowance all round.

4 Stick the wrong side of the fur shape to the right side of the felt shape with the hemming strip, or machine or slip-stitch the two fabrics together.

FAUX-SOAPSTONE FLOOR

BLACK CORK TILES covering the whole floor in this room were too severe, but when the middle section of the room was treated to this wonderful soapstone effect, they became an important part of the overall grand gesture. The cork tiles in the centre were replaced with a large piece of MDF (medium-density fiberboard), to which a maze pattern was applied. This could simply have been painted on to MDF as a two-dimensional effect, but here the surface has been enhanced by routing the maze pattern (take it to a local joiner; routing really isn't for the inexperienced) and then painted to create a soapstone effect. You could also imitate slate, by using a wave formation and the black leading that was used in the nineteenth century for cleaning cast-iron fireplaces and grates (available from specialist suppliers). Sand or prepare your floor before beginning.

YOU WILL NEED

paper

pencil

MDF (medium-density fiberboard) sheet

plastic wood or wood filler,
if necessary

fine-grade sandpaper

matt emulsion (latex) paint: white,
dark grey and mid-grey

paintbrushes

wax candle

scraper

softening brush

matt (flat) varnish

1 On a new floor, plan your design on paper, using this picture as a guide. Draw it on to the sheet of MDF (medium density fiberboard). Take it to a joiner to be routed and ask him to fix it in place on your floor. On an existing floor, draw the maze on the floor and ask a joiner to do the routing in situ.

2 Fill any damage with plastic wood or wood filler, following the manufacturer's instructions. Don't try to achieve a perfectly flush surface at this stage. Leave to dry.

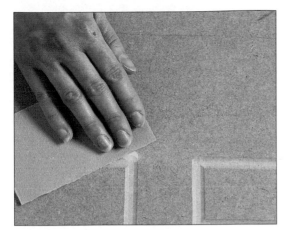

3 When dry, gently sand until you have a level surface.

4 Paint the whole surface white and allow it to dry.

5 Paint over the whole surface of the floor in dark grey.

6 Using a candle, apply a generous coating of wax with circular movements to the surface of the floor.

7 Take off most of the candle wax, using a scraper.

8 Follow this with a coat of mid-grey emulsion (latex) paint. ➤

9 Apply another coat of wax. Take off the wax with the scraper.

10 Apply white paint with a dry softening brush, to soften the whole effect. Seal with matt (flat) varnish. If you are surrounding the MDF with cork tiles, lay them at the end and butt up to the edges neatly.

RUBBER MATS

AVAILABLE FROM RUBBER MANUFACTURERS, this safety matting is valued for its non-slip and protective qualities, and since it is waterproof, it is particularly useful in, say, a shower room. Rubber matting doesn't fray when cut and will happily absorb any lumps or strange joins in a floor. Clean and seal the matting with a silicone spray polish, then fix it in place using any rubber contact adhesive. Make sure your floor is sanded, or lay an MDF (medium-density fiberboard) layer underneath before starting.

YOU WILL NEED

2 types of rubber safety mat
tape measure
metal rule or straight edge
craft knife
Pirelli rubber tiles in different patterns
rubber contact adhesive
WD-40 or silicone spray

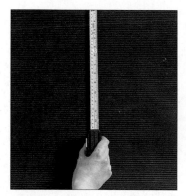

1 Measure the floor and the rubber matting and carefully trim the matting to size.

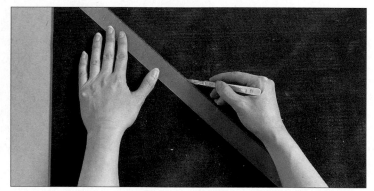

2 For the corners, cut four squares. Divide these diagonally and make four squares by placing two triangles together, with the grooves running across and top to bottom. Position these and the runners around the edge of the room.

3 Cut pieces from the other matting to fit the central section. Cut the tiles into squares, then cut holes in the mat at regular intervals to take the squares.

4 Secure all the pieces with rubber adhesive, applied to both surfaces. Spray with WD-40 or silicone spray.

CHECKED FLOOR MATS

FLOOR MATS ARE EASILY available, extremely cheap and particularly useful as you can usually cut them without their edges fraying. They are manufactured in many finishes, some even incorporating words, symbols or pictures, and all are produced in manageable rectangles. When these heavily textured grey polypropylene mats are arranged with the pile alternately running in different directions, a delightful chequer-board effect is achieved. For a different style of room, you could create a less subtle or even thoroughly funky effect by combining two or more colours. Make sure your floor surface is smooth before starting.

YOU WILL NEED

string

white crayon or chalk

tape measure

grey polypropylene floor mats

long metal ruler or straight edge

craft knife

notched spreader

floor adhesive

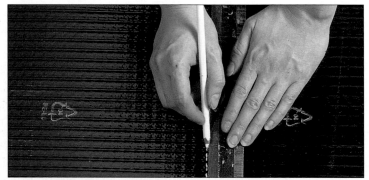

1 Use strings stretched across to find the room's centre and mark with a cross. If possible, link the opposite pairs of walls. Measure the floor and work out how many floor mats you will need. Mark the cuts with a white crayon or chalk on the reverse of the floor mats.

2 If the mats are of carpet quality, first score along the lines before cutting them with the craft knife. Then cut the mats to size.

3 Using a notched spreader, apply floor adhesive to the floor.

4 Starting at the centre, carefully lay the mats in position, remembering that, for the chequerboard effect shown here, you need to alternate the weaves.

PHOTOCOPY MONTAGE

THIS EFFECT IS REMINISCENT of the wonderful painted floors of the great European palaces. Few of us can afford to commission frescoes and floor painting, but we might still aspire to a home decorated in a style fit for Marie Antoinette. Using photocopied images on a freshly prepared floor can turn these dreams into reality. Choose any theme: the photograph shows a composition of landscapes, but architectural drawings, classical motifs, such as columns, garden urns and statues, or even still-lives of fruit or vegetables could be made into successful montages. Using the same techniques, you could create a totally modern feeling using colour photocopies of, say, flower heads; instead of stencilling the borders, add freehand leaves and scrolls if you are skilled.

YOU WILL NEED

cream and green eggshell emulsion (latex) paint

paintbrushes

photocopied images

long metal ruler

craft knife

self-healing cutting mat

artist's watercolour or acrylic paints

gum arabic tape (optional)

pencil

masking tape

acetate sheet

bleed-proof paper (such as tracing paper)

green stencil paint

stencil brush

wallpaper paste

matt (flat) varnish

1 Starting with a well-prepared hardboard or marine-plywood floor, paint on an undercoat of cream eggshell paint, followed by a top coat. Allow to dry completely.

2 Experiment with images in different sizes and settle on an arrangement that looks good on your floor. Trim the images so that you are left with just the pictures.

3 If your images are black and white, use watercolour or acrylic paints to put soft washes of colour over the prints. You may need to stretch the paper, using gum arabic tape, depending on the quality of the paper (test a small area first).

4 Arrange the images on the floor and plan and draw out the borders. Mask off the boxes for the images with masking tape. Paint between the lines of masking tape with green eggshell paint. When the paint is almost dry, gently peel off the masking tape.

5 Make the stencil from the acetate sheet. Apply the stencil to the floor with masking tape and stipple with green paint. Glue the photocopies to the floor with wallpaper paste and then varnish several times.

STENCILLED HARDBOARD

DAMAGED OR IRREGULAR FLOORS are frequently covered in hardboard and you may feel that this smooth, hard surface is especially in keeping if you have adopted a modernist, minimalist approach to decorating. If you discover hard-board in mint condition, in most instances it is not wise to lift it, as it is probably hiding some horror below. However, with several coats of varnish, hardboard has a natural patina of its own, which is very appealing and works as a neutral background as well as a wooden floor does. Introduce additional interest by using stencils, which here mimic a rather fifties-style rug, although the brown hardboard would suit different colours. The contrast of black or white works well; choose a bold, non-figurative pattern.

YOU WILL NEED

metal ruler or straight edge

pencil

paper

black water-based paint

paintbrushes

masking tape

self-healing cutting mat

acetate sheet

craft knife

pin

stencil brush

lint-free cloth or fine-grade abrasive paper (optional)

eraser

gloss varnish

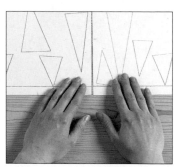

1 Draw the border motif to the desired size on paper.

2 Photocopy the design and make sure that the repeat works, by placing several sheets together.

3 Work out a right-angled section for the corners. Make sure it ties in neatly with the repeat on both sides.

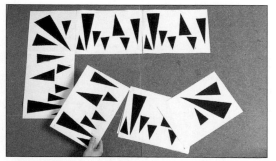

4 Black in the design and photocopy it. Lay the copies around the floor, to ensure that your design will fit pleasingly, and experiment until you have an effect you are happy with.

5 With a pencil, mark the outer edge of your border on the floor (in the photograph, this is about 13cm (5½in) from the edge of the room).

6 Draw out pencil guidelines for your border all round the room.

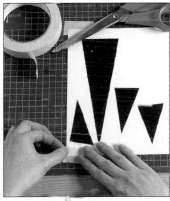

7 Stick one of the photocopies, with masking tape, to the cutting mat. Tape the acetate sheet over it.

8 Using the steel ruler and holding the knife at an angle, carefully cut out the stencil. To help get neat, sharp corners, make a pin prick just at the corner first; this also helps to prevent you from cutting too far.

9 With masking tape, attach the stencil to the hardboard, lining it up carefully with your guidelines.

10 Using a stencil brush, stipple in the neat black triangles, making sure that the paint is very dry so that it does not seep under the stencil. ➤

11 Lift up the stencil and re-position it for the next section. Remember to make sure the underside of the stencil is clear of paint. If you need to mask certain areas of the stencil so that you continue the repeat when working the corners, do this with a piece of paper held firmly in place with masking tape.

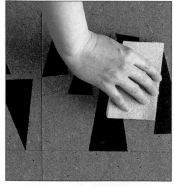

12 If you make a mistake or smudge the stencilling, rub it clean with a damp cloth or, if the surface is more porous, very gently sand away the paint when dry. Finally, remove the guidelines with an eraser and seal the floor with at least two coats of varnish.

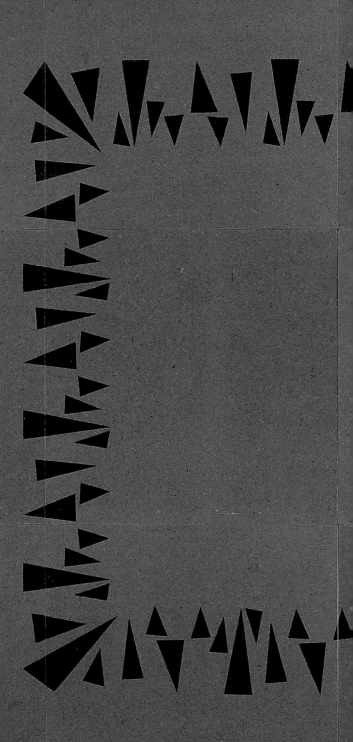

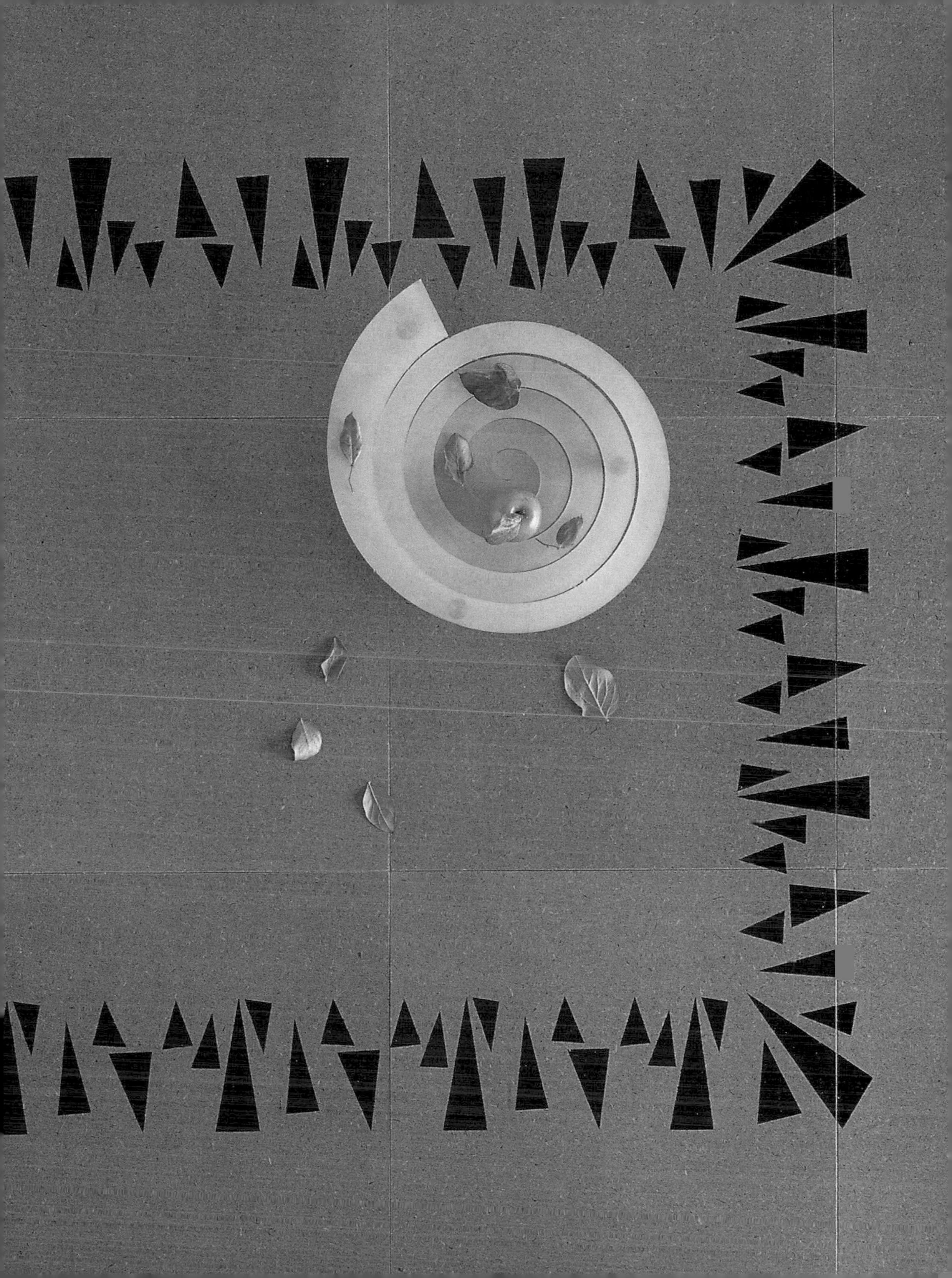

POP-ART FLOOR

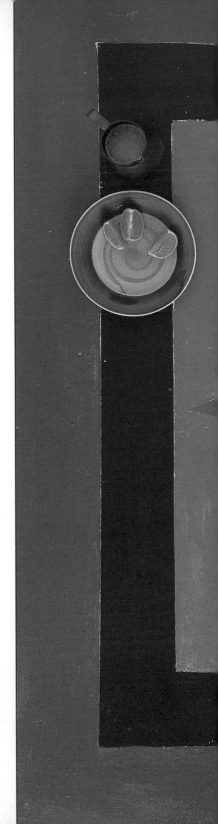

MUCH INSPIRATION for interior decoration is to be gleaned from the pop artists of this century, with their whimsical approach to art. These naïve shapes painted on a large surface make use of the pop-art conventions of boldness and simplicity, with multiple repetitions of strong images rather than intricate busyness. Dramatically discordant colours – orange and shocking pink in this case – are the most appropriate. This idea works best on a concrete floor.

YOU WILL NEED

white matt (flat) emulsion (latex) paint

paint roller

tape measure

pencil

masking tape

blue, red, shocking pink and orange matt (flat) emulsion (latex) paint

PVA (white) glue or acrylic varnish

1 Give the floor two coats of white paint, to ensure that the colours of the design ring bright and true.

2 Measure and draw out your design. Mask off the border, which needs to be crisply painted. Do the same along the outside of the star.

3 Paint the star, then fill in the area inside the border; masking may not be necessary as a little white space between the star and border and background makes it look as though silk-screening has been used – a technique common in pop art. Seal with diluted PVA (white) glue or acrylic varnish.

STUDDED FLOOR

CREATE THE APPEARANCE of the deck of a battleship in your bathroom, with studs positioned at regular intervals across the floor and painted in battleship grey. Alternatively, you could leave the wood natural and studs unpainted. The broad silver studs used here are called "domes of silence", because they are designed to fit under chair legs to help them glide smoothly across the floor without making a noise. However, you can choose any studs, as long as they are sturdy enough to withstand the traffic on the floor and they are not sharp or liable to damage shoes or furniture. Sand the floor carefully before commencing.

YOU WILL NEED
pencil
steel ruler or straight edge
studs or "domes of silence"
eraser
acrylic varnish (optional)
paintbrush (optional)
tack hammer
cloth, softwood block or
carpet scrap
wood glue (optional)

1 Decide on the spacing and pattern of the studs or domes. Draw diagonal grid lines in accordance with your design and mark with a little cross where each stud is to go.

2 Rub out all markings, except the crosses. If necessary, apply a couple of coats of acrylic varnish to the whole floor, to seal the wood.

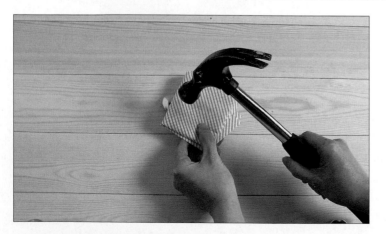

3 Using a hammer and something soft, such as a folded cloth or softwood block, to prevent damage to the studs, hammer them in over the crosses. If you use "domes of silence", which have relatively shallow teeth, hammer them in only half way to start with. Remove the domes, apply a little wood glue and then replace them and hammer them in all the way. This technique can be used on any decorative wooden floor.

BEDS AND BEDDING

You can achieve instant soft-furnishing style with minimum effort with the help of these sumptuous ideas. In the bedroom, let your personal style have a free rein and really go to town with our instant and dramatic bed-dressing effects.

We also show you how to fill the whole house with stylish and original cushions. If you don't know a four-poster from a half-tester, or have always fancied a futon but didn't know quite what to put on it, then we have the answers for you.

This is spontaneous and creative interior design for people with more imagination than skill who want the opportunity to try something a little unusual. There are lots of ideas for dressing up basic beds and none of the projects require advanced home improvement or soft-furnishing skills – but they do promise dramatic transformations. Tools and special materials have been kept to a minimum – the only two indispensable items are a staple gun and a glue gun. These provide freedom from conventional methods of construction, fixing and draping, and allow you to achieve the impossible – and keep it there. Bed dressing can mean just what the name suggests – giving a jaded divan a new set of covers – or making a bedhead, hanging up drapes or even building a four-poster frame, which isn't as daunting as it sounds! Follow our fabulous ideas with cushions to liven up a sofa or armchair or to throw them over your newly revamped bed. Whichever project you choose to do, simply follow the clear and easy step-by-step instructions and transform your chosen object for a limited outlay.

Opposite: In the privacy of your own boudoir you can be as post-modern and witty as you like, mixing spots and stripes, animal prints or tartans, to your heart's content.

LOVELY LINENS

PRETTY UP PERFECTLY PLAIN LINENS with splashes of vibrant colour. To add definition, run strips of Ric-rac edging around; for frilliness, buy broderie anglaise and sew this on to the pillowcase. You could weave tapestry wool through the broderie in place of ribbon, to add colour. Alternatively, look for linens which have a fine-holed edging and thread through this with fine tapestry wool. To complement the edges, add tiny decorative crosses to buttons sewn on to the pillowcase. A more time-consuming, but extremely effective decoration is made by scalloping the edge of a sheet and decorating with tapestry wool.

YOU WILL NEED

paper

pencil

cardboard

scissors

single or double white sheet

sewing machine

white sewing thread

small, sharp-pointed scissors

red tapestry wool

tapestry needle

plain pillowcase

3m (3 yards) broderie anglaise

dressmaker's pins

needle and tacking thread

buttoned pillowcase, with fine-holed decorative edge

glue gun and glue sticks

decorative red buttons

small cushion, with frilled-edge and centre-opening cover

1 Cut out a cardboard template for the sheet edging. Draw around it then machine satin stitch over the line. Cut along outside the sewn line.

2 Cut lengths of coloured tapestry wool and knot the ends. Sew the lengths of wool through the sheet leaving the long ends as decoration.

3 Edge the plain pillowcase with broderie anglaise. Then use a tapestry needle to thread coloured yarn through the holes in the lace. You can also use this technique to decorate pillowcases with fine-holed decorative edging.

4 You can liven up plain buttons on a pillowcase by using a glue gun to apply decorative coloured buttons on top. Decorate round cloth buttons by making neat cross-stitches over them with tapestry wool.

TRIMMED CUSHIONS

DRESS UP A PILE OF PLAIN CUSHIONS and transform the atmosphere of your bedroom in the space of an afternoon. The embellishments used here are dressmaker's trimmings, which are available in a wide range of materials, shapes, colours and sizes. Upholstery and soft-furnishing trimmings tend to be more expensive and the range is limited, so it is well worth looking out for a dressmaking specialist. Market stallholders often carry haberdashery (notions) offcuts, with short lengths of fringing, beading, braids and lace which are ideal for embellishing cushions. Tie tassels and cord around the ends of a bolster cushion, for example, or embellish a plain black cushion with an unusual motif.

YOU WILL NEED

3 cushions: 2 velvet
and 1 silk

fringing

needle and matching threads

pencil

pair of compasses

thin card

scissors

pins

black lace and fringing

black bobble trimmings

tape measure

1 For the first cushion, slip-stitch the ends of a length of fringing, so that it doesn't unravel.

2 Cut a quarter circle from thin card and place it on the cushion as a guide for the curve of the fringing. Slip-stitch along the edge of the fringing using a matching thread.

3 For the second cushion, pin three or four parallel rows of black lace and fringing on to a yellow-ochre velvet cushion.

4 Slip-stitch the trimmings in place with matching thread.

5 For the third cushion stitch two rows of black bobble trim on to an orange silk cushion. Pin one row then use a tape measure to align the second.

VICTORIAN LACE

NOTHING LOOKS MORE ROMANTIC and feminine than a brass bed covered with snowy white, lace-trimmed bed linen. Make layers of scallops and frills on sheets, bolsters, pillows and bedcovers. Start by buying a good cotton duvet cover with a scalloped edge. Trawl second-hand shops and flea markets for lace-edged tablecloths, dressing table runners, tray cloths and curtain (drape) panels. Look out for old white cotton sheets with embroidered edges to add interest.

YOU WILL NEED

plain white bed linen

selection of lacy tablecloths, tray cloths, mats, chair backs or dressing table runners

dressmaking pins

iron

iron-on hemming tape or needle and white thread

bolsters

rubber bands

white ribbon or raffia

1 Select suitably sized lace additions to make central panels or corner details on the pillow-cases and duvet cover. Pin them in position.

2 Use iron-on hemming tape and an iron to bond the two layers together, or slip-stitch them in place.

3 Roll the bolster up in a lace-edged tablecloth and bunch up the ends, securing them with rubber bands. Tie ribbon or raffia over the gathered ends and drape the lace edging.

CANOPIED BED

A SIMPLE DRAPED CANOPY is a great way to define and decorate a sleeping area without completely enclosing it. The muslin is draped over a wooden plant support. The natural rustic character of the twigs combines very well with the unfussy appearance of unbleached muslin (cheesecloth). Muslin is inexpensive, so buy more than you need – any extra will make a pretty cascade at the end of the bed.

YOU WILL NEED

at least 12m (12 yd)
unbleached muslin (cheesecloth)

iron-on hemming tape

iron

rustic plant support

rubber bands

twine

scissors

ceiling hook

1 Turn up a hem at each end of the fabric and use iron-on hemming tape to make a neat hem. Find the middle of the fabric length, bunch it up and wrap around the narrow end of the plant support at this point.

2 Pull the fabric into a pleasing shape, then secure it with rubber bands. Wind the twine to cover the rubber bands and decorate the fabric.

3 Attach a ceiling hook centrally above the bed. Hang the plant support from it. Drape the fabric either side of the support and over the bed ends.

BEACH MAT BED

A SIMPLE FOUR-POSTER FRAME can be built to fit around an existing base and mattress. Only basic carpentry skills are required, as the timber can be cut to size when you buy it, and just needs drilling and screwing together. The wood used here is basic construction timber that has been left in its natural state, but you could colour it with wood stain or paint it to co-ordinate with the decor of the bedroom. Grass beach mats are perfect for hanging around the four-poster, especially if your room is decorated with natural fabrics and earth colours. The loosely stitched grass strips allow a soothing, soft golden light to filter through and the air to circulate.

YOU WILL NEED

grass beach mats

packet of brass paper fasteners

rough twine

scissors

odd-shaped shells, pebbles and driftwood

1 Fold one short edge of each beach mat over the top rail of the four-poster frame. Push paper fasteners through the mats just below the rail and open out the prongs. Use four fasteners along the top of each beach mat.

2 The mats are edged with different coloured tape that makes fine stripes around the bed. Arrange the mats to make the most of this striping.

3 Decide how many blinds you want to tie up – maybe all, or just a select few. You will need about 1 m (1 yd) of rough twine for each mat to be rolled up. Cut the lengths required and tie some shells, pebbles and bits of driftwood randomly along the length and at each end of the twine.

4 Dangle the ties over the top rail and use them to hold back the rolled-up blinds.

ROMANTIC NETTING

EVEN IF YOU HAVE NO practical need for mosquito netting, the light and airy beauty of this project makes it ideal for the bedrooms of urban romantics who dream of being in the Punjab or on the Serengeti plains. Netting like this can be bought from camping stores and comes complete with a spoked wooden coronet that opens like a fan to support it. Here, the spokes have then been decorated with dangling glass ornaments to make the netting look more exotic than utilitarian. Plain white netting is very appealing, but it can also be dyed in any pale colour.

YOU WILL NEED

mosquito netting, with coronet and fixings

dangling glass ornaments and earrings

fine wire

long-nosed pliers

ceiling hook

1 Fan out the spokes of the wooden coronet and fit them into the channels of the netting.

2 Thread assorted glass ornaments, beads and earrings on to lengths of fine wire to make decorative pendants.

3 Thread the wire ends through the netting at the bottom of the spokes. Use long-nosed pliers to twist the ends together to secure them.

4 Attach the ring and rope provided to the centre of the coronet. Hang the net from a ceiling hook above the bed.

BLACK AND WHITE PRINTS

IMAGINE BEING ABLE to decorate soft furnishings with any image or picture of your choice. There is now a special transparent gel available which enables you to transfer black and white or colour images on to fabric. The image can then be sealed to make it resistant to wear and tear. By enlarging or reducing the images on a photocopier, you can obtain a selection of prints that will fit perfectly on to any item that you would like to decorate, such as cushions, pillows or even a quilt. You can use the same process to monogram your bed linen in royal style. However, because the image will be reversed once it is transferred, you will have to photocopy any lettering on to acetate first.

YOU WILL NEED

photocopies of chosen
images

scissors

plain-coloured cotton
cushion cover

iron

plastic carrier bag

image-transfer gel

paintbrush

soft cloth

sheet of acetate (optional)

1 Choose your images and make the required number of copies. Here, several copies of the same image are used to form a frame around the portrait.

2 Cut away all the excess paper, leaving only the images that you want to transfer.

3 To design the cushion cover, arrange the images on a flat surface. Experiment with spacing until you are happy with the design.

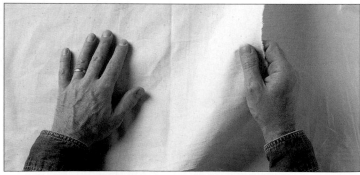

4 Pre-wash and iron the cushion cover. This is important because glazes used to stiffen fabrics may adversely affect the transfer process. Place the cover on a plastic carrier bag to protect your work surface.

5 Paint a thick layer of transfer gel on to the first photocopy, making sure that you have covered it completely.

6 Place the image face-down in position on the cushion cover and gently rub all over the back with a soft cloth. Leave the image in position.

7 Repeat steps 5 and 6 with all the images, ensuring that they are positioned accurately before you make contact with the fabric. Leave to transfer overnight.

8 Soak the cloth with clean water and then use the wet cloth to saturate the photocopy paper.

9 Keep the cloth wet and begin to rub away the paper, working from the centre outwards. The images will have transferred on to the fabric. When all the paper has been removed, leave the fabric to dry.

10 Apply a final fixing coat of the transfer gel to the prints and leave to dry completely. ➤

11 You can use the same process to monogram your bed linen. Photocopy the initials on to a sheet of acetate. Then turn the acetate over and photocopy from the acetate on to paper to reverse. Cut out the print.

12 Transfer the initials as described in steps 5 to 10. The transfer process will reverse the initials once more, so that they are now the right way round.

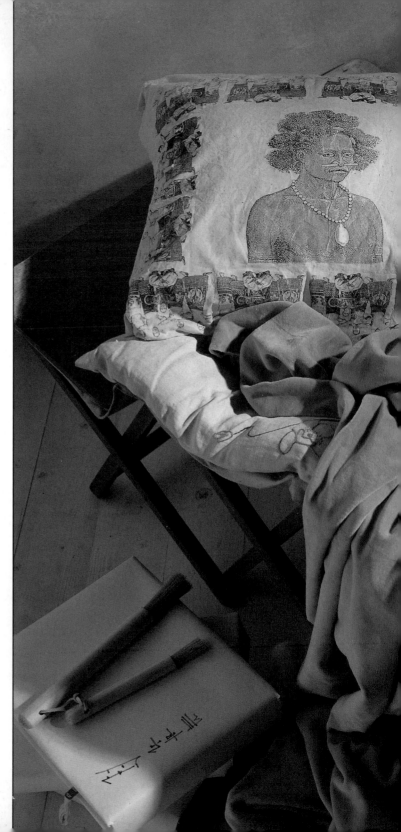

ANIMAL CUSHIONS

ANIMAL PRINTS HAVE NEVER BEEN more popular and the quality of fake fur now available is truly fantastic. It is also a delight to animal-lovers and the environmentally conscious. The distinctive boldness of the cowhide print chosen here makes great cushion covers. This low bed is draped with lengths of silky smooth velvet tiger- and leopard-skin fabric that spill over on to the floor, adding to the tactile, languorous atmosphere. This project doesn't have to be a permanent fixture, so bring out this special bedding for wild weekends – and it may bring out the animal in you!

YOU WILL NEED
card
scissors
button blanks
small pieces of black velvet
hemmed squares of cowhide print, 5cm (2in) smaller than the cushions
black velvet cushions
needle and thread
tiger- and leopard-skin fabrics

1 Cut a circle of card approximately 1 cm (½in) larger all round than the button blanks. Use the card pattern to cut circles of black velvet.

2 Cover the top of each button blank with a velvet circle, tucking in the edges so that they catch on to the spikes underneath.

3 Press the backing firmly in place to make neatly covered black velvet buttons.

4 Stitch a hemmed cowhide fabric square diagonally on each cushion. Sew a black button on to the centre, stitching through both the cowhide print and the black velvet cushion. Arrange the tiger- and leopard-skin fabrics over the bed.

DREAM TRELLIS

DRESS UP A PLAIN WALL behind a simple bed with a most unusual trellis headboard made from woven twigs and branches. The trellis is very lightweight and is easily fixed in place. Continue the theme with twig accessories, ranging from chairs to cache-pots, and complement the decor with crisply starched white sheets and pretty cushion covers. Country garden centres are always worth a visit, because trellis-work like this is handmade and producers often use local garden centres as outlets. Alternatively, you might like to try your own hand.

YOU WILL NEED

garden raffia

scissors

handmade twig trellis

masonry nails or
cavity wall fixtures

hammer

1 Divide the raffia into two bunches of approximately twelve strands each. Knot one end of each bunch.

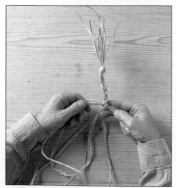

2 Plait the strands to make two braids about 10cm (4in) long.

3 Tie the plaits on to the trellis 25cm (10in) from each end. Attach the plaits to the wall above the bed, suspending the trellis behind the bed.

LOVE PILLOWS

MAKE SURE THE RIGHT message gets across by stencilling the word "love" on your pillows in both English and French, the archetypal language of romance! The type-face used is a favourite of graphic designers – Gill (bold) – chosen for its stylish simplicity and clarity. There is no doubt what is meant here. The word has been enlarged on a photocopier to 18cm (7in) long. You can adapt this idea for other messages that are completely personal and private, but if you have children, discretion may be a good idea. Choose colours that match your bedroom's overall scheme or that are your favourites. Fabric paints are available in a wide range of colours. Always wash and iron the fabric before stencilling to rid it of any glazes that could block the colour absorption.

1 Enlarge the templates to the required size. Spray the backs of the photocopies with spray adhesive and stick them on to the stencil card.

2 Cut out the letters on a cutting mat. The O, A and R need ties to retain the internal letter features, so draw them in "bridges" before you cut out.

3 Place a sheet of thin cardboard inside the pillow case, so that the colour does not bleed through to the other side.

4 Apply paint sparingly to letters. You can always build up colour later, but too much paint can cause problems. When dry, seal with a hot iron.

A E O L
M R U V

GINGHAM HEADBOARD

THIS HEADBOARD CONVERSION creates a fresh new style with added comfort. Gingham fabric always looks crisp and bright, so you will wake up bright-eyed and ready to face the day. It is available in both small and large checked patterns and in a wide variety of both bright and pastel colours. The gingham fabric is backed with quilter's wadding. Alternatively, you could use other fabrics to create a different sort of mood – a small floral print for a feminine, country cottage decor or a vibrant primary colour for a teenager's room, for example. The headboard should be rectangular in shape and can be solid or of a slatted or spindled type. Measure the width and height of the headboard, then double the height measurement so that the gingham fabric folds in half over the top.

YOU WILL NEED

iron-on quilter's wadding

dressmaker's scissors

iron

gingham fabric, width of the headboard × twice the height, plus seam allowance on all edges

iron-on hemming tape

needle and matching sewing thread

2 metres (2 yards) red ribbon

dressmaking pins

tape measure

1 Cut the wadding to the size of the headboard. Press one end of the gingham fabric on to the wadding. The other end will fold over the headboard back. Leave a large seam allowance all around the edge.

2 Fold the seams over and tuck the corners in neatly. Use iron-on hemming tape or a needle and thread to secure the edges. As the hems will be on the inside of the cover, they will not be visible.

3 To make the ties, cut the ribbon into 16 equal lengths.

4 Pin, then sew four ribbons, equally spaced, along the inside edges of each side of the cover. Fold the cover over the headboard and tie the ribbons in bows to finish.

CHINTZ HEADBOARD

GIVE YOUR PADDED HEADBOARD a new lease of life using old chintz curtains (drapes). The fabric improves with age as the colours fade and mellow, and it looks wonderful teamed with crisp white cotton, handmade quilts or plaid woollen blankets in a traditional bedroom. Use the very best section of pattern for the bedhead and tuck remaining lengths under the mattress to form a valance. If you prefer a more permanent valance, you could sew pleated lengths of the same chintz fabric around the edges of a fitted sheet.

YOU WILL NEED

pair of floral chintz curtains (drapes)

scissors

tape measure

headboard

pencil

staple gun and staples

1 Trim the curtains (drapes) to get rid of thick seams, curtain tape and bulky hems. Cut a strip of curtain long enough to fold over the front and on to the back of the headboard at the sides, top and bottom. Smooth it over the front of the headboard, then move to the back. Draw any curved corners on to the back of the fabric.

2 Cut notches in the fabric right up to the drawn line, so that the fabric will fit the curve without puckering. Staple each cut strip on to the headboard.

3 Pull down the top flap tautly and staple it on to the headboard.

4 Pull up the bottom flap tautly and staple it in place. Staple both side edges in the same way. Cut a panel of fabric to cover all the stapled edges on the back. Turn in the edges and staple the panel flat on to the backing board.

ENTWINED HEADBOARD

QUITE APART FROM BEING one of the most stylish looks around, rope wrapping is a real pleasure to do. All you need is a frame, which can be a junk-shop find or a home improvement structure made from construction timber. The wood is completely hidden by the coils of rope, so there is no need to prepare the surface in any way. Rope comes in many different twists and thicknesses, some more decorative than others. Some ropes are made from natural fibres and others, like the one used here, are synthetic. An advantage of synthetic rope is that the ends can be sealed by holding them over a flame to melt the fibres together.

YOU WILL NEED

rope

wooden-framed headboard

tape measure

pen

scissors or craft knife

cutting mat or thick cardboard

lighter or matches (optional)

glue gun and glue sticks

1 To calculate the length of rope needed to wrap each wooden post, first divide the height of the post by the thickness of the rope. Multiply this figure by the circumference of the post. Mark the rope at this point.

2 Cut the lengths of rope required to wrap all the posts. If you are using synthetic rope, seal the ends by holding them briefly over a flame. Use the glue gun to stick the end of the rope to the back of the first post to be wrapped.

3 Wrap the rope tightly around the post, keeping the coils as close together as possible. To maintain the tension, apply a few dabs of hot glue.

4 Cut short lengths of rope to cover gaps and another to cover loose ends and blobs of glue at the intersection. Glue the ends at the back of post.

5 Make sure that all the intersections are finished in the same way so that the symmetry is maintained. Finish off with rope decorations.

HAMMOCK QUILT

RECLINING IN A HAMMOCK may be the ultimate relaxation, but it is only really possible to lie back and enjoy the sway if you feel completely secure. So make quite sure that your wall fittings are sturdy and properly installed and that the wall itself is strong enough to take the strain. Use strong metal garage hooks with long screws and heavy-duty wall plugs (plastic anchors). Once the safety angle has been covered, you can then turn your attention to comfort and make this stylish and simple no-sew quilt to dress up your hammock and keep you cosy.

YOU WILL NEED

iron

2.5 m (2¾yd) iron-on wadding

5 m (5½yd) blue fabric

2.5 m (2¾yd) black cotton fabric

scissors

tape measure

iron-on hemming tape

5 m (5½yd) black iron-on mending tape

dressmaking pins

1 Iron the wadding to one half of the wrong side of the blue fabric. Then fold the other half over so that the wadding is sandwiched by the blue fabric. This will give the quilt some thickness. Next, cut the black fabric into four 14cm (5½in) wide strips to fit the quilt edges. Press a 1cm (½in) hem along the long edges. Iron each strip in half to make a long doubled strip 6cm (2¼in) wide. This will be used to border the blue cloth. Place a length of iron-on hemming tape along each edge of the blue fabric and enclose each edge with a doubled black border strip. Iron to bond the fabrics. Fold down the corners of the black edging to achieve a mitred effect. Turn the fabric over and repeat on the other side.

2 Cut twenty-four 20cm (8in) strips of iron-on mending tape and use the tape measure to position them on the quilt in four rows of three crosses.

3 Pin the crosses in place if required, then iron them in position.

TARTAN BEDHEAD

WOOLLEN TARTAN RUGS are comfort blankets, traditionally used on winter car journeys and picnics. The two rugs used in this project are doubled over, with their folded edges meeting in the middle. To complete the Highland hunting lodge atmosphere, the rugs are hung above the bedhead from a rough-hewn "branch".

YOU WILL NEED

2 matching tartan blankets
or rugs

tape measure

needle

thick contrasting thread

2.5cm (1in) wooden dowel
(slightly longer than the
bed width)

craft knife

fine-grade abrasive paper

cloth

shellac

2 iron pipe holders
(to fit 2.5cm (1in) pipe)

drill and wallplugs

screwdriver

kilt pins

1 Fold each blanket in half lengthways and pin together along the folded seam. Blanket stitch the outside edges, then stitch the blankets together along the folded edge. If you don't like sewing, hold the seams closed with three kilt pins.

2 Start decorating the wooden pole by roughly carving away both ends of the dowel with a craft knife. Sand the rough edges with abrasive paper. Use a cloth to rub shellac into the wood.

3 Screw the pipe holders to the wall. Fix the rail in place. Hang the blankets over the rail, with a 35cm (14in) overlap to make a pelmet, pinning it in place with kilt pins.

RENAISSANCE HEADBOARD

DRAMATIC EFFECTS HAVE BEEN used in this bedroom to create a distinctive atmosphere, with the large painting dominating the room. It's a good idea to visit a museum shop for the best range and quality of art posters – you are certain to find something for all tastes. You can apply a crackle glaze or antiquing varnish to the poster if you wish to add an authentically aged Renaissance look.

YOU WILL NEED

wallpaper paste

poster

MDF (medium-density fiberboard)
width of poster × height of poster
plus mattress tofloor measurement,
plus allowance for frame

paste brush

pencil

ruler

picture rail moulding (height
of poster × 2, plus width × 1)

mitring block

small saw

viridian green emulsion (latex) paint

paintbrushes

gold spray paint

fine-grade abrasive paper

glue gun and glue sticks

crackle-glaze varnish

red artist's oil colour

clean cloths

clear varnish

drill and fixtures to attach
MDF to bed frame (depending
on the type of bed)

1 Mix up the wallpaper paste. Mark the position of the poster on the MDF (medium-density fiberboard) and apply paste to that section. Smooth the poster on to the board. Any air bubbles should disappear as the glue dries.

2 Measure and mark the lengths of moulding for the frame. It goes along the top of the poster and down both sides to mattress height. Saw the corners on a mitring block. Paint a viridian green undercoat. Leave to dry.

3 Protect your work surface, then spray a coat of gold spray paint over the green. Leave to dry. Rub the frame with fine-grade abrasive paper, so that the gold is lifted on the highest ridges to reveal the green beneath. Do not overdo the sanding. Use a glue gun to stick the picture frame around the edge of the poster.

4 Paint the whole surface of the poster with crackle-glaze varnish, following the manufacturer's instructions. Leave the varnish to crackle. Use a cloth to rub artist's oil colour into the surface. Red is used here but any strong or dark colour will also work well. Rub the oil paint right into the cracks and cover the whole surface.

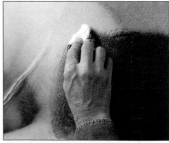

5 Rub the oil paint off the surface with a soft cloth. The colour will stay in the cracks. Apply several coats of clear varnish to the poster. When dry, attach the headboard to the bed frame, using the drill and fixtures.

CHAIRS AND TABLES

Tables and chairs are two of the most important elements in every home – they appear in most rooms and in many shapes and forms from the elegant and luxurious to the everyday and useful. Everyone needs somewhere to sit and something to eat off! As they usually grace communal spaces such as kitchens or living rooms, they can suffer more than other furniture from day to day living – from busy mealtimes, young children or family pets. They are also relatively quick to show wear and tear and very expensive to replace when they start to look a little ragged round the edges.

If you are short of time and have a limited budget, this chapter will provide simple solutions for instant, affordable and creative table and chair decoration ideas. This thrifty chic is tremendously satisfying. Easy to follow steps demonstrate how to paint, glue, tie, pin and staple a wide variety of materials, providing new looks for old favourites. Each project is self-contained and fully illustrated with clear, step-by-step photographs.

Quite often you will find that furniture needs little more than a new cover or a decorative paint effect to give it a whole new lease of life, so you certainly won't have to think of sacrificing every weekend to take on a project. And by giving a bit of tender, loving care to an old junk-shop find – bought for next-to-nothing and revamped at minimum cost – you can create an individual masterpiece of your own, giving your home a real sense of personal style. Flick through our wonderful and innovative ideas for treatments and simple embellishments, then arm yourself with a paint-brush or a staple gun and have some fun!

Opposite: From the understated elegance of a white dining room to the quirky kitch of a pink bedroom, or the eco-chic of recycled card, there are all sorts of ways to jazz up your favourite old tables and chairs.

DRESSING FOR DINNER

FOR VERY SPECIAL OCCASIONS, why not dress up your table and chairs. Choose a style of corsage suited to the style of your chairs. A simple unvarnished country chair, for instance, calls for understated trimmings, whereas a fancy French one requires something much more elaborate. Trim the table to match. The individual flower arrangements can be given to your guests to take home. These ideas could not be simpler, but will add to the festivities.

YOU WILL NEED

silk or fresh flowers
fresh greenery
florist's wire
scissors
2.5 m (2.5 yd)
organza ribbon
pot-pourri and star anise
glue gun and glue sticks
fine string
beads

A CHAIR WITH STYLE

1 Use florist's wire to join the flowers together at the stem. Silk flowers are best because they bend as you like.

2 Continue binding in flowers and greenery. Trim the stems and tuck in any ends.

3 Finish with a ribbon bow. Make a wire hook to fix the corsage to the chair.

LIVENING UP THE TABLE

1 Fill a teapot with pot-pourri. Then cut a circle from organza, fill it with pot-pourri and tie the top with string. Twist a cinnamon stick into the tie and tie the bag to the lid.

2 Make a necklace for a bottle by pulling apart a piece of fine string into separate strands and glueing star anises to one strand.

3 Decorate a decanter or jar with a piece of organza ribbon tied into bows, or threaded with beads.

PURE PLASTIC

A PLASTIC TABLECLOTH is invaluable on a table that gets a lot of use – in a family breakfast room, for example – as it can be wiped clean in seconds and doesn't stain. As a rule, however, ready-made plastic cloths tend to be very plain or extremely garish. To make an attractive as well as practical cloth, why not cut a shaped trim from plain white plastic and make a simple design along the edge using a hole punch? Inexpensive, quick and very easy to make – what could be better? You could also make a matching cloth for a sideboard or serving area.

YOU WILL NEED

tape measure
plastic fabric
dressmaker's scissors
pencil
cardboard
scissors
hole punch
ribbon, string or rope (optional)

1 Measure your table and cut the plastic fabric to the required size. Draw up and cut out a cardboard template for the scalloped edge. Draw lightly around the template on the wrong side of the plastic fabric with a pencil.

2 Cut the edging shape with sharp dressmaker's scissors, keeping the scallops rounded and even.

3 Punch out a design with a hole punch. You could thread ribbon, string or rope through the holes to add even more interest and, perhaps, a splash of colour.

TACTILE TABLECLOTH

A MASS OF ALL sorts of wonderful trimmings is now available and a trip around the haberdashery (notions) department will, with a little imagination, generate any number of ideas. Here, simple upholsterer's webbing was used to edge a plain and practical hessian (burlap) cloth. The webbing was decorated with string in very loose loops. The charm of this simple design lies in its interesting textures, so it is probably best to use materials in toning colours, as here. However, if you wish, you could make a bold statement in bright primaries or contrasting shades.

YOU WILL NEED

about 2 m (2.5 yd) hessian (burlap)
dressmaker's scissors
dressmaker's pins
needle and tacking thread
iron
sewing machine and
matching sewing thread
8 m (8¾ yd) webbing
brown string

1 Cut the hessian (burlap) to the size you require, allowing for hems. Turn under the hems and pin, tack, press and machine-stitch. Cut a length of webbing to go round all four sides. Pin and machine-stitch the webbing around the edge.

2 Lay the string on the length of webbing and twist it to experiment with different designs – a repeating pattern will look more professional.

3 Pin, tack and hand-stitch the string to the webbing, to hold it securely. It doesn't matter if there are gaps in the stitching; the looseness of the string is all part of the effect.

NEW WAYS WITH NAPKINS

NAPKINS IN JEWEL-BRIGHT colours add a wonderful and inexpensive splash of brilliance to any dining table, immediately conjuring up visions of hotter climates and more exotic places. Choose tapestry wools in strong colours to edge the napkins and trim each one in a different style, adding buttons and beads where appropriate. They will prove really eye-catching used with a plain, boldly coloured tablecloth, country-style china and chunky knives and forks.

YOU WILL NEED

coloured linen napkins

coloured tapestry wools

tapestry needle

large button

about 50 tiny multicoloured beads

tailor's chalk (optional)

1 If your napkin has an open-work edging, work cross-stitch following the decorative holes in the edge. If not, work evenly spaced cross-stitch along the edge. Attach a button with tapestry wool at one corner.

2 Work the edge of the second napkin in blanket-stitch by holding the thread under the needle and pulling the point of the needle through. Take a few strands of tapestry wool, knot them in the centre and stitch them to one corner.

3 For the bead edging, work out a design by arranging the beads on a flat surface. You could mark these on the napkin first, by chalking tiny dots where you feel the beads should be. Sew the beads securely in place.

4 Complete the edging with running stitch. Take the thread and weave it in and out of the fabric at regular intervals, to form a pretty line of stitches about 1cm (1/2in) from the edge.

EGYPTIAN TABLE-TOP

THE BEAUTY OF THIS TABLE-TOP design lies in its simplicity. Just one colour was used on a bold blue background, with three similar images stamped in regimented rows. The table used here has a lower shelf, but the design would work equally well on an occasional table. The salmon-pink prints show up well on the rich background, making it look even bluer. The stamps are pre-cut and are taken from Egyptian hieroglyphs. The finished table could be the surprising and eye-catching centrepiece of a room decorated in subdued colours.

YOU WILL NEED

3 hieroglyph rubber stamps

ruler and set square

2 card strips, one the length and one the width of the table, for position guides

piece of card or plasticr

felt-tipped pen

salmon pink emulsion (latex) or acrylic paint

small paint roller

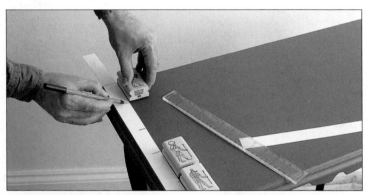

1 Use the stamps and ruler to measure out the stamp positions. Place a card strip along the edge of the table and mark as many stamp lengths as will fit along, leaving even spaces between them. Mark stamp widths along the second card strip.

2 Position the card strips at 90 degrees to each other to mark the position of the first row. Coat the roller evenly with paint on a piece of card.

3 Coat the hieroglyphs and stamp in sequence along the first row.

4 Move the wide strip up one stamp space on the short strip, check that it is at 90 degrees and stamp a second row. Continue until the table is covered.

FABRIC SWATHED CHAIR

THIS EFFECT IS STYLISH and practical and yet needs no sewing skills. There are none of the usual difficulties caused by the need for washing fitted covers, so you can capitalize on the sheer drama that is created by brilliant white. A generous quantity of fabric is the only essential; this project uses a king-size, pure cotton sheet, which is ready-hemmed, but you can use any wide, preferably washable, fabric that is soft enough to knot and tie. Why not consider this as a stunning addition to your Christmas scheme, by wrapping the dining chairs in red silk?

YOU WILL NEED

chair

fabric

sewing machine
(optional)

1 You need at least twice, and preferably three times, as much fabric as the width of your chair. Hem the fabric, if necessary. Throw the fabric over the chair and centre it.

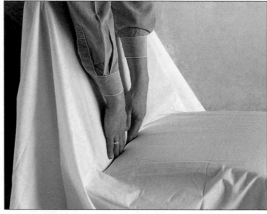

2 Tuck fabric down the back behind the seat of the chair. If the chair has arms, do this all around the seat, so that the cover doesn't pull when you sit on the chair.

3 Sweep the fabric round to the back of the chair, allowing it to drape.

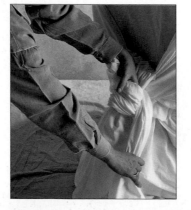

4 Tie a knot, making sure that the fabric is an even length on both sides and that you have attractive folds and drapes at the sides. Try to tie the knot confidently in one go: otherwise the fabric can look tortured and may be crumpled. Remember that the fabric should cascade down from the knot.

ASTROTURF CHAIR

CLASSIC CONSERVATORY CHAIRS are usually made of expensive hardwood and are often rather boring and conventional in design. To create a truly modern garden room, therefore, why not jazz up a cheap fifties metal chair with strips of astroturf, available from garden centres and home improvement stores. Complete the retro effect with some artificial flowers – although they are as a rule considered kitsch, their use is most definitely tongue-in-cheek here. The chair would also be an ideal talking point for a garden party, so get out your staple gun and have some fun.

YOU WILL NEED

metal chair
screwdriver
fine- and coarse-grade astroturf
staple gun
ruler
craft knife
glue gun
artificial flowers

1 Unscrew the seat pad and cut a piece of fine-grade astroturf to cover it. Staple it in place.

2 Measure and cut strips of a coarser grade of astroturf and attach to the seat with a glue gun.

3 Cut two matching pieces of coarse astroturf to fit over the central back struts of the chair. Glue the artificial flowers to the front piece.

4 Fix both pieces over the struts with a glue gun.

STOOL WITH WOOD

THIS IS A VERY SIMPLE and yet effective look, which does not involve any complicated techniques or specialist techniques. The wood mouldings used here are available in a considerable range from your local timber merchant or hardware store and are intended for embellishing doors and panelling. They give instant texture to otherwise plain objects, lending them unexpected style.

YOU WILL NEED

wooden stool

white undercoat paint, if necessary

paintbrushes

ruler

pencil

wooden mouldings

glue gun

oil-based brown paint, mixed with 2 parts matt glaze (scumble)

creamy white oil paint

dry brush

1 If your stool is already painted in strong colours, paint it white to give a neutral base colour.

2 Draw a central grid in pencil on the sides of the stool and decide on the positioning of the mouldings. Stick them on to the surface. Either curves or angles are suitable.

3 Using the brown glaze and working continuously in one direction (to simulate the grain of the wood), paint the whole stool. Allow to dry.

4 Using a pale wash of cream, paint over the mouldings. Remove some of the glaze while still wet with a dry brush, to give a limed appearance.

MAGIC CHAIR

COVERED IN NOVA SUEDE, this hard-backed chair has a split personality: a kitsch fifties dining chair by day and a theatrical throne in the evening. Throws are often used to cover easy chairs but the limitless possibilities of using them to add drama to a hard chair, totally changing its appearance, are often overlooked. Another advantage is that you can knot throws and tie them on to the uprights of a hard-backed chair and extras such as tassels or bindings can easily be incorporated. Any fabric that is wide enough is suitable for this treatment, but squashy fabrics, such as suede or velvet, are particularly stylish. Practicality is not an issue, because the covers can be whisked off to reveal the practical chair underneath.

YOU WILL NEED
hard-backed chair
large piece of plush fabric,
for example, Nova suede
tassels and bindings
(optional)

1 Drape the fabric over the chair, making sure it touches the ground at the front.

2 Take up some excess fabric from the back and form a knot over both chair pegs at the back of the chair.

3 For further embellishment, secure the corners of the fabric with tassels or bindings.

ROPE-BOUND CHAIR

COLONIAL-STYLE AND VERANDA CHAIRS have gained much popularity recently but originals are extremely difficult to find. This is a good technique for a chair whose character would be lost if it were painted or stripped and yet which needs some form of embellishment. Natural trimmings, such as twine, rope or hessian (burlap) tape, can be expensive, as you will need about 80m (90yd). Look out for less expensive forms of the same product, such as the sash cord used here. You could also use garden twine, rope, washing line or builder's scrim.

YOU WILL NEED

old chair

6 to 8 12m (12yd) bales of sash cord

glue gun

1 Starting at the back of the chair, secure the end of the rope with a small amount of glue from the gun.

2 Begin wrapping the chair with sash cord, according to your chosen design.

3 You can use two lengths at a time for the arms, starting with a slip knot.

4 When you reach the end of the length, secure it by tucking it in at the back of the chair and then glue.

SPACE-AGE CHAIRS

FOR AN OVERDOSE of the fantastic, create some space-age simplicity and make a statement in your bathroom or kitchen that can't be ignored. Vacuum-formed chairs appeared in vast numbers in our schools and offices, as part of the sixties space-craze. A twenty-first century update can be given to these forgotten and often discarded chairs by adding yet more space-age technology: shiny silver space blankets, used as emergency blankets. These are easily available from most camping stores and their silver appeal is unsurpassed. Vacuum-formed chairs themselves are the classics of their time and crying out for a facelift. Car spray paint is available in many colours if you don't want silver.

YOU WILL NEED

2 plastic chairs
silver car spray paint
PVA (white) glue
paintbrush
1m (1yd) thin wadding
1m (1yd) of 137cm (54in) iridescent lycra fabric
needle and strong thread
scissors
4 ping-pong balls
craft knife
space mat
chinagraph pencil
space blanket

1 Spray the legs of the chairs silver. Apply a coat of PVA (white) glue to the top and underneath of the first chair and stick on the wadding.

2 Stretch the lycra tautly over the chair. Gather the fabric at the back and stitch it in place. Trim off any excess fabric and turn and tack to neaten the back. Cut holes in the ping-pong balls and insert a leg into each one.

3 To line the circular hole in the second chair, use the chinagraph pencil to draw the outline of the hole on the underside of the space mat.

4 With a craft knife, cut a small circle from the centre of the outline and then make straight cuts from the inner to the outer circle.

5 Apply PVA glue to the back of the chair and press the cut sections in place. Once the circle has been centred and the glue is tacky, apply the space blanket as a continuous strip.

SHEER FABRIC CHAIR

A BEAUTIFUL CHAIR with wonderful curved legs, a ladder back and cane seat may seem to need no further treatment; yet sometimes, for a change, or for a special occasion, such as a wedding party or a Valentine's Day dinner, you might want to decorate a chair without masking its integral beauty. A wistful, romantic appeal can be given by swathing the chair in translucent fabric to give it a softness that looks really special. The transparent fabric could be coloured or use one of the metallic fabrics in gold or silver, so long as the bones of the chair show through. Tie the sash that takes up the extra fabric in a knot or a big, soft bow and leave it either at the back or on the seat, like a cushion.

YOU WILL NEED
wooden chair

tissue or pattern-cutting paper

pencil

dressmaker's pins

3m (3yd) of 137cm (54in) transparent silk, voile or organza

fabric marker

dressmaker's scissors

measuring tape

sewing machine, matching thread and iron

1 Trace the shape of the chair back rest. Use this as a template for cutting the back and front of the back rest cover, adding 2cm (¾in) all round for seams. Pin the template to the fabric, draw round it and cut out the pieces. Trace the shape of the seat in the same way. Transfer on to fabric, adding 2cm (¾in) for seams. Measure from the seat edge to the floor, for the depth of the skirt. Add 2cm (¾in) for the seams.

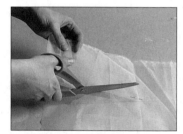

2 For the skirt, add 120cm (48in) to the circumference of the chair seat. Cut as one panel.

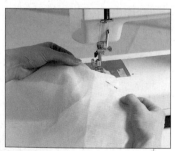

3 For the sash, allow 2m (2yd) x 40cm (16in). Right sides facing, stitch the bottom of the front back rest panel to top of the seat panel.

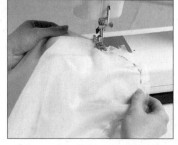

4 Press open all the seams as you go. With right sides together, stitch the front back rest panel to the back.

5 Hem bottom of skirt. Press and pin pleats. Hem top of skirt and sew to seat panel at sides and front and to back panel at back. Right sides together, fold sash in half and sew seams. Turn right sides out and stitch open end. Tie to chair.

FUN-FUR CHROME CHAIR

ANOTHER COMMON junk-shop find is the chrome-framed chair. Suppliers of second-hand office furniture should have plenty of inexpensive examples. This one was in a very bad state when found – the chrome was spotted with rust and the padding torn. The finished picture shows how even a really tatty chair can be transformed into something smart. The fun-fur covering may seem a touch bizarre but, teamed with the chrome, it turns the chair into a real one-off. You need at least twice the length of each pad in fun fur.

YOU WILL NEED

chrome chair
screwdriver
chrome cleaner
soft cloth
craft knife
foam or wadding
staple gun
fun-fur fabric

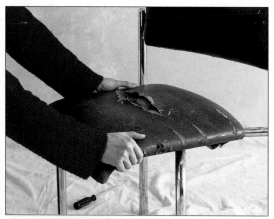

1 Undo and reserve the screws and remove the old seat pads. Clean the chrome frame with chrome cleaner.

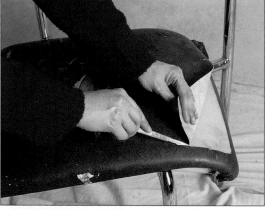

2 Cut away the old covering fabric and padding, to reveal the wooden base of the pads.

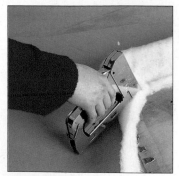

3 Cover the base and seat back with new foam or wadding, securing it with a staple gun. Replace the pads.

4 Cover the pads with fun-fur fabric, using a staple gun to attach the fabric to the wood. Take into account the nap of the fabric, so it falls nicely over the curved edge. For the hardest wear, the pile should run from back to front (i.e. it lies flat when smoothed in that direction). Fold the fabric over the chrome supports. Replace the screws.

POLYNESIAN THRONE

A SPLENDID ADDITION to your conservatory or log-cabin-style summer house, this chair festooned with wheat and rushes is not destined to be a mere garden seat, but a haven for sitting and musing. Gardening has become one of the most popular pastimes and garden centres are full of a huge variety of plants and garden paraphernalia. Customized garden furniture is much sought after and pricey, but you can make this stylish throne for very little cost, with dried grasses, craft brushes, raffia and twigs, which are available from garden centres or florists.

YOU WILL NEED

wooden chair
medium-grade abrasive paper
oil-based brown paint
paintbrush
4 large bunches of wheat
large hank of raffia
double-sided tape
craft rush brushes
saw
staple gun
dried bamboo or rushes

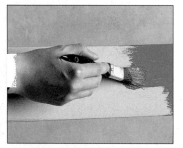

1 Sand the wooden surfaces, to provide a key for the paint. Paint the chair with the brown paint to give it a woodgrain effect. You may find it easier to remove the seat.

2 Cover the horizontal strut of the back rest with a few lengths of wheat, tying them in place with raffia. Use the double-sided tape to hold the wheat while you work (the final fixing comes later). Attach two rush brushes diagonally, by binding the stalks to the chair frame and at the crossing point with raffia. Shorten the two remaining rush brushes to the length of the vertical chair struts.

3 To cover the verticals of the back rest, bind them with several strands of raffia. Slot stems of wheat through the raffia until the wood is covered. Tie the shortened brushes to the front horizontals and verticals.

4 Bind the two side brushes with many twinings of raffia. Discreetly part the brushes and secure them at the top with a few strengthening staples. Add decorative and reinforcing raffia in crisscross fashion to the back of the chair. Knot the raffia to secure it.

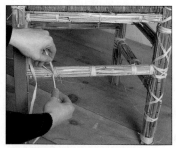

5 Choose thin, flexible bamboo or rushes to bend over the top of the legs, staple in place then bind with raffia. Staple a rough covering of wheat and rushes over the legs. As a final touch, and to help it last, knot and crisscross more raffia between your turns.

BUCKET STOOL

FLORIST'S BUCKETS in galvanized tin are widely available in a variety of heights – obviously, the taller they are, the better. Cover the metal seat pad in any fabric (a waffle towel was used here). For a bathroom you could fill PVC or clear plastic fabric with foam chips or fun sponges. Tea towels also make fun covers and a layer of dried lavender would make a lovely scented seat.

YOU WILL NEED

1 m (1 yd) heavy cord or rope
2 florist's buckets
glue gun
very large self-cover buttons
scraps of material for
covering buttons
fabric-cutting tool for
buttons
waffle hand towel
circular cushion pad
large sewing needle
matching thread

1 Attach the cord or rope to the top rim of one of the buckets with the glue gun.

2 Place this bucket inside the second bucket, applying glue to its rim, then invert both buckets.

3 Use the fabric to cover the buttons, following the manufacturer's instructions. The special tool for cutting the fabric is invaluable for this job.

4 Sew the buttons to the centre of the waffle hand towel. Then use the towel to cover the cushion pad. Instead of smoothing out the gathering in the fabric, accentuate it, using the buttons as a focus. Glue the pad to the upturned bucket.

CARDBOARD CHAIR

IT'S VERY IMPORTANT that you hunt down the correct cardboard of the heaviest weight direct from a cardboard manufacturer for this chair. Here, a substantial "treble-skinned" cardboard has been used. The template shows how to make the chair by judicious folding. Remember that, as with wood, the vertical grain is the strongest. Cardboard furniture is particularly suitable for children, because of their lighter weight. To hold your cardboard creation securely together, use gum arabic tape, as it is a deceptively strong brown parcel tape and therefore perfect for this project.

YOU WILL NEED

felt-tipped pen

metal ruler

4 sheets of treble-skinned cardboard, 2 x 1.5m (2 x 1½yd)

scissors

craft knife

self-healing cutting mat

gum arabic tape

4 thin dowels, pencils or chopsticks, 13cm (5in)

1 Draw the design directly on to the cardboard, using the diagrams on the next page as a guide. Make sure that you keep the grain of the cardboard running from the top of the chair to the bottom.

2 Using the back of the scissors and the metal ruler, score along the fold lines and, using a craft knife, cut out all the shapes and bind the edges with gum arabic tape.

3 Assemble the chair in the same way as you would make a carton, folding and slotting the cardboard into itself. The back rest of the chair has flaps that fold into the arm rests.

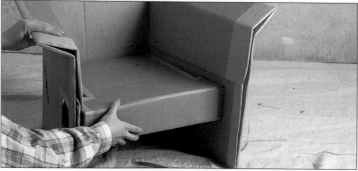

4 Slot the seat into position, making sure it is securely held in place. To give further support on the struts, peg pieces of dowel, or even pencils or chopsticks, through the cross-struts.

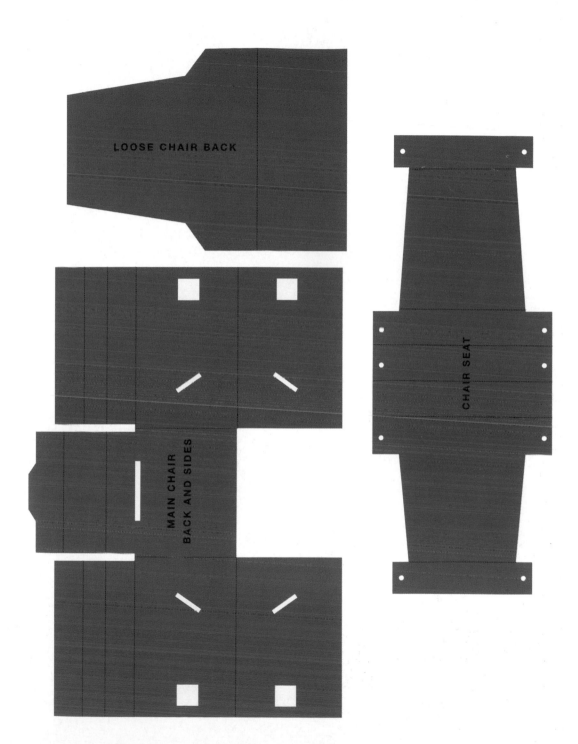

LOOSE CHAIR BACK

MAIN CHAIR
BACK AND SIDES

CHAIR SEAT

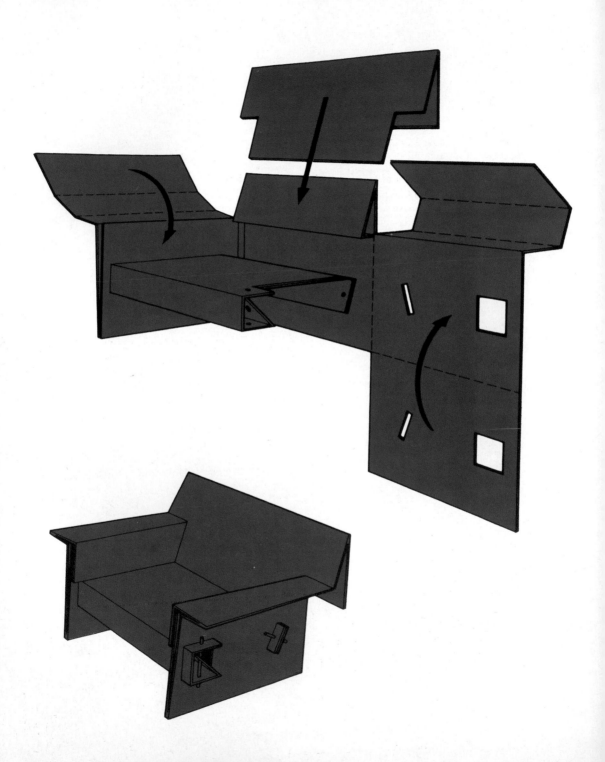

LIGHT AND SHADE

The lighting in any room is crucial as it can have a huge impact on the overall atmosphere. You can use it to highlight the contours of a room, to draw attention to desirable features and to tempt the eye away from less impressive corners.

The options for interesting lights are endless, from high-tech spotlights to traditional standard lamps and classical sconces, and in this chapter we have tried to explore plenty of alternatives. Simple, step-by-step photographs show how to transform everyday lampshades and bases by using interesting paint techniques, by embellishing them with raffia or covering them with beads. You can take a basic frame and cover it with tissue paper, or wrap it with muslin (cheesecloth), or create a table lamp from bamboo – all the projects we have chosen are clearly photographed and provide a stunning gallery of different treatments for painting, adapting and

decorating light fittings of all kinds. A good starting point is to look at the lights that are already in your home. Some of the quick projects could be just what is needed to give them an injection of style. Bases and shades can both be transformed with simple paint techniques or bead fringing, or stamped with paper designs. Patterns can be cut out of paper shades, to allow shards of light to escape, and tin shades can be drilled or pierced for a similar effect.

Old-fashioned wall lights that you no longer admire can be replaced with small spotlights and cunningly shaded with unusual objects such as baskets, colanders, roof slates… or perhaps you will come up with an original idea of your own.

Lighting is more than a practical necessity, it is one of the interior designer's most powerful tools, so use it creatively and really enjoy transforming the look of your rooms.

Opposite: Light is the easiest way to transform any environment, from the warm and comforting to the bright and lively. Try changing your current plain shades for one of these new ideas.

BENT-WIRE CHANDELIER

MAGICALLY CRAFTED FROM a roll of wire, this delicate little chandelier was twisted and curled into shape with long-nosed pliers. Making it is so much fun that you will probably want to make a pair. Bonsai-training wire, sold in garden centres and by bonsai-tree specialists, was used here. Hang the chandelier from a chain and hook so that it can twist and turn in passing air currents.

YOU WILL NEED

roll of silver bonsai-training wire

wire cutters

long-nosed pliers

roll of gardening wire

4 self-tapping screws and screwdriver

glue gun with all-purpose glue sticks

4 drawing pins (thumb tacks)

4 night-lights

large sequins

1 Cut a 35cm (13¾in) length of bonsai wire for the first kidney-shaped curl. Hold the wire with one hand, grip the end with the pliers and shape a curl. Holding the first curl in your hand, curl the other end. Make a single curl from a smaller piece of wire.

2 Make two more single curls. Each branch is made of these four pieces. Cut a 12cm (4¾in) length of gardening wire and bind the kidney-shaped curl and two of the single curls together, as shown. Wind the wire round neatly like a spring.

3 Screw a self-tapping screw into the centre of the binding, leaving at least 1cm (½in) protruding at the top.

4 Bind the third single curl on to the back of the kidney shape, winding a length of gardening wire into a neat binding as before. Snip off the end of the gardening wire at an angle, close to the binding. Repeat the above steps to make the four branches.

5 Cut a 50cm (20in) length of bonsai wire for the central column. Twist one end into a spiral and the other into a small hook. Make two small, tight curls and bind them into the top end of the column, facing inwards. Bind the four branches on to the column.

6 Apply a dot of glue to one of the screw heads and immediately sit a drawing pin (thumb tack) on it, point upwards. Repeat with the remaining screw heads. Press a night-light down on to each of the drawing pins. Thread the large sequins on to the curls.

ANGULAR UPLIGHTER

THIS UNUSUAL WALL LIGHT IS a two-coloured plastic shade slotted over a standard mini-spotlight. The two halves of the shade are simply clamped together with two shiny sprung paper clips on each side. Before fitting the two pieces together, cut a hole in the back piece to slot over the base of the spotlight. Make the hole the same size as the spotlight base so that it fits snugly and will not slip. Fit the back of the shade in position first, making sure that the bulb will remain well clear of the plastic to avoid damage to the shade and any potential accidents.

YOU WILL NEED

brown wrapping paper
pencil
ruler and set square
scissors
spray adhesive
sheet of yellow plastic
sheet of red plastic
craft knife and cutting mat
small halogen wall-light fixture
4 small sprung paper clips

1 Enlarge the template on a photocopier. Transfer it twice to brown wrapping paper. Cut out the two patterns, leaving a 2cm (¾in) seam allowance all around the edges.

2 Spray the paper patterns with adhesive and stick one on each plastic sheet. Cut out the shapes and nick the ends of the fold lines, so that they will be obvious from both sides.

3 Remove the paper, then score the fold line, but do not cut more than the surface as you do it. Practise on the off-cuts first to get the pressure right.

4 Turn the sheets over and score the fold lines again, working between the nicks at each end. Fold up the shades. Cut a hole in the back shade to fit the spotlight base, place it over the spotlight, then attach the front piece with paper clips.

PINK TISSUE SHADE

THIS BRILLIANT PINK PAPER lampshade will make a stunning centrepiece for a room and will cast a flattering pink light over everything – and everyone – at the same time. Make the size of the lampshade appropriate for your room. As it is very lightweight, it can be made quite big, which is useful if your house has high ceilings. Attach equal lengths of chain to the curled hooks and hang the light fitting in the centre, so that the hot air rises out of the top of the shade.

YOU WILL NEED

bonsai-training wire
wire cutters
thinner wire
long-nosed pliers
chains to hang the shade
glue gun with all-purpose glue sticks
bright pink, good-quality tissue paper
water-based varnish
paintbrush

1 Cut three equal lengths of bonsai wire for the struts. Bend them into wavy shapes. You can exaggerate the shape as the wire will spring back a little. Bind the ends together with thinner wire, using long-nosed pliers.

2 Attach a length of the thinner wire about 12 cm (4¾in) from the end of one strut, winding it around to secure it. Then take it around the other two struts in the same way. This will form the top of the framework. Wind around two more lengths of the thinner wire in the same way.

3 Using the pliers, curl the ends of the struts where the chains will be attached. Apply glue to one of the struts and fold the edge of a piece of tissue paper over it. Stretch the tissue across and glue it to the next strut.

4 Continue in this way, overlapping where necessary, until the framework is covered. Wind and glue a strip around the point where the three struts are joined. Brush on a coat of varnish to tighten up the paper and bond the layers.

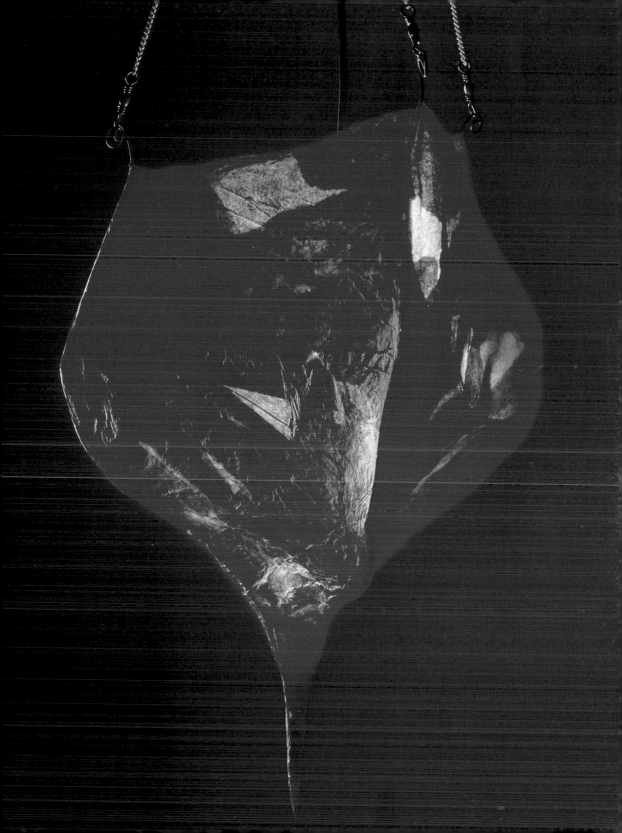

ECCENTRIC CREPE

CREPE BANDAGE IS GREAT material to work with and makes a fun lampshade. It has just enough stretch to give a good tight fit and the textured surface clings to itself as you layer the bandage. Keep an even tension as you wind it around a wire frame and use hot glue at key points, if necessary, to prevent any slipping or sagging. Make sure you leave an opening at the top, however, to allow the hot air to escape.

YOU WILL NEED

copper bonsai-training wire

wire cutters

long-nosed pliers

thinner wire

glue gun with all-purpose glue sticks

rolls of bandage

1 Cut three equal lengths of bonsai training wire and bend each one into three curves, using the pliers. The wire will straighten up when you release it, so exaggerate the shapes as you bend them.

2 Bind the three ends of the bonsai wire firmly together with the thinner wire. Be generous with the amount of wire because you need to make a solid fixture. Use the long-nosed pliers to help you to bind tightly.

3 Run another length of wire between the three struts, winding it tightly around each strut, to form the lowest of three enclosing wires that will later provide the framework for the bandage binding.

4 Wind round two more lengths of wire to complete the frame. Twist the ends of the struts into curved "feet".

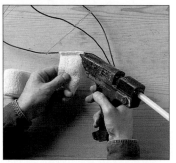

5 Glue the bandage to a strut about 5cm (2in) from the binding at the top. Wrap tightly to fix firmly. Wrap the bandage around the framework, pulling it to get the tension right. Apply glue whenever it crosses a strut.

6 Wrap and glue a small length of bandage to cover the wire binding right at the top of the framework. Use the glue gun to seal the edge and be sure to leave a 5cm (2in) gap around the top in order for the heat to escape.

BIRD CAGE

ALREADY DECORATIVE AND DESIGNED to hang at eye level, birdcages need little adaptation to turn them into unusual oriental-style shades. This charming little wooden cage was made in the Far East. However, judging by the spacing of the bars, it cannot have been intended for keeping a real bird. Look out for wooden or bamboo cages like this in gift shops, florist's or import stores and even junk shops and jumble (rummage) sales (as long as they are in good condition). If necessary, adapt the steps to suit the shape of the cage. Hang the lampshade from a chain so that it can twist in passing air currents and use a low-watt bulb for safety.

YOU WILL NEED

small wooden or
bamboo birdcage

saw

wire cutters

tissue paper

pencil

scissors

ready-mixed wallpaper paste

paintbrush

pendant lamp fitting

1 Using a saw and a strong pair of wire cutters, cut away the struts that make up the base of the cage.

2 Roll a sheet of tissue paper around the top section of the cage – here it is conical. Mark the shape in pencil.

3 Cut out the shape. Apply wallpaper paste to the inside of the struts of the top section. Roll up the tissue paper then unfold it inside the cage, pressing it against the pasted struts to form a lining. Trim away any excess.

4 Cut out a rectangle of tissue paper to line the rest of the cage. Paste the inside of the struts, then place the tissue paper inside the cage. Allow to dry. Ask an electrician to attach the pendant lamp fitting and to wire it to a flex.

CHICKEN-WIRE TORCH

THIS DRAMATIC SHADE WOULD look fabulous in an entrance hall or at the top of a staircase, especially if it is teamed with an interesting paint finish. The basic shape is a cone, but the character relies on layers of chicken wire interwoven with silver solder and copper wire. Spirals of wire, creating an unusual textural patchwork, hold the ragged, torn paper in place. The shade is hooked over a small halogen wall spotlight by means of a slit cut into the wire mesh. The light picks up the colours of the silver solder and the copper wire, adding a further layer of brilliance on top of the greyish wire mesh, and shines through the different paper textures. The shade is very lightweight, but a coat of black emulsion (latex) paint applied to the base of the cone will add visual weight and also create a feeling of substance and balance.

YOU WILL NEED

90 × 60cm (36 × 24in)
chicken wire

long-nosed pliers

hammer

wire cutters

small halogen wall-light
fixture

silver solder

copper wire

3 different, highly textured
natural-weave papers

black emulsion (latex) paint

paintbrush

screw and screwdriver

1 Roll the chicken wire into a tube with a 16cm (6½in) diameter. Using the pliers, pinch and twist the cut edges to make a firm fixing at one end.

2 Roll the tube into a cone shape, so that the unfixed end tapers down to a point. Pinch and twist the cut wire to hold the shape firm.

3 Compress the narrow end of the chicken-wire shape by hammering it on a hard surface. The wire mesh will scrunch up into a fairly solid mass.

4 Use the wire cutters to make a slit in the back of the cone. This should be large enough to fit over the base of the wall-light fixture and allow the cone to lie flat against the wall.

5 Cut two 50cm (20in) lengths of solder and weave them in and out of the mesh. Follow the shape of the cone, spiralling the wire upwards.

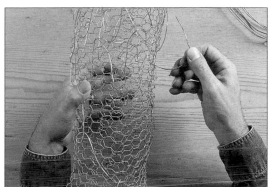

6 Cut similar lengths of copper wire and weave them through the mesh. Here a zig-zag pattern is used.

7 Wind copper wire around the outside of the cone, "sewing" it through the mesh in places.

8 Add a patchwork of chicken wire pieces. The different depths of wire will be picked out and enhanced by the light when it is switched on.

9 Tear up the three sheets of paper. The edges should be rough and ragged. Tear some pieces into strips and others into random shapes. ➤

10 Place the paper pieces randomly on the outside of the cone, and use spiralling strands of wire to bind them into place.

11 Use the long-nosed pliers to tweak and pinch the paper in places, so that it becomes a part of the structure instead of just sitting on the outside.

12 Carefully dry-brush black emulsion (latex) paint on to the base of the torch to give a matt-black charcoal finish.

13 Fit the torch over the wall-light fixture. Bend the mesh so that it fits snugly around the base and fix a screw in the wall near the top of the torch to hold it in place.

Above: Chicken wire is cheap and surprisingly easy to work with. You can form the wire into elegant candleholders, candlesticks and shimmering bead domes.

LEADING LIGHTS

STRIKE A LIGHT! Change your shade and lamp base to something unique and quite sensational within the space of just an hour. Here, a basic shade was decorated with rough string threaded through punched holes. It is very easy to punch holes around the top and base of any shade, using a hole punch, and then thread through raffia, ribbon or wool. To continue this idea, put small string bows at intervals around the shade and intersperse them with dried leaves.

YOU WILL NEED
lamp base and shade
hole punch
rough string
scissors
glue gun and glue sticks
dried leaves

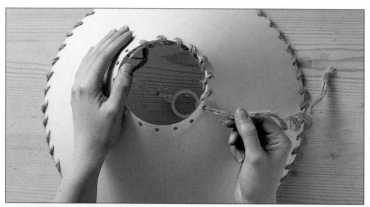

1 Punch evenly spaced holes around the top and bottom of the shade. Oversew lengths of string through the holes, top and bottom.

2 Use the glue gun to stick the leaves around the shade.

3 Tie small string bows and glue them between the leaves.

4 Put a line of glue down the back of the metal base. Starting from the top, bind a long length of string tightly around the stem. Use a second length of string to cover the base. Press to make sure the string binding is absolutely firm. Make sure that the ends are glued securely in place.

HANDMADE PAPER GLOBE

COVERING AN INFLATED BALLOON with papier-mâché may not be the most original creative technique, but the old ideas are often the best ones. You could use a variety of different papers, such as light tissue paper mixed with fibrous handmade-paper scraps, layering dried flowers and leaves between them. Keep the same thickness across the top of the balloon, but allow it to taper off towards the tied end.

YOU WILL NEED

inflated balloon

handmade paper scraps containing leaves and flower petals

ready-mixed wallpaper paste

paintbrush

cream or white tissue paper

gauze or mesh

dressmaking pin

scissors

pendant lamp fitting

cardboard ring

all-purpose glue

1 Apply paste to small pieces of paper and stick them on to the balloon in a random overlapping arrangement, beginning at the top.

2 Cover the top two-thirds of the balloon with three layers of paper, tissue paper and gauze or mesh. Leave until bone-dry; this may take several days. Use a pin to burst the balloon and remove it from the shade.

3 Cut a small hole in the top of the shade, using the light fitting as a guide to the right size.

4 Reinforce the hole by gluing a cardboard ring inside the shade. Screw the two halves of the pendant lamp fitting together, one on either side of the shade, and ask an electrician to wire the fitting to a flex.

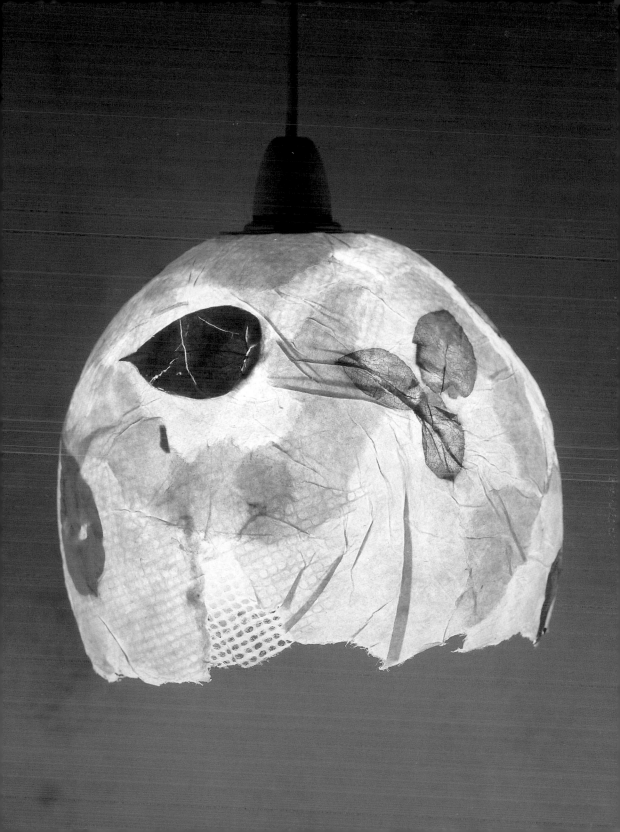

RAFFIA STANDARD

STANDARD LAMPS PROVIDE the perfect overhead light to read by without killing the atmosphere of a room as bright central ceiling lights often do. Placing one in the corner means that an individual can see what he or she is doing, while the rest of the room can be dimmed for watching television or general relaxation. Here, a turned-wood standard lamp has been enclosed in a sheath of raffia that is finished off by a "thatched" base that resembles a very clean chimney-sweep's brush.

YOU WILL NEED

turned-wood standard lamp

rubber bands

several bunches of
natural-coloured raffia

scissors

coloured raffia

1 Place a rubber band at the bottom of the pole. Unravel the raffia and cut a handful of 38cm (15in) lengths. Fold the lengths in half and tuck them under the band, so that it holds them in place just below the fold. Continue inserting folded lengths until the base is completely covered.

2 Wind a strand of raffia around the rubber band several times and tie it tightly to hold the raffia base in place.

3 Place a rubber band around the top of the lamp. Tuck bunches of raffia under it until the pole is covered. About 25cm (10in) down from the band, wind a strand of raffia around the pole. Continue at intervals.

4 At the base, tuck the raffia into the top of the base raffia, then bind to cover the join. Trim any loose ends. Cover the plain raffia bindings with coloured raffia.

TRIMMED SHADE

TURN A RATHER BORING, plain-coloured lampshade into a completely wacky extrovert by adding a dangling fringe of unusual trimmings. Almost anything non-perishable that will thread can be used – the brighter it is, the better. The choice is yours. For ideas, check out the toy store, especially the pocket money selection, where bright beads, miniature dolls and animals and fluorescent plastic balls are all waiting to be snapped up. Another good source of trimmings is the stationery store; multicoloured plastic paper clips and even treasury tags can be put to a decorative use their inventors would never have credited.

YOU WILL NEED

plain conical lampshade
square of paper or cardboard
pencil
set square
hole punch
strong thread
needle
selection of beads, toys, baubles, etc.
glue (optional)

1 Place the lampshade on a square of paper or cardboard and draw around the bottom edge in pencil.

2 Use a set square to divide the circle into eight equal segments.

3 Replace the shade on the paper or cardboard and mark the divisions around the edge in pencil.

4 Use the hole punch to make eight small holes about 1cm (¹/₂in) up from the edge of the shade, in line with the pencil marks.

5 Attach a bead securely at the end of the length of thread, as an anchor, then thread on a selection of your chosen baubles and beads.

6 Fix to the shade by sewing the thread through one of the punched holes several times, finishing with a secure knot. An extra bead can be glued to the edge of the shade to cover the thread. Decorate the rest of the shade in the same way.

TRIO OF LAMPSHADES

NOTHING COULD BE QUICKER, easier or cheaper than painting squiggles, spots or flecks of colour on a few plain lampshades to add a touch of individuality to any room. The three shades shown here have each been made using a different decorative technique. All are fun to do, and only the black-and-white stripes require a steady hand. Use plain fabric shades and experiment with colour, using it to reinforce an existing decorating theme or to add a spark of brilliance and give a quick face-lift to a monotonous colour scheme.

YOU WILL NEED

BLOTTING-PAPER EFFECT
plain fabric lampshade
paintbrushes
bright blue ready-mixed
watercolour paint
droppered bottle

PAINTED-LINE EFFECT
cardboard
cutting mat
plain fabric lampshade
scalpel
metal ruler
black acrylic paint
paintbrushes: large
square-tipped and small

FLECKED EFFECT
plain fabric lampshade
cardboard
pencil
scalpel
cutting mat
toothbrush
water-based acrylic, poster,
watercolour or gouache
paints: yellow ochre,
brick-red and cream
paintbrush

BLOTTING-PAPER EFFECT

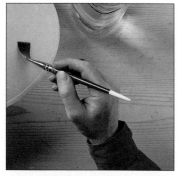

1 Dampen the whole outer surface of the fabric lampshade with water, using a paintbrush.

2 Fill the droppered bottle with blue paint and squeeze it gently to deposit one small drop on to the shade. Watch the blot spread so that you can judge where to position the next drop.

3 Turn the lampshade with your free hand and, as you do so, drop equal amounts of paint, spaced fairly evenly all around the shade.

4 Fill the spaces between the blots with a more random pattern of differently sized dots, but be careful not to cover all the original lampshade colour completely.

5 Holding the lampshade from the inside with your free hand and resting your painting hand on the work surface, paint the top and bottom rims solid blue.

PAINTED-LINE EFFECT

2 Hold the square-edged cardboard up against the shade and paint a wide squiggle to the right of it, using the large brush. After each squiggle, move the cardboard along; this will ensure that you paint vertically and don't slide off in one direction, which is very easily done when painting a shape like this.

1 Cut a right-angled piece of cardboard with one edge the same length as the height of the shade. Angle the other side to make it easy to hold.

3 Paint fine squiggly lines between the fatter ones, using the small paintbrush. Support the wrist of your painting hand with your free hand to keep it steady.

4 Finish off the lampshade by painting the top and bottom rims with a solid black line.

➤

FLECKED EFFECT

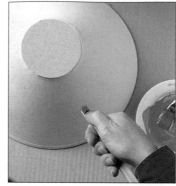

1 Place the shade upside down on the piece of cardboard and draw around the inside of the top rim. Cut this circle out, just slightly larger than the drawn pencil line, and place it on top of the shade to prevent any paint from dripping on to the inside.

2 Place the shade on a protected work surface. Fill the toothbrush with the yellow ochre paint, then draw your thumb backwards over the bristles to fleck the lampshade with colour. Try and get a fine, even covering, but allow the background to show through.

3 Clean the toothbrush, then dip it into the brick-red paint. Use the brush at an angle, to make randomly placed wedge-shaped marks at different angles over the flecked pattern. Don't try for a regular pattern: look at the example shown here to judge the effect you are after.

4 To finish the decoration, clean the toothbrush, then apply the cream paint in the same way as the red. It may not show up much but when the lamp is lit at night, all will be revealed.

INCA BIRD PRINT

MAKE AN IMPRESSION on a tall conical lampshade by stamping it all over with a strong printed pattern. The shade used here is made of thin, mottled cardboard that resembles vellum in appearance and which casts a warm glow when the lamp is lit. The stamp is based on an Inca bird design that is bold enough for a beginner to cut and is even enhanced by a slightly rough cutting style.

YOU WILL NEED

white paper

spray adhesive

high-density foam

scalpel

PVA (white) glue

flat plate

ready-made wallpaper paste

golden brown and darker brown ready-mixed watercolour paint in droppered bottle

small paint roller

conical paper lampshade

1 Photocopy the motif from this page. Spray the back of the copy lightly with adhesive and stick it on to the foam block. Cut carefully around the shape with the scalpel and scoop away the background so that the motif stands proud.

2 Put about a dessertspoonful of PVA (white) glue on to the plate. Add a similar amount of wallpaper paste and a few drops of golden brown paint and mix well. Run the roller through the mixture to coat it evenly and use it to coat the stamp.

3 Print the bird motif on the lampshade by pressing the stamp on to the surface and then removing it directly. The wallpaper paste makes the paint gelatinous, leaving an interesting texture when you lift the stamp.

4 Add a few drops of the darker paint to the mixture and stamp more motifs on the shade.

STARRY NIGHT

CAPTURE A SMALL PIECE of the midnight sky by making this cut-out lampshade. Choose the deepest of blue shades, as the effect will be best if the light is completely blocked except by the star-shaped holes. The stars should be 1–2cm (½–¾in) wide; any smaller or larger and the effect will be lost. Use a very sharp scalpel to cut the points of the stars, and always cut from the top of a point towards the middle. The lampshade is really spectacular at night, but you will get a similar effect by day with the decoration of raised metal stars. Available from haberdashery (notions) stores, these have spikes at the back that are pressed through the shade and folded flat on the inside.

1 Using the template, draw 50 stars on to white paper. Cut the paper into small squares with one star in the centre of each. Lightly spray the backs of the squares with adhesive and stick them inside the shade. Arrange them randomly rather than spacing them regularly or in a pattern.

2 Rest the shade on the cutting mat, and cut out the stars using a scalpel. Working from the right side of the shade, cut through any threads that remain and gently push the stars inwards to remove them.

3 Make sure that the spikes on the backs of the metal stars are all straight, otherwise they will not penetrate the shade. Hold a piece of dense foam inside the shade to give you something to push against, then press the stars through and fold the spikes over at the back.

GILDED PAPER PATCHWORK

GIVE TWO PLAIN LAMPSHADES a glittering new look by covering them in paper patchwork in two different styles. Although the techniques for each shade differ slightly, they have enough in common to be used as a stunning pair. The paper can be any type that is not too thick: newsprint, tissue paper, parcel wrap, photocopied typescript, sheet music or fine woven papers. Make a feature of ragged edges and avoid a regular, neat finish. The very special linking finishing touch is added with flashes of brilliant gold. The leaf used here is called Dutch metal. It is applied in the same way as gold leaf but costs much less. If you have never done gilding before, these shades are a good starting point.

YOU WILL NEED

CUT-PAPER PATCHWORK

selection of interesting paper materials: corrugated cardboard, coloured scrim ribbon, parcel wrap, handmade papers, paper mesh

scissors

plain cream fabric or paper lampshade

ready-made wallpaper paste or PVA (white) glue

household paintbrushes for applying glue, an artist's paintbrush and a firm-bristled brush

gold size

Dutch metal leaf

soft cloth

TORN-PAPER PATCHWORK

selection of interesting paper materials: photocopied typescript, paper mesh, brown wrapping paper, handmade fibre paper, handmade paper, tracing paper

shellac (button polish)

household paintbrushes for applying stainers and glue, and an artist's paintbrush

methylated spirits

water-based stain: a natural wood shade

plain cream paper lampshade

ready-made wallpaper paste or PVA (white) glue

gold size

Dutch metal leaf

soft cloth

CUT-PAPER PATCHWORK

1 Cut out "squares" from the different materials. Make them roughly equally sized, but trim them at an angle on both sides to taper slightly to fit the shade's conical shape.

2 Try out various combinations of texture and colour until you are happy with the arrangement. Apply wallpaper paste or PVA (white) glue to the backs of the shapes and stick them in place on the shade. Butt them against each other to form a solid patchwork.

3 Paint "stitches" of gold size to link the squares together. Think of patchwork stitching, and make the lines vertical on the top and bottom and horizontal on the sides.

4 Cut the Dutch metal leaf into strips, still on the backing sheet. Gently press the leaf on to the tacky gold size.

5 Use a firm-bristled brush to clean away all the excess leaf, leaving just the stitches. Burnish with a soft cloth.

TORN-PAPER PATCHWORK

1 Tear the different papers into similarly sized shapes, leaving the edges ragged and uneven.

2 Tint one-third of the shapes with shellac. It is fast-drying and will make the papers stiffer and also slightly transparent. Clean the brush with methylated spirits (methyl alcohol).

3 Tint another third of the paper shapes using water-based stain and leave them to dry.

4 Arrange the shapes on the shade, overlapping them in places and making a feature of the ragged edges. Practise with different arrangements until you are happy with the result.

5 Apply wallpaper paste or PVA (white) glue to the backs of the shapes and stick on to the shade, using the stained shapes first. Space wide apart to start and build up gradually.

6 Fill in the gaps with the untinted torn papers.

7 Paint a neat 1 cm (½in) border line all around the top and bottom of the lampshade with gold size.

8 Cut the sheets of Dutch metal leaf into strips, leaving the backing sheet still in place.

9 Press the strips against the tacky gold size along both edges. Overlap them when you need to; the leaf will only stick to the sized sections.

10 Finally, rub off any excess metal leaf and burnish the entire design to a shine with a soft cloth.

A SHADE ORIENTAL

THE GLOBAL SUPERMARKET is now well and truly a part of our lives, and strings of brightly coloured fabric birds from the orient have become as familiar to us as imports from closer to home. The lampshade made here is a combination of Chinese bamboo weaving and Indian textile work, put together in a way that is reminiscent of an Australian bush hat! The lampshade looks best when hung low over a kitchen table or anywhere that needs light combined with vibrant colour.

YOU WILL NEED

string of Indian hanging textile birds

scissors

needle

embroidery thread

assorted beads

bamboo lampshade

scrap-paper measuring strip

1 Cut the retaining bead off the string of hanging birds. Remove the cord to separate the birds and beads.

2 Thread the needle with about 30cm (12in) of embroidery thread and tie a bead at the end of the thread. Push the needle up through the existing hole in one of the birds, and then thread on three more beads.

3 Attach the bird to the shade, allowing it to hang down three finger-widths from the rim. Divide the rim into ten equal sections and attach a bird at each division.

4 Attach an inner row of birds one-third of the way up the shade. Position them so that they hang between the birds on the outer row and at a slightly higher level. Use a paper measuring strip to calculate the thread lengths required.

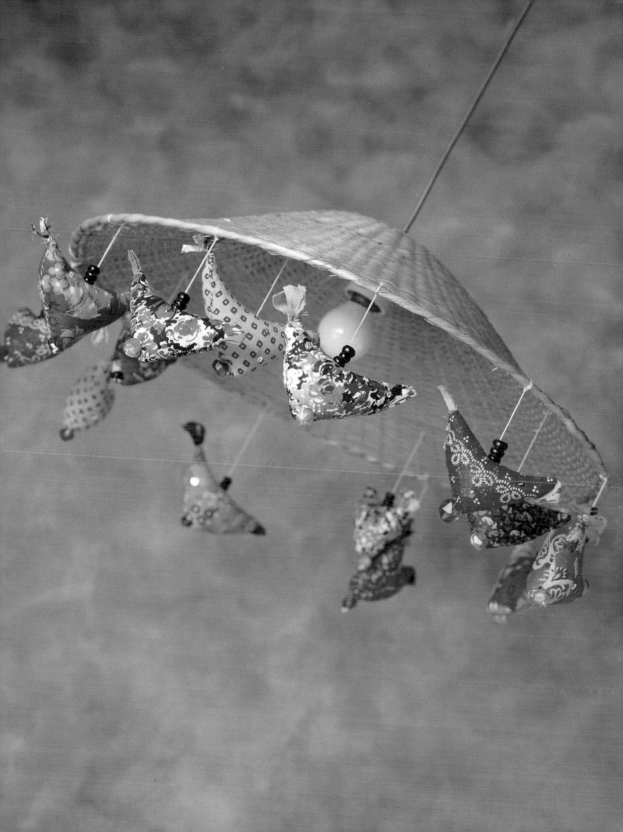

STAINED-GLASS BULB

LIGHT BULBS CAN BE PAINTED in jewel-like colours to look like little illuminated stained-glass balls and create an unusual and impressive talking point. Ordinary light bulbs can be used, but the one shown here is a large 60-watt decorative globe bulb. Painted bulbs deserve to be shown off, so hang them low over a table, with a shallow shade that will not distract attention from the pretty patterns cast by the coloured shapes. Special glass paints are available from art and craft shops. You don't need to buy much, as a little paint will go a long way.

YOU WILL NEED
waterproof marker pen
3 pieces of cardboard
light bulb
scalpel and cutting mat
strip of cardboard
adhesive tape
glass paints: pink, green, yellow, blue and black
paintbrushes

1 Draw a circle on each piece of cardboard: one the size of the widest part of the bulb, one the size of the centre of the star design and the third in between the two. Cut out the circles. Slip each piece of cardboard in turn over the bulb and draw a guideline on the glass where each sits. Carefully draw the guidelines for the rest of the design.

2 Roll up the corrugated card strip to make a base for supporting the bulb. Secure the roll with adhesive tape.

3 Begin painting the top of the bulb. Start with the central dot and radiating arms of the star. Support your painting hand with your free hand to steady it.

4 Working carefully, fill in all the different parts of the design, applying more than one coat where necessary to build up the colour. Allow the paint to dry, then paint a thick black line around each colour section to give a stained-glass effect.

WOODY NIGHTSHADE

WOOD VENEER IS A THIN SHEET shaved from a seasoned tree trunk and is sold by timber merchants who supply furniture makers. Each sheet is unique, so choose the veneer with the best grain; it will look even better with light shining through it. The lampshade shown here is made from flamed-ash veneer. The veneer hangs from a simple wooden frame but you could use a square picture frame (without the glass). Carefully remove one edge of the frame, thread on the curtain (drape) rings and glue the piece back. Suspend the veneer from the frame using clipped curtain rings. Hang the lampshade on leather thongs or cord from a ceiling hook, with a pendant lamp fitting and bulb dangling inside it.

YOU WILL NEED

4 equal lengths of wooden dowel, mitred

glue gun with all-purpose glue sticks

curtain (drape) rings with clip attachments

metal ruler

scalpel

sheet of wood veneer

4 equal lengths of cord or leather thongs

1 Join three pieces of dowel using the glue gun. Thread the rings on to the frame before glueing the last piece of dowel in place.

2 Measure the width of one side of the frame and, using the scalpel, cut four strips of veneer, one for each side. Make the length roughly twice the width; for a natural look the pieces should not be precisely the same size.

3 To finish, attach two clips to each sheet of veneer, then tie a cord or thong to each corner for hanging.

CONTAINERS

CONTAINER DECORATING PROVIDES imaginative and innovative projects for transforming old containers or creating new ones in quick, simple, stylish and beautiful ways. Put an end to cluttered shelves and overcrowded wardrobes, protect your belongings from dust, spillages or breakages and find exciting ways to jazz up your home.

If you've always thought of containers as mere practical objects in which to store anything from flowers to cookies, then you will be amazed at how cheap, everyday items can be easily made over into chic containers, bringing a personal dash of style into every room in your house. Take old paint tins, jam jars, bottles, bags, baskets or shoe boxes and give them a whole new lease of life by converting them into plant pots, shoe racks or funky chests of drawers – cover them with fabric, perhaps, or glue on buttons, beads or shells... there are no limits to what you can do. The projects we show you can serve as a source of ideas to help you add a variety of colours, textures, patterns and shapes to whatever style of organization you opt for. Whichever project you choose to make, you can simply use our suggestions as a springboard for your own creativity, so don't be afraid to amend or embellish once your confidence has grown. Adapt ideas and techniques to suit your own style and existing decor.

An afternoon spent sticking and gluing is totally absorbing and at the end of the day you will have a wonderful sense of achievement, too. All the techniques used here are clearly photographed for each project and are designed to be easy to follow. Throw inhibition to the wind and enjoy creating great-looking effects at next to no cost!

Opposite: From laundry to bric-a-brac, everything has to have a place, so make yours funky or rustic to suit your mood and your interior.

STRING BOTTLES

LIQUEUR BOTTLES HAVE SUCH lovely shapes that it seems a shame to put them into the recycling bin. This method of recycling enables you to keep on enjoying them even after you have enjoyed their contents! The bottles used here are sherry, crème de menthe and Armagnac. This project is very easy to do and it can almost seem like therapy once you've gathered together a ball of string, some glue, a pair of scissors and three interestingly shaped bottles. Make yourself comfortable, put on some relaxing music and start winding the string round the bottles.

YOU WILL NEED

ball of string

glue gun with all-purpose glue sticks
(or all-purpose glue)

3 interestingly shaped bottles

scissors

1 Coil one end of the string round like a drinks mat to make a base. Place a dot of glue in the centre of the bottle base. Heat the glue gun and apply glue in spokes over the base. Press the string on to them. Draw a ring of glue round the edge to make the base secure.

2 Circle the bottle with the string, working your way up and applying sufficient glue as you go. Make sure you get a good bonding on the bends and curves.

3 When you reach the top of the bottle, cut the end of the string and apply plenty of glue to it so the finish is neat with no fraying. Repeat these steps with the other bottles.

FANCIFUL SHOE BOX

IF YOU ARE ONE of those people who always takes the shoe box home with new shoes, only to throw it away reluctantly a while later, then this is the project for you! Your instincts to take the box in the first place are right, as shoe boxes are the perfect shape and size to make useful containers. This box was covered with brown wrapping paper – yet more good recycling – that was rolled and twisted, then unravelled and stuck on to the box to provide an interesting textured surface. The "bark" is made from torn strips of white paper, coated with wood stain to give a streaky finish. The end result is a unique, natural-looking container suitable for anything from pot-pourri to a card index system.

YOU WILL NEED

shoe box

cream emulsion (latex) paint

paintbrushes

brown wrapping paper

pre-mixed wallpaper paste, and cheap brush

scissors

PVA (white) glue

thick white paper

wood stain (such as antique pine)

thick, coarse string

piece of calico, 10 x 10cm (4 x 4in)

bulldog clips

glue gun with all-purpose glue sticks (or all-purpose glue)

1 Paint the shoe box with cream paint until all of the lettering is completely covered. Leave to dry.

2 Roll up some wrapping paper, crumpling it. Fold up, twisting as small as possible. Untwist and open out.

3 Apply a coat of wallpaper paste to the box. Place it centrally on the parcel wrap.

4 Fold the wrapping paper round the box, pressing it into the pasted surface, but not smoothing it too much. Pinch the paper along the edges of the box and cut along these. Fold the end flaps inside, sticking them with wallpaper paste.

5 Fold the wrapping paper round the sides of the box, one end at a time, pasting one on top of the other to create two large triangular shapes.

6 Fold the triangular shapes up over the sides and paste them against the inside of the box.

7 Neaten the inside by cutting a piece of wrapping paper to fit the base. Paste it over the paper edges.

8 Using a dry brush, paint a streaky coat of undiluted PVA (white) glue on the white paper. Leave some areas of the paper unpainted, to allow the wood stain to show through. Leave to dry completely.

10 Tear the paper into rough triangular shapes. If you tear at a slight angle, the paper will rip through its thickness and make the edges white and thin. Paint these white edges with wood stain so that they blend in.

9 Brush wood stain on to the white paper. It will be resisted by the PVA glue where it is at its thickest and part-resisted in other places. This gives the bark effect.

➤

11 Roll up the paper triangles, beginning with the widest part and rolling towards the point. Bundle the strips together with string and tie a reef knot. Separate the strands of string so that they bush out from the knot.

12 Fray the edges of the calico piece, then scrunch it up in the middle, using clips to hold the shape. Heat the glue gun and apply glue to the scrunched folds. Press the calico on to the centre of the box lid.

13 Remove the clips from the calico and apply more hot glue. Press the bark bundle on top of the calico.

14 If you are using the box to store a card index, write labelling on some spare "bark" paper and glue this to one end of the box.

BLANKET CHEST

YOU CAN ALMOST GUARANTEE that every interesting pine chest has been discovered by now, stripped and sold for a profit, but there are still plain, solid work chests around which can be used as a good base for this project. The blanket used for covering the chest is the utilitarian sort used by furniture removal firms as a protective wrapping. Any blanket would be suitable, but this sort has lots of "give" because of the way it is woven and so can be stretched for a smooth fit. The chest has a piece of upholstery foam on it so it doubles up as a comfortable bedroom seat. The lid is held down by a leather strap – suitcase straps or old horse tack are ideal as they come in longer lengths than leather belts.

YOU WILL NEED

wooden chest
screwdriver
pliers
tape measure
blanket
dressmaker's scissors
staple gun
upholstery foam, to fit lid
ruler
cutting board
craft knife
upholstery tacks
scrap card
small hammer
piece of leather (or card)
leather strap

1 Unscrew the hinges from the lid and remove any protruding nails or screws. Measure around the chest for the length of the blanket. Then measure the height of the chest. Double the height and add 13cm (5in).

2 Cut the blanket to size. Spread it out, and lie the chest on its side in the middle with an even amount of blanket either side and 8cm (3in) below the base. Cut from the front edge of the blanket, in a straight line, to the left and right front corners of the chest. Staple the cut section inside the chest.

3 Smooth the blanket down the side and staple it under the base. Cover the rest of the chest in the same way. Fold the blanket round from both sides to meet at the back, and staple it in place. Staple all the lining neatly inside.

4 Cut a piece of blanket about 10cm (4in) larger than the lid on all sides. Place the foam in the middle of the blanket with the wooden lid on top. Press down, pull up the blanket on one side and staple it in place.

5 Cut a triangular section off each corner. Leave enough of the blanket to fold up and staple to the lid. Fold the cut edge up and staple it across the corner.

6 Staple the side pieces over the first. Neaten by folding and trimming. Work on diagonal corners alternately.

7 Trim the chest and secure the fastening strap to the lower half with upholstery tacks. Use a card strip as a guide to keep the spacing even.

BUTTON BOX

BUTTON BOXES are an old-fashioned delight that should not be allowed to disappear altogether. There was a time when most homes had a biscuit tin filled with an assortment of buttons for sewing and knitting projects. You can make your own button box to store these little treasures. The wooden box used here is an empty tea container with a sliding lid, covered with black felt and decorated with buttons.

YOU WILL NEED

wooden box with sliding or hinged lid

black emulsion (latex) paint

paintbrush

black felt

chalk

dressmaker's scissors

rubber-based fabric glue

craft knife

cutting board

buttons

glue gun with all-purpose glue sticks (or all-purpose glue)

1 Paint the box black inside and out. Leave to dry. Then put it on the felt and draw the shapes needed to cover it in chalk: a rectangle for the base and long sides up to the grooves for the lid; a strip to cover the two ends and the base a second time; and a strip for the lid, stopping short of the runners.

2 Cut out the felt pieces. Then spread fabric glue on to the base and sides of the box and smooth the shorter strip of felt on to it. The felt will stretch a bit at this stage. Spread a thin strip of fabric glue along the top edge of the sides and fold the felt over it. Leave to it to dry completely.

3 Trim off any edges for a neat finish. Glue the longer strip of felt on to the base and up both of the ends in the same way. Trim off any excess. Cover the lid with felt, then begin arranging the buttons to make an attractive design.

4 When you are happy with the design, use the glue gun to stick the buttons in place. The glue will set straight away, so work quickly and place the buttons accurately. Decorate the sides of the box with stripes of coloured buttons.

5 Glue a row of white and pearl buttons along the top edge of the sides to complete the design.

STAR CUPBOARD

THIS ATTRACTIVE LITTLE cupboard fits in anywhere the moment you have finished it. While its style is individual, it is also understated, with that comfortable, lived-in look. It was painted, stamped, then painted again, and finally it was given a coat of antiquing varnish and rubbed back with a cloth in places. It glows from all the attention and took just one after-noon to make. This style of decoration is so simple that you might consider transforming other furniture in the same way.

YOU WILL NEED

wooden cupboard

emulsion (latex) paint (olive-green, off-white and vermilion)

paintbrushes

scalpel

kitchen sponge

PVA (white) glue

matt varnish (antique pine)

kitchen cloth

1 Paint the cupboard with a coat of olive-green paint. While the paint is drying, use the scalpel to cut the foam into a star shape.

2 Pour some off-white paint on to a plate. Dip a sponge star into the paint and print stars all over the cupboard. Leave to dry.

3 Make a mixture of two-thirds vermilion paint and one-third PVA (white) glue and coat the cupboard.

4 Finish with a coat of tinted varnish, then use a cloth to rub some off each of the stars.

LIZARD-SKIN BOXES

THESE SMART ANGULAR BOXES look crisp and exclusive, but they are, in fact, no more than paper-covered foam board! They make great containers for jewellery, hair-slides or cufflinks and they would add a touch of elegance to any desk or dressing-table. When you make your own boxes, there are no manufacturing constraints, so you can make them any shape you like, however unconventional. Foam board is light and easy to cut and stick. Buy it from art and craft suppliers, and buy lizard-skin paper from specialist paper shops.

YOU WILL NEED

foam board

cutting board

felt-tipped marker pen

ruler

craft knife

glue gun with all-purpose glue sticks (or all-purpose glue)

3 different lizard-skin papers

1 spray adhesive

1 Place the foam board on a cutting board and mark a four-sided angular shape for the base. Cut out the shape. Measure each side, then decide on the height of your box. Cut out four rectangular side sections to fit those measurements. Heat the glue gun and run a thin strip of glue along each base edge, then stick the sides on. The glue will set straight away, so work quickly and accurately.

2 Place the box on a sheet of foam board and draw round it. Add 3–4cm (1¼–1½in) all round for the lid overlap. Cut this out. Do this again, taking off 1 cm (½in) all round, for the lower half of the lid. Glue the two lid sections together. Cut a strip of lizard-skin paper wide enough to line the inside and outside of the box and to fold underneath. Apply spray adhesive to the paper, then wrap it round the box.

3 Cut down into the corners and fold the paper inside the box. Do the same underneath, smoothing the paper flat on to the box. Apply more glue where necessary.

4 Cut out paper for the lid. Glue in place and cut corners. Cut two identical shapes for a handle and glue together. Cover the handle with paper and glue to the top of the box.

MOSES BASKET

THESE GENEROUS-SIZED WOVEN BASKETS were originally designed as easy, convenient and comfortable transport for young babies. Sadly, these old-fashioned cradles do not conform to stringent modern safety regulations, so present-day newborns have safer, but rather less charming, plastic and metal contraptions instead. Moses baskets are not completely redundant, however. They are used here as fresh and airy hanging containers for clothes and also provide an attractive decorative feature for a bathroom or bedroom. Alternatively, you could use them for easy toy storage in a child's nursery.

YOU WILL NEED

plank of wood

tape measure

saw

abrasive paper

drill, with wood and masonry bits

1 long or 2 short branches (or poles)

penknife (or wood carving knife)

dowel (optional)

2 Moses baskets

wood glue

hammer

wall plugs (plastic anchors) and screws

screwdriver

1 Cut two squares of wood at least 12 x 12cm (4¾ x 4¾in) and 5cm (2in) deep. Sandpaper the edges and drill a hole through the middle of each square, slightly smaller than the diameter of the branches. Carve away the branch ends so that they fit tightly into the holes. Sandpaper them slightly.

2 Use dowels or offcuts from the branches for the pegs. Taper the ends.

3 Measure the distance across the basket, between the basket handles, and drill two holes the same distance apart on top of each branch. Apply wood glue to each branch and tap them into each square.

4 Apply wood glue to the peg ends and fit them into each branch. To fix the top branch to the wall, drill holes in the four corners of the square of wood, and four corresponding holes in the wall. Using the wall plugs (plastic anchors) and screws, screw the branch to the wall. Fix the lower branch to the wall allowing about 10cm (4in) clearance between the two baskets.

PRETTY POTS

MINIATURE TOPIARY WILL LOOK both eye-catching and charming on a windowsill or collected together on a table, but don't forget to make the most of their containers. Terracotta pots have their own special appeal, but can also be treated to a variety of embellishments, from tassels to tape. Subtle, natural colours are best as they tone with the pots themselves and with the small pebbles used to conceal the florist's foam.

YOU WILL NEED

florist's dry foam block

sharp knife

3 old terracotta pots

2 straight twigs

glue gun and glue sticks

2 florist's dry foam balls

fresh foliage, such as box or privet

selection of pebbles

curtain (drape) weight

fine string

string tassels

masking tape

craft knife

self-healing cutting mat

matt (flat) varnish

paintbrush

1 Cut the florist's foam blocks in half and cut each block to fit into the pots. Position the foam in the pots. Insert the twigs and then glue them in place, to act as the stems of the trees. Glue the foam balls on top.

2 Cut small pieces of foliage to the required size and insert them at random in the foam balls, to create a casual, carefree effect.

3 Cover the foam in the pots with a layer of small pebbles so that it is completely concealed.

4 Thread the curtain (drape) weight on to string and tie it around one of the pots. Decorate the other pots with tassels or designs cut from masking tape with a craft knife. Varnish to make the masking tape secure.

ALL BOXED UP

THERE IS A HUGE VARIETY of boxes available, ranging from plain and simple white wooden boxes via shoe boxes to oval trinket boxes. Make a toning set of three using easily available natural materials. However, boxes can be trimmed with almost anything you like: bottletops, paper clips, string, rope or a collage of stamps. Linen tape (used in upholstery or for tags) is available from haberdashery (notions) departments.

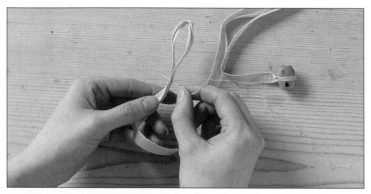

1 Measure the plain wooden box. Allow an extra 2cm (¾in) at one end for the toggle and about 7.5cm (3in) for the loop and tag. Cut two lengths of linen tape to this length. Sew a loop in the end of each tape and attach the wooden beads to be used as toggles.

2 Secure the tape to one end of the box with glue, leaving the toggle and loop free so the lid can be opened. Repeat on the other side. Glue a larch twig to the top of the lid, as a decorative "handle".

3 For the slatted wooden box, sort through the pot-pourri and choose the items you would like to use. Glue them to the lid. Glue the dried leaves and cones to the Shaker box, and glue linen tape around the sides.

ORIGAMI BOXES

ORIGAMI IS THE JAPANESE ART of paper-folding, where the most extraordinary three-dimensional objects are made from a single folded square of paper. This little box is a suitable project for a beginner, but it may take a couple of practice attempts before it suddenly "clicks". You can make the boxes any size you like, and use any paper that is not too flimsy. Brown wrapping paper is good as it creases well and is cheap and strong.

YOU WILL NEED

sheet of paper

scissors

double-sided tape
(this breaks all the rules!)

selection of paper squares
for practice (optional)

1 Fold and trim a sheet of paper to make a perfect square. Fold the square corner to corner. Open it to show the creases of four equal triangles. Turn it over and fold into four square quarters. Unfold it so you can see the creases of eight equal triangles. The centre of the paper is Point A.

2 Hold the model in the air and push all the sides together so that the corners meet in the middle. Flatten the model. Point A is now a corner of the flattened model. Keep it facing you.

3 Fold the point opposite Point A over to meet it. Crease it along the mid-line. Now fold it back up to the mid-line and crease the fold. Unfold it again. Fold the same point up to the last crease, then fold it over again, up to the mid-line. Turn the model over and repeat this step.

4 With point A still facing you, take the top layer of the left-hand corner and fold it over on to the right-hand corner. You are now faced with a square. Fold the left-hand corner and the top layer of the right-hand corner into the centre point, and crease. Bring the right-hand top layer over on to the left. Turn over and repeat.

5 Point A now forms the base of a smaller triangle. Fold this up at the point where it meets the sides. Crease, fold it in the other direction and crease. Unfold. Insert your hand and splay your fingers while pushing up the bottom of the model, Point A. Fold down the two pointed sides level with the others and tuck the ends under. Secure with a small piece of tape.

ALL THE TRIMMINGS

CHOOSE THE CHEERFUL PRIMARY colours of blue and red and team them with white for a crisp, clean look with a slightly nautical feel. Equally, you can trim black with white for classic appeal or use toning colours for adding a subtle lift. Felt is an easy, lovely and inexpensive way to trim plain fabrics, whether on shoe bags, linen bags, throws or cushions. You can add as much or as little decoration as you choose.

YOU WILL NEED

round template

2 squares of red felt, about 20 x 20cm (8 x 8in)

2 squares of blue felt, about 20 x 20cm (8 x 8in)

dressmaker's pins

fabric marker

pinking shears

blue cord

string

needle

matching sewing thread

fabric item, such as a shoe bag or quilt

1 Find a round template: it could be a tin lid, coin or anything similar. Place the template on the felt, and draw round the template with a fabric marker. Cut around the circle with pinking shears.

2 Pin two circles together, knot short lengths of cord and sew them on to the circles.

3 Repeat with lengths of string. Sew the circles on to your shoe bag, quilt or other fabric items.

NEWS ON SHOES

 SPECIAL SHOES DESERVE a home of their own and these sturdy wooden wine boxes can be made stylish enough to house anything from country brogues to Cinderella's glass slippers. The boxes were lined with different types of newsprint, which was layered and stuck down like papier mâché. Select your newsprint to suit your shoes – put leather lace-ups in the pink financial pages, party shoes in comic strips and velvet pumps in the arts and literary review pages.

YOU WILL NEED

wooden wine crates
abrasive paper
PVA (white) glue
paintbrushes
variety of newsprint
craft knife
clear matt varnish
(or shellac button polish)

1 Sand down the wine crate. Then mix PVA (white) glue with water (50:50) and apply a coat to the inside.

2 Apply another coat of the diluted PVA, then smooth newsprint over the inside. Apply undiluted PVA along the top edges and smooth the paper over it. Leave to dry before applying more paper and glue at random.

3 Leave to dry, then trim the paper along the outside top edges with a craft knife. Varnish the whole box with either clear matt varnish or, if you want an "aged" look, shellac. Leave to dry, then re-coat at least twice.

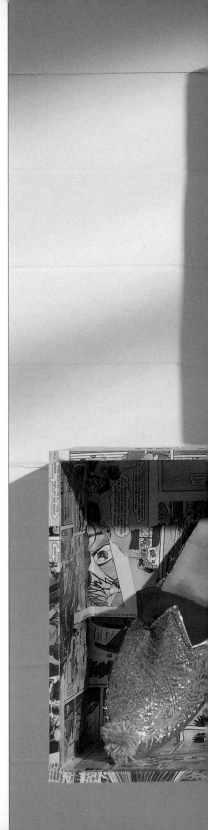

GILDED BOXES

THERE IS NO PAINT OR SPRAY that gives a finish to compare with gold leaf, or its cheaper counterpart, Dutch metal leaf. It glows and glitters and can be burnished with a soft cloth to leave a gleaming surface. The art of gilding is surrounded by mystique because it requires a great deal of skill to lay the fragile sheets of gold leaf on to gold size or glue. This design was created using a kit suitable for beginners, which can be bought from art and craft suppliers. The flat surface of the box makes it easy to apply, but it is important to follow the manufacturer's instructions as the drying time is crucial to the success of the project.

YOU WILL NEED

design tracing or photocopy
spray adhesive
high-density foam
craft knife
round painted wooden box
with lid
fine-grade abrasive paper
pencil
gold leaf kit
paintbrush
plate
small foam roller
cotton wadding
fine wire wool (optional)

1 Select a suitable design or motif from a source book, and photocopy or trace to size. Spray the back of the design with adhesive and stick it on to a block of foam.

2 Carefully cut out the design, starting in the middle. Then cut around the outside.

3 Once the cutting is complete, carefully peel off the paper pattern.

4 Rub the entire surface of the painted box lightly with fine-grade abrasive paper to make a rough surface for applying the gold size.

5 Draw a pencil line around the top edge of the lid. Use your fingers to keep the line an even distance from the edge.

6 Carefully paint a strip of gold size between the edge of the box lid and the pencil line.

7 Put some size on to a plate and run the roller through it until it is evenly coated. Using the roller, coat the foam stamp thoroughly and evenly.

8 Stamp an even pattern round the side of the box, re-coating the stamp after each print. Stamp four shapes inside the lid border line and one in the centre.

9 Leave the size until it has the right degree of "tack" (according to the manufacturer's instructions), then invert the lid on to a sheet of gold leaf. Smooth the gold leaf over the edges so that it is in contact with all of the size.

10 Holding the box at an angle, apply the sheets of gold leaf round the sides in the same way.   ➤

11 Rub the surface with cotton wadding. All the "un-sized" gold will flake off, leaving the design behind.

12 If the brand new gleaming design overwhelms you, rub the box lightly with wire wool to create an antiqued look.

PUNCHED METAL BUCKET

THE IDEA OF DECORATING metal objects with raised punched patterns has been around ever since sheet metal was invented about 300 years ago. Silver is probably best-known for this decorative treatment, but cheaper metals can also look very impressive. Bare metal buckets are ideal for this sort of pattern-making, and all you need is a pen to draw your guidelines and a hammer and blunt nail for the punching. You can practise your technique on any can to find the ideal sort of tap needed to make a good bump without piercing the metal.

YOU WILL NEED

bare metal bucket

felt-tipped marker pen
(not water-based)

blunt nail
(or centre punch)

hammer

rag

lighter fuel
(or similar solvent)

1 Draw your pattern on the inside of the bucket. These motifs come from South America, but any repeated curves or angles are suitable.

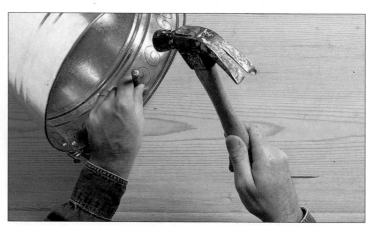

2 Rest the bucket on a piece of wood to protect your work surface. Tap the nail with a hammer, keeping the dents regularly spaced. About 1cm (½in) is fine.

3 Continue hammering the pattern all over the inside of the metal bucket.

4 Use a rag and lighter fuel to clean off the marker pen pattern that is left between the punched marks.

CIRCULAR PAINTED BOXES

THIS PROJECT EXPERIMENTS with three different paint effects. The first, rust, looks especially good when used on a material that doesn't naturally rust, such as wood. Verdigris is a natural substance that forms on the surface of weathered brass and is a beautiful turquoise-green colour. The third finish used here is crackle glaze (craquelure) which looks a bit like lizard skin. This is the most time-consuming of the three paint effects because of the drying time needed between coats.

YOU WILL NEED

3 wooden boxes, with lids

water-based paints: dark grey,
2 shades of rust, green-grey, stone,
2 shades of green and maize yellow
(according to required finish)

handful of fine sand

plate

paintbrushes

3 foam sponges

clear matt varnish,
craquelure base varnish,
craquelure varnish

alizarin crimson oil paint

2 rags

white spirit (paint thinner)

THE RUST FINISH

1 Mix sand into the dark grey base coat for texture. Apply two coats of paint to the box. Leave to dry. Dab on the darker rust colour with a sponge. Cover most of the background.

2 Dab on the lighter rust colour. If you are in any doubt about how it should look, find some real rust and copy it. Finally dab in just a touch of green-grey. Do not overdo this as it should blend in rather than stand out as a sharp contrast.

THE VERDIGRIS FINISH

Paint the box with the stone base coat colour. Dab on the lighter green with a sponge. Cover most of the background with this. Dab on the other green using a sponge. Apply a coat of clear matt varnish to protect the surface.

THE CRACKLE GLAZE FINISH

Paint a yellow base coat and a coat of craquelure base varnish. When dry, apply a coat of craquelure varnish. Leave to dry. Rub crimson oil paint into cracks with a rag. Dip a rag in white spirit (paint thinner); rub the surface so red paint stays in the cracks.

CAMEMBERT NUMBERS

THIS PROJECT SHOULD be linked to a wine and cheese party or the befriending of a French restaurateur as it involves nine Camembert boxes. It is always a relief to be able to recycle packaging and these empty boxes are certainly given a new lease of life in the form of a stylish set of containers. Enlarge the numbers on a photocopier so they fit your boxes and cut them out as stencils. If you find the task too daunting, trace the numbers on to the boxes and paint them in.

YOU WILL NEED

9 Camembert boxes

fine-grade abrasive paper

clear matt acrylic varnish

paintbrushes: medium, stencilling, fine-pointed and square-tipped

number templates

craft knife

cutting board

spray adhesive

stencilling plastic or waxed stencil card

enamel paint: 9 colours plus silver

pair of compasses and pencil (optional)

shellac button polish

1 Remove any paper labels from the boxes. Rub the wood with abrasive paper to get rid of any rough edges. Apply a coat of clear matt acrylic varnish to all the boxes.

2 Take the templates or, to make your own, enlarge them on a photocopier so the numbers are 8cm (3in) high (or to fit within a border of about 1.5cm (⅝in). Cut each one out.

3 Stick the photocopies on to the stencil material with spray adhesive. Stick them underneath stencilling plastic, but on top of stencilling card. Cut out, making the incisions away from the corners.

4 Stencil a number on each lid in different colours. With a fine-pointed brush paint a band about 1.5cm (⅝in) wide around each lid. (If necessary, use a pair of compasses). With a square-tipped brush, paint a band of silver around the edges. When dry, rub them down lightly and apply button polish.

1 2 3 4 5 6 7 8 9 0

SNOWFLAKE STORAGE JARS

ALMOST EVERY KITCHEN COULD DO with a face-lift every now and then. Rather than pay over the odds for a completely new look, why not just cheer up your storage jars, simply and inexpensively, and give your kitchen a breath of fresh air? You can create a whole new atmosphere, and a really individual look, by stamping patterns on your jars with acrylic enamel paint. The finish is quite hard-wearing and is tough enough to stand up to occasional gentle washing, but take note that it will not withstand the dishwasher.

YOU WILL NEED
pencil
tracing paper
spray adhesive
upholstery foam
scalpel
kitchen cloth
glass storage jars
white acrylic enamel paint
plate
tile

1 Trace your chosen pattern shape, lightly spray it with adhesive and place it on the foam. Cut around the outline with a scalpel. Cut horizontally into the foam to meet the outline cuts and remove excess foam.

2 Clean and dry the glass jars. Spread a coating of paint onto a plate and make a test print on to a tile to remove excess paint from the stamp.

3 Holding the jar steady, press the foam around the side of the jar.

4 Rotate the stamp 90 degrees and make the second print directly below the first. Continue in this way, alternating the angle of the print.

SUPPLIERS AND USEFUL ADDRESSES

UNITED KINGDOM

Axminster Power Tool Centre
Chard Street
Axminster
Devon EX13 5HU
Tel: 01297 33656
Power tools supplier

Black and Decker and Dewalt
210 Bath Road
Slough
Berkshire SL1 3YD
Tel: 01753 567055
Power tools supplier

Colour Centre
Offord Road
London N1
Tel: 020 7609 116
Paints and do-it-yourself
equipment supplier

Foxell and James
Farringdon Road
London EC1M 3JB
Tel: 020 7405 0152
Wax, oil, varnish and finishing
products supplier

Heward and Dean
Grove Park Road
London N15 4SP
Tel: 020 8800 3447
Tools supplier

HSS Power Tools
25 Willow Lane
Mitcham
Surrey CR4 4TS
Tel: 020 8260 3100

James Latham
Leeside Wharf
Mount Pleasant Hill
Clapton E5
Tel: 020 8806 3333
Timber supplier

Plasplugs Ltd.
Wetmore Road
Burton-on-Trent
Staffordshire DE14 1SD
Tel: 01283 530303
www.plasplugs.com
Tiling tools, fixings and
fasteners supplier

Record Tools Ltd.
Parkway Works
Kettlebridge Road
Sheffield S9 3BL
Tel: 0114 244 9066
Hand tools supplier

Ronseal Limited
Thorncliffe Park
Chapeltown
Sheffield S35 2YP
Tel: 0114 246 7171
www.ronseal.co.uk
Ronseal, Colron, Thompson's
products

Spear & Jackson
Neill Tools Ltd.
Atlas Way
Atlas North
Sheffield S4 7QQ
Tel: 0114 261 4242
Tools supplier

Stanley Tools UK Ltd.
Beighton Road East
Drakehouse
Sheffield S20 7JZ
Tel: 0114 276 8888
Tools supplier

Vitrex Ltd.
Everest Road
Lytham St. Annes
Lancashire
FY8 3AZ
Tel: 01253 789180
Tools and clothing supplier

Woodfit Ltd.
Kem Mill
Whittle-le-Woods
Chorley
Lancashire PR6 7EA
Tel: 01257 266421
Furniture fittings supplier

UNITED STATES

**Compton Lumber &
Hardware Inc.**
P.O. Box 84972
Seattle, WA 98124-6272
Tel: (206) 623-5010
www.comptonlbr.com

Constantine's
2050 Eastchester Road
Bronx, New York
NY 10461
Tel: (718) 792-1600
www.constantines.com

The Cutting Edge, Inc.
7123 Southwest Freeway
Houston,
TX 77074
Tel: (981) 9228
www.cuttingedgetools.com

Northern Tool and Equipment
Corporate Headquarters
2800 Southcross Drive West
Burnsville, MN 55306
Tel: (800) 533-5545
www.northerntool.com

AUSTRALIA

BBC Hardware Stores
Hardware House
For details of your nearest store
in either of the above two
chains, contact (02) 9876 0888.

Mitre 10
For details of your nearest store
contact (03) 9703 4200.

Bunnings Warehouse
For details of your nearest store
contact (03) 9607 0777.

Thrifty-Link Hardware
See you local state directory for
your nearest store.

USEFUL ADDRESSES

British Cement Association
Century House
Telford Avenue
Berkshire RG45 6YS
Tel: 01344 762676
www.bca.org.uk

**British Wood Preserving and
Damp-proofing Association**
1 Gleneagles House
Vernon Gate, South Street
Derby DE1 1UP
Tel: 01332 225100
www.bwpda.co.uk

**Conservatory Association/
Glass and Glazing Federation**
44–48 Borough High Street
London SE1 1XB
Tel: 01480 458278
www.ggf.org.uk

Energy Saving Trust
21 Dartmouth Street
London SW1H 9BT
Tel: 08457 277200
www.est.org.uk

**Home Energy Efficiency
Scheme**
Eaga Partnership
2nd Floor, Eldon Court
Eldon Square
Newcastle-upon-Tyne
NE1 7HA
Tel: 0800 316 6011

Kitchen Specialists Association
12 Top Barn Business Centre
Holt Heath
Worcester WR6 6NH
Tel: 01905 726066
www.ksa.co.uk

**Laminated Glass
Information Centre**
299 Oxford Street
London W1R 1LA
020 7499 1720
www.martex.co.uk/prca/condor

**National Association of Loft
Insulation Contractors
and
National Cavity Insulation
Association**
PO Box 12
Hazlemere
Surrey GU27 3AH
Tel: 01428 654011
theceed@computer.com

National Fireplace Association
6th Floor
The McLaren Building
35 Dale End
Birmingham B4 7LN
Tel: 0121 200 1310

**RIBA (Royal Institute of
Chartered Architects)**
66 Portland Place
London W1B 1AD
Tel: 020 7580 5533
www.architecture.com

SALVO
(Directory of Salvage Yards)
PO Box 333
Cornhill on Tweed
Northumberland TD12 4YJ
Tel: 01890 820333
www.salvo.co.uk

**The Association of Noise
Consultants**
6 Trap Road
Guilden Morden
Hertfordshire SG8 0JE
Tel: 01763 852958
www.association-of-noise-
consultants.co.uk

**The Institute of Electrical
Engineers**
2 Savoy Place
London WC2R 0BL
Tel: 020 7240 1871
www.iee.org.uk

The Institute of Plumbing
64 Station Lane
Hornchurch
Essex RM12 6NB
Tel: 01708 472791
www.plumbers.org.uk

GLOSSARY

Architrave (trim) A type of timber moulding, used mainly around openings in walls for doors.

Batten (furring strip) A straight length of timber, used for temporary or permanent support, e.g. of roof tiles, wall tiles or for setting concrete.

Bevel An angled edge on, for example, a piece of wood. Also see chamfer. Also a carpenter's tool for setting an angle.

Bolster (stonecutter's) chisel A flat-bladed chisel used for cutting masonry. Used widely by electricians, plumbers and paving contractors; can also be used for levering up floorboards.

Building regulations Legal requirements in the UK and other countries for the ways that houses are constructed (and modified).

Butt joint A joint between two pieces of timber when one piece simply meets the other, such as in an L-shape or a T-shape or end-to-end.

Casement window A window (or light), which is hinged at one side or at the top.

Caulking gun A device for squeezing sealant or adhesive out of a cartridge.

Cavity wall A method of house construction, where the outer walls of the house consist of two "leaves" (typically one of brick and one of lightweight block) with a gap (cavity) between them.

Centre point The sharp point of a twist drill bit or a metal plug put into a dowel hole to transfer its position to a second piece of wood.

Chamfer An angled edge to timber, usually smaller than a bevel.

Chipboard (particle board) An inexpensive manufactured board consisting of timber scraps and glue.

Clearance hole A hole drilled to take the full size of a screw.

Consumer unit The modern term for an electrical fuse-box. It may contain miniature

circuit breakers rather than fuses depending on its age.

Combination ladder A ladder that can be used in two or more ways. Uses include: step-ladder, straight ladder, stair ladder and extending ladder.

Cornice, Cove (crown molding) A decorative timber, plaster or polystyrene (styrofoam) moulding to cover up the join between wall and ceiling.

Counterbore To enlarge a hole, for example to take a bolt or screw head.

Countersink An angled recess to take the head of a countersunk screw. Also tool for making the same.

Damp-proof course An impermeable layer put in exterior walls to prevent damp rising up the wall.

Damp-proof membrane An impermeable layer put in floors to prevent damp rising.

Depth stop A device attached to an electric drill to limit the depth of a hole being drilled.

Door furniture A general term for the bits screwed on to doors, such as handles, knockers and knobs.

Dovetail A woodworking joint, where angled pins in one piece of wood fit into identical angled recesses in the other. Also describes fine-toothed backsaw used for making same.

Dowel A circular timber peg used for reinforcing woodworking joints.

Duckboard Used in bathrooms, a low slatted timber platform for standing on.

Eaves A general term for the wood pieces where the roof meets the house walls. Consists of soffit and fascia board.

Emulsion (latex) paint Water-based paint for covering walls.

End grain The fibres at the end of a piece of wood that are highly absorbent.

Fascia (board) The vertical timber boards at the eaves. Gutters are usually fixed to these.

Fillet A thin narrow strip. Usually applied to strips of mortar used in paving.

Flashing Strips cut from lead or zinc sheet used to seal roofing junctions.

Float glass The modern replacement for sheet glass and plate glass (so called because in manufacture it is floated out of the furnace on molten tin).

Flush panelling Covering moulded doors with hardboard to make them flat.

Former A word for a mould around which something else shapes itself.

Fungicide A chemical treatment for removing mould and algal growth.

Fused connection unit An electrical fitting allowing electric equipment to be permanently wired in.

Gable The pointed walls, sometimes found at the ends of a pitched roof.

Galvanized Coated with zinc to prevent steel from rusting.

Gloss paint An oil-based paint with a shiny finish used on wood and metal.

Grain The texture of timber created by the annual growth of a tree.

Grout A filling to go into the gaps between tiles.

Handed Refers to hinges (for example, rising butt hinges) attached to either the right or the left of the door.

Hardcore A mixture of stones and rubble used to provide a base for paving and concrete.

Housing (also housing joint) A wood-working joint where one piece of wood fits into a slot (housing) in another piece.

Jamb Vertical timbers that form the sides of window and door frames.

Joists Large pieces of timber used in house construction to support floors, ceilings and flat roofs.

Knot A dark coloured circle in wood where a branch grew out of the tree. It can exude resin or can fall out.

Laminate Wooden flooring made in layers; the thin sheeting applied to the tops of worktops; and glass made with a plastic interlayer.

Lath-and-plaster An old-fashioned way of constructing ceilings and partition walls. The plaster is applied to thin timber strips (laths), which are secured to vertical studs (walls) or horizontal joists (ceilings).

Leaded light A window where small panes of glass are held between lead strips.

Light Another name for a window, usually in a roof.

Lipping A thin strip (often of hardwood) applied to the edges of a timber board (e.g. a shelf or a countertop).

Mastic (caulking) A non-setting and flexible waterproof sealant.

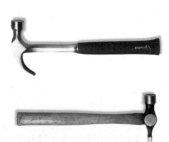

MDF (medium-density fiberboard) A manufactured board consisting of timber fibres and resin. Has smooth surface and will take screws and nails.

Melamine An easy-to-clean plastic often used for covering chipboard (particle board) to make shelving boards.

Mitre A joint made by cutting two pieces of wood at 45 degrees, such as for making picture frames.

Mitre fence A platform on a fixed sander to support mouldings while the mitred end is sanded.

Mortise A deep slot cut in timber, for example, for a mortise lock. A mortise chisel is a strong type for levering out the wood. See also tenon.

Ogee A particular, popular shape of ornate moulding or gutter profile.

Oilstone A flat abrasive stone used with oil for sharpening chisels and knives.

Overflow An essential part of a sink, basin or bath or a pipe attached to a water tank.

Party wall The wall between two semi-detached houses or two terraced houses.

Pilot hole A small hole drilled to guide a larger drill or to take the point of a screw that then cuts its own thread.

Pitch The slope of a roof or a staircase.

Planning permission Local authority consent needed in the UK and other countries to build a house or for certain extensions and alterations.

Plasterboard (gypsum board) Sheets consisting of solid plaster contained by heavy paper sheets, used for constructing partition walls and ceilings.

Plywood A man-made board consisting of thin sheets glued together. Alternate sheets have the grain running at right angles, which gives the board exceptional strength.

Pointing Using extra mortar to finish the joints between bricks in a wall.

Polyurethane varnish A very tough varnish (paint without colouring), which will withstand heat and which is resistant to stains.

Prime/primer The first coat of paint applied to bare wood or metal.

Punched Applied to nail heads to mean that they are pushed below the surface of timber with a nail punch.

PVA (white) glue Strictly polyvinyl acetate: a type of adhesive used for wood-working, also used in concreting work to reduce the absorbency of surfaces.

Rafters Sloping timber members of a roof.

Rebate (rabbet) A slot cut out of the corner of timber to hold something.

Render A mixture of sand and cement used to coat external walls.

Residual current device An electrical safety device that prevents electric shock.

Reveal The rectangular hole in a wall in which a window or door is fitted.

Rim lock (rim latch) A lock (or latch) that is attached to the surface of a door unlike a mortise lock, which fits into a slot cut out of the door.

Rising butts Hinges that lift a door as it is opened.

Router An electrical woodworking tool that cuts a slot or a recess.

Sash A name for a window, usually applied to sash windows where each window slides vertically.

Screed A thin layer of sand and cement applied to concrete floors.

Set The way in which alternate teeth on a hand saw are bent away from the blade. This makes the saw cut wider than the saw blade and so prevent the saw from sticking.

Shuttering A framework of timber boards used to hold concrete while it sets.

Silicone A flexible non-setting plastic used in sealants.

Skew (toe) nailing Driving nails in at an angle to provide a stronger bond.

Soffit The horizontal timber boards used at the eaves.

Soil pipe The large vertical drainage pipe in houses taking the toilet waste.

Spigot A projection designed to fit into a recess.

Stile The vertical timber pieces of a door or window.

Stopcocks Valves fitted to water pipes to stop the flow of water through them.

Stopping A filler used for repairing wood.

Stud A vertical timber strut, which are used to frame internal partition walls.

Template A guide for drilling or cutting.

Tenon A reduced section on one piece of wood designed to fit into a slot (mortise) in another.

Tongued-and-grooved A method of joining planks (such as floorboards or cladding) edge to edge – a tongue on one piece fits into a groove in its neighbour.

Trap A device fitted in the waste pipe under a bath, basin or sink to prevent foul air and small animals getting in.

Twist drill bits Drills for making holes in wood and metal.

Veneer A very thin layer of expensive timber attached to a cheaper base.

Waste Any piece of material that is cut off and not used.

INDEX

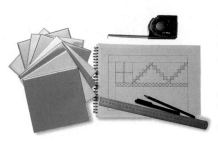

ACKNOWLEDGEMENTS

The publishers would like to thank Jan Eaton for devising and writing the Soft Furnishings section; Fiona Skrine for devising and demonstrating the special paint effects on pages 58-63; and Pat Murphy for demonstrating the carpet laying sequences on pages 134-7. Many thanks also to New Islington & Hackney Housing Association for the use of one of their properties that was awaiting repair. In addition, the publishers would like to thank the companies listed below for their generous help in either loaning or providing materials and equipment for use in the production of this title. For more details, see the Suppliers and Useful Addresses list.

J D Beardmore & Co Ltd
Black & Decker
Crown Paints
Fireplace Designers Ltd
Forbo Nairn Ltd
General Woodwork Supplies Ltd
Gripperrods plc
Hobbs & Co Ltd
Hodkin & Jones (Sheffield) Ltd
Ideal-Standard Ltd

H & R Johnson Tiles Ltd
Junckers Ltd
Kosset Carpets Ltd
Mosley-Stone
Oracstar Ltd
Plasplugs Ltd
Daniel Platt Ltd
Stanley Tools
Whincop & Son Ltd

The publishers would also like to thank the following companies for their kind permission to reproduce the following pictures in this book; they apologize for any unintentional omissions and will be happy to rectify this in future editions.

t = top; b = bottom; c = centre; l = left; r = right.

Addis Ltd: page 203 cl.
The Amtico Company Ltd: page 99 br.
Laura Ashley: pages 152 tl, 202 br, 182 t, 184 r, 187 br, 190 bl, 199 br.
Richard Burbidge Ltd: pages 20, 152-5, 194.
Castelnau Tiles: pages 98 br, 151 tr.
Concord Lighting Ltd: pages 24 b, 25 cl cr b, 29 tl b,30 r, 31 bc br, 33 br.
Corres Mexican Tiles: page 96 cr.
Cliffhanger Shelving Systems: pages 202 tl, 203 tr.
Crown Paints: pages 36, 40 tr cr, 68-9, 69 cr br.
Cuprinol Ltd: pages 41 bl br, 125 b.
Dulux: pages 14, 16 b, 17 tl, 21 tr, 22 tl,

38, 39, 40 tl, 41 t, 150, 152 b, 185 br, 194 bl, 204 b, 213 t.
Cristal (H & R Johnson Tiles) Ltd: pages 18 b, 96 bl, 205 tr.
Crucial Trading Ltd: pages 123 b.
Fired Earth Tiles plc: pages 94, 96 tr, 97, 98 t bl.
Fireplace Designers Ltd: page 151 tl.
Forbo–CP (Fablon) Ltd: pages 16 t, 28, 66 b, 68 l, 69 bl, 153 b.
Forbo–Kingfisher Ltd: pages 18 t, 66 t, 67 t, 173 r, 195 tr.
Forbo–Nairn Ltd: pages 99 t, 123 tr, 124 t, 141.
Harlequin Wallcoverings Ltd: 21 tl, 64, 67 b, 152 b, 191 t, 192 br.
Harrison Drape: pages 21 b, 180 t, 181 t.
Hayloft Woodwork: pages 17 b, 204 t.
Heuga: pages 123 tl, 135 bl br.
Junckers Ltd: pages 19 b, 27 cr, 124 b, 125 t, 147, 211.
Kevin MacPartland: page 153 tr.
Mazda Lighting: pages 24 t, 25 t, 26, 27 tl tr cl, 29 tr, 30 l, 31 t bl, 32, 33 t.
The Merchant Tiler: page 114.
MFI: pages 17 tr, 19 t, 202 bl, 205 tl.
Monkwell Fabrics and Wallpapers: page 23 b.
Mr Tomkinson: pages 120, 122.
Philips Lighting Ltd: page 33 bl.
Sanderson: pages 22 tr b, 133 b, 186 t, 198 t.
Muriel Short Designs: page 193 br.
Silver Lynx Products: page 205 c.
Spur Shelving Ltd: pages 203 b, 205 b.
Today Interiors: pages 23 t, 174.
Wicanders: pages 99 cr, 124 c.
Elizabeth Whiting and Associates: page 189 br.